Contents

INTRODUCTION	**1**
Using This Guide	2
Geography	3
Climate	3
Ecology	4
History	7
Government	16
Economy	17
People	17
Culture & Customs	18
Travel	20
Getting Here	20
By Air	20
By Car	23
By Bus	24
Getting Around	25
By Bus	25
By Car	28
Car Rentals	31
By Taxi	31
Customs	32
Entering	32
Returning	32
Entry Requirements	33
Passports	34
To Apply	34
Lost or Stolen Passports	34
Passport Agencies	35
Practicalities	37
Time, Measurements & Electricity	37
Pack Small or Bring it All?	39
Disabled Travelers	41
Communications	41
Making Calls	42
Mail	43
Bathrooms	43
Laundry	44
Money	44
Currency	44
Taxes	44
Traveler's Checks	45
Credit Cards	45
Health	45
Common Ailments	45
More Serious Diseases	46

Medical Insurance	47
Vaccinations	48
Safety & Crime	48
Checkpoints	49
Emergency Assistance	49
Breaking the Law	49
Shopping	50
Tipping	51
When to Go	52
Holidays	53
National Holidays	53
National Celebrations	54
Festivals & Events	55
Food & Drink	57
Where to Eat	57
Regional Specialties	60
Local Fruits	61
Spices	62
Drinks	62
Accommodations	63
Hotel Expectations	64
Camping	66
Adventures	66
On Foot	66
Hiking	66
Caving	67
Hunting	68
Archaeological Discoveries	68
On Water	69
Fishing	69
Boating	70
Rafting/Kayaking	70
Beaches	71
On Wheels	71
Biking	71
Entertainment	72
Information Sources	73
General Information	73
Place-Specific Websites	74
Tampaulipas	74
Veracruz	74
Tabasco	75
Chiapas	75
Oaxaca	75
Embassies & Consulates	75
TAMAULIPAS	**77**
The Border	77
Nuevo Laredo	78
Orientation & Practicalities	78

Getting There & Getting Around	79
By Air	79
By Bus	79
By Car	79
On Foot	80
Sightseeing	81
Adventures	81
On Foot	81
On Water	81
Festivals & Events	82
Shopping	84
Where to Stay	84
Where to Eat	85
From Nuevo Laredo to Reynosa	85
Reynosa	87
Orientation & Practicalities	87
Getting There & Around	88
By Air	88
By Bus	88
By Car	88
Sightseeing	88
McAllen	89
San Juan	89
Mission	90
Festivals & Events	90
Where to Stay	90
Where to Eat	91
Matamoros	92
Getting There & Around	92
By Air	92
By Bus	93
By Car	93
Orientation & Practicalities	93
Sightseeing	94
Brownsville	95
Adventures	95
On Foot	95
On Wheels	97
On Water	97
Festivals & Events	97
Where to Stay	98
Where to Eat	99
The Coastline - From Matamoros to Aldama	99
Where to Stay	101
Aldama	101
Adventures	102
Cenotes	102
Fishing	103
Where to Stay	103
Ciudad Victoria	103

Orientation & Practicalities	104
Getting There & Around	104
By Air	104
By Bus	104
By Car	105
Sightseeing	105
Adventures	105
On Water	105
On Foot	105
Where to Stay	106
Where to Eat	106
Reserva de la Biosfera de El Cielo	107
Adventures	107
Hiking	107
How to Get There	107
Where to Stay	108
Xicoténcatl	108
Ocampo	108
Ciudad Mante	109
Where to Stay	109
Tampico	109
Orientation & Practicalities	110
Getting There	112
By Air	112
By Bus	112
By Car	113
Getting Around	114
Sightseeing	114
Museums	115
Zoo	117
Adventures	117
On Foot	117
City Walking Tour	118
The Pyramid	120
Golf	120
On Wheels	121
On Water	121
Lagoons	121
Beaches	122
Fishing	123
Festivals & Events	123
Shopping	124
Nightlife	124
Where to Stay	125
Where to Eat	127

VERACRUZ 129
Northern Veracruz 130
The Road To Tuxpan 131

Tuxpan (or Tuxpam)	132
Orientation & Practicalities	132
Getting There & Around	133
Sightseeing	133
Adventures	134
On Water	134
Archaeological Discoveries	134
Festivals & Events	135
Where to Stay & Eat	135
Poza Rica	136
Orientation & Practicalities	136
Getting There & Out	136
Where to Stay	137
Central Veracruz	138
Papantla	139
Orientation & Practicalities	139
Getting There	140
By Car	140
By Bus	140
Adventures	142
On Foot	142
Cultural & Eco-Travel Excursions	143
El Tajín Archaeological Site	144
Festivals & Events	149
Shopping	151
Nightlife	151
Where to Stay	151
Where to Eat	152
Costa Esmeralda	153
Getting There	153
By Car	153
By Bus	154
Adventures	154
On Water	154
Fishing	154
Boat Launches	154
Beaches	155
Archaeological Discoveries	155
Cultural & Eco-Travel Excursions	156
Festivals & Events	156
Where to Stay	156
Camping & RV Sites	157
Where to Eat	158
Tlapacoyan	158
Adventures	159
Rafting	159
Archaeological Discoveries	160
Along the Coast: Villa Rica to Cardel	161
Ruins of Quiahuiztlan	161
Spanish Settlements	161

Sulfur Springs of Tinajitas	162
Birding in La Mancha	162
Ruins of Zempoala (Cempoala)	163
Dunes in Chachalacas	164
Birdwatching in Cardel	164
Veracruz	**165**
Orientation & Practicalities	165
Getting There	166
By Air	166
By Bus	167
By Train	169
By Car	169
Getting Around	169
Car Rentals	169
Local Transit	171
To San Juan de Ulúa & Boca del Río	171
To Mandinga	171
Sightseeing	171
Adventures	174
On Foot	174
Town Walks	174
Golf	176
On Wheels	176
Bus Tour	176
Bike Rentals	176
Coastal Drive	177
On Water	177
Beaches & Lagoons	177
Boat Tours	178
Diving	179
Fishing	179
Sailing	179
Kayaking/Rafting	179
By Air	180
Archaeological Discoveries	180
El Zapotal	180
Festivals & Events	180
Carnaval	180
Festival Internacional Afrocaribeño	181
School Holidays	181
The Fiesta de Santa Ana	181
Shopping	181
Nightlife	182
Dancing	182
Nightclubs	182
Where to Stay	183
Where to Eat	185
Tlacotalpan	**187**
Orientation & Practicalities	188

Getting There & Around	188
Sightseeing	188
Shopping	189
Adventures	190
Festivals & Events	190
Where to Stay	191
Where to Eat	191
Xalapa	191
Orientation & Practicalities	192
Getting There	194
By Air	194
By Car	194
By Bus	195
Getting Around	196
To Coatepec & Xico	196
To Jalcomulco	196
To Perote	196
Sightseeing	198
Adventures	198
On Foot	198
Town Walk	198
Hikes	200
Tour the Churches	201
Wandering the Alleys	202
A Daytime Stroll	203
Sports	204
On Wheels	204
Bus Tour	205
Drives	205
On Water	205
Archaeological Discoveries	206
Cultural & Eco-Travel Excursions	207
Art Galleries	207
Visit a Hacienda	208
Learn the Lost Art of Goldsmithing	209
Theaters	209
Study Abroad	210
Festivals & Events	210
Shopping	210
Nightlife	211
Where to Stay	211
Where to Eat	213
Perote	215
Orientation & Practicalities	215
Getting There & Around	215
Adventures	216
Hiking	216
Where to Stay	217
Where to Eat	217

Coatepec	218
Orientation & Practicalities	218
Getting There & Around	218
Sightseeing	218
Adventures	219
Eco-Travel	219
Festivals & Events	219
Where to Stay	220
Where to Eat	220
Xico	220
Orientation & Practicalities	220
Getting Around	222
To Cascada de Texolo	222
To Coatepec/Xalapa	222
Adventures	222
On Foot	222
Town Walk	222
On Wheels	224
On Water	224
Waterfalls	224
Festivals & Events	226
Shopping	226
Where to Stay	226
Where to Eat	227
Jalcomulco	227
Orientation & Practicalities	227
Getting There & Around	228
Adventures	228
Outfitters	228
On Foot	230
Hike	230
Rappeling	230
Gotcha	231
On Wheels	231
On Water	231
In the Air	231
On Horseback	232
Festivals & Events	232
Where to Stay	232
Where to Eat	232
Orizaba	233
Getting There & Around	233
By Bus	233
By Car	234
Orientation & Practicalities	235
Sightseeing	237
Adventures	238
On Foot	238
Hikes	238

Beer Tour	239
Caving	239
Mountain Climbing	240
On Wheels	241
On Water	241
In the Air	241
Cultural & Eco-Travel Excursions	242
Nightlife	243
Where to Stay	243
Where to Eat	244
Fortín de las Flores	245
Orientation & Practicalities	245
Getting There & Around	246
Adventures	246
On Foot	247
Festivals & Events	248
Where to Stay	248
Where to Eat	248
Córdoba	249
Orientation & Practicalities	249
Getting There & Around	250
By Car	250
By Bus	250
Sightseeing	250
Where to Stay	251
Where to Eat	251
Southern Veracruz	251
San Andrés Tuxtla	252
Orientation & Practicalities	252
Getting There & Around	254
Sightseeing	254
Adventures	256
On Water	256
Beaches	256
Waterfalls	257
Lagoons	258
Archaeological Discoveries	258
The Olmecs	258
Where to Stay	259
Where to Eat	260
Catemaco	260
Orientation & Practicalities	260
Getting Around	261
Adventures	261
On Wheels	261
On Water	263
Boat Rides	263
Kayaking	264
Waterfalls	264
Spas	265

Where to Stay	265
Camping	266
Where to Eat	266
Santiago Tuxtla	267
San Lorenzo Tenochtitlán	267

TABASCO — 269

Villahermosa	269
Orientation & Practicalities	270
Getting There	272
By Air	272
By Car	272
By Bus	272
Getting Around	274
Sightseeing	275
Adventures	279
On Foot	279
On Wheels	280
On Water	280
Archaeological Discoveries	281
Cultural & Eco-Travel	282
Nature Park	282
Chocolate Plantation Tour	283
Festival	283
Where to Stay	283
In Paraiso	285
Where to Eat	285
The Coast	286
Western Tabasco	288
Adventures	288
Archaeological Discoveries	288
Cultural & Eco-Travel	289
The Sierras	290
Eastern Tabasco	291
Adventures	292
On Water	292
Archaeological Discoveries	292

OAXACA — 295

Tuxtepec	295
Orientation & Practicalities	295
Getting There & Around	296
Adventures	297
Drives	297
Valle Nacional	297
Monte Flor	298
Jacatapec	299
On Water	299
Where to Stay	300
Where to Eat	301

Ixtlán de Juárez	301
Guelatao	302
And Beyond…	302

CHIAPAS 303
Palenque	304
Orientation & Practicalities	304
Getting There & Around	304
By Air	304
By Bus	304
By Car	304
Cautions	306
Tour Operators/Travel Agents	306
Adventures	307
On Water	307
Archaeological Discoveries	309
The Ruins of Palenque	309
Where to Stay	311
Where to Eat	312
Farther into Chiapas	312

APPENDIX 313
Useful Words & Phrases	313
Bibliography	317

INDEX 319

Maps

States of Mexico	inside front cover
Tamaulipas State	facing 82
Matamoros	94
Greater Tampico	111
Central Tampico	116
Veracruz State	facing 130
Papantla	141
El Tajín	145
Veracruz & Vicinity	170
Veracuz Downtown	172
Xalapa	193
Xalapa's Historic District	197
Xico	221
Orizaba	235
Los Tuxtlas Region	253
San Andrés Tuxtla	257
Villahermosa	271
Tabasco State	facing 274
Historic Villahermosa	278
Tuxtepec & Vicinity	296
Palenque	305
Palenque Ruins	308

Acknowledgments

This book could not have been written without the invaluable help of the many travelers, shop owners, tourism officials, and locals who without hesitation opened their doors and hearts to share the secret treasures and natural beauty of their states. My sincerest thanks go to all the aforementioned, and particularly to the following for the extra time and effort they spent sharing their expertise: Maestro José Luis Gómez Lima, Patricia Caraza Cerda from the Subsecretaria de Turismo in Veracruz, Miguel Angel Ramirez from the Direccion de Turismo Municipal in Orizaba, Raymundo Alvarado from Desafio, the folks at the Coyame spring water factory, Chevy Rodriguez from Aventuras Sin Limite, Gerardo Reyes from Servimont, Mélida Barbee of Río y Montaña Expediciones, Margarita Fararoni of Faraventuras, Pablo Migueles Moreno from Puros Santa Clara, the delightful Yolanda from the Hotel Figueroa, Ma. de los Angeles Pérez Cabrera of the Departamento de Difusión del Centro INAH Veracruz, Christine Garsault from the Mexican Tourism Board, and Miguel Camarillo Berzunza of the Preservación y Proyectos del municipio de Tampico. I'd also like to give a special thanks to Mary Taylor for skillfully editing a town, Neena Philip for rescuing me from disgruntled workers, fellow traveler Alyssan Barnes for always being there with advice, Ezra Johnson for his geographic expertise and reliability in times of crisis (my computer couldn't handle it, but yours could...), my wonderful mother Joan Shauchunas for her continual support and encouragement, particularly when all seemed bleak, and finally, and most importantly, my father Orlando Sánchez who traveled with me on my adventures, and whose knowledge and encouragement guided me through every city, jungle, and mountainside.

Dedication

To all who wonder where the crooked street leads and what's around the next bend... I'll be waiting for you right around that last turn.

Introduction

Volcanoes... rainforests... ruins... throw in a few colossal stone heads, some world-renowned birding locations, an island filled with monkeys, and festivals culminating with bulls running the streets – and you've only begun to glimpse all that Mexico's Gulf Coast has to offer. If you know of anyone who's been here, that's probably why you've picked up this book. You've heard their remarkable tales: of rafting through untouched jungle past ancient ruins, of easily sumitting one of the tallest peaks in North America, of swinging through the treetops in a remote jungle village. And maybe you've heard the tales from their friends as well: of sitting in a *zócalo* (a central square) sipping coffee and listening to guitarists play late into the night, of eating fresher-than-fresh seafood on the beach, of an exhilarating outing to an ancient Indian burial ground. Are you ready to make those memories yours?

IN THIS CHAPTER	
■ Using This Guide	2
■ Geography	3
■ Climate	3
■ Ecology	4
■ History	7
■ Government	16
■ Economy	17
■ People	17
■ Culture & Customs	18
■ Travel	20
■ Practicalities	37
■ Health	45
■ Safety & Crime	48
■ Shopping	50
■ Tipping	51
■ When to Go	52
■ Holidays	53
■ Food & Drink	57
■ Accommodations	63
■ Adventures	66
■ Entertainment	72
■ Information Sources	73
■ Embassies & Consulates	75

The region, which includes the states of Tamaulipas, Veracruz, and Tabasco, is a little bit country, a little bit rock and roll. Roads to some of the best places are little-touristed, and located in the middle of villages (not cities). And so you find large four-legged beasts wandering across the road, prices that are truly inexpensive, and natives that are unlikely to speak much English (or, in some cases, Spanish!) You'll find biosphere reserves and remote areas that still host toucans, jaguars, and monkeys, as well as stretches of coastal grasslands that have nothing (save the occasional vulture) as far as the eye can see. And then you can go back to your hotel in a huge, colorful, cosmopolitan city with an endless assortment of restaurants, events, and action.

A popular destination of locals, the region is starting to get more interest from European visitors too, but is often overlooked by many travelers due to the popularity of Mexico's mega-resorts. For those seeking an unforgettable cultural experience, this is truly too bad. Culturally, the region is unparalleled – from the rhythmic dance and music of Veracruz (the birthplace of the famous song *La Bamba*), which will have hips grooving to the beat – to the world-class museums and art galleries of Xalapa. Local festivals and events take place in many towns and are not to be missed.

The more adventurous traveler will be well-rewarded too. With several large rivers, Mexico's tallest mountain, and miles of coastline, the area offers unsurpassed opportunities for river rafting, kayaking, mountain biking, diving, fishing, and camping – to name but a few. Archaeology buffs will enjoy the many ancient ruins, including one of Mexico's most important archaeological sites – El Tajín. Even movie producers have celebrated the area's pure natural beauty. Check out the jungles in *Romancing the Stone* and *Medicine Man*.

So are you ready for an unforgettable visit and a remarkable adventure? Why are you still reading? Pack your bags; you're going to the Gulf Coast!

Using This Guide

Many folks choose to drive through the Gulf Coast region – some simply on a weekend exploration trip from the Texas border, while others are in it for the longer haul – using a drive as a cheap alternative to get to the Yucatán. But there is no need to wander around aimlessly or drive so far – this book starts at the border (with the state of Tamaulipas) and heads south through the states of Veracruz and into Tabasco. It shows you how to explore the entire eastern coastline of México.

One of the Gulf Coast's more attractive features is that the region is a little bit wilder than other well-touristed spots – it's therefore less accessible and a bit underdeveloped. You won't find many international flights into the region, so your trip is going to require careful planning, beginning with entry through either one of the aforementioned airports, or through México City. Plan on basing yourself in a large city (at least initially), and from there you can take either local buses to surrounding sites or rent a car. Check out the travel agencies; some of them can arrange transportation to and from México City or the Puerto de Veracruz.

Geography

Of the more than 6,000 miles of coastline in México, the Gulf Coast accounts for about 15% of the total: some 900 miles, starting at the Texas border (which is formed by the Río Bravo del Norte, or Río Grande), and continuing down to the end of Tabasco and the beginning of the Yucatán. Three states comprise the coastline. In the north there's the short squat state of **Tamaulipas**, then the long, narrow state of **Veracruz** (dominating the central portion) and, at the southern end, the tiny state of **Tabasco**.

The Gulf coastal plains are marshy and flat, for the most part populated by fishermen and ranchers. The farther south you travel, the more rainfall you see, and vegetation and jungle increase proportionately; the shrubby plains of Tamaulipas cross the Tropic of Cancer, and eventually turn into swampy jungle-covered marshlands in Tabasco. Until about 50 years ago, much of the swampy area along the coast was infested with mosquitoes and flooded. However, the construction of dams, drainage of swamps, and cultivation of lands has controlled much of the problem. In Tabasco, particularly outside of the main cities, you'll still want to wear plenty of insect repellent.

To the east, always within view, the land rises up, forming a natural barrier between the coastline and the rest of the country. This is the **Sierra Madre Oriental**. The mountains are lush and tropical; rivers flow down from them to the ocean – a huge attraction for rafters. On the other side of the mountain range is the **Altiplano Central**, where a large percentage of the Mexican population lives. Near San Andres Tuxtla, a volcanic area emerges, the **Cordillera Neovolcánica**, connecting the Sierra Madre Oriental with the more westerly **Sierra Madre Occidental**. The highest mountains in México are here, including the **Pico de Orizaba** (Citlaltepetl) rising up more than 18,000 feet. There is still some volcanic activity here as well – the most recent volcano emerging in 1943 in the western state of Machoacan. Earthquakes are a fear throughout the entire chain, and many cities, including Xalapa and Orizaba, have suffered destruction becaue of them.

Climate

Over the extensive length of the Gulf Coast, there is something to please just about every taste. The northern section of Tamaulipas lies above the Tropic of Cancer in a mild climate of dry flatlands. South of the line, it becomes hot and humid along the coast, with large amounts of rain year-round, but particularly during the rainy season (May-October). Some of the bigger ports during these months can be absolutely stifling, and you'd be well-advised to pay the few extra dollars for a room with air-conditioning. As you travel inland, the elevation rises, and the temperature drops; summer months in Xalapa, for example, may require a light sweater in the mornings, while winter requires hat and mittens. The whole coastline is also subject to hurricanes (defined as storms with winds exceeding 74 mph), a constant threat to the coast during the hurricane season, which runs from around August to October. If a storm hits full-force, you don't want to be around the coastline at all. Roadways are flooded and completely disappear, houses and hotels are soaked inside and out with water, and everybody is holed up for days.

Hurricanes are rated in categories. A Category 1 hurricane is the smallest type, and therefore causes the least amount of damage. Categories 2-4 become progressively stronger (a 4 can be devastating), and a Category 5 hurricane is the strongest and most frightening of them all, with winds exceeding 155 mph. If a Category 5 hurricane is headed your way, clear out!

Ecology

There are two things you'll notice when you visit Tabasco or Veracruz. The first, is how green and lush the surroundings are (they'll become greener and more lush the deeper into Tabasco you go). The second is the amazing degree to which much of that beautiful foliage has been cleared out to make way for ranches, plantations, and fields. The plentiful flora and fauna are disappearing. The huge flocks of parrots that you could once see flying overhead have mostly disappeared, the large mammals that once called much of the jungle home have retreated, the toucans are now so rare you probably won't see one. Even the jungle itself is seen only while traveling on secondary roads; many main roadsides have been cleared off for industry. Deforestation has had a huge impact on the environment – approximately 95% of Tabasco's jungles alone have been destroyed thanks to the ugly problem. Much of the more exotic wildlife has now retreated to the remote reaches of Tabasco bordering with Chiapas. In Veracruz, the wildlife has moved back as well. You'll now find the greatest diversity near the border with Oaxaca. In Tamaulipas, the **Reserva de la Biosfera El Cielo** has a number of different ecosystems, including a tropical forest and a cloud forest, and is home to some of the wilder animals you might be hoping to find (such as wildcats). What the Gulf Coast does still have, however, is a huge variety of birds – wetlands along the coast of Tamaulipas, Tabasco, and Veracruz (in particular) are well-known for the vast numbers of migratory birds. In addition, the **Reserva de la Biosfera de Centla** in Tabasco has proved an excellent refuge for wetland animals, including many that are nearing extinction.

■ Fauna

The most exciting local wildlife for many people are the wildcats native to the region. Unfortunately, however, though they are still around, they now live only in the most remote reaches of the jungle. Among them is one of México's most popular animals – thanks to its importance in the ancient Maya culture – the **jaguar**. A huge feline that can measure more than six feet in length and weigh more than 300 pounds, the jaguar is one of the most beautiful and most powerful predators in the jungle, identified by its short yellowish-brown pelt covered by small black spots. Slightly smaller than the jaguar is the **cougar** (also known as the panther, mountain lion, or puma) – a huge feline predator with a long tail and a reddish, grayish, or brownish pelt. The nocturnal **ocelot** is another beautiful cat that is incredibly difficult to find as it's currently on the endangered species list. Ocelots are delicate-looking felines with a short cream-colored pelt marked by large brownish spots. The smaller cats include the **jaguarundi**, which is about the size of a house cat and has a short, dark-colored pelt, and the **tigrillo** (also known as the margay), which is a beautiful cat with a small body (about the size of a house cat) and a short golden pelt with black spots.

Other large mammals you'll find in remote regions of the jungle include (among many others) the **black bear** – often black, but sometimes brown, and quite large, weighing in at around 300 pounds. There's also the **grey fox**, the **coyote**, the **white-tail deer**, the **red deer**, the **spider monkey**, the **armadillo**, the **iguana**, **snakes** (even boa constrictors!) and the **collared peccary** (an animal similar to a wild pig).

Because there are so many wetlands along the Gulf, you're likely to find a few **crocodiles**. In most cases, your boat tour guide will simply mention that they are out there. If you want a shot at actually seeing one up-close in the wild, however, visit Tampico, where they hang out on a sandbar right in the middle of a lagoon near downtown. The **manatee** is another animal that lives in the lagoons and mangroves of Tabasco. This gentle aquatic animal with flippers has a whiskered face with a snout. You're unlikely to see one, however, as they are an endangered species. You'll also find all kinds of fish, which has made the area very popular with sport fishermen. Among the various kinds you'll find is the unique **pejelagarto**, a carnivorous fish found in Tabasco that has a long tooth-filled jaw similar to that of a crocodile. The pejelagarto is a popular dish, favored for the delicate flavor of its meat. As for **turtles**, parts of the Gulf serve as one of the only nesting grounds for the endangered species of sea turtle known as the **Kemp's Ridley** (the smallest of the sea turtles).

The wetlands draw a huge variety of migrating and local birds. Among them are **falcons**, **hawks**, and **eagles** by the thousands. If you're interested in something a little less familiar, the marshlands of Tabasco have a few **jabirú**, huge storks that stand four to five feet tall, There are so few of them, however, that you are unlikely to spot one. **Yucatecan parrots** were once much more common than they are today, but you can occasionally still spot some of the beautiful green birds in untouched streches of jungle. The **toucan** is another bird commonly associated with México. It is easily identified by its long colorful beak. Remote patches of jungle still have some toucans. And the list doesn't stop there, but includes more exotic varieties as well as **vultures**, **crows**, **buzzards**, **herons**, **gulls**, **ducks** and **geese**. Birdwatchers, keep your eyes open!

■ Flora

The diversity of both wild and cultivated plants growing in the jungles and marshes is amazing. You'll find trees such as **cedar**, **mahogany**, **oak**, and the sacred **ceiba** (a tropical tree also known as the silk cotton tree, believed by the Mayans to connect the earth with the heavens). There are also plenty of fruit trees, including all kinds of exotic and not-so exotic varieties (see *Local Fruits*, page 61), as well as huge cultivated plantations of **banana** and **coconut**. Unfortunately, some of the coconut palms that are so thick along the Tabascan coastline have succumbed to lethal yellowing, a disease that quickly kills them. **Mangroves** (manglares) are found in abundance along the shore – the thick, intertwined trees with their roots half-in and half-out of the water are much loved by aquatic animals and boat guides. **Cactus** takes well to the dry regions in Tamaulipas. There's an endless variety of flowering plants, including **orchids**, both wild and cultivated. The most famous orchid of all produces the vanilla bean.

> *The symbol of the eagle and cactus on the Mexican flag is based on an ancient Aztec legend that said that the god Quetzalcoatl appeared before the Aztecs and told them to found their city in a spot where they saw an eagle with a snake in its mouth perched on top of a cactus. The Aztecs found the place and that is where they built their capital Tenochtitlán.*

History

A long, long, time ago... The story of the Gulf Coast begins thousands of years before the birth of Christ. In the land that is today the southern section of Veracruz, a civilization started to emerge. The year – around 2000 BC. The **Olmecs** as we call them (we don't know what their original name was, but have adopted a name given them by archaeologist George Vaillant) emerged and flourished in the hot, mosquito-filled swamplands of the Gulf Coast. They are remembered for the sophisticated levels they reached – creating religious centers, huge sculptures and inventing a numbering system and a calendar. They lived as farmers, growing the staples of corn, beans, and squash; they were hunters and (thanks to the region in which they lived) fishermen as well. Evidence suggests that the Olmecs traded widely – objects reflecting the Olmec culture have been found as far away as Honduras, El Salvador, and Guatemala. It is also believed that they were deeply spiritual, venerating the eagle and jaguar, and using ball game sacrifices in their religious beliefs. Eventually, however, around 400 BC, due to either revolts or invasions (it's not quite clear), their cities were destroyed and abandoned. The culture started to come to the attention of the modern world in 1862, when a huge basalt head – one of the most familiar trademarks of the Olmec civilization – was discovered in Veracruz. In 1925, more Olmec remnants were found by Frans Blom and Oliver La Fage in Veracruz' Laguna de Catemaco.

	TIMELINE	
Early Preclassic	2000-900 BC	Early settlements, Olmecs (San Lorenzo)
Middle Preclassic	900-300 BC	Olmecs (La Venta, Tres Zapotes)
Late Preclassic	300 BC-300 AD	Capital Teotihuacán built by unknown group (possibly Totonacs or Olmecs); Mayans emerge

Early Classic	300-600 AD	Mayans flourish
Late Classic	600-900 AD	Mayans
Terminal Classic	700-900 AD	Mixtecs & Toltecs emerge
Early Post Classic	900-1200 AD	Toltecs flourish
Late Post Classic	1200-1521 AD	Aztecs

After the Olmec civilization, others emerged in the Classic period (300-900 AD); some of these do not have a physical connection with the Gulf Coast, but did influence its culture. Among them is the unknown civilization that created the city of **Teotihuacán** (located near present-day México City and dated at 250-750 AD). The city would have a big impact upon the later Aztec civilization. Teotihuacán was huge in its day, housing a population of around 150,000 people in a massive complex of buildings that were both residential and religious. It dominated much of Mesoamerica until its downfall in 750 AD. No records have been left to help decode its inhabitants, rulers, original name, language, or history.

Other great cultures to emerge in central México include the **Toltecs** (900-1200 AD), who arose in central México, and the **Zapotecs** (300 BC-950 AD), who dwelt in southern México – specifically, the Oaxaca Valley. Interestingly, many Zapotec reliefs show a strong Olmec influence. The most famous site of this culture is **Monte Albán**, which had an elite ruling class and a peasant working base. They had established a calendar, and left behind hieroglyphics; here, too, many ball courts have been discovered, indicating that the game was extremely important.

Perhaps one of the most intriguing cultures was the **Mayan** (250-900 AD), a magnificent, highly sophisticated culture that developed in southern México (you'll find some Mayan ruins in Tabasco, though most are in the Yucatán, Chiapas, and Guatemala). From 1839 to 1842, John Lloyd Stephens and Frederick Catherwood brought the civilization to the attention of the modern world with the publication of their adventures and explorations in México, *Incidents of Travel in Central America, Chiapas, and Yucatán* (published in 1841), and *Incidents of Travel in Yucatán* (published in 1843). They were an adventurous and remarkable duo – Stephens the writer, and Catherwood the artist (who sat for hours in the middle of jungle-covered ruins sketching images of what he saw). There had been little or no knowledge of the culture here since the Spanish arrival in the New World, and what was discovered was amazing – evidence of a highly sophisticated civilization. The Maya traded over long distances, built huge temples, and had complex religious beliefs. The Mayans were also sophisticated in mathematics and astronomy. Their calendar was amazingly accurate and, until modern times, there has not been one to match it. Curiously, it is unknown why the many great cities were abandoned and where the Mayans disappeared to.

In the Post Classic period (900-1521 AD), things took a turn with the arrival of the **Aztecs** in 1111 AD. Their homeland was a mysterious place called Aztlán (archaeologists have not come to a consensus on exactly where this was, although some believe it to be an island in a lagoon in northwest México). The Aztecs were nomads for some 200 years before arriving at Lake Texcoco in around 1319. At that time, the area was inhabited by other indigenous groups, among them the Acolhua and the Tepenacs. Though the Aztecs were not very welcome, they were eventually granted the right to stay in the least desirable area – Tizapan – and, to the consternation of the other tribes, they flourished. One day, they approached a ruler of one of the tribes and asked him if he would allow them to honor his daughter by allowing her to marry the god Huitzilopochtli (the God of War). The ruler agreed, but had no idea that he would later find her killed, skinned, and being worn by the priest. The Aztecs were immediately engaged in battle, and eventually found the spot foretold to them by the god Huitzliopochtl. They built a capital – Tenochtitlán, a huge sophisticated city – and went about conquering the cultures of most of central México. Finally, in 1502, at the age of 34, the most famous of Aztec rulers came to power: **Moctezuma Xocoyotl**, also known as Moctezuma II. Shown at right, he would reign for 18 years, and see the coming of the Spaniards and the downfall of his empire.

Quetzalcoatl

Quetzalcoatl was a god worshipped by (among many of the ancient cultures) the Aztecs. He's often depicted as being light-skinned, having a beard, and in some accounts, having come from a foreign land across the seas to the east. He was said to have set sail on a raft of serpents headed back in the same direction. Legend said that he would one day return – specifically, in the year 1519 – coincidentally the same year that Cortés arrived.

The Spanish Arrival

In 1517, **Francisco Fernández de Córdoba** was the first to discover México – a storm had thrown him off course, landing him on the banks of the Yucatán. He set sail to further explore the new land, eventually making it down to Campeche, where he was attacked by natives, lost half his crew, and sustained severe injuries. He set a return course for Cuba (which had a Spanish colony), where he would soon die, but not before reporting that he had seen great wealth in the new world.

The governor of Cuba, **Diego Velázquez** decided that Córdoba's findings should not be left uninvestigated. Another expedition was sent out in 1518, this time headed by general **Juan de Grijalva**. He reached the Yucatán, searching for a way around the "island," but eventually discovered that it was in fact a continent. Along the way, he found and named the Río Grijalva, the Isla de Sacrificios, and San Juan de Ulúa (both in the state of Veracruz); he also learned from the natives that farther inland he would be able to find gold.

A third expedition was organized upon Grijalva's return. This time, Velásquez picked **Hernan Cortés** as his general. Cortés set sail from Cuba, and in 1519 landed on the Yucatán, where he was approached by a pair of castaways who had been stranded there for eight years – Jerónimo de Aguilar and Gonzálo Guerrero. Aguilar, who had been a servant of a Maya chieftain, became invaluable to Cortés for his language skills. Guerrero, who had become a Maya chieftain himself, was by this point married with children, and stayed behind. The company continued down the coast to the town of Centla. Here, Cortés defeated a local Maya chieftain and was given as tribute a horde of 20 women, among them a woman named **Marina** (sometimes called La Malinche or Malintzín), who would become pivotal to the Spaniard's campaign. A captured princess, she spoke Náhuatl (the language of the Aztecs), as well as the Mayan language. With Aguilar's Spanish and Mayan skills, Cortés now had a means to communicate with the Aztecs.

Aztec emperor Moctezuma II had been watching the coast carefully, and had seen the arrival of Grijalva. Fearing him to be the god Quetzalcoatl, he had sent gifts of immeasurable wealth to the coast, only to find that Grijalva had disappeared. When Cortés finally arrived, a lavish reception awaited him. Cortés, eager to meet with the ruler Moctezuma, was discouraged by the ruler's terms. But ever-resourceful Cortés formed an alliance with the Totonac leader of Cempoala, who had complaints of his own against Moctezuma. His ambition was limitless. Though Cortés had no charter to colonize, and was being encouraged to return home by some of his crew, he pressed forward, unwilling to lose the wealth he knew he would find. He founded the colony of Villa Rica de la Vera Cruz, then drew up a petition that was sent to the Crown directly, requesting rights to New Spain, superceding those given to Velásquez. In order to ensure none of his troops got other ideas, he burned all his ships. Now, with (in some cases reluctant) support from his troops and aid from Cempoala, he set out on a march to México, against Moctezuma II.

A First Taste of Chocolate

Moctezuma gave the Spaniards their first taste of a drink from the xocoatl plant. When Cortés first tried the drink, it was hot and bitter, with an unknown taste and an unfamiliar name; but it was good. Others liked it too. Doing their best with the pronunciation, they called it chocolate. The scene at left is from the Nuttall Codex where a cup of foaming chocolate is exchanged at the marriage in AD 1051 of two Mixtec nobles.

Though his troops numbered fewer than 800 (under 500 Spaniards, plus around 300 Cempoalans), Cortés had one advantage over the Aztecs and the six million people that Moctezuma ruled – horses, never before been seen in the New World. As he advanced, his cavalry proved crucial in battle, convincing Moctezuma to negotiate.

Hernan Cortés

The son of a Spanish infantry captain, Cortés had no interest in school, but was fascinated by adventure. When he was 17, he had the opportunity he had been hoping for, but hurt himself climbing a wall to meet with his lover. The trip to the New World with Nicolas de Ovando, was put off for two years, until 1504, when Cortés set out for Santo Domingo. Five years later, when Diego Velásquez was sent to Cuba, Cortés accompanied him, and eventually was granted the mayorship of St. Jago, where he became wealthy, thanks to farming and gold mining. When Velásquez (who had become governor of Cuba) started organizing the expedition to follow Grijalva's discoveries, Cortés, who would be able to fund most of the trip with his own money, was chosen to head the campaign. So it came to pass that in 1519, at the age of 34 years, Cortés set out for México – an expedition that forever changed the continent.

 When Cortés reached the Aztec capital of Tenochtitlán, Moctezuma, left, welcomed him, and housed and fed his troops. After five days at the capital, however, Cortés discovered that his colony had been attacked, and several Spaniards had died. He confronted Moctezuma, who denied involvement and Cortés eventually convinced with death threats to stay in the Spanish quarters, in order to guarantee his safety. Moctezuma went. At this point it was over for Moctezuma – his allegiance to Spain was publicized, his governors were summoned to do the same, and Cortés was given free movement throughout the empire.

Meanwhile, back in Cuba, Diego Velásquez intercepted Cortés' men, who were bringing the petition to New Spain. In anger, he organized yet another expedition, picking **Pánfilo de Narváez** as his general and ordering him to find Cortés. Narváez made it to New Spain and learned all about what Cortés' had done. He quickly sent word to Moctezuma that Cortés was an outlaw, with no backing from Spain. Moctezuma informed Cortés.

With an army of thousands (many Indian recruits), Cortés marched back across the country in search of Narváez, who was at Cempoala. He arrived and attacked in the middle of a rainy night, when Narváez was certain Cortés would not be coming. In a few hours, with minimal casualties, Cortés had won. Half of Narváez' troops joined Cortés. Narváez' impact on the course of Mexican lives does not end here, however. It turns out that on his ship, Narváez had an African slave who was infected with smallpox. A huge number of Indians would die in the widespread epidemics that broke out.

Back in Tenochtitlán, Pedro de Alvarado, who had been left in command, was approached by Moctezuma, who requested that he be allowed to organize the annual harvest ceremony for his people. Alvarado authorized the event, but became suspicious of a plot, and launched a violent attack on the worshippers, slaughtering a group of ceremonial dancers and spectators; the city rose against him and, for weeks, an angry mob besieged the palace. When Cortés finally arrived (having received word of the events while in Cempoala), he tried to control the uprising by bringing Moctezuma in front of the people. When Moctezuma appeared, he was viciously stoned; a terrible strike to his head led to his death a few days later.

The Spanish had a few more battles to fight but, for the most part, the Aztec rule had come to an end. The Spanish continued exploring and spreading Christianity. In 1523, Franciscan friars arrived, followed some years later by the Augustinians, and years after that by the Jesuits. These religious groups went about setting up churches and spreading religion to the "heathens," in many cases by associating new beliefs with old ones, and in some cases by military strength.

It's important to note that African slaves brought by the Spanish from their homeland were used as a labor source in the New World. A huge percentage of the native population was dying from newly introduced diseases. African slaves filled that hole. Vera Cruz saw thousands of slaves arrive yearly. Eventually, a mixed population of mulattos (Spanish-black) and zambos (Indian-black) emerged.

■ Independence

As society became divided, with the superior attitude of the Spanish, resentment grew. Creoles (Spanish blood born in México), mestizos (mixed Spanish-Indian blood), and Indians were all part of the lower classes, and tired of it. Civil war followed, starting on September 16, 1810, when **Father Miguel Hidalgo y Costilla**, a mestizo, issued the Grito de Dolores (Cry for Dolores), a call for independence. Though it took years, many more years of rebellion (and many deaths, including Hidalgo's), the day is now celebrated annually as Mexican Independence Day. Independence was finally declared on August 24, 1821, with the Treaty of Cordoba.

■ War

In 1833, **General Antonio López de Santa Anna**, who had been driving the Spanish from San Juan de Ulúa in Vera Cruz, gained control of the government and was elected as the third president of México. During his tumultuous career he lost much land to the United States. When Texas declared its independence in 1835, he marched against them and won (remember the Alamo?). Shortly thereafter, he was captured in the **Battle of San Jacinto**, and granted Texas its independence. In 1845, when Texas sought to join the United States, México claimed such actions a violation of the terms of its independence, and declared war. The **Mexican-American War** of 1846 was the result; its outcome was the signing of the Treaty of Guadalupe Hidalgo, where Santa Anna lost California, Utah, Arizona, Nevada, and sections of Wyoming, New México, and Colorado to the United States. Eventually, with the uprising of liberals, Santa Anna was removed from office, and the **War of Reform** (1858-1861), an attempt to regulate the powers of the church, was underway.

During this time, one of the leaders who was fighting for equality, a Zapotec Indian named **Benito Juárez**, established a liberal government in Vera Cruz, fought against the conservatives, and eventually won the war; he was elected president in 1861. Facing a devastated, bankrupt nation, Juárez saw no choice but to suspend interest payments on foreign debts until the country could get back on its feet. France, Britain, and Spain became upset by México's indebtedness to them and refusal to pay up; they sent ships to México to collect. Only France's emperor, however, took things a step further – Napoleon III decided to invade México, as good an excuse as any to establish France in the Americas.

Surprisingly, on May 5, 1862, the French were defeated in Puebla by General Ignacio Zaragoza. The day came to be celebrated as **Cinco de Mayo**. It was an amazing victory, as the French had a much stronger military. They did not give up, howver, and sent more troops in. Finally, on June 10, 1863, the French took control of México City, installing Austrian Maximilian of Hapsburg as emperor.

Three years later, under pressure from the United States and facing trouble from Prussia, France withdrew, and Juárez, who had fled, returned to power. The French Maximilian was executed, and reconstruction began; the economy revitalized and education improved. Juárez was appointed to a fourth term as president in 1871, but died from a heart attack the next year.

■ Revolution

Juárez' successor was **Porfirio Díaz**, a liberal who pursued economic development for the next 35 years. During this time, the oil industry along the Gulf Coast boomed, much of it owned by foreign companies; acres of land around Poza Rica, Tampico, and Tuxpan belonged to foreign investors. Díaz also implemented policies that led to social inequalities – he gave power back to the church, and preference to the wealthy.

As the presidential election of 1910 drew near, **Francisco Madero**, a liberal from Coahuila campaigned; fearing a loss, Díaz jailed him. Released from jail after Díaz was re-elected, Madero fled to the United States and plotted a revolution, with the idea that México needed to elect its own president. The call went out, and the cry was heard on November 20, 1910 (today marked as the Day of the Mexican Revolution). Two revolutionaries rose to the challenge – revolutionary (and bandit) **Doroteo Arango** (aka Pancho Villa) with rebels in the north and revolutionary **Emiliano Zapata** with rebels in the south.

The revolution was eventually victorious, and León de la Barra became interim president until a formal election by the people could be held. Zapata's rebel forces, however, were calling for land that had been taken up by the haciendas to be returned to the villagers and de la Barra, to the disappointment of Madero, sent troops in to disarm them. This set the stage for Zapata to turn against Madero and, when Madero was finally elected president in November of 1911, he was confronted with Zapata's Plan de Ayala, which called for the turnover and restoration of local lands from the rich to the poor villagers, and the overthrow of Madero.

Though Madero tried to make good on his talk about reforms, he had kept many Porfirsts around him, and his ideologies became impossible to attain. Unable to come to terms with the revolutionaries, Madero was murdered in 1913. Rebellions and unrest followed, including an incident in 1914 with the United States. An American ship's crew sailing along the Gulf Coast came ashore in Tampico, which was under siege. The Americans were arrested, but immediately released; things escalated, resulting in an American attack on Vera Cruz, and hundreds of deaths.

Eventually, under president **Venustiano Carranza**, the new Constitution of 1917 was in place, and the revolution, for the most part, had ended. Zapata ended up being killed in 1919 by Carranza, and Villa was killed in 1923 while raiding an American city.

■ Post-Revolution

In the years that followed, the United States made the sale and consumption of alcohol illegal. Prohibition boosted development around the border. Americans crossed over, spent their money, and border towns grew, but not without consequences. Prostitution, gambling, and late-night bars gave the area a nasty reputation.

In 1938, under President Lázaro Cárdenas, the oil industry along the coast, which had been foreign-owned, was nationalized. The **Petróleos Mexicanos** (Pemex) was established to run the petroleum industry; foreign companies were paid market value for the seized property. México's economy continued to expand; it built relations with the United Stated by aiding its efforts during World War II, it expanded educational services nationally, and stabilized politically.

■ The Zapatista Movement

On January 1, 1994, in the state of Chiapas, a new movement was born. The **Ejército Zapatista de Liberación Nacional** (Zapatista National Libaration Army, EZLN), an Indian uprising led by a man referred to as **Sub-Commandante Marcos**, decided that it was time for political and economic reform. The EZLN was going to do something about México's poverty. Purposely planning their first action on the day of the implementation of NAFTA (the North Atlantic Free Trade Agreement), they took control of a number of cities in

Chiapas (including San Cristóbal de las Casas), drawing attention to their cause. They then retreated to the Lancondonian Forest, where they established a rebel military and waged war to better the lives of the impoverished people of Chiapas. Their goal was to overturn the corrupt, wealthy leaders and do something about the discrimination and poverty that had resulted in many of the indigenous groups being without education, food, work, and land. Marcos started to become something of a folk hero, spreading word through the Internet, and garnering a following on the rich-poor issue, which the government had a hard time effectively handling. In the intervening years between then and now, the government has made some concessions, including putting money into roads and social services in Chiapas to improve life for the indigenous population. It is, however, a battle in progress, and today the rebels are still fighting for their cause from the jungles of Chiapas.

Government

The Estados Unidos Mexicanos (United Mexican States) is México's official name; it is comprised of 31 states and a Federal District. Its main political party is the **Partido Revolucionario Institucional** (PRI), which was organized in 1929 originally under the name Partido Nacional Revolucionario. The PRI has had a political monopoly for much of its existence, plagued with controversy and accusations of bribery and fraud. The 1988 presidential election, for example, was a close race – the PRI officially received only around 50% of the votes; the FDN (**Frente Democrático Nacional**, founded in 1986 by Cuauhtémoc Cárdenas) came in second, receiving around 30% of the vote. Many claimed election fraud – in a suspicious coincidence, the computers that tallied the scores broke down (they were PRI computers). Other parties that have taken power in municipal government have, at various times, been squelched by PRI state legislatures. Recently, however, the conservative **Partido Acción Nacional** (PAN) has had some success, as has the **Partido de la Revolución Democrática** (PRD).

México is a federal republic with an executive, judicial, and legislative branch. The chief executive is the president, who serves a six-year term. The congress has a 128-member senate (each of whom serves a six-year terms), and a law-making Chamber of Deputies (one member for each 250,000 people).

Economy

In Catemaco, a man struggled his way up into the back of the pickup/taxi I was in. His working tool was a machete, thrown in first, then he followed, cradling a useless arm, the tendons of which had long ago been severed by the slip of a machete. I had not the heart to ask if it was by his own hand or someone else's. The machete is scary. But it is the tool of working life for many in rural México. The Gulf Coast region is filled with plantations and fields. If you drive even a short distance from the towns you are likely to come upon plantations – field after field of sugarcane, coffee (Veracruz is a big exporter), bananas, fruit (especially citrus of all kinds), and vanilla. Besides **agriculture** (which takes up about a fifth of the nation's lands), the economy is dependent upon a number of other activities. **Cattle raising** is one. The quality of cattle in Tabasco and the quantity of cattle in Veracruz are particularly noteworthy. **Fishing** is a big industry for much of the Gulf Coast as well. As for **oil**, the entire country looks to the Gulf Coast, and you'll see plenty of evidence when you travel – rigs, PEMEX stations, cities-turned-industrial. **Mining** is also important, as is, for the border towns specifically, the **maquila** industry, where factories in México partner with factories in the United States to provide cheap labor for product assembly.

People

Mexicans are renowned as a loving and friendly people, particularly valuing family relationships. When you see the coastline get crowded during Semana Santa, it's for the most part with families – parents, grandparents, great-grandparents, kids, uncles, aunts. Everyone's invited and everyone goes; you'll see cars on the highway laden with people, food, and drink.

Most of the population that you'll see driving around is coming from an urban area, which is where about 70% of the population lives. The official language is Spanish, although a large number of indigenous languages are spoken. Many indigenous groups live in small villages and have kept their traditions alive over the years, including arts, crafts, music, and cuisine. Festivals are a particularly good time to see different aspects of the culture, including traditional costumes as well.

In Tabasco, three indigenous groups you're likely to find include the **Chontal Maya**, who are from the western and central portion of the state, and probably comprise the largest indigenous group within Tabasco. Their festivals reflect their prehispanic heritage, among them colorful dances to mark the harvest. Then there are the **Zoques** (from the Sierra portion), who today represent only a small population (mostly in remote areas), with a deep love of nature. Finally, there are the **Chol**, from the southeast.

In Veracruz there are the **Totonacs**, and the **Náhuatl** speakers (descendants of the Aztecs). In Tamaulipas, you'll find the **Huastecs**; in Oaxaca, the **Zapotecs** and **Mixtecs**; and in Chiapas, the **Maya**.

Culture & Customs

■ Hello? Goodbye?

Mexicans observe a few formalities in greetings. It's polite to greet people with the appropriate temporal acknowledgement – *buenos días, buenos tardes*, or *buenos noches*. When you pass someone on the street and they nod and greet you, just smile and give the same greeting in return. If you plan on addressing someone whose name you don't know, it's appropriate to use their title – *señor* (for men), *señora* (for women), *señorita* (for young women), or *maestro/maestra* (for a skilled professional). Someone with whom you're more familiar is likely to greet you (if you're a woman) with a kiss on the cheek. If you make phone calls, instead of an *hola?*, you'll likely be greeted with a *Bueno?*, the common phone greeting.

■ Is this a Line?

For some reason, there is just no such thing as a neat orderly line to receive goods and services. You think you've done it, you've gotten to the concert, bus station, or bank before the ticketperson's there, the bus has arrived, or the exchange counter opens. You think you can get a good seat or get in and out quickly; there's a crowd behind you, but you're second in line and unconcerned. Unconcerned? As soon as whatever you're waiting for opens, a crowd of people will appear from nowhere – most of them in front of you, pushing and edging their way to the entrance. It's not rudeness here, it's just the local custom. You'll either have to be polite and do your best to maintain your own little piece of line, or square your shoulders and join in the fray.

■ Is It Open?

Ever heard of the Mexican mañana and wondered whether or not it's true, whether or not it's exaggerated, and whether or not you could ever live that way? You're about to find out. There is no such thing as punctuality in México. Mexicans simply don't allow time to rule their lives. Punctuality should never be assumed, store hours are never adhered to, and if someone says they'll get to something tomorrow – well, that could be tomorrow, or the following day, or the following week.

This attitude is reflected in all aspects of life, but for the everyday visitor, it will be most apparent in store hours – many shops, banks, and even government offices take a mid-day break, most famously known as the siesta. It's meant to give workers a break during the worst heat of the day. Throughout the region covered in this book, many places follow this custom. Typically, this means that between the hours of 2 or 3 pm and 4 or 5 pm, many offices will be closed, re-opening for another three or so hours in the late afternoon. And don't be too alarmed if the shop doesn't open up exactly when it said it would – the owner will be along in good time. Don't assume either that a bank, tourist office or shop is open from 9 to 5 – you're in México and anything goes. I encountered a government office whose hours were 9 am to 12 pm, Tuesdays, Wednesdays and Fridays. Check hours before you make a specific attempt to go somewhere distant (especially on a Sunday); printed hours can and do change.

■ Where Can I Find...?

Mexicans are friendly, kind, and helpful, but perhaps a deadly combination of the three when you're lost. If you ask a villager for directions, he may point you in the right direction. Often, however, if he doesn't know, he is more likely to point ahead in the direction you were going, and nod agreement, preferring to encourage you (even if it is wrong) than to be unfriendly. It's strange, but true. Often, you'll be able to tell. Some clues give it away – like the fact that the local villager might not even speak Spanish (which you discover of course only after you've hailed him down), and yet he's eagerly and kindly directing you on. Just drive on and ask the next person, you'll get to where you're going eventually.

■ How Do I Dress?

Most anything you would normally wear at home is fine to wear out in public. However, short-shorts, cropped shirts, and mini-miniskirts will bring extra attention. Most Mexican men stick with long pants and most Mexican women wear dresses. This is especially true of indigenous women, though it does not apply to the young crowd (especially in urban areas), who are incredibly fashion-conscious, follow current trends, and will probably be decked out better than your teenager at home. At church, men should wear slacks, and women a dress (to be most respectful, your dress should not be open-backed or with bare shoulders). You'll notice that, during evenings, women especially get dressed up to go out. Even if it's just to the mall or to the movies, you'll find makeup set, hair fixed, perfume out, and heels on.

Travel

■ Getting Here

By Air

Though you'll probably connect through Texas or Florida, you can get to the Gulf Coast directly from the United States; international airports are located in the Puerto de Veracruz, Tampico, and Villahermosa, and each offers at least one direct route. Other than that, most people find themselves connecting through México City, which to us small city folk (México City is one of the largest cities in the world!) is a bit intimidating. Just be sure to keep your eye on the kids and your hand on your wallet. Keep in mind when you book your flight that some stateside airlines have code sharing agreements with Mexican airlines; if you book all your flights in advance of your trip, they often offer a discount on Mexican domestic flights that you'll have to take. Definitely worth investigating.

Another option you'll want to look at is the **Mexipass** – an airpass designed for use by foreign tourists mainly on Mexicana domestic flights. The Mexipass allows for drastically reduced airfare between cities. The rules are a bit confusing, but what it seems to boil down to is that discounts are given only on domestic flights, and you must book more than two domestic segments in addition to having a roundtrip international flight (on any airline) in order to receive the discount. You also must be traveling inside México for a minimum of three days, and a maximum of 90 days. You do not have to purchase or pay for the Mexipass – you simply tell the agent when you're booking your domestic flights that you are interested in the Mexipass discount; you should then be offered a lower rate than you might otherwise receive. Not every reservations agent is completely familiar with the Mexipass (and indeed, it took a couple of agents until I found one who was); you may get a silent reaction at first, followed by a few grunts of incomprehension. Don't worry, you'll eventually be put on hold and a knowledgeable agent will come to your aid. Even if you've booked your incoming international flight on a different airline, if you're flying around México on Mexicana, don't forget to ask about the discount when booking your tickets. (The use of a different airline simply requires three domestic segments instead of two).

Each appropriate city in this book has a *Getting There – By Air* section, where I've listed the major airlines that service the airport. For convenience, all relevant phone numbers are listed below.

AIRLINES SERVING THE GULF COAST

- **Aeroméxico**, ☎ 800-237-6639; www.Aeromexico.com

You can find international service with them from cities including Atlanta, Baltimore, Barcelona, Baton Rouge, Boston, Budapest, Charlotte, Chicago, Cincinnati, Cleveland, Columbus, Dallas Fort Worth, Detroit, El Paso, Hartford, Houston, La Vegas, Lubbock, Madrid, Ontario, Orlando, Raleigh, San Jose, Tampa, Vancouver, Washington/Dulles, Washington D.C., and Zurich. Nationally, they fly to most major cities. Aeroméxico has code-sharing agreement with Delta airlines.

- **Mexicana Airlines**, ☎ 800-531-7921; www.mexicana.com

Mexicana flies to most major destinations throughout Latin America, including Acapulco, Cancún, Carmen City, Cozumel, Durango, Guadalajara, Guatemala, Havana, Hermosillo, Huatulco, Leon, Manzanillo, Mazatlan, Merida, Mexicali, México City, Minatitlan, Monterrey, Morelia, Nuevo Laredo, Oaxaca, Panama, Puerto Vallarta, Saltillo, San Jose Costa Rica, San Jose del Cabo, Tampico, Tijuana, Tuxtla Gutiérrez, Veracruz, Villahermosa, Zacatecas, Zihuatanejo. They also have service to New York, San Francisco, San Antonio, Miami, Los Angeles, Denver, and Chicago (among others). They have a code-sharing agreement with United airlines.

Regional subsidiaries of Mexicana also are in the code-sharing agreements, including **Aerocaribe/AeroCozumel**, ☎ 800-531-7921, which fly to some smaller cities.

- **Aeroliteral**, ☎ 800-531-7921; www.aerolitoral.com.mx

Flights include to/from México and Las Vegas, Houston, Los Angeles, El Paso, and Salt Lake City; in México some of the flights include Tampico, Poza Rica, Reynosa, Veracruz, Villahermosa, and México City.

- **Aeromar**, ☎ 800-531-7921 or 0800-237-6627 (MX); www.aeromar.com.mx

When you travel on Aeromar you can earn frequent flyer points on Mexicana, Aeroméxico, or United Airlines (you can also use any you might have). They fly turboprop planes to: Campeche, Ciudad Victoria, Colima, Xalapa, Lazaro Cardenas, México City, Monterrey, Morelia, Poza Rica, Puebla, Querétaro, Reynosa, Salina Cruz, San Cristóbal de las Casas, San Luis Potosi, Tepic, and Unuapan. They have one daily flight on Fri., Sat., and Sun. from Laredo, TX to México City.

- **Aerocalifornia**, ☎ 800-237-6225

This carrier has international flights from Los Angeles to Veracruz or Tampico (with a connection in Guadalajara) and also services other major Mexican cities.

- **Continental Airlines**, ☎ 800-231-0856; www.continental.com

Includes service to México City, Monterrery, Cancún, Mazatlan, and service from the Puerto de Veracruz to Houston.

- **United Airlines**, ☎ 800-241-6522; www.united.com

United doesn't offer service to the Gulf Coast, but does fly directly from some U.S. cities to México City, including direct service from Los Angeles, San Francisco, and Washington DC.

Code-sharing agreement with Mexicana airlines.

- **American Airlines**, ☎ 800-433-7300; www.aa.com

American doesn't offer service to the Gulf Coast, but does fly directly to many Mexican cities where you can get a connecting flight, including Monterrey, México city, Cancún, Guadalajara, Aguascalientes, San Jose del Cabo, Acapulco, Puerto Vallarta, and Guanajuato.

WORD TO THE WISE

Did you know that many Mexican airlines offer discounts to students, children, and senior citizens? Aeroliteral, for example, offers as much as a 50% discount to students. When you make your reservation, be sure to ask.

By Car

Driving into México is convenient. Coming from Texas, there are a number of border crossings. In the mornings or afternoons, you'll find long lines of cars waiting to cross the bridges over the Río Grande and into México. Traffic moves pretty quickly and, aside from perhaps a brief glance into your car on the Mexican side, Customs is a breeze. The most convenient spot to cross into the coastal region is near the Gulf at the Brownsville (US)-Matamoros (MX) crossing; from here, you just follow Highway 180 straight down into Tamaulipas and the rest of the Gulf Coast. Other major access points to the coast include McAllen (US)-Reynosa (MX), a little farther west, and, still farther west, Laredo (US)-Nuevo Laredo (MX). This last is a popular access point to Monterrey; from there you can cut across to Ciudad Victoria (in central Tamaulipas) on Highway 85.

Regulations & Permits

Your US driver's license is valid in México. If you plan on going more than 20 km/12 miles into México, you'll need to obtain a Temporary Vehicle Importation Permit, except in the Free Trade Zones (Baja California and Sonora). When you cross the border, stop at the Customs office; you'll need to present proof of citizenship, your tourist card, a valid driver's license, the car's registration or title, and a major credit card. First you'll be sent to make copies of the documents (there's usually an office right there doing it for a small fee), then you'll have to go to the Vehicular Control Module, run by the Banco del Ejército (Banjército), where you present your papers, pay the processing fee (around US $25), and present your credit card as a guarantee. (Card details are recorded; if you fail to bring your car back to the US, you can be charged a duty and lose future importation rights.) If you don't have a credit card, you can post a cash deposit (refundable when you exit the country in the authorized time) of US $200-$400, depending on the year of the car. You'll be given a permit document, as well as a hologram sticker for your car. Once you have the permit, you can use it for up to six months to exit and enter the country. After the permit expires, if the car is being driven in México, it can be (and more than likely will be) confiscated. Be sure when the time is up (or when you leave the country), to stop at the Banjército at the border Customs office to terminate the permit. Get a receipt!

When you finally cross back over the border to the United States, you'll be asked your citizenship, and whether or not you have any items to declare; a few people are randomly stopped and inspected.

Insurance

Unfortunately, your American car insurance is not valid in México, although many insurers do cover a few miles into the border zone (check with your insurance company for the specifics of your coverage). So the question then becomes, to insure or not to insure? Contrary to popular belief, Mexican insurance is not mandatory in México. But this does not mean that you should throw caution to the wind. If you get into an accident, the police can (and will) detain everyone involved (regardless of who caused the accident) until all details are worked out. When you purchase insurance, you don't have to worry about every crazed bus driver, tired trucker, or speeding taxi that you see – you're covered (in many cases you're also given the name of a lawyer to contact for help). It's worth it for the peace of mind.

A well-known company offering insurance is **Sanborn's**, ☎ 800-222-0158 (US), www.sanbornsinsurance.com, which provides coverage for cars, RVs, trailers, motorcycles and boats. You can even receive a quote and purchase coverage online. They have agents in Illinois, California, Arizona, México, and Texas (some of the cities where you can stop by in person include Dallas, El Paso, Laredo, McAllen, and San Antonio). If you don't plan ahead of time, no problem. In the US border towns you'll see signs advertising Mexican insurance – the closer you get to an international bridge, the more you'll see. They'll be able to hook you up on the spot.

By Bus

Greyhound Bus Lines, ☎ 800-229-9424 or 402-330-8552, www.greyhound.com, offers a convenient way to make it to the border. Typically, the bus will drive over the border crossing, stop at the Customs office (where luggage is inspected and you get your tourist permit), then continue to the border city in México. From there, you can connect to a huge network of Mexican bus lines and destinations (see *Getting Around*, below). If you're planning on traveling into México by Greyhound, particularly around the border towns, look into the **Ameripass**, which you purchase for a specific time frame – four (US $140), seven ($199), 10 ($249), 15 ($289), 21 ($339), 30 ($379), 45 ($429), or 60 days ($519); it allows for unlimited bus travel during those times. The catch is that the number of Mexican cities it serves is very limited – Matamoros, Nuevo Laredo, and Tijuana. However, in addition to these cities, it also allows for travel within the US and some Canadian cities, so if you're doing a lot of traveling, it might fit into your plans. There are discounts for students, seniors, and children.

■ Getting Around

By Bus

Traveling by bus in México is not the same as in the United States. It's much more common than flying or taking a train. As for long-distance bus travel, it can be a luxurious affair. A word of caution – you'll want to travel during the daytime whenever possible. It's pretty safe along the Gulf Coast, but in Chiapas and some sections of Oaxaca hijackings and robberies have been reported on overnight travels. If you're heading to these areas, travel by deluxe bus, or at least first class – these buses use the toll roads where such incidents are less frequently reported.

There are many different bus lines in México. The main first-class line on the Gulf Coast is **ADO**, and for second-class service you'll mostly see **AU**. Between companies, first-class and second-class service is pretty comparable.

Deluxe

For long-distance trips, take the deluxe bus service (*lujo*) whenever possible, also known as *ejecutivo* (executive service). At the top of this category is **UNO**, with its top-notch luxury service. There are about 25 seats for the entire bus (compared to twice that many in a normal bus), meaning there will be plenty of leg room and personal space, beverages and a movie (four TVs in the bus) are complimentary, seats are assigned and they recline extra-far; there is a bathroom, trips are air-conditioned (bring a sweater) and buses are dependable. They do adhere to printed departure and arrival times. Sometimes you even get a first-class lounge at the bus station. And you will always find that the drivers are dressed in suits and ties – that little extra touch adds a lot. Unfortunately, however, UNO travels to only 20 or so destinations, mainly servicing the long-distance market. It's also 30-50% more expensive than regular first-class service, but well worth it.

Right under UNO, still in the executive class, are **ADO GL**, **Maya de Oro**, and **ADO Plus**. These lines are still luxurious (much more so than first class), but a little less extreme than UNO. There are a few more seats (40), but you still get beverages, frigid air-conditioning, a bathroom, and movie after movie. Maya de Oro's main destinations in this category include San Cristóbal de las Casas and Tuxtla Gutiérrez (both in Oaxaca). ADO Plus main destinations head into Chiapas and Oaxaca (Arriaga, Oaxaca, Tapachula, etc.). Finally, for the purposes of this book the main line you'll see in this category time and time again is ADO GL (which even has both a men's and women's bathroom).

BUS DESTINATIONS
UNO Destinations (☎ 0800-702-8000, www.uno.com.mx)
Cardenas, Ciudad del Carmen, Coatzacoalco, Cordoba, Xalapa, Juchitan, Matamoros, México City, Minatitlan, Oaxaca, Poza Rica, Puebla, Orizaba, Reynosa, San Cristóbal de las Casas, Santa Cruz, Tampico, Tapachula, Tuxpan, Tuxtla Gutiérrez, Veracruz, Villahermosa.
ADO GL destinations (☎ 0800-702-8000 www.adogl.com.mx)
Acatlan, Acayucan, Campeche, Cancún, Cardenas, Ciudad del Carmen, Chetumal, Coatzacoalcos, Cordobas, Huajuapan de Leon, Huatulco, Huixtla, Ixtalepec, Ixtepec, Xalapa, Juchitan, Lagunas, Matias Romero, Merida, México City (Norte, Sur, TAPO), Minatitlan, Oaxaca, Orizaba, Playa del Carmen, Poza Rica, Puebla, Putla, Salina Cruz, Tampico, Tapachula, Tehuantepec, Tlaxiaco, Tonala, Tuxpan, Tuxtla Gutierrerz, Veracruz, Villahermosa.

First Class

The first-class buses (*primera classe*) you'll see most often are the ADO buses (www.ado.com.mx). Besides mainly servicing the Gulf, ADO also has some destinations in the Yucatán, including Cancún and Merida. First-class service is about the equivalent of what you would find on a Greyhound – it's comfortable and dependable. Seats are assigned when you buy your ticket, buses are air-conditioned, and most of the time you'll have an en-route movie. Buses tend to have different movie selections, so you probably won't have to watch the same movie twice. Most have bathrooms, though on shorter trips you might find them locked. They are pretty consistent with scheduled arrival and departure times, though they do get off-schedule a bit more than the deluxe or ejecutivo. Many cities have hourly departures. You're likely to make a couple of stops getting from Point A to Point B (particularly if it is a long journey). The ticket agent can tell you where and how many stops there will be; often, it's only a five- to 10-minute stop for people to get on and off.

Another first-class line you see in the northern section (Tamaulipas) is the **Omnibus de México**, www.omnibusdemexico.com.mx, which has buses around Tamaulipas and Northern Veracruz (as well as other states such as Durango, Aguascalientes, and Guanajuato). **Cristóbal Colon**, www.cristobalcolon.com.mx, serves the southeast portion of the country, including Veracruz, Oaxaca, and Chiapas. If you are heading into Oaxaca, you'll see **Altos** (with lots of service to San Cristóbal de las Casas and Tuxtla Gutiérrez), and if you're coming from the Yucatán, you'll have seen **Riviera**. **Estrella de Oro**, www.estrelladeoro.com.mx, which serves mainly the Pacific coast.

Second Class

Stepping down a notch or three, you have the second-class buses, which are cheaper, slower, and more crowded. The lines you'll see most often will be **ADO Economico**, **AU**, **Cuenca**, **TRT**, and **Sur**, although (particularly in larger cities near a state border) you'll see a number of other lines as well. Though these buses travel the same routes as the first-class lines, the trip is anything but the same. Second-class buses are frequently crowded, often not air-conditioned, don't have a bathroom, and are always slow. Printed times are almost never adhered to; you'll want to add at least an hour onto the time you are told. As soon as the bus leaves the station you'll understand why. It is not necessary to pre-purchase a ticket; in fact, people actually stand a block or two from the station and flag the bus down. Before you've even left the city, you've made a half-dozen stops to pick up other travelers. Bus drivers can also be a bit wilder than on the first-class or deluxe buses. One driver was so anxious to get nowhere, that he actually attempted to pass a line of six cars while going around a tight curve, unable to see the other lane. Everybody on board (aisles packed) was grabbing the handholds for balance, and we were so top-heavy that if a car actually had come head-on at us, the bus would have toppled over with the turn before we actually hit anything.

Sometimes you have no choice but to take a second-class bus – you might be traveling during a holiday and everything is booked, or first-class service might not stop in the village you want to get to. In such cases, don't despair. Yes, you might have continual stops, but at least you have cushioned seats and a fairly modern bus. It could be far worse – you could be on a local city bus.

Local City Buses

As for local city buses, just about anything goes. You can always expect the bus to be old, the ride to be bumpy, the drivers to speed, and tickets to be cheap. Now, the degree of each of these does vary considerably – in some cities the ride is hardly anything worth talking about, while in some villages, you can find yourself on an ancient school bus on an adventure you'll be talking about for years. The usual method of catching a bus is to find the route it travels, then flag it down at the nearest corner. Be sure to have change (you might find that difficult), and be sure that if you do need change returned, you get it. Ask for and keep your ticket/receipt – not only to make sure you were charged the correct price, but because ticket inspectors sometimes pop in to make sure everyone has paid. If you don't show your ticket, you're probably going to have to pay again.

Getting Tickets

You can buy your ticket at the bus station right before the scheduled departure. In most cases, if there's not a holiday or event taking place, you should have no problems. During these times however – most especially if you want a deluxe or first-class ride – you should book well in advance; if you change your mind, tickets are refundable. (This does not, however, necessarily apply to second-class service.) Just bring your unused ticket to the bus station agent . One of the most convenient ways to check bus schedules and times – particularly if you are trying to do it from home before you go, is to consult **Ticketbus**, ☎ 0800-702-8000 or 5-133-2424, www.ticketbus.com.mx. Their helpful website comes in both Spanish and English, and gives you a lot of information for the routes that you specify, including prices, number of stops, lines that service the route, distance, and duration. A toll-free number is listed for tickets. It's an excellent resource, particularly for information on UNO, ADO, and AU lines.

By Car

The main highways in México are notorious for being nerve-racking and slow. In almost all cases, they are a single lane each way with little or no shoulder, no official rest stops, and no option but to follow the road and slow your car through the numerous local villages. For obvious reasons then, the highways (which are really not that different from what you'd find in some rural sections of the US) start to pose problems for the safe driver. Where can you stop to stretch? Where do you pull off if you break down? The solution is not to dismiss driving, but simply go prepared with equipment and knowledge. Be sure you have spare tires, jacks, know how to change a tire, and take warning triangles to put in the street if you break down. Be aware of drivers that pass you going in the other direction – often, they can see any obstructions or breakdowns around the bend before you can. I narrowly avoided hitting a broken-down fruit truck on one trip thanks to passing drivers flashing their lights.

Driving in México has improved by leaps and bounds in the past 10 or so years. The federal government has put in place many federal tollways (*autopistas*) that bypass the narrow single-lane highways, small villages, and slower speeds that were the nightmares of some drivers. You now drive on fast, smooth, wide tollways light-years ahead of their no-fee predecessors. Of course, convenience does come with a hefty pricetag – the tolls are not cheap, and segments can cost anywhere from $1 to $15. Add to this the outrageous price of gas – at the time of this writing it was 5.98 pesos a liter (equivalent to about $2.26 a gallon), and you'll wonder if you should adjust your budget.

So, should you take the tollway or not? Well, in some cases, you don't even have a choice. Where you do have a choice, you'll really have to weigh speed over time. On the *libre* (free highway) you'll encounter dogs, chickens, farmers, locals, vendors – while the *autopista* will get you where you need to go quickly, and with no *topes*.

So you want to drive? Here are 10 things you should know:

- When you see the word **tope**, slow down. The *tope* is a Mexican speed bump; every village has one – at its entrance, at its exit, and often in-between. The bumps are more often much bigger than you might expect. Some will scrape the bottom of a heavy car, some will scrape the bottom of a light car. They can be made out of anything, but most commonly you'll see thick ropes or cement humps. Most of the time the sign is long before you see the bump – the kindest of villages give you ample warning – at 1,500 feet, at 600 feet, at 300 feet , then the sign right over it. One thing about the *tope* is certain: if you miss slowing down for one, you'll never forget it.

- Since most of the *libre* highways are single lane each way, **to pass someone**, you'll have to cross into the oncoming traffic lane. Many times, the person that you are trying to pass will turn on his or her left turn signal, and move slightly to the shoulder (if there is one), this is a signal to you that it is OK to pass.

- If you break down on the highway, take heart. The major highways are regularly patrolled by the Secretaría de Turismo's **Ángeles Verdes** (Green Angels), a patrol of bilingual mechanics who provide breakdown assistance free of charge. (A raised hood is a good way to signal that you need help.) You can also call for their assistance toll-free at ☎ 0800-903-9200.

- **Driving at night** can be dangerous. The major problem is that, when night comes, most highways become completely black. There are no streetlamps and usually no road reflectors. Curves and turns in the road can be difficult to see, animals can appear unexpectedly, and if a car breaks down on the *libre*, it often will stop partially (or totally) in the middle of the road (bad in the daytime, extremely dangerous at night).

- You'll quickly become familiar with Pemex, the government-owned stations where all **gasoline** is sold. Gas is bought by the liter, you'll see *magna sin* (unleaded), *premium* (super unleaded), and *super* (leaded). With the exception of the border towns (which are often differently priced), as you get into México, gas pricing is consistent. You'll need to have cash (credit cards are generally not accepted), know how much you want (it's full-service, so to fill her up, simply say *lleno*), and watch carefully to make sure you are not cheated. Sometimes the attendant will "forget" to zero out the gas pump from the last person – charging you for more gas than you receive. It won't happen all the time (in 20 fill-ups I encountered one incident). Just pay attention; if you're looking, they'll be forced to charge you correctly. While you're being filled up, you'll also get an unsolicited window cleaning – it can be practically impossible to stop the attendant. A small tip is generally expected for this service.

- If you need a **parking lot**, look for a sign saying *estacionamiento*. If hotels don't themselves offer parking, many can direct you to the nearest lot. Around the border – and especially if you have boxes, luggage, or a fancy car – don't leave your car parked outside overnight. Sometimes in the parking lots, or when you park in front of a store, a "parking attendant" (I use the term loosely) will wave you in. Even if you're the only car in the lot, your helpful friend has done you a service he believes warrants a tip – a few pesos is fine.

- Think preventatively when it comes to car accidents. Get **insurance**. In the event of an accident (assuming the other person stops), once the police get there, both parties are committed to hours of detainment, and most likely a trip down to the station. Some people, wishing to avoid the involvement of the police, if the accident is clearly their fault, will try and arrange a deal with you to get it fixed before the police arrive; if you have insurance, you don't have to worry about any of that. Notoriously, bus drivers are the worst when it comes to driving – they have absolutely no regard for anyone else on the road and often use intimidation tactics to make you yield to them. I've seen more than a few cars fall victim to their wheels. Unless you have nerves of steel, you're probably not going to want to call their bluff.

- If you didn't pay attention to #1 on this list (the *tope*), you'll probably be forced to pay attention to this one – the *taller mecanico* (**mechanic/repair shop**). You might also need to find a *vulcanizadora* or *llentera*, who can fix your tires.

- When you stop your car at a light in a city, it's more than likely a **windshield washer** will take it upon himself to clean the filth from your windows; he expects a tip in return. If you don't want his assistance, when you see him approaching, firmly say no and shake your head (he may or may not take the hint – if he doesn't, you're probably not being firm enough!).

- When you come across a **military checkpoint** (you'll see a few if you drive south along the coast), don't be alarmed by the uniformed military men with their guns in view. They are looking for weapons and drug traffickers and, aside from maybe a brief look in the car, will do little to detain you. Don't take pictures!

Car Rentals

Renting a car in México can be expensive. A week-long rental in Xalapa, for example, runs from US $500 to $700 for a small car; border-town rates are a bit less expensive. Sometimes, however, even though you can get just about everyplace (given time and patience) by bus, having your own set of wheels to bump around the countryside is worth it for the freedom it gives you. Compare prices among agencies, and check the weekly rates (which are often much cheaper than daily rentals). Many agencies offer four-wheel-drive rentals.

By Taxi

You'll easily be able to find taxis in most mid-sized to large towns. If you are wary of exorbitant fares, you just might be in for a pleasant surprise. Taxis can be quite affordable – usually just a couple of dollars can get you to most places in town. If you're more than one person traveling, a taxi may even be as cheap as a bus – three or more people and it's almost certainly so. Before you get in, agree on the fee with the driver, as taxis throughout México are not metered. There are established fees to drive from Point A to Point B. Since you're a foreigner, however, you won't know what those rates are. It's important for both you and the driver to have the same figure in mind from the get-go. It's not uncommon for a taxi driver whose cab is half-full to stop if you hail him and ask where you're going – if you're going in the same direction, you just share the cab with the other passengers. If it's you in the half-empty cab, and someone is flagging him down, the driver will likely ask you if it's okay if he stops to pick them up.

■ Customs

Entering

When you enter México, you can bring your personal items duty-free, including clothing, toiletries, a CD player, a personal computer, 12 rolls of film, a VCR, and a cell phone. Some items are restricted by quantity – over a certain amount and you'll have to pay a duty. This includes alcohol (three liters per person) and cigarettes (20 packs per person). Plants and seeds are usually restricted. If you have prescription medicine, bring the prescription. Drugs and firearms are big no-nos. (If you're going hunting, see the Mexican Consulate about regulations and permits.)

Before you leave Customs, you'll have to decide if you have items to declare or not. If so, go to the appropriate line and pay your duty. If not, you press a button under a red and green stoplight to determine if your luggage will be searched. Simply press the button next to the immigration official and, if the light is red, you're pulled aside to have your bags searched (they're looking for undeclared items); if the light is green, you've started your Mexican adventure! The red light/green light system applies to all – those coming by air, by car, and by foot.

Returning

When you return to the United States by air, you'll probably fill out a Customs declaration form where you declare the value of anything you've picked up on your travels. The immigration officer will ask if you have anything to declare, how long you've been abroad, and he'll want to see your passport. You're allowed $800 duty-free purchases (if you've been gone for longer than 48 hours), which includes one liter of alcoholic beverages; you are not allowed to bring back fruits or vegetables of any kind. The **US Customs Service** (www.customs.ustreas.gov) can give you more information on exemptions and declarations. Canadian and British citizens can consult the appropriate Customs office – **Canada Customs and Revenue Agency**, www.ccra-adrc.gc.ca, or **HM Customs and Excise** (for British citizens), www.hmce.gov.uk.

Entry Requirements

For US citizens, entrance into México for less than 72 hours involves no legalities – all your need is to cross the border, and provide proof of citizenship (a current passport or birth certificate accompanied by a picture ID). For periods longer than 72 hours (or to go beyond the Border Zone), you'll need to get a **tourist permit** (*Forma Migratoria para Turista – FMT*). The tourist permit is good for up to 180 days; the immigration official will stamp the permit, and write on it the length of time he's approving you for. Normally, you're given the full amount, but if for some reason you're not, and you'll be in the country for awhile, ask for it. If you aren't given the maximum and it later turns out that you need it, visit an immigration office a few days before it's about to expire and you can get an extension. Before you exit the country, you'll need to pay the tourist card fee (approximately US $20); the fee can be paid at any time during your stay at any of the Mexican banks listed on the back of the permit. Be sure you get a stamp marked "Paid." Keep the card with you at all times – if you're stopped at a checkpoint or by the police, you'll probably need to show it. If you lose it, contact an immigration office or your consulate for assistance; it's a hassle, but a duplicate can be issued. If your passport gets lost or stolen, contact the closest US embassy immediately (see page 75).

If you're coming into México via plane, normally the price of the permit (and any applicable departure fees) are included in the price of your ticket.

WORD TO THE WISE

If you're traveling with a minor (under 18), and both parents aren't there, you'll need to provide a notarized letter of consent allowing the one parent to travel with the child or, if the child is traveling alone, a letter of authorization from both parents. If a parent has sole custody, bring documentation to that effect. The rules can be a pain, but they're there to protect against child abduction.

US citizens planning on living or working in México should contact the nearest Mexican consulate about an FM-2 or FM-3. If you're a student and want to spend more than six months studying there, you'll need to apply for a student visa; contact your embassy for further details. In general, it requires that you fill out the appropriate paperwork and submit photos, an acceptance letter from the school you're attending, proof of financial resources, and fees.

Passports

To Apply

The easiest way to enter México is by providing a current US passport (see *Entry Requirements*). Unless expedited, it takes around six weeks to receive your passport, so be sure to allow plenty of time. Applications are accepted at many post offices, public libraries, courthouses, and municipal government buildings. To download an application, find more information, and view a listing of the designated places where you can apply, visit the US State Department website: http://travel.state.gov.

The procedure and application for getting a passport is very easy – you'll need to fill out form Form DS-11, Application for Passport (which you can obtain either online or from an issuer's office). Provide proof of US citizenship (a certified birth certificate, an expired US passport, a certificate of citizenship, or a naturalization certificate), present proof of ID (an expired US passport, a driver's license, a government ID, a military ID, a certificate of citizenship, or a naturalization certificate), provide two copies of a passport photo and pay the passport fee. At the time of this writing the fee was US $85 for applicants aged 16 and older, and US $70 for under 16 years of age. If you cannot provide any of the listed proofs of citizenship, there are alternate procedures – consult the US State Department's website for more information. Passports are valid for 10 years if received when you are 16 or older, and five years if 16 or younger.

If you need to renew your passport, you can do so if you submit your expired passport with your application (Form DS-82). Your old passport will be returned to you, and you'll get a new one as well. The current renewal fee is US $55.

If you need your passport application expedited (under either new or renewal conditions) add an extra US $60 to the application fee. Expedited passports arrive in around two weeks.

Lost or Stolen Passports

If your passport is lost or stolen, report it immediately. You'll need to fill out an application and a Statement Regarding Lost or Stolen Passport (Form DS-64) and bring them to a passport issuer. If you do not need it immediately, send your documents in the mail: US Department of State, Passport Services, Consular Lost/Stolen Passport Section, 1111 19th Street, NW, Suite 500, Washington, DC 20036, ☎ 202-955-0430.

If your passport has been lost or stolen while outside the country, contact the nearest embassy or consular office immediately. They'll

Above: Tamaulipas ruins reflected in the water
Below: Cenote in Tamaulipas (see page 102)

Above: Tampico, Tamaulipas, boat tour (see page 122)

ow: Playa de Miramar before the crowds arrive, Tampico, Tamaulipas (see page 122)

Above: Veracruz ladies in traditional dress
Below: Fiesta in Zococalco, Veracruz

be able to assist you. It's a good idea when you go traveling to make two photocopies of your passport. Leave one copy at home with your family and bring one copy on your trip (carried separately from your original passport). It can help reduce the headache of any unforeseen passport disappearances.

Passport Agencies

If you're down to the wire and you need a passport immediately, your local passport agency can help you. All of them assist those traveling within two weeks, or those needing a foreign visa. All agencies listed below have automated appointment phone numbers – it's best to use them to ensure you don't end up wasting the whole day; some offices even require it. The New York office, for example, does not take walk-ins at all – it's by appointment only.

BOSTON
Region: Upstate New York, Vermont, Maine, Massachusetts, Rhode Island, New Hampshire.
Thomas P. O'Neill Federal Building
10 Causeway Street, Suite 247
Boston, MA 02222-1094
☎ 617-878-0900
Open Mon.-Fri., 9 am-4 pm

CHICAGO
Region: Illinois and Michigan
Kluczynski Federal Building
230 S. Dearborn Street, 18th Floor
Chicago, IL 60604-1564
☎ 312-341-6020
Open Mon.-Fri., 9 am-4 pm

CONNECTICUT
Region: Connecticut, Westchester County New York
50 Washington Street
Norwalk, CT 06854
☎ 203-299-5443
Open Mon.-Fri., 9 am-4 pm

HONOLULU
Region: Hawaii, Guam, American Samoa, Commonwealth of the Northern Mariana Islands, Koror, Kolonia, Majuro, Kwajalein and Johnston Island
Prince Kuhio Federal Building
300 Ala Moana Blvd., Suite 1-330
Honolulu, HI 96850
☎ 808-522-8283
Open Mon.-Fri., 8:30 am-3:30 pm

HOUSTON
Region: Texas, Oklahoma, Kansas, and New Mexico
Mickey Leland Federal Building
1919 Smith Street, Suite 1400
Houston, TX 77002-8049
☎ 713-751-0294
Open Mon.-Fri., 8:30 am-3:30 pm

LOS ANGELES
Region: California (all counties south of and including San Luis Obispo County, Kern and San Bernardino), and Clark County, Nevada
Federal Building
11000 Wilshire Blvd., Suite 1000
Los Angeles, CA 90024-3615
☎ 310-575-5700
Open Mon.-Fri., 8 am-3 pm

MIAMI
Region: Florida, South Carolina, and US Virgin Islands
Claude Pepper Federal Office Building
51 SW First Avenue, 3rd Floor
Miami, FL 33130-1680
☎ 305-539-3600
Open Mon.-Fri., 8:30 am-3:30 pm

NEW ORLEANS
Region: Alabama, Arkansas, Georgia, Indiana, Iowa, Kentucky, Louisiana, Mississippi, Missouri, North Carolina, Ohio, Puerto Rico, Tennessee, Virgina (except Arlington, Alexandria, Fairfax, Loudon, Prince William, and Stafford counties), and Wisconsin
One Canal Place (corner of Canal and North Peters Streets)
365 Canal Street, Suite 1300
New Orleans, LA 70130-6508
☎ 504-412-2600
Open Mon.-Fri., 8:30 am-3:30 pm

NEW YORK
Region: New York City and Long Island
376 Hudson Street
New York, NY 10014
☎ 212-206-3500
Open Mon.-Fri., 7:30 am-3 pm
Walk-ins not accepted, you must call to make an appointment beforehand.

PHILADELPHIA
Region: Pennsylvania, New Jersey, Deleware, and West Virginia
US Custom House
200 Chestnut Street, Room 103
Philadelphia, PA 19106-2970
☎ 215-418-5937
Open Mon.-Fri., 9 am-4 pm

SAN FRANCISCO
Region: Arizona, California (all counties north of and including Monterey, Kings, Tulare, and Mono), Nevada (except Clark County) and Utah
95 Hawthorne Street, 5th Floor
San Francisco, CA 94105-3901
☎ 415-538-2700
Open Mon.-Fri., 9 am-4 pm

SEATTLE
Region: Alaska, Colorado, Idaho, Minnesota, Montana, Nebraska, North Dakota, Oregon, South Dakota, Washington, and Wyoming
Henry Jackson Federal Building
915 Second Avenue, Suite 992
Seattle, WA 98174-1091
☎ 206-808-5700
Open Mon.-Fri., 8 am-3:30 pm

WASHINGTON
Region: Washington, DC, Maryland, and Virginia (counties of Arlington, Alexandria, Fairfax, Loudon, Stafford, and Prince William)
1111 19th Street, N.W.
Washington, D.C. 20524
☎ 202-647-0518
Open Mon.-Fri., 8 am-3 pm

Practicalities

■ Time, Measurements & Electricity

The Gulf Coast is on **Central Standard Time**, and observes **daylight savings time** between the first Sunday in April and the last Sunday in October.

Going Metric

To make your travel a bit easier, we have provided this chart that shows metric equivalents for the measurements you are familiar with.

GENERAL MEASUREMENTS

1 kilometer = .6124 miles

1 mile = 1.6093 kilometers

1 foot = .304 meters

1 inch = 2.54 centimeters

1 square mile = 2.59 square kilometers

1 pound = .4536 kilograms

1 ounce = 28.35 grams

1 imperial gallon = 4.5459 liters

1 US gallon = 3.7854 liters

1 quart = .94635 liters

TEMPERATURES

For Fahrenheit: Multiply Centigrade figure by 1.8 and add 32.

For Centigrade: Subtract 32 from Fahrenheit figure and divide by 1.8.

Centigrade	Fahrenheit
40°	104°
35°	95°
30°	86°
25°	77°
20°	64°
15°	59°
10°	50°

Units are measured using the metric system (a *medio kilo* of tortillas should satisfy a family of four during lunchtime, and 96 kilometers/60 miles is about an hour's drive).

Time is often measured using military standard time (the 24-hour clock), so 2 am is 2:00, noon is 12:00, 6 pm is 18:00 and midnight is 24:00. Dates are often expressed in DD/MM/YYYY format.

If you're coming from the US or Canada, you're not going to need a transformer. Electricity is on the 100V system. Most outlets, however (except for the very newest), have only two prongs, so if you're bringing any appliance with a three-pronged plug, you should buy an adaptor before you leave.

■ Pack Small or Bring it All?

Almost anything you forget to bring, you'll be able to buy in México – in fact, in some cities, you can even go over to the local Wal-Mart (though you'll pay premium for sure). There are some things, however, that you're going to want to bring plenty of, because you'll have to dig deep into your wallet to buy them once you're here – examples are suntan lotion, camera film, and insect repellent (with DEET). When (and if) you can find them, they'll be outrageously priced. Suntan lotion, for example, averages more than US $10 per bottle, and a 24-exposure roll of Kodak film will run you around US $6.

WORD TO THE WISE

Do you hate the sweating that accompanies humidity and heat? Stop by a supermarket or fabric store and buy a paliacate *(handkerchief). Locals like to keep one in hand to wipe the perspiration away. It'll be crisp, rough, and unabsorbent when you purchase it, but one quick wash in the sink, and it'll become soft and usable.*

A basic packing list should include:
- ❐ Walking shoes
- ❐ Sandals
- ❐ Clothing
- ❐ Sweater (specifically if you're traveling by long-distance bus, which can be frigidly air-conditioned)
- ❐ Swimsuit
- ❐ Hat
- ❐ Camera, batteries and film
- ❐ Toiletries (toothbrush, toothpaste, comb, Q-Tips, contact lens solution, women's products, razor, etc.)
- ❐ Sunglasses

- ❏ Money belt
- ❏ Suntan lotion
- ❏ Insect repellent
- ❏ Notebook
- ❏ Pen
- ❏ Light rain jacket (especially if you're visiting the sierras)
- ❏ Phone Card
- ❏ Spanish-English dictionary
- ❏ Money and passport (including photo ID)
- ❏ Credit and debit cards
- ❏ Driver's license
- ❏ Shower shoes (even in moderately priced hotels, bathrooms just aren't the same here; you'll feel much better with a good cheap pair of shoes on your feet)
- ❏ Watch (although you could just go native and get there when you get there)

If you plan to spend some time hiking in remote corners, or exploring the villages, add the following:

- ❏ Towels (some rustic lodgings might have nothing but tiny squares of non-absorbent material)
- ❏ Soap and shampoo (even though most budget lodgings seem to have them, some remote cheapies may not)
- ❏ Toilet paper (some remote facilities aren't well-stocked)

On the flip side, there are some things that are incredibly easy to find:

- ❏ Medicines. Most towns have at last one *farmacia* selling any medicine you need, though mostly generic names.
- ❏ Shoes. You'll see *zapateria* after *zapateria* selling any make and model shoe you could want, from nice leather ones and sandals to the more popular cheap imitations of brand names and newest styles, which are mostly uncomfortable but come at bargain prices.
- ❏ Batteries. Go to any market or ask a vendor; the custom is to pull out a pack, open it, and sell you the batteries individually, at good prices.
- ❏ Underwear and outerwear. It is common for some supermarkets to have a section dedicated to fabrics and clothing.

A final word on clothing. Strangely, it's just not very common for locals to run around in shorts (even in extreme heat); most men wear jeans or slacks, while women wear skirts or dresses. If you're going to the coast, however, you'll want to wear shorts and T-shirts; it'll probably identify you as a tourist, but the heat, especially in the summer, can be extreme, and in most well-visited areas, other tourists (and some locals too) do the same. You won't attract much attention unless you're wearing shorts up to here and skirts up to there. If you're visiting the Sierras, add a light sweatshirt and a pair of jeans to your packing list – mornings especially can be a bit chilly, and in the winter you won't get away with shorts (they even sell hats and mittens in the bus stop in Xalapa).

■ Disabled Travelers

Handicap accessibility is rare. Disabled travelers, especially with wheelchairs, will find things a bit difficult. Few hotels, stores, or public facilities were built with you in mind. The best thing to do is plan your trip carefully. Check out any of the big chain hotels such as Holiday Inn or Best Western. Often, they are more likely to offer facilities. You'll find most people are friendly and happy to help if you find yourself in a jam. Instead of using city streets where sidewalks are often narrow and full of curbs, look for options away from the streets, such as a *malecón*, where pathways are wide and clear. Rent a car so you don't have to rely on the crowds, bumpiness, and general craziness of local buses.

■ Communications

You'll find plenty of **public pay phones** around, almost all of which require a phone card, which you can buy at many local stores and pharmacies. Pay phones are operated by the phone company – **Telemex** – and the cards are often identified as **Ladatel** (long distance telephone). With the cards, you can make long distance phone calls out of the country; generally, however, the rates are not the best. A 50 peso card, for example, is just enough to give your fam a quick update on how things are going. You can also make phone calls in a shop which just has phones for making calls, known as a *caseta*. If you plan on using the phone from your hotel, make sure you check to see what surcharges might be added.

By far, the best and cheapest way to keep in touch with home while you're in México is through e-mail. Cyber cafés are widely available in even the smaller villages. For an hourly rate averaging around US $1 you can send and receive e-mails, surf the Internet, or chat online. Typically, these cafés have printers, scanners, and often fax machines as well. Another place to look if you need to send or receive a fax, is in a *caseta*.

CALLS TO MÉXICO	CALLS WITHIN MÉXICO
International access code-52 (México country code)-area code-phone number	Local: number without area code Long distance: 01-area code Toll-free: 0800-phone number International: 00-country code-area code-phone number
From the US, 011-52-area code-phone number; to the US, 00-1-area code-phone number	

Making Calls

Phone numbers within México can be very confusing, especially since access codes were changed a few years ago. Most printed information has been changed, but you can occasionally run into some business cards and printed material that hasn't been updated. You'll notice that all local phone numbers written in this book (with the exception of México City) have seven digits. If you encounter printed material showing five digits, that is an old number. To update it, you'll need to add the last one or two digits of the area code to the phone number, to complete the seven digits. Another confusing thing about the phone numbers is the way that they're written. This varies according to local custom; as long as you find the proper number of digits, you're fine.

Numbers you'll find in this book have been streamlined for simplicity. The first three digits are the city area code, while the next seven digits are the local phone number. To dial a local number in the town where you are, simply dial the seven-digit number without the area code. If you're in México, but you're trying to call another town in México, you'll need to use 01, followed by the city area code, then the local phone number. If you're making an international call and you're within México, dial 00, then the country code, the area code and phone number. To call into México from the United States, dial the international access code (011), followed by México's country code (52), followed by the area code and phone number.

COUNTRY CODES	
US	1
Canada	1
UK	44
Australia	61
Belize	501
New Zealand	64
France	33
Germany	49
Spain	34

Mail

The post office is known as the *oficinas de correos*; one can be found in almost all towns, and certainly every city. The office will have a slot for you to deposit outgoing mail (don't bother looking for external postal boxes, it's a fruitless search), and a counter from which you can purchase stamps (*estampillas*). The postal system is notoriously slow and very inconsistent – an outgoing postcard might get to its destination in a week or a month, or it might never get there at all. As for mail being sent to you, do not expect packages of any kind to make it – those more often than not have a tendency to disappear. You can also receive mail at a post office, by marking it as *lista de correos*. So for example, a letter would read: Your Name, *lista de correos*, city, state, zip code, country. You'll need to show up in person with ID to pick up the mail. Letters might or might not get to you – it's really anyone's guess. If you're wondering how normal people and businesses operate in México if mail is this way, many deliver by courier and everyone pays bills in person. I actually did have the pleasure of seeing some mail arrive at a house in México. I was in the yard, and picked up a balled up piece of trash from the ground. It was the mail delivery. Apparently the easiest way to reach the door had been to ball it up and toss it over the gate!

■ Bathrooms

If you have to use the bathroom, and you are far away from your hotel, you could be in for a long, agonizing search. The best advice is to do your business before you leave the hotel. Sometimes, however, emergencies do strike. In such cases, one place where you can often reliably find public facilities is in the bus station; it should be noted, however, that occasionally the restrooms are located in the loading and unloading dock, and are thus only available to ticketed passengers. In an emergency, another spot to look is at the *mercado* (market). You can sometimes get lucky here, although the facilities are not the cleanest, or in the best of shape. As a last resort, you'll have to find a nice, clear, brush-free spot on the side of the road.

There will be a fee (typically 2-5 pesos) for bathroom use. You'd think that some of this fee would go to bathroom upkeep, but don't count on it. Be prepared for the worst conditions – unflushed toilets, littered floors, dirty seats, etc. Occasionally, you can hit the jackpot and find a halfway decent place. After you pay the fee to the bathroom attendant (stationed like a guard at the door), you'll typically be given a roll (or wad) of toilet paper to use.

■ Laundry

In all major cities, you can find plenty of shops dedicated to laundry. Your garments will be weighed, and you're given a ticket for pick up of the cleaned, dried, and folded laundry the next day. Prices are usually given by the kilo, averaging around $1 US per kilo. While it is certainly nice to get all your clothes clean, be aware that it's not uncommon for a sock or two to turn up missing. And sometimes an item will take on a slightly different color due to bleeding.

■ Money

Currency

The Mexican unit of currency is the **peso**, and it's indicated in México with the dollar sign ($).

One peso equals 100 centavos, which are given as coins. Bills come in denominations of 10, 20, 50, 100, 200, and 500 pesos (at the time of this writing US $1 is equal to about 10 pesos). There are also some 10 and 20 peso coins. They are thicker and larger than the lower-denomination centavos. Take a look at exactly what change you have. It can be easy to overlook the few dollars you might have received as change. When you exchange your money, you'll receive larger bills – if you're in a bank, it's a good idea to ask for some of it in smaller denominations. In most places, a 500 peso bill can be almost useless as hardly anyone will have change. Even a 200 peso bill can be hard to use in a village, and a local bus can't handle anything over a 50 peso bill (which is also pushing it). Do your best to spend larger bills in hotels and restaurants, and keep change for buses, local stores, markets, etc.

All price listings in this book are in pesos unless otherwise noted. Hotel and restaurant price charts, however, are based upon US dollar equivalents.

In some of the larger touristed cities, dollars are often accepted in place of pesos. You will, however, invariably get a horrible exchange rate; if you have time, it's best to exchange your money in advance.

Taxes

You may notice an IVA (*Impuesto de Valor Agregado*) is added to your hotel rate or restaurant meal. This is a 15% tax that is added onto most purchases.

Banks do not like to accept US bills that have any kind of a tear or mark on them. Many bank tellers scrutinize the bills very carefully, and if there is the slightest imperfection, they'll flat out reject it. Before you leave for your travels, take a look at your bills.

Traveler's Checks

You should also be aware that in the Gulf Coast region, because of the relatively low level of American tourism, it might be hard to exchange traveler's checks. It's probably a good idea therefore to bring your ATM card. This can be an excellent way to get money, since you can find ATMs in just about every mid-sized to large town, you don't have to deal with bank hours or holidays, and you get local currency at the best exchange rate. It's best not to withdraw or exchange too much money at once. Carry only small amounts of cash.

Credit Cards

Credit cards (Visa, MasterCard, and American Express) are widely accepted in the larger cities. You'll need to be careful, however, when it comes to hotels – you'll be surprised by how many don't take credit cards. Usually at larger cities you'll encounter the least problem, but in smaller towns even the nicer hotels might not accept them. Ask when you're making your reservation to be sure. When it comes to eating, aside from the largest cities, you'll find few restaurants that accept credit cards. Gas is, by and large, a cash-only affair. Be sure to let your credit card company know you'll be using the card in México. I encountered a tourist who found his card unusable because the company thought it strange that it was being used in another country and so froze his account.

Health

■ Common Ailments

Probably the biggest fear that people have when they think of traveling to México, is getting sick. Their first question will be: Can you drink the water? I think Moctezuma would be pleased he's stricken such fear into the hearts of foreigners. But things aren't as bad as you might believe.

You probably shouldn't drink the water. Even though some of the larger cities' public services have come a long way, for the most part, you're probably better off sticking with bottled water. Most hotels supply a bottle of water for each guest when you check in, others have tanks in the lobbies. *Agua purificada* (purified water) is available everywhere. Many urban restaurants make their ice out of purified water – if you're uncertain, go without; as for juices, be wary – if water has been added, it might not have been purified (especially if you're in a small village). If you're in a real jam, you can purify water yourself by bringing it to a rolling boil for one full minute (higher altitudes require about three minutes); another option is to drop in some tetraglycine hydroperiodide tablets (you can purchase these at sporting or camping good stores at home).

Turista is diarrhea, which may or may not be accompanied by severe stomach cramps, nausea, and fever. It can have even the strongest traveler curled up in a ball for a day or two. But *turista* often has more to do with changes in climate and diet, not to mention tress. Do your best to ease into the exciting food and spices you'll encounter. Interestingly, Mexicans visiting the United States reportedly are affected by *turista* as well.

As far as food is concerned, traveler's diarrhea can come from bacteria in uncooked meat and seafood, unsanitary cooking conditions, and raw, unwashed, fruits and vegetables. Your most effective means of prevention is to pay attention to where and what you eat – street vendors, markets, and questionable restaurants should be avoided; you're probably better off eating only raw fruits and vegetables that can be peeled.

Usually, *turista* cures itself pretty quickly. Within three days you'll probably be better, and within five to seven days, almost all people are back on their feet. While you're sick, drink plenty of water to rehydrate yourself. You can go to a *farmacia* and buy a few capsules of immodium. Even the generic-brand discount stores are familiar with the name and will pull out its equivalent and sell you pills by the capsule for a few pesos each.

> **EMERGENCY!! WHO ARE YOU GOING TO CALL?**
>
> The Mexican equivalent of 911 is ☎ 060. In an emergency, another option is to call the ***Cruz Roja*** (Red Cross) or the local hospital (listed under *Orientation & Practicalities* throughout the guide).

■ More Serious Diseases

More than likely, the only problems you'll have in México will be a few stomach upsets. Other far less common illnesses that you may hear of include:

- **Hepatitis A** – a viral infection of the liver resulting from poor sanitation of food and drink. Symptoms include abdominal cramps, nausea, fever, and malaise. The risk highest for those in rural areas, but it can also acquired in well-touristed areas.
- **Rabies** – a virus caught from an animal bite (most especially in carnivores and bats). Symptoms include muscle spasms, delirium, convulsions, and, eventually, coma and death. Animal bites should get prompt medical attention.
- **Typhoid** – a febrile illness caused by a bacterium typically found in food or drink. Symptoms include high fever, nausea, headaches, and infections.
- **Hepatitis B** – a virus caught typically through blood or sexual activities. Symptoms include nausea, vomiting, abdominal cramps, and jaundice, and can eventually lead to liver scarring, liver cancer, or liver disease.
- **Yellow fever** – caught through infected mosquitoes, with symptoms ranging from mild to severe (fever, hepatitis, flu, etc.). Insect repellent with DEET is highly recommended as a preventative measure.
- **Malaria** – caught from infected mosquitoes. Symptoms are flu-like, appearing four to 10 weeks later, and include headaches, diarrhea, and vomiting. In the geographic area this book covers, the National Center for Infectious Diseases has identified a risk in rural Chiapas and rural Tabasco. There is no cause for concern in ports along the Gulf Coast, or in any border cities.
- **Diphtheria and tetanus** – the first is a bacterial disease of the mucous membranes, the second is a disease causing severe muscle rigidity. Vaccinations are advisable.

For more information on disease symptoms, cures, and risks throughout México and the world, visit the website of the National Center for Infectious Diseases: www.cdc.gov.

Medical Insurance

Check with your insurance agency to see if you have medical coverage while abroad and, if so, what is covered. If you're not covered, you can get travel insurance, which often covers medical expenses too. Be aware that in México is that payment is due at the time of medical consultation (doctor's office or hospital).

If you need a medical evacuation, expenses can be extremely high, and the US embassy cannot front you the money for it (the most they can do is give you a list of hospitals and doctors to consult, and contact family members back home). Also be aware that if you're on social security, international medical assistance is not offered to you.

The State Department's website, www.travel.state.gov, in the medical section, has long lists of both travel insurance companies and US- and foreign-based Air Ambulance/Medical Evacuation companies.

WORD TO THE WISE

If you have a medical emergency, 060 is the equivalent of 911, and can be called from any phone. Additionally, hospital and red cross phone numbers are listed in the Orientation and Practicality section of each town.

■ Vaccinations

As for other basics, there are no required vaccinations to travel to México, and the majority of people travel back and forth with hardly a thought to malaria or yellow fever. If you want be extra-sure, however, you can always consult your doctor regarding your trip. Typically, immunizations are administered during childhood for diphtheria, tetanus, polio, typhoid, and hepatitis A.

Safety & Crime

The safety measures you should take here are about the same as those you would take anywhere else – simply be aware of yourself and your possessions. In general, crime is not excessive (with the notable exceptions of México City and some areas in the border cities). Don't carry large amounts of money, don't leave your bags unattended, and keep valuables such as camera and binoculars secured while you're walking around. Many people wear a money belt and keep valuables in it tucked against the body. This is effective and protects against purse-snatchers.

Most hotels have a safe where you can keep valuables.

Chiapas deserves a special comment as well. Unrest due to the Zapatista uprising has been on and off. Especially in this area, highway robbery can sometimes occur. Travel by road only during the daytime. If you're heading deep into Chiapas by bus, use a deluxe (or at the very least first-class) bus. If you plan on exploring by foot, stay away from remote and isolated paths; travel with groups of other people wherever possible.

No matter where you travel, be sure to check the State Department's travel advisories at http://travel.state.gov/travel_warnings.html for current safety conditions.

■ Checkpoints

If you drive or take the bus, you're likely to come across military checkpoints. The very idea of the military, armed and inspecting, causes concern to many potential visitors before they even set foot in México. The military is there, however, for your safety, and is nothing to be concerned about unless you are involved in illegal activity. At these checkpoints (which are usually a barricade in the road requiring cars to slow down and pull over), vehicles are inspected for drugs or weapons. Most cars are simply waved through with only a cursory glance (tourists aren't what they're concerned about); those that are pulled over will usually get a quick look in the back seat, or an inspection of the trunk. It usually takes a couple of minutes, and then you're on your way. If you're on a bus that passes through a checkpoint, the bus will pull over and stop. A uniformed and armed member of the military will come on board, walk to the end of the bus, glancing at overhead bins and passengers, and then get off; the bus is on its way again within five minutes. The whole process is painless. Remember, though, never to take pictures at a military checkpoint; that could cause trouble.

■ Emergency Assistance

The Mexican Ministry of Tourism has a 24-hour toll-free hotline set up to provide emergency assistance if you need it: within México, ☎ 0800-903-9200; from the US, ☎ 800-482-9832. In addition, you can contact your local embassy for support (see *Embassies & Consulates*, page 75).

■ Breaking the Law

You do not want to end up in a Mexican prison. Overall conditions are very poor, food is not always a given (and must be paid for), and medical attention is minimal. And then there is the fact that México is based on Roman and Napoleonic law, which means that you're guilty until proven innocent. A sentence can take six to 10 months to be issued. Do your best not to break the law in México – especially when it comes to drugs and firearms, as this is where you'll find the most severe penalties. A charge for possession of drugs could put you behind bars for 25 years, while slipping across the border with a .22 caliber (or higher) firearm or ammunition could put you there for 30 years. If you smuggle a child into or out of México, you're looking at five years. If you're even suspected of breaking these laws, expect a long detainment.

So, what should you do? If you're bringing a prescription medicine into México, have your prescription with you, and if you really have to have your gun with you, contact the Mexican Embassy (before you leave home) about getting a permit. If you somehow you do end up getting arrested, notify your embassy immediately. You can also contact a lawyer to help with your case – the embassy can provide you with a list of them.

If you're arrested for a vehicular accident, and you bought an auto insurance policy that covers México, it too probably includes a name and phone number for a lawyer to help you out. Good luck.

Shopping

One of the more interesting places to shop is in the town market. Almost every town will have one – big, small, outdoor, indoor, fancy, slummy, dedicated to food, dedicated to crafts – there are endless variations on the theme. Almost all, however, will have things that you've never seen before, and most are pretty inexpensive. Look around and you'll find some fun treasures. There are huge bags of spices that you can browse through to find cures for everything from knee pain to cancer. You'll find disembodied heads and feet of chickens, cows, pigs, and other no-longer identifiable animals. Or delicate hand-crafted clothing made by the women that are selling it to you, and religious shops so over-the-top you'll stop and stare (soap, candles, incense, matches, cards, books, crosses, statues, busts, clothing – all in the name of God). When you have your eye on something, it's a particularly good idea to shop around and compare prices. If you're in a market, and what you want is unmarked, it's not uncommon for the vendor to jack the price up a bit; the shop next door might sell the exact same thing at a lower price. In some big markets, the fine art of bargaining is common. The vendor will say one price, you offer another, and the dance goes back and forth until an agreement is made. Usually, just at the point when you decide something is too expensive, and you start to walk away, the price drops.

While you're shopping – be it in a market or a more traditional store, keep your eye out for local specialties. Veracruz in known for its superb coffee. In the Tuxtla area of Veracruz, stop by a cigar factory and pick up some cigars, or while in Papantla buy some pure vanilla (go ahead and throw out that artificial extract). In Tamaulipas, in the border towns, you'll find a lot of silver jewelry, as well as leather goods, such as belts, purses, boots, gloves, and saddles. In the villages of Tabasco and Veracruz, there are exquisitely made handicrafts, among them hats and mats made out of palm fronds and reeds, or elaborately designed *jicaras* (gourds).

Tipping

Just about anyone who does a service for you – wanted or unwanted – expects a tip. If you've been waited on in a restaurant, it is customary to leave a tip of 10-15% (the upper figure if you've received good service). The tip is not usually added to the bill, though there are exceptions.

When you get gas, an attendant will quickly emerge out of nowhere with a squeegee to clean your windshield (whether or not it is dirty and always without your request); he or she expects a tip (a few pesos is fine). Gas stations will also check your oil or inflate your tires if you request – this is also tip-worthy. The actual gas pumper, however, does not need anything extra.

It is not necessary to tip a taxi driver. If you're driving your own car, however, and you receive the assistance of a "parking attendant" (a man waving a rag, signaling you into a space), he is expecting a tip. Again, a few pesos is fine, usually given when you are ready to leave the space. Clowns that you might see performing in the *zócalo* are expecting a tip if you enjoy their performance, and kids that bag your groceries in the supermarket are waiting for tips as well (a couple of pesos is fine; often they are not paid at all, but work solely for tips). If you've received a private boat tour and particularly enjoyed your guide, a tip is a nice gesture. You'll also want to tip the hotel porter a few pesos.

Although the government has been working to clean up its act, there is still the chance that you might run into a slightly crooked police officer here or there, asking for a *mordida*. Generally what happens is that you are pulled over on a minor traffic offense (pay careful attention to one-way roads and don't run any stop signs or traffic lights). If the officer talks to you for an abnormal length of time, and seems to be making a federal case out of running a stop sign (threatening you with fines or a trip to the station), it is likely that he's angling for a bribe. Typically, the officer will not directly ask for such a thing (that, after all, would clearly be wrong), but you are expected to come up with a creative way to give him the money without acknowledging that it is a bribe. If that happens, you're faced with a couple of options. You can agree to go to the police station and pay for your infraction. If the officer sees he's not going to get anything from you, he might just give up and let you go on your way. If you are being mistreated, harassed, or wrongly accused, be sure that you get the officers name, badge number, and patrol car number to pursue a complaint, and if you've paid a fine, make sure that you get a receipt. Remember, getting angry, loud, or violent will make things incredibly difficult – staying calm, collected, and extremely polite will get you in and out of the situation the fastest and with the least amount of mental anguish. Your other option, of course, is to pay the *mordida*. That, however, perpetuates the problem.

When to Go

You'll find the most action and tourism during holidays, festivals, and summers. Visiting during festivals in particular, can be a wonderful way to immerse yourself in the culture of a place – including dances, music, processions, and rituals that you might never see at another time of the year. Often, it can be unforgettable (you'll be hard-pressed to find someone who's ever been to and forgotten the Puerto de Veracruz' Carnival). The only thing you should be wary of, however, is that hotels, restaurants, roads, buses – everything – will be crowded, and hotel prices are likely to be elevated. Summers are also a great time to visit, and this is the time that many foreign visitors take vacations. You'll just want to be prepared for heat and humidity (higher elevations such as Xalapa can still be quite pleasant). If you can't take the heat, visit during the winter months, when the coast can be quite nice temperature-wise (just be sure to keep your eye on hurricane season, and be aware that towns and villages in the mountains get downright nippy).

Each color on the Mexican flag is representative of something: red stands for union, white stands for religion, and green stands for independence.

Holidays

Banks and government offices (including the post office and tourism office) close on national holidays, and often on the days surrounding them. Generally, a note pasted on the door of the bank will let you know when it will reopen. Galleries, museums, ruins, and stores may or may not be open; if in doubt, you're probably better off assuming they're closed, since, if they can, they most certainly will be. National holidays tend not to be as much fun as religious festivities. There are parades (especially on Labor Day and Independence Day) and, possibly, military displays, but otherwise they're marked by family outings. If your vacation falls around one of these dates, book hotels, buses, and domestic flights well ahead of time, especially along the coast or its port cities, since visitors from inland flood beaches during holiday-time.

■ National Holidays

January 1: **New Year's Day**
February 5: **Constitution Day** (commemorating the Constitution of 1917)
February 24: **Día de la Bandera** (Flag Day, in honor of the Mexican flag)
March 21: **Birthday of Benito Juárez** (commemorates the1806 birthday of Juárez, most famous president of México.)
May 1: Labor Day
May 5: **Cinco de Mayo** (anniversary of the 1862 Battle of Puebla, when Mexicans defeated an invading French army.)
September 16: **Independence Day of México** (celebrations of México's independence include parades, fireworks, and parties. The famous *El Grito Viva México!* is issued by the president.
October 12: **Día de la Raza** (celebration of Columbus' discovery of the New World)
November 20: **Anniversary of the Revolution of 1910**
December 25: **Christmas Day**

The Virgin de Guadalupe

The legend of México's Patron Saint begins in the year 1531 with an Aztec Indian named Juan Diego. At this time, the Spanish missionaries had just settled into their work of spreading Christianity to the local Indians, and Juan Diego was on his way to his lessons. On his walk, he passed by a hill known as Tepeyac and, feeling an urge to climb it, he did. At its top, to his surprise, he had an apparition – a

woman surrounded by a halo of light and beautiful music. She spoke to him in his native language (Náhuatl), addressed him by name, and said that she was the Blessed Virgin Mary, Mother of the Lord Jesus Christ, and that she wanted him to tell the bishop to build a church in her honor at that spot on the hill. Juan Diego, in shock and excitement, ran to the bishop's house, but was rejected by disbelievers at the door. He returned to the Virgin, and she bade him try again; so he did. This time, he convinced one of the assistants, who went to talk to the bishop. The assistant soon returned, however, and told Juan Diego that the bishop had just laughed at his request. Dejected, he returned to the Virgin who went to a nearby dead bush and produced a healthy rose when no rose should have bloomed. She gave it to Juan Diego and bade him return to the bishop. With his proof, the Aztec Indian went again to the church. The assistants saw the flower and believed him; then the bishop saw the flower and believed him as well.

The church was built on the hill of Tepeyac, and the cloth that was used to carry the flower (where the bishop had seen an image of the Virgin) was placed at the back of the church.

■ National Celebrations

The following, while not national holidays, are important traditional festivals that are marked by an assortment of activities, including fairs, parades, offerings, and dances. You can expect most businesses and government offices to be closed.

February/March .... **Carnival**
Takes place three days before Ash Wednesday (46 days before Easter) as a final celebration before the beginning of Lent. The biggest celebrations take place in the Puerto de Veracruz, which becomes a madhouse of festivals and people. Festivities include parades, music, dancing, fireworks, and fairs.

March/April .... **Semana Santa**
Holy week takes place from Palm Sunday to Easter Sunday, with the main celebrations starting on Good Friday. The coast especially gets flooded with vacationers during Semana Santa.

November 1............................ **All Saint's Day**

November 2 . . . . **Day of the Dead**
This is a festive holiday instead of a somber, depressing one. Gravesites are visited. Gifts and foods are prepared for the deceased.

December 12 . . . . **Day of Our Lady of Guadalupe**
Celebration of the Patron Saint of México. Pilgrimages are made to churches, and some children get dressed up to honor Juan Diego.

December 16-24 . . . . **Posada**
Candle-lit processions through the streets in reenactment of Mary and Joseph's search for lodging. Children have parties and break piñatas.

December 24 . . . . **Christmas Eve**

December 31 . . . . **New Year's Eve**
General celebrations and parties.

After holidays and festivals pass by, things go back to business as usual, although it can be hard to understand what business as usual really means in México. In smaller villages, it is not uncommon to find regular bank or government hours totally sporadic. Some places may be open three hours on Monday, Tuesday and Wednesday, closed weekends, and open only afternoons on Thursdays and Fridays, for example, and I've seen worse. Around major cities, however, normal business hours won't be that bad, though they will usually include the afternoon siesta.

■ Festivals & Events

After I described the American fireworks, cookouts, and general merriment on the 4th of July to a new Mexican friend, she nodded and said, "Aaahhh... like any normal day here then?" And it is just about true. Any day is a reason to celebrate in México. Possibly it has something to do with the generations of family living together or close by. That can give rise to aunts, uncles, and cousins stopping by, which can just as easily lead to food, drinks, and all-night music. A Mexican family party of this sort is a treat to attend; worries are thrown aside, and it's all about enjoying each other's company and having a good time.

But it doesn't stop at national holidays and informal family parties. With around 90% of the population of México Catholic, religious festivals take a prominent role in village life. The main festivals are dedicated to the village's patron saint, who is honored yearly with one or several days of festivities. Annual birthday parties are also held for people on the day of their particular patron saint (the one they were named after).

Even for the non-religious, a visit during one of these holidays can be a real treat. The Santa Maria Magdelena fiesta in Xico, for example, culminates with a bull running through the streets! During any one of the religious festivals, local businesses close, and villagers celebrate with all kinds of processions, fairs, folk dances, exhibitions, and cultural events. The non-religious events below are celebrated with gifts and parties, and, though not official holidays, you're likely to find people with a holiday attitude. Some of the more outstanding festivals, as well as some national (non-holiday) events are listed below.

January 6 . . . . **Día de los Reyes Magos**
Day of the Three Kings. Celebrates the arrival of the three wise men. Christmas presents are given to children. It's traditional for parties to have a rosca de reyes, a ring-shaped, fruit topped pastry with a figurine baked inside. Whoever receives the piece with the doll is supposed to hold a party on February 2, Candlemas Day.

February 2 . . . . **Candlemas Day**
Celebrated with a couple of days of activities including processions and bullfights. Tlacotalpan's celebrations are particularly festive and highlight a running of the bulls at its end.

February 14 . . . . **Valentine's Day**

April . . . . **Expositions in Xalapa**
Concerts, art exhibits and displays.

April 30 . . . . **Children's Day**
Children are honored with gifts and celebrations.

April/May . . . . **Tabasco's State Fair**
Takes place at the end of April and the beginning of May in Villahermosa. The city goes all out, with fairgrounds, fireworks, cultural events, music and dances.

May 3 . . . . . **Celebration of the Black Christ of Otatitlán**
On this date, Otatitlán's patron saint, the Cristo Negro or Black Christ is honored with dancing, singing and people seeking the "miracles" that the figure is thought to offer.

May 10 . . . . **Mother's Day**
Both mother's and father's day are taken seriously and parents are honored with flowers and gifts. You'll see an abundance of flowers in the markets, most of which will be bought up by sons, daughters, and friends to give to mothers.

May 15 . . . . **Teacher's Day**
Día del Maestro is dedicated to recognizing teachers with festivities and gifts.

June 1 . . . . **Navy Day**
Coastal towns celebrate with tournaments and competitions.

June . . . . **Father's Day**
Third Sunday in June; fathers are honored with gifts.

Mid-June . . . . **Corpus Christi Festival**
Festivities honoring the Body of Christ. Celebrations at El Tajín and Papantla are particularly famous.

July 22 . . . . **Festival of La Magdalena**
Dedicated to Xico's patron saint; marked with a bull run at its end.

July 25 . . . . **Festival of Saint James Apostle**
Dedicated to Xalapa's patron saint, marked by processions and music.

September 29 . . . . **Festival of San Jerónimo**
Dedicated to the Coatepec's patron saint.

Food & Drink

■ Where to Eat

It's unbelievable that anyone would go to México and not sample its flavors, but the cautious tourist often avoids exploring the culinary world altogether. McDonalds, KFC, or Dominoes Pizza (which can be found easily in most large cities) are a safe haven for those craving the taste of home, or an escape from possible stomach upsets. Even if you think you know Mexican food, the way it isprepared and eaten in México is a horse of a different color. You'd be missing out by not trying it. This is not to say that in order to fully enjoy your visit you have to resign yourself to a bubbling stomach.

DINING PRICE CHART	
Price per person for an entrée, not including beverage or tip.	
$	Under US $5
$$	US $5-$10
$$$	US $10+

The first thing to understand is what you're up against. Most worries that plague tourists involve the water, food, hepatitis B, and malaria. Rumors and exaggerations surround all stories about these illnesses. See the section on *Health* for more details on what you can expect.

Now, let's really talk about eating. The cheapest eats are generally found in the city **markets**. Most markets are mazes of open-air stalls that sell what you would expect (fruits, vegetables, meats), and what you may not expect (beautiful hand-made clothing, recently konked-out chickens, live talkative parrots), plus what you probably need (shoe repairs, sodas, and hot meals).

There are pluses and minuses to eating in the market. On the plus side, you're likely to find yourself eating with all the locals, the food is tasty, and often authentic to the region, service is quick, and prices are the best you'll find in the city or town. On the minus side, not all the vendors hold themselves to the same sanitary standards. My advice is simply to be aware. At most places you'll be able to see them making and serving the food; you'll quickly get a feel for what places are best avoided. If, however, your stomach is already feeling a bit odd, it's best to stay away all together.

Just about anywhere you go, you will hear the cries of the **street vendor**, another source of cheap eats, selling everything from "*Elotes!!*" (corn on the cob) to "*Tamales!*" (steamed corn *masa* stuffed with meat and wrapped with banana leaves). Although in many cases quite tasty, unless you have a hardy stomach, it's probably best to steer clear of the meat-filled items. The exception here are the vendors of sweets, such as *churros* (fried sugar-coated dough, sometimes stuffed with *cajeta*, something similar to caramel), and *meringue* (sugar and egg whites beaten into a froth) are just way too good to pass up.

These sweets are not to be confused with those you find at the *panadería*, or **local bakery**. Sugar-coated, fruit-topped, and cream-filled pastries, along with the most affordable rolls (*bolillos*) you're likely to see anywhere, make *panaderías* a nice place to stop for breakfast. Just a word of warning: I have always found that the prettiest-looking choices are often the most disappointing. Chocolate-covered donuts aren't sweet enough, beautifully decorated cakes tend to be very dry and oddly flavored. Stick with the ones you might at first overlook, or have never seen before, and chances are you won't be disappointed.

DID YOU KNOW?

More than 300 million tortillas are consumed daily in México! They're eaten with breakfast, lunch, and dinner, by the rich and the poor, by the roadside or at the formal dining table.

As for **restaurants**, most are easily found around the main square, and, in the Gulf Coast region of Veracruz, Tabasco, and Tamaulipas, well-prepared meals remain pretty cheaply priced. A tasty belt-loosening *comida corrida* cruns about US $4, and is often your best choice for lunch. Regardless of the local specialty, your order will almost always come with tortillas, the Mexican equivalent of bread, typically made from maize (mah-EES) or corn, and either chilis or chili sauce (red or green). On some menus you'll find an assortment of *antojitos* (or light dishes) such as *gorditas* (a flattened, stuffed, and fried *masa*), *tortas* (sandwiches), and *tostadas* (fried tortillas covered with any number and variety of toppings). The most famous *antojito* of all is the taco, which is found on most menus, and is generally sold individually. An order of four or five is about what you need to fill you. They are inexpensive, tasty, and loaded with goods, but often smaller than their Americanized cousins. Common side items regardless of region include *arroz* (rice) and *frijoles* (beans). Be aware that, in most places, restaurants are likely to close pretty early, so if you have not eaten by 8 or 9, you might be hard-pressed to find a hot meal, particularly in a smaller village. In large urban areas like Xalapa or the Puerto de Veracruz, however, you'll easily find places open late into the night.

THE LEGEND OF MAIZE

An old Aztec legend says that the god Quetzalcoatl was in search of a food source for humans. He found a tiny ant carrying a piece of maize who showed him a big horde of more maize hidden away in a mountain (known as Tonacatepetl). Quetzalcoatl solicited the aid of the Tlaloloc Gods to burst open this Mountain of Sustenance; and thus, maize came to the Aztecs.

Finally, for the budget traveler, long-term visitor, or stomach-sensitive, there is always the *supermercado*, or **supermarket**. The most familiar names you'll see, such as Chedraui, sell just about everything that you can get at home (of course non-Mexican items like peanut butter are likely to be outrageously priced). Most supermarkets have a deli counter (ham and cheese are great if you're on the go), a *panadería* (where you'll always find me at breakfast-time), and hot ready-to-serve meals (these tend to disappear quickly by early afternoon as Mexicans load up for the midday meal).

Mexicans are all about sampling. If you're at the deli counter or in the fruit section, and you're not quite sure what you want, ask for a sample. They will give you a bit of the meat or cheese in question, or cut out a piece of the fruit for you to try. This also applies to fruits in markets. Vendors have knifes at the ready to slice out a section as an encouragement to buy their goods. Smaller villages may have nothing bigger than a *mini-super,* a store that sells the most popular items (sodas, chips, canned goods, etc.). Don't buy your tortillas at the supermarket or mini-super, however. Instead, head where all Mexicans go – to the *tortillería*, an establishment dedicated to making corn tortillas. They are made fresh throughout the day and, when you buy them, they are often hot. If you want a real treat, eat a fresh, hot one. They're addictive, and absolutely nothing like what you might get at home.

Estimates in the price chart are based on the average price of a single entrée without beverages or tips.

POP-PHIZZZZZZ

Soda, or more specifically, Coca-Cola, is so engrained in the day-to-day lives of most Mexicans, that it is more common to see bottles of Coke on a dinner table than jugs of water – even in the smallest villages. Surprisingly, however, the greenish (depositable) glass bottles that were until recently associated with México, have mostly disappeared, replaced by their plastic counterparts. It's a change that brings its own set of problems, as plastic litter accumulates even along remote mountain roadsides (thousands of bottles in some sections).

■ Regional Specialties

The regional specialties of the Gulf Coast, not surprisingly, have a lot to do with seafood. You'll see many dishes (especially in ports or fishing villages) with *langostina* (lobster), *camarones* (shrimp), *camarones gigantes* (prawns), *jaiba* (crab), *cangrejo* (large crab), and different types of *pescado* (fish). Depending on where you are, the fish might be *mojarra* (perch), *huachinango* (red snapper), *robalo* (sea bass), and, the strangest one of all, *pejelgarto* (an ugly fish with huge teeth and jaws), savored for its delicate white meat. This last one is found in Tabasco.

Mole is a thick brown sauce often made with bitter chocolate, spices, and chilis, and served over chicken. There are some excellent types of *mole* sauce in Veracruz (in Xico you'll find many different kinds). You might find *pozole* on the menu, which is a soup made by boiling corn with a pig's head (and other parts) to create a thick stew.

There are also some distinctive ways things are prepared here. You'll find the entire country trying to imitate styles of cooking named for the area. Some of the most popular menu items are seafood dishes that have been prepared *a la veracruzana*, which means they're in a tomato-based sauce made from olive oil, onions, olives, capers, tomatoes, spices, and, often, jalapeños. Keep an eye out for the tasty and popular *huachinanga a la veracruzana* (a red snapper dish). You'll also find dishes cooked *a la tampiqueña* – which means it's a thin meat sautéed with slices of onion and often served with guacamole and enchiladas. Another popular dish you'll see is *carne asada a la tampiqueña* (flank or skirt steak).

■ Local Fruits

The variety of fruit throughout México is amazing, and if you go into the markets, you're likely to see just about anything. Fruits you might see at the supermarket back home, this country produces in huge quantities. But here they're bigger, juicier and more colorful. Keep an eye out for orange (*naranja*), grapefruit (*toronja*), lime (*lima*), apple (*manzana*), pineapple (*piña*), pear (*pera*), banana (*plátano*), tamarind (*tamarindo*) and coconut (*coco*).

The lands of Veracruz and Tabasco are especially rich and well-suited to plantations and orchards, which you'll see lining the roadsides and on hillsides. In the markets, you'll see the results – the common fruits, yes, but also exotic fruits you've never seen or heard of. You can buy some there, or just pick them up on the road – as you slow down for the village's *topes*, you'll find kids there selling bags of fruit, often plucked right out of the trees in their yards.

Capulín: A type of cherry. You'll find them in Veracruz and Tabasco; fruits appear in the markets in the late summer months.

Castaño: Also known as the fruit from the breadfruit tree. Keep an eye out for them in Tabasco.

Caujilote: Also known as the cucumber tree fruit. You can find them in some parts of Tabasco.

Guanabana: It's a green fruit whose skin has prickles or spines; the meat is whitish, has many seeds (big enough to pick out), is somewhat fibrous, and very aromatic and flavorful – a very different, musky, pungent taste. It's known as the soursop in the US.

Guayaba: Also known as the guava, a sweet musky-flavored fruit.

Mamey: It's shaped like a football, with a rough outer brown skin, one large almond-shaped seed in the middle, and an orange meaty interior, sweet and tropical in flavor.

Marañon: A cashew nut.

Mango: You will find this one at the supermarket at home. It's typically red/orange when ripe, and has a meaty, flavorful interior.

Nance: A sweet-tasting fruit with a pit, similar to a cherry.

Pitahaya: A delicious, exotic-looking fruit, with a taste and interior very similar to a kiwi (except it's much bigger). They're the fruit from a cactus, and have tough, red overlapping pieces that can be pealed away to expose the delicate white interior. Also known as the dragon fruit.

Zapote negro: Also spelled *sapote*, and also known as the chocolate pudding fruit. It's similar in appearance to a tomato with a green (or brown when very ripe) skin. Inside, it is soft and dark-brown/black in color. They are sweet, and eaten as-is for dessert; often they're used as a dessert ingredient as well.

Papaya: A sweet yellow-green fruit that resembles a huge pear in shape.

■ Spices

Mexicans like their food spicy, and you'll find no shortage of **chilis** that are added in (or eaten whole and raw on the side) to do the job. The spiciest chili of all is the ***habañero***, a round chili that comes in shades from green to orange. This little guy packs a powerful punch – if you don't like things *picante* (hot and spicy), steer clear. If you do end up trying it and can't take the heat, besides grabbing for your drink, sometimes a little bit of salt helps ease the burning on your tongue. Sauces are often made with chilis, including (listed from milder to hotter) ***puya***, ***piquín***, and ***de árbol***. The **Serrano** chili is perhaps the most usual ingredients in traditional salsa, and is not all that hot. Jalapeños are very well-known across the border; the short, fat, green chilis, are at a mid-range of hotness. On a menu, you might see *chili poblano*, which is not all that hot, and is usually served stuffed with meat. ***Chipotle***, on the other hand, is very spicy. It's a dried chili that you can often find canned.

As for herbs and seasonings, you can often find *epazote*, which is an herb sometimes used to flavor black beans; *achiote*, which is a red paste made from a combination of spices; and oregano, an herb used in many dishes.

A final word. If you don't want something spicy, say you don't want it *picante*. If you say you don't want it *caliente*, that means you don't want it warm.

■ Drinks

Everyone drinks soft drinks, so you'll find a huge variety of *refrescos* – both familiar names and unfamiliar names. Be sure to try a ***toronja*** (grapefruit) soda, as well as a ***sangria soda*** (despite its name, this soda does not have alcohol). *Sangria* is a tasty dark soda, and has a flavor that is a combination of bitter and sweet. Once you finally find one (they're not available in every store), they're very addictive. If you're tired of carbonated beverages, it won't be hard to find purified bottled water in just about any store.

Juices (*jugos*) are also plentiful, and you won't want to go home without trying some. You'll find formal juice shops as well as market vendors who will cut and blend (or squeeze) juice straight into your glass while you watch. Don't be surprised if you go to a stall and they don't provide a cup (money-saving tactic). Instead, you might get a clear plastic bag full of juice, with a straw inserted. At that point you'll really know you're in México!

In restaurants, you might be told they have an assortment of *aguas*. This does not mean they have different kinds of waters; *aguas* refers to drinks made from fruit (and sometimes grains), along with water. A tasty *agua* to try is **jamaica**, made from dried hibiscus flowers; it tastes and looks like cranberry juice but with a more subtle flavor, and without the acidity. Tamarind is a popular flavor in México (you'll see lots of tamarind candies), and you can find it in a drink as well – try an *agua de tamarindo*. All sorts of fruits are made into *aguas*; for example, you could get an *agua de sandía* (watermelon water); or try one made from grains, such as *horchata* (a delicious rice and cinnamon drink). Besides restaurants, you'll see plenty of vendors walking the streets with carts, or set up in markets with huge jars of *aguas*. If you don't fancy a light, refreshing *agua*, you might want to try a true Mexican drink – **atole**, a thick sweetened beverage made of *masa* (a dough made from dried, boiled and ground corn kernels). *Atole* is definitely worth trying, but it takes some getting used to.

México has some world-renowned **beers**, including Dos Equis (XX), Corona, and Superior (among a long list of others). Wines, while not traditionally one of the country's strong points, aren't bad from the Baja California region. **Tequila**, on the other hand, is universally known as being very Mexican, and you'll find a nice selection in most bars; you drink it either with salt and lime (lick salt, suck lime, then take the tequila) or with *sangrita* (a spicy tomato juice that helps temper the strength of the tequila).

Accommodations

Accommodation prices in this book are rated on the same scale from place to place. All rates are based on double occupancy, so if you're one person traveling alone, prices will usually be lower – perhaps even down a whole notch on the price chart. In some places, you'll also be given different options that can raise or lower the price you might pay. Common extra-cost options include air-conditioning, two beds or a television. During the summer months, specifically in the big cities on the coast, I recommend air-conditioning – the weather gets hot, humid, and unpleasant. The TV choice is a personal one – if they have cable, you'll find plenty of movies in English with Spanish subtitles. As for beds, a double bed, as opposed to two singles, can be a money-saver.

HOTEL PRICE CHART	
Rates are per room based on double occupancy. Rates lower if single occupancy or sharing a bed. Higher rates on holidays.	
¢	US $10-$20
$	US $21-$40
$$	US $41-$60
$$$	US $61-$80
$$$$	US $81-$125
$$$$$	Over US $125

■ Hotel Expectations

Hotels are surprisingly affordable. In most places covered by this book, you can get a nice place to stay for around US $30. In larger cities such as the Puerto de Veracruz or Villahermosa, however, you will pay a bit more. Along the coast, the summer months often bring elevated prices, and everywhere you'll find prices bumped up quite a bit during the holidays (see *Holiday* section for dates) – most especially during *Semana Santa*. During the holidays, you'll need to reserve your hotel ahead of time whenever possible. Unfortunately, less expensive hotels often don't take reservations – they work on a first-come, first-served basis. In this case, head to the hotel as soon as you get to your destination. Many smaller places don't have a specific check-in time, and will allow you to check in as soon as you get there. Another thing to be aware of is that many hotels, especially in smaller towns, do not accept credit cards.

DON'T FORGET

- Ask to see your room before you take it.
- During holidays, try to make an advance reservation, especially in the coastal cities during Semana Santa.
- Credit cards are not always accepted.

It's essential that wherever you decide to stay, you ask to see the room before committing to it. The lobby can be beautiful, clean and air-conditioned, the hotel clerk kind and friendly, but you never know what's behind the door to your room. It could be as simple as a bit of stuffiness, or it could be as uncomfortable as saggy and worn beds. Or it could be worse.

> *April 23 – We checked into our hotel today, I couldn't believe how lucky we were to get a room at such a good price and right on the zócalo too! After we dropped off our stuff, we went right out to explore. When we finally got back after dinner, it was late, and we started to unpack. Then I saw a little roach running across the floor. I don't particularly like bugs, but I stepped on it, and as I leaned down to pick it up and throw it away, a little bit of movement at the edge of my vision made me turn my head. I saw dozens of tiny roaches pouring out of a hole in the front door. I don't know why we didn't see it before when we checked out the room. But they were everywhere, and by this point it was too late to get another room. So here I am now, at midnight, sitting in the zócalo writing this and waiting for the Raid bomb we bought to finish smoking the room. I'll look more closely next time. I hate bugs.*

Hotels should let you see the room before you take it. If they have a problem, you're probably better off not staying there.

The least expensive hotels should be clean, small, and without much by way of amenities. You'll find that beds are often well-worn, bathrooms are ancient, and towels are threadbare. Often, however, they can be good values, especially if all you're looking for is a place to bed down for the night. Mid-level hotels generally have a few more amenities, and often an on-site restaurant. The most expensive hotels will have everything from room service and laundry service to pools and tennis courts. If you're a fan of chain hotels, there are many of them in this more expensive category, including Holiday Inns and Best Westerns. Most hotels (including the least expensive ones) have bathrooms that come with soap and towels (although many times they are rather thin and unabsorbent). As the price goes up, you'll usually find shampoo and conditioner as well. It never hurts, however, to bring a travel bottle with you.

Except for the most expensive places, the bathrooms, for some strange reason, are crazily designed, and often one of the more memorable parts of the hotel. Toilets may not have seats. Sometimes there is no shower door or shower curtain. The water pressure is either way too weak, or the hot water is only lukewarm, or – my particular favorite – half the water ends up on the other side of the bathroom. I've seen one too many bathrooms where the showerhead spurts water in every direction except down onto you. Be prepared for anything when it comes to bathrooms – and don't forget to bring a cheap pair of shower shoes.

■ Camping

There aren't many formal campgrounds in the areas covered by this book. The one notable exception is the portion of Gulf coastline known as the "Costa Esmeralda," which has a number of private campgrounds with full-service hookup spots for RVs, as well as areas for tent campers. Because of this, the area is particularly popular with campers and, if you're headed there during a holiday, be advised that things book up fast.

Adventures

The adventures in this book run the gamut from easy, spur-of-the-moment walks around town, to exciting, must-plan-ahead white-water rafting trips. There's something to fit every level and every interest. Be sure you're prepared – the best adventure, is one where you don't end up recovering in the hotel for three days! Wear comfortable shoes, bring maps (if necessary) so you don't get lost, carry water so you don't get dehydrated in the hot sun, hire a guide if you want to go inside a darkened, deserted cave and, above all, be sure you select activities at your skill level. Don't head out on a Level IV white-water rafting trip when you've never even been on a boat).

■ On Foot

Hiking

There are a few national parks and biosphere reserves in the region. But you'll find few maps or guidebooks to the trails and mountains. Getting to the hiking paths of the protected areas usually involves an outing to a village at the park's border. If you don't have a car, this means you'll be on a rickety, second-class bus. Once you get there, you'll often find a huge network of paths from which to choose – typically well-worn, narrow and winding. They can be exciting for explorers and a nice outing for hikers, but a little rustic for those who like things a little more organized (no signs, few facilities and no rangers). You'll need a good sense of direction (bring a compass), as the number of trails means it's easy to get lost. Don't be ashamed to turn around if you think you're forgetting the way home.

Hiking does offer an unforgettable chance to see a part of México you might not otherwise experience. In these protected areas, you'll find wildlife, such as wildcats and exotic birds, that has retreated to these undeveloped patches as deforestation occurs.

You're typically pretty safe on an independent hike, and are unlikely to encounter any harassment. You probably won't even see many people. The notable exception is in Chiapas, where you don't want to get out of the well-touristed areas (or even out of view of other people). If you're not keen on hiking independently, you can find outfitters that will take you on guided day (or overnight) outings. If you plan on a hike up the Pico de Orizaba, you'll want to get a guide as well.

When you head out for the day, it's a good idea to bring a backpack with the necessities. Water and snacks are mandatory (you won't find any in the jungle). A compass can be very useful, as can a Spanish-English dictionary (if you don't know much Spanish, and you need to ask for directions, you won't find anyone that speaks English). Bring toilet paper (unless you like using leaves) and water purification tablets are useful. Insect repellent and suntan lotion should not be forgotten, and a first aid kit and a light jacket (it gets cool at higher altitudes) are good items to bring along as well. A good pair of comfortable boots is the final touch.

Caving

It can be absolutely thrilling to explore a dark, mysterious hole that leads deep into the earth. Bats, curious rock formations, underground rivers and lakes – there's a whole world in there ready to be discovered. Speleologists – those people addicted to the excitement of cave exploration – know this. There are a number of interesting caves that you can visit – all three states have offerings. My favorite by far, simply for its name, has to be Tabasco's Cave of the Blind Sardine, which actually has blind sardines.

Some caves are fine for exploring on your own, and are clearly marked, with roads leading right up to them. Others are not formally set up for tourists and are not well-lit (or lit at all), do not have paid admittance, and are reached only by a dirt path. These caves are best seen with the aid of a guide, who can organize a hike, set up a swim in a submerged cavern, or lead you to into little-known spots.

A resource curious cavers should consult before leaving home is the National Speleological Society (NSS), www.caves.org. Its *Journal of Cave and Karst Studies* offers articles on some Mexican caves (it has a project on the caves of Tabasco), including research, accidents, and explorations; information can be searched and read online. The NSS also offers brochures on tips for responsible caving, a brochure on bats, reference lists on caving books and websites, as well as conventions, events, and discussion boards for more avid cavers. Although not all of the links on the Proyecto Espeleológico Purificación (PEP) website work (www.purificacion.org), it still has some good, interesting information on the 25-year history of caving in the Purificación Karst Area, which covers the southern section of Tamaulipas and Nuevo Leon.

Hunting

The **Secretaría del Medio Ambiente, Recursos Naturales y Pesca** (SEMARNAP) is México's federal agency in charge of hunting regulations. Sport hunting is particularly popular in northern México, and hunting licenses are issued for the activity. Tamaulipas is known by hunters for the quality of its bird hunting, specifically white wing doves, although quail, ducks, and geese are plentiful, as are deer. The wing season runs from summer to early fall for most birds; January and February are the months for quail. There are regulations on numbers and size of killings, as well as the number of rifles you can carry and amount of ammunition. You must get a permit to hunt as well as a permit to carry a gun. Be forewarned – firearm possession in México is a criminal offense. You don't want to end up in jail, so follow all rules.

There are a number of different types of hunting permits, including waterfowl, duck, mammals, other birds, limited, and special. Permits (gun and hunting) cost several hundred dollars and you'll still need to be accompanied by a licensed Mexican hunting guide. To get the permit, you'll need a certificate from your consul, which is issued once you provide a letter of clearance from your local police department, a special visa, and a military gun permit. You'll also need proof of US citizenship. A good option is to get a list from the local Mexican Consulate of licensed hunting outfitters, many of whom specialize in setting up all the necessary permits.

Archaeological Discoveries

Archaeological sites in México are operated by the government-run **Instituto Nacional de Antropología e Historia** (INAH). In many places, excavations are ongoing, with sections roped off or hidden under canopies for protection. This gives you a first-hand look at the recovery process. At El Tajín, for example, underneath a small, makeshift hut you can see a beautiful mural slowly emerging from an ancient ruined building. When you return in a few years, there will be more buildings to explore!

Larger INAH sites generally have restrooms, a museum, and a place to buy sodas, water, and light snacks. Sites are open specific hours and charge an admission fee (though don't expect a site map or pamphlet to come with it). There is usually an extra charge for the use of a video camera. Admission on Sundays at some sites is free or half price; occasionally the Sunday discounts are given to Mexican citizens only. Mexican students regularly receive discounted admission; if you're a student, it never hurts to show your ID and ask. The smallest sites have nothing but a ticket person and a book for you to sign. It's a good idea to bring your own water as on-site prices can be exorbitant. Wear plenty of suntan lotion; the main paths are usually cleared of vegetation and offer little shade. Have a hat and bring insect repellent with DEET. Do not think about removing any archaeological stones, no matter how small. Such actions are illegal and can land you in jail (have you read the section on criminal penalties yet?).

■ On Water

Fishing

The Gulf Coast is a sport fisherman's paradise. You can do everything from simply throwing a line in the water to going on a competitive multi-day fishing tournament. Most villages along the coastline are home to fishermen, and it won't be hard to find someone to take you out in a boat. A laid-back daytrip, in which your guide supplies the fishing gear and bait, can be pretty inexpensive, as well as an enjoyable way to spend the afternoon. A day out with the family putzing around the waters and waiting for the fish to bite could be just what you need to de-stress from the hassles of everyday life.

The waters along the coast of **Tamaulipas** in particular are quite popular with more serious fishermen. At **La Pesca**, you can find huge fish, including marlin, red snapper, sea trout, bass, tuna, tarpon, and mackerel. Throughout the year fishing tournaments are organized to see who can catch the biggest one out there. And they grow big – a 1991 club record for an Atlantic blue marlin in the Club de Yates of Tampico was 521 pounds! Besides the coastline, look to the *presas* (dams) in Tamaulipas for fishing opportunities (especially bass). Many Texans drive across the border to fish in these rich waters; bait shops, picnic tables, and fishing campgrounds are near them.

If you're in a small village and you're going out in the local fishermen cooperative boat, you will not be bothered with regulations and licenses. Officially, regulations state that if you are in a private boat, there is fishing gear on board, and you are 16 years old or older, you must have a sport fishing license issued by the Mexican Department of Fisheries (Oficina de PESCA). In other words, if you're on a charter or you bring your own boat in, you should get a license before you leave for México. If you're fishing from shore, a license is not required.

You can purchase licenses from PESCA itself – Oficina de PESCA, ☎ 619-233-6956 (US), 2550 Fifth Ave., Suite 101, San Diego, CA, 92103. If you call them, they'll fax you an application, which you complete and fax or mail back with a check. Permits are sold in daily, weekly, monthly, or annual increments. You can also buy licenses at some bait shops in México (although these might be difficult to find in some places). There is no limit to the amount of fish you can catch and release. However, if you are keeping them, there's a daily limit of 10 fish, with no more than five of a specific species. Exceptions include marlin (you're limited to one), and sailfish, halibut, dorado, and tarpon (limited to two). There is a higher limit if you are out at sea for a few days.

The fishing license requirement is irregularly monitored. You could meet people who have never been stopped and have never purchased one. I would not recommend taking the risk.

Boating

If you visit the Gulf Coast by boat, boat and fishing clubs provide docking services. A boat permit is required for all trailerable or non-trailerable boats – you'll need the title, proof of citizenship, and the title for the trailer if you arrived by land. You'll then pay a fee to a Customs officer for a permit (which is good for 12 months). For more specific, and the latest, information, contact the closest Mexican consulate or the Mexican Tourism Board (www.visitmexico.com) before you depart for México.

Rafting/Kayaking

Veracruz has some of the best white-water rivers in the country, and a large number of agencies specialize in rafting trips at all skill levels, from beginner to extremely advanced, and some combine them with camping as well. Outfitters will work with you to figure out what level you're at, and what trip would be best for you. The geography of Veracruz is such that every trip is spectacular, so there is no need for you to overstate your skills or sign up for a trip you're not qualified for – you'll find it a thrill at any level. Check with outfitters before you arrive in the country. Some offer transportation to and from the airport or your arrival city.

Some of the same agencies that offer rafting have kayaks as well, although the sport is far less popular and kayaks are a bit harder to find. If you've driven in and brought your own boat, there's a limitless number of rivers where you can put in. But be sure to consult with locals and/or tourism officials, so you know what to expect. You don't want to go over a waterfall or into a cascade of rapids. Ocean kayaking along the coast of Tamaulipas in the Laguna Madre can be particularly pleasant. The lagoons form a barrier between you and the open ocean, and they draw a fabulous variety and quantity of birds that migrate through the area. Some parts are also comfortably shallow. The only drawback is that there are a few villages along the way.

Beaches

The Gulf Coast is not known for quality beaches, although you can find a few good ones. Typically, be prepared for brown sand, dark churned waters, and strong surf. Almost every decent beach draws excessive crowds during holidays. Plan your beach vacation for an off-peak time, because even if you don't mind the people, they bring loads of trash that ends up littering the sand. It's especially bad during Semana Santa, but does get cleaned up over subsequent weeks. Since beaches are public, camping is allowed on them.

■ On Wheels

Biking

If you like to mountain bike, the best way to enjoy yourself is to contact a local outfitter (you'll find a couple listed in this book), who can provide you with bikes, guides and transportation. Be aware that you will find no dedicated bike paths, either on the streets or in the jungle. Biking on streets is permitted, and can be enjoyable; but be prepared to ride on the shoulder of narrow roads, which can be a bit frightening, particularly when big buses zoom by. Local drivers are used to bikers, however. In villages, bikes are used for transportation by men, women, and children. Although this means that drivers won't be totally surprised to see you, it doesn't make a long-distance ride any less nerve-racking. Your best bet is to go to a village, and from there bike local roads to other nearby villages. The smaller and bumpier the road, the better it is for you, as you'll see fewer cars and those that you do see will be driving slower. The scenery in such places can be absolutely gorgeous.

You can bring your bike into México on a plane without a problem, but it will be a bit expensive. Continental Airlines, for example, charges US $100 one-way (the bike is not part of the free baggage allowance). Their requirements state that bikes should be packed in sealed cardboard boxes (check their website if you need a box) with handlebars turned sideways and pedals removed. The $100 fee is a flat rate, regardless of oversize and overweight boxes. Check with each airline for embargoes. Continental, for example, has embargo periods during holidays. Usually, this applies November 15-January 15, June 4-August 31, and from nine days before Easter until the Wednesday after Easter.

Entertainment

You can often find a lot of activity, day or night, in the town's *zócalo*, or main square. The best have entertainers of all types, including clowns, with faces painted, and other performers. My favorite was a "professional" boxer, a skinny short man with boxing trunks and boxing gloves, who called himself *El Negrito*. He boasted he was the absolute best in the country. He waited while the "ring announcer" recruited an audience member (a girl) to take him on. The match was over after a look from the girl downed the boxer in a hilariously comical sequence. You'll see musicians (in some places the nighttime brings out mariachis) and vendors of all kinds. Sometimes there's nothing more entertaining than going from stall to stall trying every exotic treat you find. And if that's not enough, almost every *zócalo* will have a number of shoeshiners where you can set yourself up in their chair and watch in utter amazement as they take your 20-year-old, worn, filthy shoes and make them look brand-spanking new again.

There's also more formal entertainment. All major cities have at least a couple of nightclubs, discos, and late-night bars to keep night crawlers amused. If you like music, but don't care for discos, busy city centers (Villahermosa and Veracruz, for example) or restaurants will sometimes have live music. Dances, music and theater performances are scheduled during the weekends. Check with the tourism office or at theaters for schedules of events. If you want a taste of home, it'll be easy to find movie theaters in most major cities. Rates are usually lower than in the US, and movies are typically released in English with Spanish subtitles.

The Internet café is another good option for evening entertainment, especially since even the smallest villages that don't have much else going on will usually have one. Besides using e-mail and the Internet, you can use chat programs and play online games. Some of the better cafés may also have TVs where you can play video games. Before the Internet, people went to arcades, and in many towns you'll still find shops filled with old-fashioned stand alone Pac-Man, Donkey-Kong, and Tron machines; many have updated and you'll see newer shooting, racing, fighting, and sports games.

Along the border, you'll find bullfight rings and *charrerías*. A traditional bullfight (*corrida de toros*) is a show that involves three different bullfighters who fight two bulls each. Typically, the bull is initially evaluated for strength, *picadores* then enter the ring and prick the bull with a lance, *banderilleros* follow and stick the bull in the back, and finally the bullfighter begins his traditional dance with the bull, enticing it to rush past him with a red cape. At the very end, he will kill the bull. The bull arena is usually called the *plaza de toros*. If this show seems gruesome, you may be more interested in a *charrería*, México's version of a rodeo. The show is performed in a *lienzo* (arena) by *charros* and *charras* (male and female cowboys), and is basically a show of horse-riding skills. The show is marked by equestrian competitions and highly choreographed shows, performed by riders in elaborate costumes.

Information Sources

■ General Information

México's tourism department has a helpful website (www.visitmexico.com), where you can find information on hotels, restaurants, and cities throughout México; it's available in both Spanish and English. They also have an information hotline (☎ 800-446-3942) where you can talk to a live person. Another source is your local Mexican consulate. They sometimes have a few pamphlets on México – most, however, tend to be very general.

There are a number of websites that provide useful information on México. **México Connect** (www.mexconnect.com) is an e-magazine with forums as well as a collection of articles about food, places, culture, etc. **México Online** (www.mexonline.com) has good information in English, including bulletin boards, articles, accommodations, food and culture. **The México Channel** (www.trace-sc.com) has links to an assortment of information, including links to online news about México.

Before you actually travel, check out the State Department's **Department of Consular Affairs** website (http://travel.state.gov), which has a section devoted to travel warnings and consular information sheets on many different countries. If you don't have an Internet connection, you can call ☎ 202-647-5225 to hear their advisory. Get the latest update on road conditions, crime activities and public announcements, as well as information on visas, passports, medical assistance and health. For health information, consult the **National Center for Infectious Diseases** at ☎ 1-800-311-3435, www.cdc.gov.

When you're in México, besides the local tourism offices in each city, each state on the Gulf has a **State Tourism Office**, offering a lot of good printed material covering more of the state than the local offices can provide. In Tamaulipas, the office is in the state capital, Ciudad Victoria; in Tabasco, there is one in the capital Villahermosa (although many of the tourism booths in the city are just as good, and can give you a complete state map and state visitors guide). There is also excellent information at the Veracruz state office in its capital of Xalapa (they have a couple of books covering specifically the coast around Veracruz, and the area around Xalapa).

■ Place-Specific Websites

Tampaulipas

Tampico's graphic-heavy website is **www.tampico.gob.mx**. It has a lot of good information on the city, including contact phone numbers and e-mail addresses of tour operators, travel agents, restaurants, and hotels (in Tampico).

You can also try **www.tamaulipas.gob.mx**, which is much more orderly and a bit boring. You can get some information on the history, municipalities and climate of the state, and, if you hunt around, information on towns and museums. Everything is in Spanish.

Veracruz

Available in both Spanish and English, **www.veracruzturismo.com.mx** provides good information on various areas throughout Veracruz, but has only minimal information on hotels and restaurants. You can find maps, information on the different regions, and travel agencies at **www.veracruz.gob.mx**.

Tabasco

A busy site that's done a nice job of supplying information is **www.tabasco.gob.mx**. It includes a map of the state and its capital, information on politics, education, culture, and the state, as well as photographs, links to hotels with websites, a current month calendar of cultural events in Villahermosa, information on museums, and much more. The only problem is that it is only in Spanish.

Chiapas

Basic information on services is online at **www.chiapas.gob.mx**. For more information on the Zapatista movement, visit **www.ezlnaldf.org**, where you can learn about the uprising through Marcos' letters and writings, some of which have been translated into English.

Oaxaca

There is good information in English on hotels, restaurants, festivals and events, as well as a newsletter you can subscribe to at **www.oaxacainfo.com**. Also try **www.oaxaca.gob.mx**; it's a little bit slow, but the tourism link does eventually get you some information.

WORD TO THE WISE

> *If you visit a Spanish-language website and you need help, do a search for it under Google. When you find the site, instead of clicking on the link directly, click on "Translate this page." You'll then be linked to the translated page; translations won't be perfect, but if you had absolutely no idea what was going on in the other language, it can certainly help.*

Embassies & Consulates

Your embassy can help with emergencies such as notifying your family if you become seriously ill, helping you find appropriate medical assistance, providing you with a list of attorneys, and assisting if your passport was lost or stolen. Embassies are located in México City, and consulates or honorary consulates elsewhere. In the Gulf Coast (and México City) there are the following.

US Embassy in México City
Paseo de la Reforma 305
Colonia Cuauhtemoc
06500 México, D.F.
☎ 5-080-2000
From the US: ☎ 011-52-55-5080-2000
Hours: 9 am-2 pm and 3-5 pm, Mon.-Fri. Consular section closed last weekday of each month. Also closed on US and Mexican holidays. If it's an after-hours emergency, call and notify the switchboard that you need to speak with an officer.

US Consulate in Matamoros
Ave. Primera 2002 y Azaleas
Matamoros, Tamaulipas 87330
☎ 868-812-4402
Hours: 9 am-12 noon and 1:30-3:30 pm, Mon.-Fri.

US Consulate in Nuevo Laredo
Allende 3330
Col. Jardín
Nuevo Laredo, Tamaulipas 88260
☎ 867-714-0512
Hours: 8 am-12:30 pm and 1:30-5 pm, Mon.-Fri.

US Consular Agent in Reynosa
Calle Monterrey No. 390 (corner with Sinaloa)
Col. Rodríguez
Reynosa, Tamps., 88630
☎ 899-923-9331
Hours: 9 am-noon and 1:30-3:30 pm, Mon.-Fri.

British Embassy
Consular Section
Río Usumacinta 30
Colonia Cuauhtemoc
06500 México, D.F.
☎ 5-242-8500
Hours: 10 am-2 pm, Mon.-Fri.

Canadian Embassy
Consular Section
Calle Schiller No. 529
Col. Bosque de Chapultepec
Del. Miguel Hidalgo
C.P. 11580, México D.F.
☎ 5-724-7900
Hours: 9 am to 12:30 pm and 2 to 4 pm, Mon.-Fri.

Tamaulipas

State Capital: Ciudad Victoria

Tamaulipas is an interesting state to visit, though you're really going to have to look hard for your touristic reward. You'll find a few goodies – some *cenotes* (deep natural wells) along the border of Veracruz, fishing along the border with Texas, wildlife watching along the coastline, but they're buried in places with few facilities and few other attractions. For the adventurous among you, this poses little problem. Faced with the dry, arid plains of Highway 101 south from Matamoros, you'll rise to the challenge, and head down that bumpy dirt road to see what there is to be seen. No facilities? No problem! You'll bring a picnic and enjoy the same grounds that endangered sea turtles and manatees call home. The cloud forest is hidden up a dirt trail too? No problem! Hire a guide to show you the hidden waterfalls and caves, and do your very best to see that elusive jaguar that is said to live in the area.

IN THIS CHAPTER	
■ The Border	77
■ Nuevo Laredo	78
■ Nuevo Laredo to Reynosa	85
■ Reynosa	87
■ Matamoros	92
■ Matamoros to Aldama	99
■ Aldama	101
■ Ciudad Victoria	103
■ Reserva de la Biosfera de El Cielo	107
■ Tampico	109

The border cities are an animal of their own, and you'll quickly find out whether the busyness, grime, and crowds are for you. Other cities in the state, with the exception perhaps of Tampico, are for the most part a means to an end – stops for a pleasant overnight, or to access the nearby coastline, *presas*, or rivers.

The Border

The Río Grande separates México's border towns from US border towns geographically, but certainly not culturally. Perhaps México's side has become a little bit more American, or the US side has become a little bit more Mexican. Both sides thrive off one another. The Mexican border towns are paired up with border towns on the US side (Tamaulipas-Matamoros with Brownsville, Reynosa with McAllen, and Nuevo Laredo with Laredo). Residents of each drive to and from all day; Americans spending their money on cheap souvenirs, cheap liquor, and the excitement of a "foreign" visit, and Mexicans crossing to buy American products. Also contributing to the interactions and the economies of the two cultures are the *maquiladoras* (factories set up in México to provide cheap labor and product assembly for their partner factories on the US side). Border cities have big industrial parks, particularly Matamoros and Reynosa, where there are thousands of *maquiladora* workers.

Crossing is cheap and easy (US citizens staying in the border zone for less than 72 hours don't need a tourist card), adding even more attraction to a quick trip across. Tamaulipas' border cities are, by and large, bases for these day-trips. A daytime trip can be enjoyable – there are a few good fishing spots, you can have some good Mexican food, and you'll feel that you've been into México (even though there is still that Tex-Mex atmosphere), but there isn't much for the tourist by way of other real attractions. A nighttime stay can be a mixed bag. Set yourself up before it gets dark; parts of some cities can be dangerous and ugly at night (drug trafficking problems persist, prostitution is an issue, and bars can get rowdy).

Nuevo Laredo

Nuevo Laredo has a huge number of visitors that cross its border – in fact, it receives more border crossers than any other city. US visitors find the "Dos Laredos" (Nuevo Laredo in México and Laredo in the US) a convenient access point, with major tollways connecting the twin cities to the busy capital of Nuevo Leon (Monterrey) on the México side, and San Antonio on the Texas side. The city was established thanks to the Mexican-American War that created the Río Grande as the US-México border. It's attractive to shoppers and diners looking for a little more of the Mex in Tex-Mex.

The river that forms the border between the United States and México is known as the Río Grande in the United States, and as the Río Bravo del Norte in México.

■ Orientation & Practicalities

Avenida Guerrero is the main street in town, going from International Bridge #1 through the downtown. **Plaza Hidalgo** is the main square, and is located on Ave. Guerrero and Gonzalez. The bus station is out to the south.

Emergency Services: Cruz Roja/Red Cross, ☎ 867-712-0989; Hospital, ☎ 867-714-8199.

Exchanging Money: There are a couple of banks (including a Banamex) on Ave. Guerrero near Plaza Hidalgo. Many places will take US dollars, but do your best to change it beforehand or you'll lose out to shop or hotel owner's exchange rates.

Post Office: The *correos* is a block east of Plaza Hidalgo, behind the Palacio de Gobierno on Camargo.

Tourist Information: The tourist information office is at the corner of Ave. Juárez and Herrera, eight blocks south of Plaza Hidalgo. For tourist information in Laredo, contact the Laredo Convention and Visitor's Bureau, ☎ 800-361-3360, 501 San Agustin, Laredo, TX 78040.

■ Getting There & Getting Around

By Air

Nuevo Laredo has a small airport serviced by Mexicana's subsidiary, **Aerocaribe**, ☎ 800-531-7921, which offers flights to México City. The airport is south of town.

By Bus

The bus station is at the corner of Anáhuac and Ave. America, south of the center. This is a main bus station, and you should have no problem finding a bus to take you anywhere you want to go (México City, Zacatecas, Ciudad Victoria, Durango, Guadalajara, etc.). **Omnibus de México** and **Futura** are the primary first-class buses serving this area. There's a **Greyhound** bus station nearby on Matamoros.

By Car

If you're driving from the United States, the main access point is over the Río Grande at the International Bridge #1, crossing over from Laredo on the Texas side. There is a vehicle toll both ways. If you don't plan on being here longer than 72 hours and you're not leaving the border zone, you won't have to stop for a tourist card or vehicle permit, and can continue into Nuevo Leon. If you do plan on staying longer or traveling farther, you'll need to follow the signs to the Customs office right after the bridge crossing. You are not required to make this stop, so you'll have to seek it out if this applies to you (see *Customs*, pages 32-34, for more information). Traffic on the bridge is particularly bad on holidays,

Sundays, and during morning and evening commutes; do your best to avoid these times.

Once you cross the bridge, you'll be on Ave. Guerrero, which is Nuevo Leon's main avenue. You'll find most of the action here, as well as on the main square, Plaza Hidalgo, a few blocks up. Keep an eye on the roads, which are often one-way, can be loaded with traffic and have a speed limit of only around 25 mph. There are parking lots around downtown that charge a fee for a few hours or the day's use.

An alternative to crossing at Bridge #1 is to use International Bridge #2, which is about five blocks east. Bridge #2 is for vehicle-only traffic; on the Mexican side, it outlets onto Blvd. Luis Colosio, and is used mainly by those wishing to bypass downtown. If you want to go farther into México, the tollway, Highway 85D, heads north towards Monterrey, or you can take the free Highway 85, though it's slower. Highway 2 (and its companion Highway 83 on the US side) follows the US-México border, heading west, as well as east to Reynosa and Matamoros. Highway 1 is a secondary road that cuts from Nuevo Laredo across the state of Nuevo Leon, connecting up with Highway 30.

Car Rentals

You have many options for car rentals. Be sure you are properly insured.

Budget Car Rental, ☎ 867-717-4180 (5530 Reforma); 800-472-3325; www.budget.com

Milennium Rent A Car, ☎ 867-719-0519 (2450 Chihuahua)

Jardin Auto Rental, ☎ 867-715-5403 (3048 Juárez)

Direct Auto Rental, ☎ 867-715-0976 (3051 Aquiles Serdán)

Fast Auto Rent, ☎ 867-714-3232 (4036 Chihuahua)

On Foot

You can walk across the border on International Bridge #1 (International Bridge #2 is vehicle traffic only). There is parking on the US side if you want to leave your car; if it's a nice day, this might be a better option – you won't have to deal with the traffic, the tolls, or the parking issues on the Mexican side.

> **NEED HELP?**
>
> There's a **United States Consulate** in Nuevo Laredo, ☎ 867-714-0512, 3330 Allende. Office hours: 8 am-12:30 pm/1:30-5 pm.

■ Sightseeing

The Republic of the Río Grande Museum is in an old, thick-walled adobe building that once served as the capitol for the Republic of the Río Grande. It has historical exhibits covering frontier times. The museum is at 1000 Zaragoza St, Laredo, TX. ☎ 956-727-3480. Hours are Tues.-Sun., 10 am-5 pm.

While you're in Laredo, stop by **Fort McIntosh**, which was dates to around the time of the Mexican-American War. The fort was established when the US Infantry (led by Lt. Egbert Ludovicus Vielé) was sent to protect the area from Indian raid in 1849. The troops set up camp in this strategic spot next to the Río Grande, and it eventually became known as Fort McIntosh. During the US Civil War, the fort was abandoned by the North, and used by Confederate troops fighting against Union attacks. During World War II, the fort was again used – this time as barracks for troops. It was finally abandoned on May 31, 1946.

■ Adventures

On Foot

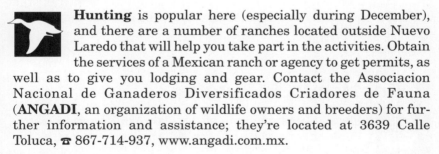

Hunting is popular here (especially during December), and there are a number of ranches located outside Nuevo Laredo that will help you take part in the activities. Obtain the services of a Mexican ranch or agency to get permits, as well as to give you lodging and gear. Contact the Associacion Nacional de Ganaderos Diversificados Criadores de Fauna (**ANGADI**, an organization of wildlife owners and breeders) for further information and assistance; they're located at 3639 Calle Toluca, ☎ 867-714-937, www.angadi.com.mx.

On Water

One of the more interesting places to visit is south of Nuevo Laredo, off Highway 2. The Presa Falcón (Falcon Dam) was built over the Río Grande as a project of both the United States and México, and inaugurated in 1963.

Because of the dam's construction and the flooding that resulted, the town of Guerrero, founded in 1749, was abandoned and its inhabitants transferred to a nearby site that would be above water. The new town became known as Nueva Guerrero (and the flooded town referred to as Guerrero Viejo, or Old Guerrero). Today, Nueva Guerrero still sits at the southern end of the waters formed by the *presa*. The original town of **Guerrero Viejo**, however, though flooded, refused to disappear from sight, and when the water levels are low, you can see the tops of some of its buildings. Among these, you can often see (and, if there is a severe drought, walk up to) much of Nuestro Señora del Refugio, the town church that stood in the main square. It's a structure similar to the Alamo at first glance. Also visible are many other ruined buildings surrounding the main square. Guerrero Viejo is about 33 km/20 miles before you reach Nueva Guerrero (at the end of the lake). You'll see a hand-painted sign and a bumpy road heading several miles through a few gates, before it eventually reaches the old town.

The **Falcon Dam** (Presa Falcón) is very popular with fishermen; the lake is filled with largemouth bass and catfish, has a fair amount of striped bass, and a few white bass. Fishing is good most of the year. The notable exception, however, is during the summer months. If it's been a dry year, droughts can also decrease the number of fish.

Nueva Guerrero is at the end portion of the lake; here you can find an international crossing to the United States (the Lower Río Grande Valley), as well as tourism facilities and shops, which should help get the fisherman on his way. There are camping, fishing, and boating facilities across the border as well, at the **Falcon State Park**. Farther south, near Ciudad Miguel Aleman, the **Presa Marte R. Gómez** is another dam with a large reservoir. Fishermen enjoy bass fishing here. It is, however, a bit more remote than the Falcon Dam (take the turnoff to the south from Ciudad Miguel Aleman). Ask at the tourism office in Nuevo Laredo (or a local bait shop) to see if you need a fishing permit.

■ Festivals & Events

A hot international event is **La Carrera Panamericana**, an automotive road rally that involves a race across the country. The original road race was in 1950, developed by the Mexican Government in celebration of the completion of the Panamerican Highway. In its time, it was incredibly popular, attracting world-famous international road-racers. The races lasted only a few more years before they were discontinued. In the past 15 years or so, however, the race is once again being held. The race starts far south in Tuxtla Gutierrez, Chiapas, and continues to the

Rock climbing in Veracruz (see pages 239-40)

Above: *Pico de Orizaba, Veracruz (see page 240)*

Below: *Pyramid of the Niches, Veracruz (see page 148)*

Wild rivers lure rafters in Veracruz

finish line in Nuevo Laredo – around 3,200 km (1,984 miles). Countries from all over the world participate; the race takes about six days, and is typically held near the end of October. To find out more about the current schedule, route, history, or (heaven forbid) the application procedure, go to www.lacarrerapanamericana.com.mx. To enter the race, you've got to have an F.M.A.D. license and, if you're under age, you can only go as a co-driver and must have your parent's consent).

So maybe you have a little extra money in your pocket that's looking for a way out? You can help it on its way by stopping to do some **track betting**. If the gambler in you just has to be heard, visit **El Turf Club**, ☎ 867-712-04-94, located at Bravo and Ocampa (five blocks north of Plaza Hidalgo). You can bet remotely here on live (Mexican or US) greyhound or horse tracks. There's a restaurant and bar at the club as well.

From February until November, you can stop by one of the five *Lienzos Charros* in Nuevo Laredo (Rancho Media Luna, Rancho Nuevo Laredo, Nueva Santander, Río Grande or Río Bravo) and see a *charrería* – a type of Mexican rodeo with performances by *charros* or *charras* (cowboys). Both the men and the women are highly skilled riders, dressed in elaborate costumes. The men wear the typical wide Mexican hat, while the women are in wide-skirted, colorful dresses, riding side-saddle. They put on an exciting coordinated show of turns, jumps, and maneuvers. The riders love what they do, practice hard, and it shows. To find out about scheduled events during your visit, stop by the tourist infromation office.

You can watch **bullfights** at the Plaza de Toros "Lauro Luis Longoria," ☎ 867-712-7192 or 1-888-240-8460 (US). They have different shows throughout the season, ranging from a traditional bullfight (with a cape), to non-traditional (no cape), as well as midgets and clowns. Sometimes the ring hosts concerts, wrestling, or boxing matches as well. The bullring is at 411 Ave. Monterrey. Buy your tickets when you get there; they range from US $10 to $55, depending on which row you prefer, and whether or not you want shade. Or you can call and reserve them beforehand. Children under 10 are often free, and sometimes promotions will include transportation to and from the International Bridge. Shows are seasonal; contact the office to see what upcoming events are scheduled.

On February 22nd (and surrounding days), the US and México celebrate **Washington's birthday** on both sides of the river. Events include parades, fireworks, and general celebrations.

For still more events, you can contact the tourism board in Laredo, TX. Laredo often has a busy schedule of events and festivals celebrating both cultures; though many of the following events are one-time affairs, this gives you an idea of the kind of selection and diversity the city offers.

This past year they had:

- A Noche Mexicana Saturday;
- An International Fair and Exposition;
- A night's concert tribute to Mexican classical and contemporary music;
- A day when Mexican manufacturers and distributors from Guanajuato came to sell their products.

■ Shopping

The main street in Nuevo Laredo, **Ave. Guerrero**, has all the action – much of which is focussed around shopping. Most things will be slightly overpriced (as you'd find in any well-touristed place), and there are lots of cheap souvenirs. But you can also find some nicer items in the surrounding area, including hand-blown glass (**The Glass Shop**, 503 Calle Ocampo), custom-made furniture (**Luis Medina Custom Furniture**, 3351 Calle Anahuac), jewelry, leather goods, and – for the kids – *piñatas*. Take your time browsing through the shops, then visit both of the city's markets to see if you can find a better price or a more interesting item: **Mercado Herrera** (located nearby at Ocampo and Hidalgo) and the **Nuevo Mercado** (off Guerrero, a couple of blocks south of the International Bridge), which is the more popular and larger of the two.

■ Where to Stay

The **Hilton Garden Inn Nuevo Laredo**, ☎ 867-711-4600 or 0800-003-1400 (MX) at 5102 Ave. Reforma, will require a car to reach. This new hotel with handicap accessibility has an indoor pool, gym, air-conditioning, and either standard rooms or suites. $$$

At 5530 Reforma is the **Hacienda Real Fiesta Inn**, ☎ 867-711-4444 or 0800-718-7470 (MX), a modern

HOTEL PRICE CHART	
Rates are per room based on double occupancy. Rates lower if single occupancy or sharing a bed. Higher rates on holidays.	
	US $10-$20
$	US $21-$40
$$	US $41-$60
$$$	US $61-$80
$$$$	US $81-$125
$$$$$	Over US $125

hotel with restaurant, pool, gym, tennis court, room front parking, and rooms with a/c and cable TV. $$$

The Hotel Reforma, ☎ 867-712-6250, 822 Guerrero, is an old hotel with slightly worn rooms, but the staff is friendly, rooms are clean, and prices are fair. $

The Motel del Centro, ☎ 867-712-1310, 3330 Héroes de Nacataz, has clean rooms at good prices. $$

■ Where to Eat

The most popular (and touristed) spot is the **El Dorado Bar**, at Belden and Ocampo, just north of Plaza Hidalgo. The restaurant/bar dates back 80 years, and is a lively place (particularly at night) with a nice range of good drinks. $$$

DINING PRICE CHART	
Price per person for an entrée, not including beverage or tip.	
$	Under US $5
$$	US $5-$10
$$$	US $10+

If you're in the mood for "typical Mexican" food, try **México Típico**, two blocks south of Plaza Hidalgo at 934 Ave. Guerrero; you'll find a good sampling of Mexican dishes here. $$

Around five blocks northwest of Plaza Hidalgo, the **Cadillac Bar** (at Matamoros and Victoria) is a lively place at night, especially on weekends (11 am-1 am), when they have live music. $$-$$$

A little out of the downtown, but very popular with locals, is **El Rancho**, at 2134 Guerrero; there is regional music Tuesdays-Sundays, and plenty of Mexican dishes (especially tacos). $

El Rincon del Viejo, at 4835 Dr. Mier, also has live music (including trios and mariachis) and serves some good local dishes. $$

From Nuevo Laredo to Reynosa

A drive south along Highway 2 towards Reynosa can be a pleasant way to spend the day, particularly if you like to get off the beaten track. The route is about 256 km (158.7 miles) and pretty much parallels the Río Grande. Across the river is the southern part of the state of Texas, referred to as the Río Grande Valley, sometimes just called The Valley. A number of border crossings give Texans easy access to this portion of México, and you'll likely see a few (but not many) other adventurous tourists during your drive, which passes by and through ranches and villages.

Some of the places along this route are worth exploring. **Nueva Ciudad Guerrero** (see above, page 82) is followed by **Mier**, a historic town with a few old churches and a stone prison. It was founded in the mid-18th century. In the 1840s, 17 Texans were executed here after attemping a raid across the Río Grande. The group of 176 men was captured, imprisoned, and made to pick beans to determine which 17 of them would die – those with the black beans lost.

Ciudad Miguel Alemán is noteworthy for its suspension bridge, which was built in 1928, and is a National Historic Landmark in both México and the United States.

Across the river from Ciudad Miguel Alemán is the American town of **Roma** – an old steamboat port that has been designated a National Historic District, and where parts of the movie *Viva Zapata*, starring Marlon Brando and Anthony Quinn, were filmed. The movie is the story of Mexican revolutionary Emiliano Zapata and Marlon Brando received an Academy Award nomination for his role.

Roma also has a few historic buildings, as well as the **Roma Bluffs** (three acres of riverland). The Bluffs are a good place to spot a number of birds (including three kinds of kingfishers), and has birding tours, canoe trips, and history tours. Walking trails are free and the site is open daily; ☎ 956-849-4930. While you're in Roma, you can visit **Roma Historical Museum**, located in a building dating to around 1840 that was built as a chapel. There are some exhibits of both Mexican and American historical artifacts, including a Straub Machinery Co. cotton gin. Hours are Mon.-Fri., 9 am-4 pm.

Just north of Roma, on the banks of the International Falcon Reservoir, is the 572.6-acre **Falcon State Recreation Park**. The park offers a range of outdoor activities, including swimming and fishing (largemouth bass, stripe bass, white bass, and catfish). Summer is the only poor fishing season. Consult the park about getting a fishing license, unless you are here on the first Saturday of June, which is the annual Free Fishing Day, when no one needs a license. There is camping (both basic tent areas and full RV hookups), aswell as a boat ramp, biking and hiking nature trails, restrooms, and playgrounds. For more information, contact ☎ 956-848-5327. The park is handicapped-accessible. To get to the park from Roma, head west on US Highway 83 for 15 miles (24 km) until you reach FM 2098. From here, turn onto Park Road 46 and look for the park.

The next stop in México is **Camargo**, a historic town dating to the mid-1700s. Stop by its historic downtown plaza, and visit the **Church of Santa Ana**. Here you'll also find a border crossing to the old US town of **Río Grande City**. In 2001, Las Caminos del Río (the area of the Lower Río Grande Valley in Texas between the cities of Laredo and Brownsville), was designated by the National Trust for Historic Preservation and the History Channel as one of America's 11 most endangered historic places. Right in the center of it is Río Grande City, which has a number of historic buildings.

When you reach **Ciudad Díaz Ordaz**, you'll find the Los Ebanos Ferry, the only hand-drawn ferry along the border. You can cross over as a pedestrian or with a vehicle (it carries only three cars) to the town of **Los Ebanos** for a very small fee; look for an unpaved road to the dock where the ferry leaves. Hours are 8 am-4 pm.

Reynosa

The border town of Reynosa was founded in 1749 under the name of Nuestro Señora de Guadalupe de Reynosa. Some 50 years later, the town was flooded and had to be moved. Today, it sits 150 miles downriver from Nuevo Laredo. Its twin city across the border is McAllen, TX. Reynosa is a busy place that sees its share of visitors eager for a little shopping and Mexican food, but it's also a big commercial and petroleum center. Like many border towns, Reynosa does not have much by way of historical attractions... its oldest buildings were taken over by water.

■ Orientation & Practicalities

The Zona Rosa (or Pink Zone) starts across the street from the International Bridge. This is where most of the restaurants, nightclubs and stores are located. The main park is only a few blocks down from here at the corner of Zaragoza and Juárez.

Exchanging Money: Banks and money exchange offices are in the area around the Plaza Principal.

Post Office: The *correos* is five blocks south of the main square at the corner of Colón and Hidalgo.

Tourist Information: You can get tourist information from the Customs office near the bridge at the border. If you plan on visiting McAllen, contact the McAllen Chamber of Commerce for updates on events; ☎ 956-682-2871 (US). They're at 1200 Ash Avenue in McAllen.

■ Getting There & Around

By Air

Reynosa has a small airport, the Gen. Lucio Banco Airport, a few miles outside of town; you can find rental car booths there. It is serviced by **AeroMéxico**, ☎ 800-237-6639, www.aeromexico.com, which flies to and from México City, Villahermosa, and Veracruz, and **Aeromar**, ☎ 800-531-7921 or 0800-237-6627 (MX), www.aeromar.com.mx, which flies to Poza Rica.

By Bus

The bus station is six blocks south and six blocks east of the main park, on Colón. You can catch an **ADO**, **Omnibus de México** or **Frontera** (among others) to connect you with the rest of México.

By Car

In the United States, Highway 281 comes down to the border and the International Bridge.

From Reynosa, you can take toll Highway 40D (or the free Highway 40) southwest to Guadalupe. Alternatively, Highway 97 heads south to connect with Highway 101/180 towards Ciudad Victoria, or you can take toll Highway 2 towards Matamoros (around 104 km/64.5 miles).

National Car Rental has a counter at the airport, ☎ 899-923-0716, as well as downtown, ☎ 899-925-5190 (Col. Prolongacion Rodriguez); prices start at about US $55 a day with unlimited mileage.

> **NEED HELP?**
>
> There's a **United States Consular Agent**, ☎ 899-923-9331, in Reynosa at 390 Calle Monterrey.

■ Sightseeing

Just about the only thing to do in this border city is explore the downtown. Most of the restaurants and bars in the area are right by the International Bridge known as the Zona Rosa; shops can be found there, and also around the Mercado Zaragoza (the corner of Guerrero and Hidalgo), and on up to the main square (along Hidalgo).

McAllen

Sightseeing nearby in McAllen can be interesting as its culture is very much entwined with that of Reynosa.

The **International Museum of Art and Science** has temporary and permanent collections of Mexican folk and contemporary art, as well as interesting crafts. The permanent exhibit includes one of the largest collections of Latin American folk art (masks, pottery, textiles) in the country. It also has a library with a number of books on Latin American art (the Rosita C. Alcorn Library). The museum is at 1900 Nolana. Call to see what temporary exhibits or events are scheduled, ☎ 956-682-1564. Hours: Tues.-Sat. 9 am-5 pm, Sun. 1-5 pm, Thurs. 12-8 pm, closed Mondays. Admission: US $3 for adults, $2 for children and seniors.

Quinta Mazatlan is an old adobe hacienda, known for bird watching in its eight acres of surroundings with trails. You currently need to make a reservation to visit, but they do plan to reopen for drop-in visitors soon. There are plans to open viewing towers, an art gallery, and workshops. The hacienda is at 600 Sunset Avenue in McAllen; contact the McAllen Parks and Recreation Office, ☎ 956-682-1517, for more information. Admission is by appointment only; hours are Mon.-Fri., 7:30 am-5:30 pm.

San Juan

Take Highway 83 east of McAllen to San Juan and the **Virgen de San Juan del Valle Shrine**. Today the church is a huge modern building, but it was originally built in 1920 as a mission of St. Margaret Mary Church. In 1949, church director Father Joseph Azpiazu brought into the church an image of Our Lady of San Juan, which had the desired result of giving the Mexican-American community a place to worship. The church was enlarged in 1954 thanks to the huge number of parishioners it was attracting. Then, bizarrely, on October 23, 1970, in the middle of prayer, and when the church was full of parishioners, a small plane crashed through the roof of the sanctuary. No churchgoers were killed, thanks to the sturdy roof, but the pilot was. The image of the Virgin was rescued from the rubble, and a gigantic new sanctuary was built.

Today, the basilica has 30 life-size bronze statues (the Stations of the Cross) on its grounds and a huge mural entitled "Jesus Presents His Mother" on its walls. The McAllen Chamber of Commerce claims it is one of the world's largest mosaics. The Stations of the Cross are placed throughout the grounds and depict the journey of Jesus, starting with Jesus being condemned to death, and continuing with images such as Jesus falling for the first time, and being stripped of his clothes. The church is at 400 North Virgin de San Juan (in San Juan). Weekday masses are scheduled at 6:30 am, 11:30 am, and 5:30 pm, while Saturdays there's an extra service at 9:30 am, and Sundays there's a service every two hours from 6:30 am until 12:30 pm, then others at 3:30 pm and 5:30 pm. ☎ 956-787-0033.

Mission

La Lomita Mission is a cute adobe chapel dating to the turn of the century. The surrounding area is ideal for an outing or picnic. The mission is by the Río Grande on FM 1016 in Mission, TX (yes, the town was named after La Lomita), and is open during daylight hours. ☎ 956-580-8760

■ Festivals & Events

Every border town has to have a bullfight ring, and Reynosa's **Plaza de Toros Monumental** attracts many Texans. The tourist information office can tell you about current events.

■ Where to Stay

The **Holiday Inn Reynosa**, ☎ 899-921-6500, 703 Emilio Portes, is a nice place to stay if you have a car. It's about five minutes from the International Bridge). They have a restaurant, pool, parking, and handicap facilities. $$$$

HOTEL PRICE CHART	
Rates are per room based on double occupancy. Rates lower if single occupancy or sharing a bed. Higher rates on holidays.	
	US $10-$20
$	US $21-$40
$$	US $41-$60
$$$	US $61-$80
$$$$	US $81-$125
$$$$$	Over US $125

A little bit less expensive, but with the same amenities, the 100-room **Best Western El Camino**, ☎ 899-923-0791, at 1480 Boulevard Hidalgo, sees its share of business travelers. It has a gym, pool, and air-conditioned rooms with cable TV. You also get a complimentary continental breakfast and a nightly cocktail. $$

Hotel San Carlos, ☎ 899-922-1280, is right on the main square at 970 Hidalgo and offers air-conditioned rooms with cable TV and phone. $$

Hotel Internacional, ☎ 899-922-2330, 1050 Zaragoza (near the International Bridge), also has good clean rooms with air-conditioning and cable TV. $

A little bit outside of town, **Hotel Engrei**, ☎ 899-924-2830, is at Km 213 on the Highway 40 towards Monterrey. Amenities include room service, a restaurant, pool, playground, and tennis court, as well as cable TV and air-conditioning. $

■ Where to Eat

The **Café de Paris** at 815 Hidalgo is a popular spot for breakfast, coffee, and rolls. $$

DINING PRICE CHART	
Price per person for an entrée, not including beverage or tip.	
$	Under US $5
$$	US $5-$10
$$$	US $10+

One of the most popular places to eat in the city is **Sam's Restaurant & Bar** (at Allende and Ocampo 1100), which was established as a wooden restaurant in 1930 and has since grown into a popular place with a couple of event halls and a full bar. It has a wide range of dishes, including lunch specials and regional plates, plus seafood and steaks, $$-$$$

La Cucaracha (at Aldama and Ocampo) is also popular and serves good traditional Mexican dishes. And the traditional song of the region will no doubt come to mind as you eat here. $$$

> *La cucaracha, la cucaracha*
> *Ya no puede caminar*
> *Porque no tiene, porque le falta*
> *Marijuana que fumar.*
> *Ya la murió la cucaracha*
> *Ya la lleven a enterrar*
> *Entre cuatro zopilotes*
> *Y un ratón de sacristán.*

> The cockroach, the cockroach
> Now he can't walk anymore
> Because he doesn't have, because he's missing
> Marijuana to smoke.
> The cockroach just died
> And they carried him away to be buried
> Among four vultures
> And a sexton's mouse.

Nuevo Progresso

On the highway from Reynosa to Matamoros, is the town of Nuevo Progresso, which has a border crossing to Progresso on the US side. Many people find this town a calm alternative place to shop and eat compared to the much bigger, busier, and rowdier cities of Reynosa and Matamoros. There are shops, restaurants, and bars here, as well as a number of Texan tourists.

Matamoros

Matamoros is the typical border town – big, crowded, and industrial. Much of it is dedicated to the *maquiladora* industry and there are many factories here. Cattle, fishing, and agriculture are important as well. From its very beginnings, Matamoros was industrial and one of the early attractions to the area was its cattle-raising potential. Slowly, the settlement grew and developed to what you see today, changing its name from Los Esteros Hermosas, to Nuestro Señora del Refugio de los Esteros (1793) to Matamoros (1826) to H. Matamoros (its official name). H. stands for "Heroic," which it was thought to have earned in 1851 after residents defended the city from attackers.

■ Getting There & Around

By Air

Matamoros has an airport, Aeropuerto Gral. Servando Channels, south of town off Highway 180 on the way to Ciudad Victoria. It is serviced by **AeroMéxico**, ☎ 800-237-6639, www.Aeromexico.com, which has two flights a day to México City, as well as service to Guadalajara, Oaxaca, Villahermosa, and Cancún. **Aerocalifornia**, ☎ 800-237-6225, flies to México City and Ciudad Victoria.

Alternatively, the airport in nearby Brownsville, TX is serviced by **Continental Airlines**, ☎ 800-231-0856, www.continental.com, which flies to and from the big hub of Houston).

By Bus

Once you're there, you can get around using the "maxi-taxi" or *pesero* (just flag one down). The bus station is about nine blocks south and four blocks east of Plaza Hidalgo on Canales next to Calle 1. Buses depart to a number of cities, traveling as far south as Villahermosa; there is both first- and second-class service, including **ADO** and **Transportes del Norte**.

By Car

Matamoros is connected to the US by the busy International Bridge. On the United States side, the connecting Highway 77 on the Texas border goes directly north from Brownsville and Harlingen to Corpus Christi; you can walk across as well. A secondary crossing is at the B & M Bridge. Take Highway 180 south to reach Ciudad Victoria, Tampico, and points south along the coast (it follows the coastline, more or less). If you're going inland, Highway 2 heads west towards Reynosa and on to Guadalupe. You can rent a car from **National Car Rental**, ☎ 868-811-5000, downtown at 5001 Ave. Pedro Cardenas (they close at 3:30 pm on Saturdays and Sundays). Or try **Budget**, ☎ 800-472-3325 (US), at Km 9 of the Ciudad Victoria Highway.

■ Orientation & Practicalities

To get to downtown from the bridge, follow Ave. Obregón; the **Plaza Principal** is the main square, and is at the corner of Gonzalez and Calle 6. The cathedral is on one side, and a number of banks are all around the square (including a Banorte on Morelos and a Bancomer on Matamoros and Calle 6). There's an **American Express** office, ☎ 868-812-0722, at Morelos 5 and 6 94-107, open Mon.-Fri., 9 am-5 pm. A few blocks west of the main square is a pedestrian zone with shops and restaurants. A tourist information office at the Customs building near the International Bridge can provide you with information brochures. You can also get information (about Charro Days, for example) from the **Brownsville Tourist Information office**, ☎ 800-626-2639 (US), across the border in Texas at the junction of US Highway 77/83 and Farm Road 802, by the city entrance.

■ Sightseeing

 The **Museo Casamata** is in a neat old fort dating to 1845, that was used in the Mexican-American War. Today it's a historical museum of the city and local area. To get there from the main square, go south down Calle 6 one block, then turn left (east) on Guerrero. After about five blocks you'll reach Degollado; the museum is two more blocks down at the corner of Guatemala and Santos Degollado. Open Mon.-Fri., 8 am-4 pm, Sunday, 8 am-2 pm; free.

The **Museo Agrarismo** is dedicated to the farming history of the area. Four time periods are covered: El Porfiriato (political, economic, and social aspects), La Revolución Mexicana, La Reconstrucción Post-Revoluciónaria, and El Cardenismo (the 1930s era of President Lázaro Cárdenas). The museum is at Km 6.5 on the highway toward the beach (Ejido Lucio Blanco). Hours are Tues.-Sat., 9 am-5 pm, and Sun., 9 am-2 pm.

From the Plaza Principal, head west four blocks on Gonzalez, then turn right onto Calle 10 to get to **Mercado Juárez**, a fun place to browse around. You'll find a network of shops selling textiles, jewelry, clothing, hammocks, and other merchandise.

Brownsville

The **Brownsville Museum of Fine Art**, ☎ 956-542-0941, occasionally has some interesting exhibits and events. It recently hosted an international student art show, entitled "Down on the Border." The museum is at 230 Neale Drive in Brownsville, and is open Tues.-Fri., 9:30 am-3 pm, Sat., 10 am-4 pm.

NEED HELP?

There's a **United States Consulate** in Matamoros, ☎ 868-812-4402, at Ave. Primera 2002 and Azaleas. Office hours: 8 am-12 noon and 1-5 pm, Mon.-Fri.

■ Adventures

On Foot

If you want to do something a little bit more active, the **El Saucito Club Multideportivo** (a sports club), ☎ 868-812-3030, has a good 18-hole golf course, as well as four tennis courts, a basketball court, a gym, and a swimming pool. It's just outside of town at Km 12 on the highway toward Ciudad Victoria. Call for more information.

This area is a magnet for birders. One option is to contact **Birds Galore**, ☎ 956-546-5771, at 814 Hackberry Court, Brownsville, TX. They offer day-trip bird excursions, as well as private guides – in northern México as well. Another option is the **Sabal Palm Audobon Center and Sanctuary**, ☎ 956-541-8034, not far outside of Brownsville. The center's 527-acre protected forest sanctuary is the place to see a number of birds (including hummingbirds, chachalacas, and thrashers) and is also home to larger animals, such as bobcats and the endangered jaguarundi. There are a number of self-guided nature trails to explore, including the 10-mile, handicap-

and wheelchair-accessible "Forest" trail, the half-mile "Native" trail, and the one-mile "Resaca Loop" trail. The visitor's center is open daily, 9 am-5 pm, and the trails are open 7 am-5 pm. Admission costs US $4 for adults, US $3 for students and children. If you're interested in a special tour, call to make an appointment. There is a charge of US $6 for special tours. To get to the sanctuary from Brownsville, take US 77/83, and exit east onto International Boulevard. Turn right onto FM 1419 (Southmost Road), and after six miles you should see a sign on your right.

If you spot a rare bird just across the border in Texas, notify Texas wildlife officials at the Rare Bird Alert line, ☎ *956-584-2731.*

If you're still unsatiated, visit the website of the **World Birding Center**, www.worldbirdingcenter.org, which will give you information and website links to nine different locations in Texas' Río Grande Valley dedicated to birds. They include 2,500 acres of the **Bentson-Río Grande Valley State Park** (in Mission), with trails for bikers, hikers, campers, walkers, and guides for those interested in nature tours, ☎ 956-519-6448. There's also the **Edinburg Scenic Wetlands**, 40 acres of wetlands in Edinburg, which offer walking trails and nature tours, ☎ 956-381-9922. The **Estero Llano Grande State Park** is another one, with 200 acres of wetlands in Weslaco and with bird and nature tours by reservation only, ☎ 956-519-6448. **Harlingen Arroyo Colorado** (aka Hugh Ramsey Park) in Harlingen has well-cleared, wide walking trails through 55 acres of woodlands, ☎ 956-427-8873.

The Old Hidalgo Pumphouse is a neat museum that has information on steam-powered irrigation pumps, as well as hummingbird and butterfly gardens. Adjacent to the museum, the US Fish and Wildlife service has a refuge with bike and hiking trails. The museum is in the town of Hidalgo at 902 S. Second St., and is open Tues.-Fri., 11 am-6 pm, and Sun., 2 pm-6 pm. General admission is US $3 or $1 for seniors and children. ☎ 956-843-8686. Other attractions are the **Quinta Mazatlan** (an old hacienda, see page 89 for more information); the **Resaca de la Palma State Park**, 1,700 acres of park in Brownsville which has abandoned river beds and ponds (admission and tours by reservation only, ☎ 956-519-6448); the **Roma Bluffs** (see page 86); and the **South Padre Island Birding and Nature Center**. This last is 50 acres of salt marshes, dunes, and intertidal flats with free boardwalk nature trails as well as birding tours. Contact the SPI Convention & Visitor's Bureau for more information, ☎ 800-SOPADRE.

On Wheels

You can arrange a long, multi-day bus tour of towns along the Gulf Coast through **Vamanos Travel**. The agency offers a US $515 six-day trip that takes you to Tampico, the Costa Esmeralda, the town of Tuxpan, Papantla, the ruins of El Tajín, and the village of Tecolutla. There is also a nine-day Veracruz bus tour for US $539. It visits Veracruz, Xalapa, Tampico, and Coatepec, among other smaller destinations. The agency arranges these trips based on group bookings. They also have planned, scheduled trips to a number of Mexican destinations, among them a multi-day tour to Tampico. You can reach them at ☎ 956-428-1392 or visit their website, www.vamonostravel.com, where you will find descriptions of current outings and prices.

On Water

Matamoros' beach, **Playa Bagdad**, is about 35 km (21.7 miles) east of town. The beach is typical of the Gulf Coast – a long strip of packed brown sand, with dark churned-up waters. It's actually a bit nicer than you might expect, especially since it is pretty much devoid of development (except for a few restaurants and *palapas*). The beach was originally referred to as "Washington," the name of a boat that was abandoned for years on its shores. Eventually, it was named Playa Bagdad after a port that was once in the area (it was destroyed by hurricanes).

Hunting and fishing is popular in the surrounding areas, and the **Tiradores, Cazadores, y Pescadores Asociados de Matamoros A.C.** (Gunners, Hunters and Associated Fishermen of Matamoros, A.C.) attends to these needs. The club hosts tournaments in both. White tail deer is popular among hunters. Contact the office for more information or details on joining the club. ☎ 868-816-2960, Calle CD de México at the corner of Calle 3, 200.

■ Festivals & Events

The **Teatro de la Reforma** (built in 1866) regularly hosts productions of opera, ballet, and theater. It's just north of the Plaza Principal on Calle 6 and Abasolo; call them to see what current events are showing, ☎ 868-812-5120.

During the last weekend in February, a four-day celebration is dedicated to *charros* (Mexican cowboys). The celebration, known as **Charro Days**, has been taking place since 1938, a joint event between Matamoros and Brownsville, TX. It's a big festival. Some of the events include music, street dancing, parades, and eating contests. People get dressed up in traditional Mexican garb. A parade starts in Brownsville and makes its celebratory way through the streets to Matamoros. Contact the Charro Days Headquarters for more information on scheduled events, ☎ 956-542-4245 (US). If you want to see *charros* in action during other parts of the year, ask the tourist information office about the schedule of events for the *charrería* (Mexican rodeo).

From mid-June to July, Matamoros celebrates an **Expo Feria**, a huge cultural event of parades, arts and crafts, and music. In October, there is the **Festival Internacional de Otoìo**, which celebrates the performing arts, with many events filling the Teatro de la Reforma.

In mid-October, Brownsville's Society for the Performing Arts hosts a **Latin Jazz Festival**, a multi-day event with activities such as Latin-themed movie nights, dance nights (shows and competitions), Latin-jazz concerts and bands, and a free street party. The indoor concerts generally have a cover charge. Contact the Brownsville Tourist Information Office at ☎ 800-626-2639 (US), for a full schedule of events.

■ Where to Stay

Hotel Ritz, ☎ 868-812-1190, at Matamoros 612, is a very good hotel just two blocks north of the main square. Amenities include a lobby bar, a gym, and discounts on rental cars if you stay there. Rooms are clean and well-maintained. Breakfast is included. $$$

HOTEL PRICE CHART	
Rates are per room based on double occupancy. Rates lower if single occupancy or sharing a bed. Higher rates on holidays.	
$	US $10-$20
$	US $21-$40
$$	US $41-$60
$$$	US $61-$80
$$$$	US $81-$125
$$$$$	Over US $125

Hotel de México, ☎ 868-814-1410 or 0800-881-8800, is a plain-looking building with 43 rooms, but it has a restaurant, bar, pool, and parking. Rooms are air-conditioned, with cable TV; arched doorways and colorfully painted walls give it a charming old-time feel. The hotel is on Lauro Villar at the corner of Marte R. Gómez 1210. $

If you're on your way out of town, try the **Fontana Inn**, ☎ 868-816-4123, at Km 3 of Lauro Villar, for a basic option with air-conditioning and cable TV (Lauro Villar is Highway 2 and heads from downtown east). $$

Also on Lauro Villar, at the corner of Fco. Villa is the small, 32-room **Road Runner**, ☎ 868-816-4220. $

The **Gran Residencial Hotel**, ☎ 868-813-9440 or 0800-718-8230, is right outside of the main square on the way to or from the International at 249 Obregón. It's a step up on the niceness scale – a pretty hotel with swimming pools, air-conditioning, and 114 spacious rooms. $$$

The 46-room **Hotel Roma**, ☎ 868-816-0573, three blocks west and three blocks north of the main square (1420 Calle 9 between Bravo and Matamoros), has rooms with air-conditioning, cable TV, and phones. $

If you're really going budget, **Hotel Majestic**, ☎ 868-813-3680, at 131 Abasolo between Calles 8 and 9, is in the middle of the action near the market. It has 29 old and worn, but acceptable rooms. $

The **Holiday Inn**, ☎ 868-811-5000 or 0800-221-9775, at 5001 Bird Pedro Cardenas, has 192 air-conditioned rooms. $$$$

■ Where to Eat

In the downtown, **Los Norteños**, at 109 Calle Matamoros 8 and 9, has been around for more than 50 years; they specialize in northern Mexican food, including goat. $$

DINING PRICE CHART	
Price per person for an entrée, not including beverage or tip.	
$	Under US $5
$$	US $5-$10
$$$	US $10+

Nearby, **Café Paris**, 125 Calle 6 near Gonzalez, is popular, especially for a good coffee. They serve some basic Mexican dishes as well. $

La Fogata, Ave. Hidalgo and Calle 9N, is a good steakhouse with a piano bar. $$

A little bit outside of the immediate vicinity, **Los Portales**, Calle Sexta and J.S. Elcano 136, is another spot to find typical northern Mexican cuisine (try the *cabrito*, aka goat). $$

Garcia's, at Ave. Obregón 82, is a popular place for both Mexican and non-Mexican dishes. $$-$$$

The Coastline - From Matamoros to Aldama

As you follow Highway 101 south from Matamoros, the entire coastline until you reach Tampico is riddled with lagoons and river outlets (though the highway is so far inland you won't see them). Since the flat dry plains leave nothing to the imagination, you will see that most of the surrounding area is fairly untouristed and offers few facilities.

If you want to get to the coast, in almost every case you'll have to detour several miles down bumpy narrow roads, at the end of which you'll find small, rustic fishing villages. You can hunt down a local fisherman to take you out onto the water, you can poke around the shore, or just find a local restaurant that sells fresh seafood. The waters along the coastline are Gulf Coast dark, somewhat churned up, and not altogether appealing for swimming.

There are many inland lagoons, but the coastline is dominated by the **Laguna Madre**. It is huge, and is actually formed by part of the world's longest system of barrier islands, continuing along the coastline of Texas and Louisiana. According to the Nature Conservancy, this is one of only five hypersaline estuary systems in the world, making it unusually attractive to fish and birds alike. The area is a nesting ground for the endangered Kemp's ridley sea turtle (see below), and an especially good spot to see birds migrating and wintering. It's also especially popular with sport fishermen.

Turtle Country

The region between the **Río Soto La Marina** and the **Barra El Tordo** is famous for the turtles that nest here. The area, nicknamed the Barra de la Tortuga Lora, is a sanctuary for the endangered sea turtle known here as the **Tortuga Lora** (*Lepidochelys Kempi* or Kemp's ridley). Between March and July, the turtles come here to nest, females slowly scraping their way ashore to lay their 100 to 120 nest of eggs. In an effort to protect the hatchlings, the Mexican and US Governments, along with different ecological organizations, have jointly set up research centers along the coast. During nesting season, technicians collect the eggs from their original location and put them into corals for protection. Once the eggs hatch (a month and a half to two months later), the baby turtles are released back onto the beaches to make their way to the ocean.

At the northern end of this section is **La Pesca**, a fishing village at the mouth of the Río Sota La Marina, a little north of the Tropic of Cancer. A turtle research center has been set up near the beach here. La Pesca is also a very popular spot for sport fishermen (with tons of trout and sea bass), and you can find a number of accommodations (including spots for RVs) on the road to it, as well as on the waterfront. Another spot where you might see the turtles is at the **Barra del Tordo**, a pretty village at the mouth of the Río Carrizal; this is a good spot for fishing as well.

To get to La Pesca, head south on Highway 180. When you reach Soto la Marina, take the bumpy turnoff to the left (east) toward the coast. Barra del Tordo can be reached by continuing south on Highway 180 (past Soto la Marina); at the town of Aldama, you'll see the road, narrow and bumpy, heading off to the left (east).

Stop & Look!

Keep an eye out for the sign on the side of the road indicating that you've crossed over the Tropic of Cancer (latitude 23½ N). The invisible line marks the northern end of the tropical zone that continues all the way to the Tropic of Capricorn (23½ S), at the southern end of the tropics. If you're standing here during the summer solstice, June 21-22, the sun will be straight above your head.

■ Where to Stay

You'll find a number of places to stay on the road towards La Pesca. All are geared towards fishermen, and can arrange boats, guides, and often a place for you to grill your fish. One such spot, **La Gaviota**, ☎ 818-336-4940 (Nuevo Leon), www.lagaviotaresort.com, has a fishing pier, and 12 full RV hookups at bargain prices. Their hotel includes a room with two queen-sized beds. These are meant to accommodate two adults and two children; if you have more adults, there's an extra charge. They offer air-conditioning and hot water. $$$. If you're coming as part of a group, they also have a two-bedroom suite with a kitchen, three bathrooms and a living room. $$$$$

Aldama

Traveling south down Highway 180, the last town of note before hitting Tampico is Aldama. It's about 36 km (22.3 miles) before you join up with the tollway. Founded in 1790, the town itself has little to offer; nearby, however, there are a couple of environmental attractions formed by natural pools and rivers, most famously five *cenotes*, where the more adventurous can have fun hiking, swimming, and exploring.

Adventures

Cenotes

Perhaps the most famous feature in the Aldama area (especially for divers) is the *cenote* **El Zacatón**. Explorations of the *cenote* began in 1990 and, since then, it has been discovered to be incredibly deep, at over 1,000 feet. World records in depth diving have been set here – men's by Jim Bowden, and women's by Ann Kristovich. The *cenote*'s waters sit in a large circular pit 70 ft down and, interestingly, are sulfuric, averaging a warm 86°F. Another interesting feature are the islands floating around its surface. They are substantial pieces of land, even growing grass!

Cenotes *are natural water-filled sinkholes, formed when the earth collapses over an underground cavern, forming a deep well.*

Nearby, are four other *cenotes*, all with sulfuric waters, including the **Poza Verde**, which is not far from El Zacatón, and also has warm waters averaging 83°F. Instead of having a steep cliff dropping to the water's surface, however, this *cenote* is swimable; it is level with the land, and resembles an oasis – a beautiful pool of water surrounded by greenery in an otherwise dry, arid, and flat landscape. Hidden in the vicinity as well are the **Poza Caracol**, **Poza Azufrosa**, and the super-warm **Poza La Pilita** (averaging 93°F).

The *cenotes* are on private property – on the grounds of the Rancho Azufrosa. According to the tourism department, the owners allow visitors to hike over to El Zacatón as long as they don't litter or destroy the area. To get there, follow Highway 180 south to Aldama. Just past town, at Km 27 (about 10 km/6.2 miles from Aldama), turn left toward Ejido La Colmena. *Ejidos*, or commonly-owned lands, have communities of people who are familiar with the area and whom you can ask for directions. At this point the road gets pretty rough, but continue for three km (1.9 miles) until you reach the Ejido El Nacimiento (about five km/3.1 miles), where you can ask for directions to El Nacimiento (a pretty spot at the mouth of a river). From El Nacimiento, it's a short hike up to El Zacatón. You need special permission to dive or fish here; you can also ask for directions to the nearby waterfalls of El Salto. Another option is to visit the tourism office in Tampico (a one-person booth in the Plaza de Armas) or Aldama. They can direct you to a good guide who will take you around the area.

Fishing

North of Aldama, at Km 78 on Highway 180, is the **Presa República Española** (a dam), which is a popular spot for bass fishing. There are a couple of places to stay in the area, including El Paraíso (see below) and **Mayo Tours de México**, ☎ 833-248-8665 or US 318-396-5250, which has a few rooms and boats to take you fishing. They are at Km 79.5 on Highway 180 near Aldama.

Another dam, the **Presa Ramiro Caballero**, is a bit to the west of Aldama, and is gaining popularity with sport fishermen and hunters (duck and geese) alike. It is a bit remote, however, so you might be better off contacting and staying at one of the listings below, who can get you what you might need. Contact **La Misión Tamaholipa**, ☎ 833-211-7400 (in González) for fishing.

To get to Presa Ramiro Caballero from Aldama, head south on Highway 180; at the intersection of Highway 80, turn right and drive north. At Gonzalez, continue on Highway 180 west until you reach Magiscatzin. A few more kilometers, and you'll see a dirt road turnoff to your left heading toward the dam (21 km/13 miles).

■ Where to Stay

If you want to stay near the Presa República Española, **El Paraiso**, ☎ 836-213-9956, offers 14 cabanas with air-conditioning, private bath, and hot water, plus a large swimming pool, on an island in the middle of the Río Carrizal. The daily rate includes meals and use of paddle boats. They also have trails for hiking, waters for fishing, plenty of birds for watching, and boats for touring around the lagoon; the *cenotes* are nearby as well. El Paraiso is only open on weekends, and reservations must be made in advance. $$$$

As for other hotels, you'll have a better selection a little farther south in Tampico; there are, however, a couple of hotels in Aldama, including the **Hotel Rancho Viejo**, ☎ 836-274-0236 (404 Méndez y Reforma), and the **Hotel Central**, ☎ 836-274-0150 (203 Libertad y Centenar). $

Ciudad Victoria

The state capital of Tamaulipas is a modern city, whose nearby fields produce cattle and henequén (which is used for crafts made out of hemp). The city was founded in 1750 under the name Santa Mariade Aguay. The name was later changed to honor the first president of México, Don Guadalupe Victory. The town sits near the Sierra Madre Oriental, and has a year-round average temperature in the '70s. The nearby Vicente Guerrero Dam attracts fishermen and hunters.

■ Orientation & Practicalities

The modern **Plaza Hidalgo** is in the city center at the intersection of Colón and Hidalgo (on Sundays you can sometimes hear the state band playing there). The **market** is two blocks to the east on Hidalgo and Diaz, and the **Palacio de Gobierno** is to the southwest on Juárez, between 5 de Mayo and Manuel Gonzalez. To find an address, you should be aware that streets are named both with numbers and names, for example Calle 16 is also known as 5 de Mayo.

Emergency Services: Red Cross, ☎ 834-316-2077.

Exchanging Money & Internet Cafés: There are a couple of banks and Internet cafés in the area around Plaza Hidalgo.

Post Office: The *correos* is at the corner of Plaza Hidalgo (Tijerina and Morelos).

Tourist Information: The state tourist information office is a little south of the immediate downtown at the end of 5 de Mayo, at 272 Rosales; they can provide some good information on the area. Open daily, 9 am-8 pm (closed for lunch from around 3:30 to 6:30 pm).

■ Getting There & Around

By Air

The city has a domestic airport (**Aeropuerto Nacional Gral. Pedro José Méndez**) several miles to the east of town at Km 18.5 of the Soto la Marina Highway. The airport is serviced by **Aerocalifornia**, ☎ 800-237-6225 (with service to many Mexican cities including México City, Merida, Matamoros, Guadalajara, and Durango); **AeroMéxico**, ☎ 800-237-6639 (with two daily flights to México City; and **Aeromar**, ☎ 834-316-9696 or 800-950-0747 (US), flying to México City only.

By Bus

For long-distance travel, the bus station is on the far east side of town at the end of Carrera Torres, and is serviced by first- and second-class buses, with regular trips to

México City, Monterrey, and all the border towns (among others).

By Car

Ciudad Victoria is well-connected by highway, and is at the intersection of Highway 85 (from the north and south), Highway 101 from the northeast and southwest, and Highway 70 from the east. It's about a four-hour drive from Matamoros (310 km/192 miles), and a five-hour drive from Monterrey (292 km/181 miles).

■ Sightseeing

There isn't much for sightseers here, but the few things you can do include visiting the Rectoria of the University of Tamaulipas, where you can see the **Museo de Antropología e Historia** (a block north of Plaza Hidalgo on Colón; free). Another interesting building is the **Santuario de Guadalupe**, situated on the Hill of the Dead. It's a nice spot to view the city, located south of the center, up the hill on the other side of the river. **Tamatán Park** in the southwest of the city, alongside Highway 101, has a zoo and a lake where you can take boat rides. Nearby to the north, the **Paseo Pedro José Méndez**, by the river on 5 de Mayo and Gutiérrez de Laba, is a large, historic* *(what makes it historic?)plaza.

■ Adventures

On Water

About 12 km (7.4 miles) northeast of Ciudad Victoria, is the **Presa Vicente Guerrero**, a dammed lake popular with fishermen because of the abundance of bass in its waters. You can find some fishing services in the main town close to the Nuevo Padilla Dam ("New Padilla"). The original Villa Padilla, founded in 1749, was on the banks of the Río Purificación. In 1970, more than 200 years later, the town had to be moved because the construction of the Presa Vicente Guerrero (built to control the waters of the Río Corona, Río Purification, and Río Pilón) caused flooding of the area. You can still see the rooftops of some of the buildings in the waters.

On Foot

The **waterfalls of El Chorrito** are also the site of an important religious sanctuary in Tamaulipas, honoring the Virgin of the Chorrito. The sanctuary is at a cave, which has a stalactite resembling the virgin, and is visited daily by hundreds of believers. Celebrations here are March 17-19, Semana Santa, and December 12. To get to El Chorrito, follow Highway 85 north from Ciudad Victoria; at El Tomaseño (about 75 km/46.5 miles) from Ciudad Victoria), take the turn left (west) toward Villa Hidalgo/El Chorrito. You'll find the Presa El Chorrito here as well.

■ Where to Stay

There are a number of good places throughout the city, and especially right downtown around Plaza Hidalgo (intersection of Colón and Hidalgo). The 74-room **Best Western Santorin**, ☎ 834-312-8938, at Cristobal Colón Nte. 349, is just two blocks north of Plaza Hidalgo. It offers standard comfortable rooms up to presidential suites. There is a restaurant and bar on the grounds, as well as a video club to rent movies, a travel agency, and parking. $$-$$$

Five blocks southwest of Plaza Hidalgo, **Hotel Fiesta Plaza**, ☎ 834-312-1761, Benito Juárez 401, is a comfortable place with parking and nice rooms, with air-conditioning and cable TV. $$

Hotel Posada Don Diego, ☎ 834-312-1279, at Juárez Ote. 814, is two blocks south of Plaza Hidalgo. It has parking, a restaurant, and offers basic rooms at a pretty good price. $

Hotel Los Monteros, ☎ 834-312-0300, 962 Hidalgo Ote., is right on Plaza Hidalgo; it's a nice hotel with worn rooms. $

More familiar names in the city include the **Holiday Inn Express**, ☎ 834-318-6000, at Blvd López Mateos 909 Ote., which is a little bit pricey, but has large, comfortable rooms, a gym, and an indoor pool. $$$

Or try the **Howard Johnson Hotel**, ☎ 834-312-4050, at Calle Colón 126 Nte, which is a modern, pleasant choice with air-conditioning and cable TV. $$

■ Where to Eat

Though it's out of the center, a good place to go for high-quality traditional grilled Mexican food is **El Mezquite Grille**, near the northern end of Tijerina at 1801 Boulevard Tamaulipas. They serve

DINING PRICE CHART	
Price per person for an entrée, not including beverage or tip.	
$	Under US $5
$$	US $5-$10
$$$	US $10+

some international food as well, and often have music. $$

Closer to downtown, you'll find **Daddy's** at 148 Cristobál Colón, right on Plaza Hidalgo in the Hotel Everest. You can get comfort foods here, such as burgers, sandwiches and soups. $

Another place you can try is **Restaurante El Granero**, 509 Carrera Torres Ote, which serves Mexican dishes. $$-$$$

Reserva de la Biosfera de El Cielo

South of Ciudad Victoria is a huge biosphere reserve that covers 144,540 hectares (357,000 acres) and is home to a wide range of flora and fauna. The reserve was originally private property; in 1890 it was claimed and, later, Rancho El Cielo was built on it. In the 1940s, the owner of the property opened it up for researchers. In 1987, on the heals of severe deforestation that had occurred during the '70s, UNESCO declared it a reserve in their network.

■ Adventures

Hiking

If you're looking for a hike into the wilderness to commune with nature, this is the place. Besides being home to an endless variety of plants, the reserve has also documented animals such as the wildcat, jaguar, ocelot, cougar, deer, black bear, skunk, and weasel. Hikers are welcome, but there are not a lot of services and the reserve's interior is quite remote.

■ How to Get There

The best way to reach the reserve is by going to the village of Gómez Farías, and from there following a dirt road 11 km (6.8 miles) up to Alta Cima; here you should register at the SEMARNAP (Secretaría del Medio Ambiente, Recursos Naturales y Pesca), before continuing on into the cloud forest.

To get to Gómez Farías from Ciudad Victoria, head south on Highway 85. When you reach the split to Highway 81, just continue on Highway 85. Right after you pass over Río Sabinas, you'll see a turnoff on your right for the village. From Gómez Farías you can drive up the dirt road to Alta Cima or take one of the infrequent buses from the village. A guide can help you explore the reserve (helping you find some of the hidden caves, waterfalls and wildlife, even providing 4x4 transportation; ask in Alta Cima or Gómez Farías.

■ Where to Stay

 If you're interested in staying the night in the reserve, contact the rustic **Cabañas San José**, ☎ 832-232-6018, in the reserve past Alta Cima in Canindo. In Gómez Farías, try the **Hotel Posada Campestre**, ☎ 836-836-232-6671, Calle Hidalgo s/n, which has eight older rooms and areas for camping. $

Or try the **Casa de Piedra**, ☎ 834-316-6941, Calle Hidalgo s/n. $

For more information about where to stay, the reserve, or guides, contact the Secretaría de Desarollo Urbano y Ecología, ☎ 834-312-6018, Ciudad Victoria, 13 Guerrero y Bravo 374.

■ Xicoténcatl

South of the turnoff for Gómez Farías (heading south on Highway 85), a road on the left goes past sugar cane plantations to the village of Xicoténcatl. The most interesting thing in Xicoténcatl is on the edge of town – a huge tree known as El Laurel de las Gallinas, which is more than 200 years old, and has a diameter of over 100 meters (328 feet). It's huge and beautiful, but you'll just have to drive past as it's on private property.

■ Ocampo

Just past the turn for Xicoténcatl (heading south on Highway 85), you'll reach a turn on the right to the village of Ocampo. The village has a few archaeological remnants, including a museum (**Museo Rufino Muñiz Torres**), an old decaying and destroyed mission (**Misión de Nuestra Señora de la Soledad de Igollo**), and some unrestored overgrown ruins known as **Los Cuisillos**. A nearby spot to get outdoors is **El Cañon de la Servilleta** (Napkin Canyon), where you can hike around the river bottoms and even find a few caves. You'll see the sign signaling the right turn to the Canyon 13 km (eight miles) after turning off Highway 85 for Ocampo.

■ Ciudad Mante

This is a huge sugarcane processing center. On May 10 you can even see what it does best in its annual **Feria del Azúcar** (Sugar Fair). It has a few restaurants, some nice hotels, and is a good spot to break a journey. You can do some hikes nearby around attractions like **La Aguja**, a swimming hole formed by a dam with shallow waters for wading and tables for picnicking, and **El Nacimiento**, a sunken cave where you can swim, or rent a boat to explore its waters.

The city is at the intersection of Highway 85 and Highway 80. From here, the access to La Aguja is right outside town; you'll have to hike about four km (2.5 miles) along a trail to get to it. El Nacimiento is four km farther down the trail.

Where to Stay

For accommodations here, try the **Hotel Mante**, ☎ 831-232-0990, at 500 Guerrerro. It's a charming hotel with a nice pool, restaurant, and clean spacious rooms with air-conditioning and cable TV. $$

Tampico

It's unfortunate that so many people do their best to bypass Tampico. The industrial urban tri-city sprawl of Tampico, Ciudad Madero, and Altamira, with its petrochemical plants, booming population, and humid weather, scares off most wayfarers by reputation alone. And though the tourist department is doing its best to pull it from the brink of an industrial wasteland like some of the Gulf's port cities, in many foreign visitors' minds there is not much difference – crowded and best avoided, it represents the final marker of the arid wasteland that is Tamaulipas. But let me stop here, before I scare off the few brave folks who have read this far, and say this: Tampico will surprise you.

The interesting thing is, Tampico at one point had a heyday, and its downtown plazas still proudly flaunt French and Art Nouveau buildings constructed during the oil boom of the '20s – buildings that would seem to be far more at home in New Orleans. When oil was discovered here, the world focused its attention on a city that might otherwise have forever remained off the maps. The movie filmed here during the '40s, *Treasure of the Sierra Madre*, starring Humphrey Bogart, depicts hopefuls flooding town with schemes of making it rich, a hope not far from reality. Oil fields sprang up, the city soon gained a role in the international business world, and with it came restaurants and hotels. Today, Tampico is one of the most important industrial ports in the country.

Then there are the other oddities. A prehistoric pyramid sheltered in the city's center; crocodiles sunbathing wild and free within blocks of downtown; the huge, pink, one-of-a-kind kiosk in the Plaza de Armas; surprisingly litter-free streets and the beach (though beach fans would be well-advised to read on and know what they're getting into).

None of this is to say that you will love Tampico, for there isn't much to do. Unless you are a sport fisherman or a boat racer (Tampico is known internationally for both), it's unlikely that you would plan an extended visit here. Other cities have more museums, better beaches, livelier nightlife, more beautiful architecture, extensive ruins. But still, there is a quality to Tampico that is stimulating, especially for those who enjoy urban life, at least for a day.

■ Orientation & Practicalities

Unlike most other cities, Tampico's downtown area (known as the "Zona Centro") centers around two main parks within a block of each other – the traditional **Plaza de Armas**, and the more distinctively-styled **Plaza de la Libertad**. Most hotels can be found here or north along Ave. Hidalgo, which runs past two large lakes – **Laguna del Chairel** and **Laguna del Charro**. A third lake, **Laguna del Carpintero**, abuts the Zona Centro on its eastern side.

To the south, **Río Pánuco** separates Tampico from the state of Veracruz before emptying into the Gulf, while the northern and eastern boundaries are somewhat more blurred, as Tampico merges with the nearby cities of Altamira and Ciudad Madero, forming what is known as the Zona Metropolitana.

Emergency Services: Cruz Roja/Red Cross, ☎ 833-212-1333. Hospital, ☎ 833-213-2035.

Exchanging Money: Banks with ATMs are easy to come by, as this is a major city; many can be found in the streets around the Plaza de Armas. You can also find an **American Express** office, ☎ 833-213-1332, at Ave. Hidalgo 2000 Local A.

Internet Cafés: Surprisingly hard to find for a city this size, these tend to be small and not as clearly marked as in other large cities. Check out the side streets of the Zona Centro for some options.

Post Office: The *correo* is in the Plaza de la Libertad, 309 Madero, between Calles Juárez and Aduana.

Orientation & Practicalities ■ 111

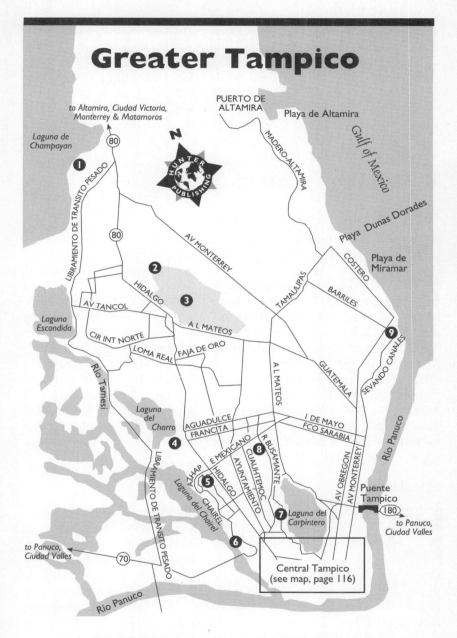

1. Club de Golf Lagunas de Miralta
2. Museo Fotográfico Aviación
3. International Airport
4. Club Campestre de Tampico
5. Pirámide de las Flores
6. Club de Regatas Corona
7. Parque Metropolitano
8. Bus Station
9. Malecón

© 2004 HUNTER PUBLISHING, INC   NOT TO SCALE

Tourist Information: A one-person booth is stationed in the Plaza de Armas and, though quite small, has a surprising number of maps, pamphlets, and event information. If you are interested in something specific, ask. The staff person may well have the information you want. Though many of the maps and pamphlets include an English translation, the staff is unlikely to be bilingual. Open daily, 10 am-6 pm. An office is also a block away on 20 de Noviembre, near Obregón.

■ Getting There

By Air

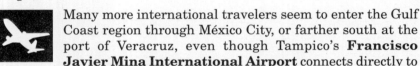
Many more international travelers seem to enter the Gulf Coast region through México City, or farther south at the port of Veracruz, even though Tampico's **Francisco Javier Mina International Airport** connects directly to the United States (albeit with only one flight a day). The airport does, however, see its share of tourists and businesspeople and therefore does offer flights to the rest of México. The airport is serviced by **Mexicana**, ☎ 833-213-9600, **Aerocalifornia**, ☎ 833-213-8403, **Aeroliteral**, ☎ 833-228-0856, and **Aeroméxico**, ☎ 0800-021-4000 (MX). Those airlines link Tampico with México City, Monterrey, Ciudad Victoria, and Veracruz. It's also serviced by **Continental Airlines**, ☎ 0800-900-5000 (MX), which connects it with Houston, TX – an hour and 40 minute flight. The airport is about 20 minutes from downtown in the northern part of the city, so you'll have to take a taxi to your hotel.

By Bus

The bus terminal is on Rosalio Bustamante (near Ave. Ejercito Mexicano), a few miles north of the downtown (pick up a taxi in front of the terminal). If you're just here for the day, there is luggage storage for 6 pesos/hour, or 40 pesos for 24 hours. There are a number of first- and second-class lines to choose from, servicing routes all across México. Lines include the deluxe **UNO** and the first-class **ADO**, as well as **Transpais**, **Estrella Blanca**, **Transportes Lineas del Golfo**, and **Omnibus de México**.

TYPICAL BUS FARES

Destination	Bus Line	Fare	Trip Time
Cordoba	ADO	331 pesos	9 hours 50 minutes
Costa Esmeralda	ADO	191 pesos	5 hours 35 minutes
Matamoros	UNO	330 pesos	6 hours 25 minutes
	ADO	253 pesos	6 hours 25 minutes
México City (Norte)	UNO	474 pesos	9 hours
	ADO GL	339 pesos	9 hours
	ADO	289 pesos	7 hours 50 minutes
Oaxaca	ADO	534 pesos	14 hours 50 minutes
Orizaba	ADO	343 pesos	10 hours 20 minutes
Pánuco	ADO	25 pesos	1 hour
Poza Rica	UNO	249 pesos	4 hours
	ADO GL	180 pesos	4 hours
	ADO	150 pesos	4 hours 30 minutes
Reynosa	UNO	393 pesos	7 hours
	ADO	257 pesos	6 hours 30 minutes
Soto la Marina	ADO	115 pesos	2 hours 40 minutes
Tuxpan	ADO	122 pesos	3 hours 40 minutes
Veracruz	UNO	470 pesos	7 hours
	ADO GL	338 pesos	7 hours
	ADO	265 pesos	10 hours 15 minutes
Villahermosa	ADO GL	676 pesos	14 hours
	ADO	562 pesos	14 hours 15 minutes
Xalapa	ADO	278 pesos	8 hours

By Car

Tampico is well connected by land and a number of highways converge here at the coast. You can reach the city from the north (Matamoros) or south (Tuxpan or Poza Rica) by following Highway 180; from Ciudad Victoria in the northwest via Highway 81; or from Ciudad Valles to the southwest by Highway 70. If you're coming from the border, it's a six- to seven-hour drive through mostly flat shrublands on a (mostly straight) two-lane highway.

■ Getting Around

Chances are that you have either driven here from the Texas border (about six hours) or that you have rented a car with plans to head into the bordering state of Veracruz. In either case, your best bet is to park your car and tour the downtown area on foot. Local city buses are very frequent and normally have their destinations plastered on the windshield, although you are unlikely to need one unless you make the (probably wise) decision to leave your car at the hotel. Most buses criss-cross the downtown streets; to get on one, don't bother looking for a stop, but instead stand on any corner and flag it down, as you would a taxi.

RENTAL CARS	
National (at the airport and downtown)	☎ 833-228-0573; www.nationalcar.com
Dollar	☎ 833-227-2575 or 0800-712-094 (MX), www.dollartampico.com.mx
Alamo	☎ 833-228-7559; www.alamo.com
Avis	☎ 833-228-0585; www.avis.com
Budget	☎ 833-227-1880; www.budget.com
Auto Rentas Rayto	☎ 833-228-0659

Rates are competitive. At the time of this writing, Dollar, for example, offers an economy car for about US $21 a day or a compact for $31 a day, both with 100-150 free km.

■ Sightseeing

Tampico sits next to two other cities – Altamira and Ciudad Madero. Combined, they make up what is called the Metropolitan Zone. **Altamira** was founded in 1759 during colonization of the coast. In 1823, to create a commerce port, a number of families left from Altamira (off the Laguna de Champayan) to found Santa Anna de Tampico (today's Tampico).

To the south is **Ciudad Madero**, which was originally named Villa Cecilia after a woman who first settled in the area in 1807 named Cecilia Villarreal; the name was later changed to Ciudad Madero, after former Mexican president Francisco I Madero. Both cities are big urban areas with not a lot to offer the tourist. Madero has a beach and a museum, while Altamira has a tiny museum (see below).

Linking Tamualipas with the state of Veracruz is the huge, modern **Puente Tampico**, which spans the Río Pánuco. There are good views of the river and surrounding countryside from the top of this bridge.

Museums

There are a few museums in the cities of Tampico, Altamira and Ciudad Madero. For the most part, though small, they do offer a glimpse into culture of the local indigenous group – the Huastecas. I wouldn't bother heading out of Tampico specifically to visit them, but if you're in the area anyway, or have a particular passion for such things, they're interesting, and probably one of the few chances you'll have to learn about the Huastecas. The most easily accessible is in Tampico, out north of downtown (past the end of the Laguna del Chairel, off Ave. Hidalgo). **Casa de la Cultura** (105 Calle Lauro Aguirre) has a museum on its first floor, currently dedicated mainly to exhibiting a few pieces from the Huasteca culture. It's open 10 am-7 pm, Mon.-Sat. Free.

THE HUASTECS

The Huastecs are thought to date back to about the 10th century BC. Their language was similar to Mayan, suggesting some connection between the two groups. The Pre-Columbian Huastecs built step-pyramids, carved standing sculptures, and produced painted pottery. They were one of the few cultures that attained civilization and built cities yet usually wore no clothing.

About 1450 the Huastecs were defeated by Aztec armies under Moctezuma I; after that they paid tribute to the Aztecs, but retained much of their local self-government.

The Spanish conquered them between 1519 and the 1530s. With the imposition of Catholicism, they were required to wear clothing.

The Huastec language is still spoken, especially in rural areas, and the people still practice their music and dance traditions. There are currently some 80,000 Huastecs in Mexico.

Out a little farther, in Ciudad Madero, is the **Museo de la Cultura Huasteca**, another museum with a number of artifacts, including a couple of huge Huastecan sculptures. The museum is in the Instituto

116 ■ Tampico

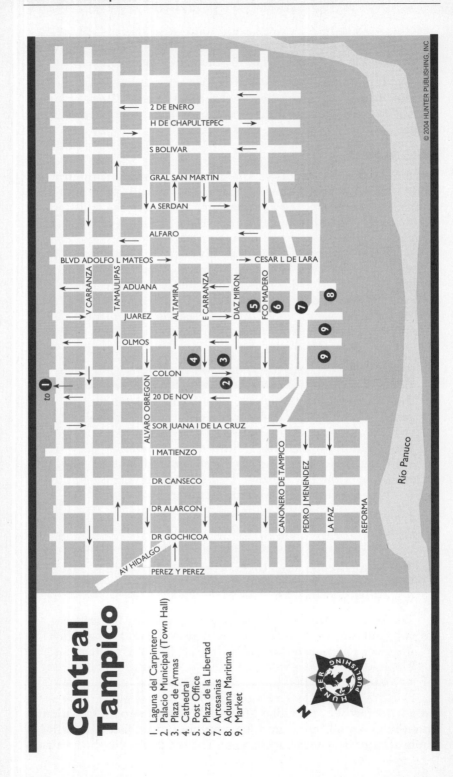

Tecnológico de Madero (at the corner of Calles 1 de Mayo and Sor Juana Inés de La Cruz); open Mon.-Fri., 10 am-5 pm, and Sat., 10 am-3 pm; free.

And a bit of a drive away, in Altamira, under the kiosk in the Plaza de la Constitución (main square), is the **Museo José Reyes Meza**. It's nothing more than one room, devoted to a sculpture of the Huastecan goddess Ixcuina Tlazolteot, the goddess of fertility. She is portrayed from mid-thigh up, standing two meters (6.5 feet) tall; her hands are clasped in front of her, and she wears a huge headdress. Open Tues.-Sun., 9 am-8 pm; free.

Zoo

If you want to get away from the city, head to the souped-up zoo outside of Tampico – the **Centro de Convivencia Ecológica El Solito**, ☎ 833-216-6924. You can join a walking tour to see various local animals or a trolley ride that visits the more exotic beasts, such as giraffes, zebras, and antelopes. This is definitely something the kids will enjoy. It's about 20 minutes away from Tampico (actually at the very north of the state of Veracruz); you can pick up a bus to the zoo in front of the Plaza de la Libertad at 11 am, 1 pm, and 3 pm. The zoo is open Sat. and Sun., 10 am-6 pm; 50 pesos for adults, 35 pesos for children.

TAAAXXXI!!!	
Grupo Forza Internacional. . .	☎ 833-227-1102 (Tampico)
Segutaxis	☎ 833-214-2240 (Tampico)
Ecotaxis del Golfo	☎ 833-216-8066 (Tampico)
Base de Ecotaxis Nuevo Milenio	☎ 833-210-6250 (Ciudad Madero)

■ Adventures

On Foot

The most appealing area to walk around is the Plaza de Armas and Plaza de la Libertad. Be sure to check out the **Cathedral** (the interior of which is exceptionally beautiful) and its supposed swastica floor (see below). The **Kiosko** in the Plaza de Armas is another must-see – it's one of the most elaborate you're likely to come across anywhere (see below). Then there is the **Edificio de la Aduana**, which has historical importance for the city, and will at the same time take you to the waterfront (see below).

City Walking Tour

For those wanting to know a bit more of the city, the walk below takes you past some of the more important buildings, many of which have been declared historic landmarks. You won't want to walk the last portion – towards the riverfront – at night; the run-down area here may be interesting during the daytime, but quickly becomes ugly as darkness sets.

Start your walk in city's main square, the **Plaza de Armas**, left, at the corner of Diaz Mirón and Colón. Surrounded by government buildings, the square is a bustling place of shoeshiners, birds and people. At its center, surrounded by fountains, is the huge, beautiful, rose-colored Kiosko; it was built in 1945, and is one of the largest and prettiest kiosks that you will see in the whole region.

After you finish walking around the square, behind you on Colón, facing the Plaza, is the **Palacio Municipal**, constructed from 1925-1933; inside are a couple of interesting and colorful murals. Adjacent to the Palacio, at the corner of Carranza and Colón, is the hard-to-miss Art Nouveau **DIF building**. Built in 1917, it has been at different times Tampico's city hall and a jail; the building currently houses the offices of the Desaroyo Integral de la Familia (DIF), which gives free social services to families. Next to the DIF (on Carranza) is the **Templo de la Inmaculada Concepción** (1831). The church has an ornate interior, complete with vaulted ceilings and beautiful paintings, but the most interesting aspect is on the floor by the entrance, where you can see designs that resemble swastikas. If you look carefully, however, you'll see that they are, in fact, pointing the opposite direction from the Nazi symbol, making them a Christian symbol. Part of the floor was removed before that was realized. You can still see some of the designs on the main aisle heading up to the pulpit.

From here, turn and head up Carranza walking up behind the Palacio Municipal one block; turn left onto Ave. 20 de Noviembre. On the right side, at the corner of Diaz Mirón, is an interesting house with a dome, constructed during the city's oil boom period. Back on Carranza, continue up one block to Calle San Juana Inés de la Cruz, and at the corner on the right (215 E. Carranza), you'll see a building that shows a mixture of architectural styles. Built in 1904, the building today is one of the most beautiful in the city. Continue up Carranza two more blocks until you reach the building between the streets of Canseco and Alarcón, which is the **Hospital**. Built in 1942, it was known at the time for having the luxury of continuous hot water.

Head back down Carranza toward the Plaza de Armas and take a right onto Colón; three blocks down, right after the intersection of Madero, you'll see on your right a salmon-colored building, the **Casa Járuregui**, at 206 Colón. Constructed in 1897, it was named for the political figure Don Amado Nicasio Járuregui, and was used during filming of the Mexican movie *Muelle Rojo*, a film about the Mexican dock workers' union. The building today is one of the oldest that has been conserved in Tampico. Next door (216 Colón) is an old building in the Art Deco style, while at the block's corner with H. del Cañonero, is the old **Hotel Riviera**. Built during the oil boom era, it was later abandoned when the area started to degenerate.

Turn left onto H. del Cañonero and walk two blocks to reach the **Plaza de la Libertad**. This plaza is a huge, beautiful square, surrounded by Art Nouveau buildings replete with balconies and patios, giving the whole plaza a distinctive New Orleans atmosphere. Under the arcades are restaurants, hotels, and local businesses, while underneath the plaza is a parking lot. Among the buildings, on your left at 304 Benito Juárez, is the iron-balconied **Hotel Posada del Rey**, where the surrender of troops under Spanish general Don Isidro Barradas was signed in 1829. Adjacent is the old **Restaurant La Troya**, followed by a typical oil boom building, the **Edificio Obregón** (at the corner of Juárez and Madero). Next to it is the *correos* (post office), built in 1907, the *Telégrafos*, built in 1908, and finally the *Edificio Alicia* (1884).

Curious about the exceptionally clean streets of Tampico? You won't see all those trash cans in every city you visit! Here, it's all part of Tampico's forward-thinking program to eliminate trash.

Around the corner on Aduana is the **Edificio Mercedes**. Besides displaying the typical Art-Nouveau feel of the Plaza, it was also the spot where parts of the movie *Treasure of the Sierra Madre* were filmed; inside, the "Manhattan" bar was installed for the movie. A little farther down, under the patios, are some displays on the city's history. If you read Spanish, there's a good amount of information here, including details about the Huastec culture (the indigenous people of the area), the city's history, Tampiqueño musicians (Cuco Sánchez, Mario Kuri Aldana, Severiano Briseño), and about B. Traven and his *Treasure of the Sierra Madre*.

When you're done examining the displays, you can continue your tour of the city, starting with the round building bordering one side of the Plaza (on H. del Cañonero). This is the **Edificio La Luz**, constructed between 1918 and 1924 out of material shipped here from

England and India. There are a couple of other visually interesting buildings behind the plaza. Take a left onto H. del Cañonero, and one block down at the corner of López de Lara is a pretty corner building, the **Edificio Diligencias** (1950). Continue straight one more block, and at the intersection of Alfaro, on opposite sides of the street, there are two old corner buildings. Turn left onto Alfaro, and one block down at the corner of Madero is the **Edificio Alijadores**. Finally, continue down one block, and turn left onto Diaz Mirón, heading back toward the plaza; on your way, you'll pass another oil-boom building at the corner of Lara, **El Águila** (1920). From here, head to the waterfront to finish the tour. From Diaz Mirón, turn left onto Aduana, once again passing by and through the Plaza de la Libertad. Continue to the end of Aduana and things start to get a little bit rougher, with more street vendors, crowds of people and cars, markets, and plenty of old, run-down buildings. On the left, just before you hit the waterfront, you'll pass by a cream-colored building that will probably have a guard out front. This is the **Estación del Ferrocarril** (train station, not accessible to the public).

A few steps farther, you've reached your final destination, the **Edificio de la Aduana Maritima** (Maritime Customs Building), in front of the Río Pánuco. Built in 1902, this is a landmark in Tampico, as well as one of its most important historical buildings. From its balconies, there is a good view of the river; you can also occasionally find art exhibits on its second floor. Outside, adjacent to the building, is a huge plaza where the tourism department sometimes sets up tents displaying information about the port's history. The Customs building is open daily, 9 am-12 pm and 4-6 pm.

The Pyramid

Disappointed you haven't seen any archaeological sites? You're in luck! Right in the middle of the city is the **Pirámide de las Flores** (Pyramid of the Flowers). It's not much more than a round mound with a staircase, protected from further deterioration. The pyramid was built, probably by the indigenous Huastecas, around 1000 BC, and is made up primarily of sand and shell. It's north of the downtown center, a block off Ave. Hidalgo (near the corner of Clavel). Open Tues.-Sun., 9 am-5:30 pm; free.

Golf

If you like to putt around, you've got two options here. The first is the **Club Campestre de Tampico**, one of México's oldest golf courses, dating back to 1925. It's frequented by México's upper class, and has a pretty nine-hole course adjacent to the Laguna del Chairel. The other option is the much newer **Club de Golf Lagunas de Miralta**, which is especially convenient if you are staying in Altamira at the Club Maeva (the golf course is in Altamira, and partners with the club, which can arrange shuttles to the course for you). The club was founded in 1991, originally as a nine-hole course. Club Campestre Tampico is at 603 Miraflores (in Tampico between the Laguna del Chairel and the Laguna del Charro, ☎ 833-213-6688). The Club de Golf Lagunas de Miralta is at the Laguna de Champayán (in Altamira, ☎ 833-224-0677).

On Wheels

You can tour the downtown by picking up an open-air tour trolley at the *malecón* on the Laguna del Carpintero. The tour takes you around the historic district and lasts around 30 minutes. Buses leave once per hour (or when they're full), and cost 15 pesos for adults, 10 pesos for children. They run Mon.-Fri., 9 am-9 pm, Sat. and Sun., 10 am-10 pm. The bus might stop operating earlier if there are no customers.

On Water

When it comes to water activities, you've got two choices: the lagoon or the beach.

Lagoons

The huge **Laguna del Carpintero**, which abuts the downtown center, is the closest option, and only a short walk from the center. The area around it is manicured and landscaped and a pathway leads along the water, a pleasant spot that attracts joggers and walkers. You'll also find the Parque Metropolitano along its banks, which is a center for activity, and very busy on weekends. Here you can pick up a bus (see *On Wheels*) for tours of downtown, rent a bike, take a boat tour, have a picnic (there are tables) or eat an ice cream. There's also a playground for your kids. It's small and in the sun, but it does have slides, swings and lots of other kids.

If you follow the waterfront path to its end (a short walk), there is a lookout over the lagoon where you can see, just offshore, a group of large crocodiles – more than 60 of them live here! I never have seen one come in to the shore, however. The canal next to the picnic *palapa* is filled with hundreds of turtles, but no crocodiles.

Bike rentals run about 20 pesos per half-hour from a stand called Tricicletas Quintos, open 11 am-11 pm, daily. You can also rent an adult or child's *trici-bike*. This contraption is pedaled by one person, and enjoyed by the rest who sit in the bench at the back. Open 11 am-11 pm, daily.

Boat rides run about 25 pesos per person (children 10 and younger, 5 pesos). They run 9 am-8 pm, with hourly departures. You're likely to see clowns at the dock trying to recruit as many passengers as possible (almost everywhere in México, you'll see clowns promoting one thing or another). The boat goes around the lagoon on a ride that lasts 30 minutes, and it's a good way to cool off in the summer.

Just west of Altamira, is the much larger **Laguna de Champayán**, where you can pick up a boat launch for fishing or just enjoying the scenery.

Beaches

Playa de Miramar is the most popular beach and, if it's a holiday, you will know it long before you see the water. At the entrance, parking lots gleam with the reflection from row upon row of cars. The long, wide brown sand (which extends for 10 km/six miles) can and does handle hundreds of people – tourists, locals, and vendors. Rows of *palapas* line the sand, most rented out by the nearby restaurants, and each one taken up by picnicking families relaxing in their hammocks or in their chairs, listening to music and snacking on lunch. Some of the *palapas* even have "palapa service," where you rent from the restaurant, order your food from their menu (stuffed crab, crab hash, octopus, seafood cocktails, shrimp) and they bring it out to you. An endless number of vendors roam the beach, selling shovels, hats, floats, ice creams, drinks, toys and foods. Kids play in the water, and adults who fancy a swim wade far out – the water stays warm and shallow for a good distance. That's Playa Miramar during the holidays – the beach version of the city.

Off-season, things calm down. Far down at the southern end of the beach, where the Río Pánuco flows into the ocean, is a *malecón* with a lighthouse, a popular spot with fishermen.

Playa Miramar is in the adjacent city of Ciudad Madero, to Tampico's east, about a 30-minute drive away. To get there, flag a bus down from downtown that indicates it's going to the "Playa." The ride costs about 4 pesos; or you can take a taxi for about 25 pesos. Be sure to avoid rush hours (between 5 and 7 pm) during holidays, when most of those people on the beach will be trying to cram into the buses as well.

More remote is the **Playa de Altamira**, north of Tampico in the city of Altamira. It's a rocky beach that's good for beachcombers or birdwatchers; there's a lighthouse here as well. This isn't the usual tourist destination, and you won't find much when you arrive. To get here, follow the Industrial Corridor along the coast towards

Altamira, eventually turning onto Boulevard Soto La Marina, and then onto an unpaved road.

Fishing

The waters surrounding Tampico are a major attraction for sport fishermen, who have caught a variety of species, including tuna, marlin, mako shark, red snapper, sea trout, snook, sea bass and black bass, tarpon, and kingfish. Yearly local and international tournaments are hosted by Tampico's fishing clubs, including a tournament in December, and a *robalo* (snook) fishing tournament in April. **Club de Regatas Corona**, ☎ 833-213-0788, is at the Laguna del Chairel, and the **Club Internacional de Yates de Tampico**, ☎ 833-212-2784, is on the Pánuco River at Km 45 of the Tampico-Valles Highway. The Club de Yates has docking facilities for boats up to 50 feet.

■ Festivals & Events

Tampico's **Laguna del Carpintero** has been used for power boat racing for about 10 years, and currently hosts an annual boat race – **La Nauticopa**. Events bring thousands of spectators to the lagoon for two days of activities, usually in April or May. Contact the tourism office (☎ 833-212-0007) for current schedule. The Union Internationale Motonautique has been organizing the event, which involves T-1 tunnel race boats. In 2003, Champ boats (the fastest outboard powerboats) were used in an exciting 50-lap race with over 100,000 pesos in prize money. Events bring thousands of spectators to the lagoon for the two days of activities, usually in April or May.

During the month of April, huge celebrations take place in Tampico. **Semana Santa** and **Carnaval** are marked with parades, fireworks, and general revelry, in addition to fishing tournaments for the abundant sea bass. Also, the **Repoblación de Tampico** is celebrated from April 12 to 27, and is marked with a number of cultural events and a huge carnaval fair replete with merry-go-round, games and food. So much happens in April, that the tourism office usually puts out a program outlining the day-by-day events. In addition to the fair, happenings range from bands playing at night in the Plaza de la Libertad, to special theater productions during the weekends, folk dances in the downtown plazas, art exhibitions, literary exhibits and book readings. Much of the focus is the Huastec culture.

■ Shopping

If you forgot something at home, there are plenty of places to pick it up in the **Zona Dorada**, a busy street filled with modern department stores, large supermarkets, banks, restaurants, hotels – not unlike the busiest commercial areas you'd find at home. There is even a Wal-Mart and a Subway here! The Zona Dorada is at the intersection of Ave. Hidalgo and Paseo Lomas de Rosales.

If you're looking for something more along the lines of a souvenir, the **Mercado de Artesanías**, two blocks from the riverfront at the corner of Juárez and H. del Cañonero, might have what you're looking for. Many of the souvenirs are based on seashells (and are a little bit cheesy). There are necklaces, bracelets, and all sorts of crazy shell-made knicknacks.

If you want to pick around in a real Mexican market, go behind the Mercado de Artesanías, on H. de Nacozari and Juárez, to the **Mercado Municipal**, which sells flowers, foods, bags of spices, *piñatas*, and fresh fish (huge and small, including snapper, cod, and trout). There are also a number of counters selling cheap *comida corridas* (pre-set meals with an entrée, drink and dessert), seafood cocktails, and fried fish. And if you decide to try something here for lunch, getting sick won't be a concern. Just hop right across the street to the **Farmacias Similares** (a discount pharmacy), where you can buy any kind of stomach medicine you need! It's cheap as well (Immodium caplets, the generic version, will only cost you about 10 pesos for 10 capsules). They close at 3 pm on Sundays.

■ Nightlife

There are a number of bars to keep you entertained late into the night, though most of them are out of the downtown area. There are several near the Universidad Autonoma de Tamaulipas on Ave. Universidad (near the airport); you'll need a taxi to get back and forth however. Among them is **Liquid Music Bar** (713 Ave. Universidad), which sometimes has a live band, and **Puerto Rico & Bermudas** (310 Ave. Universidad), a lively spot. A little closer, but in the same area, **Arquimias** (101 Ayuntamiento, at the corner of Ejército Mexicano) is a salsa and meringue discoteque, and **La Cigarra** (202 Morones Prieto, near Ave. Universidad) has good music. If you don't want to take a taxi, you can stop by the **Restaurant/Bar Palacio** near the Plaza de la Libertad (at the corner of Aduana and Héroes del Cañonero, which has live music and couples dancing nightly. A little more lively is the meringue and salsa bar, **La Cueva del Son** (621 Obregón). Alternatively, check with **La Fe Music Hall**, ☎ 833-224-6307, to see what events they might be showcasing. They are on Ave. Champayán out by the Laguna de Chairel.

■ Where to Stay

During Semana Santa, rooms in town fill up quickly, and prices are marked up for the holiday; less expensive rooms get snatched up first. You'll want to check in early to make sure you get a room. Some of the budget hotels don't take advance reservations, but it doesn't hurt to call anyway.

HOTEL PRICE CHART	
Rates are per room based on double occupancy. Rates lower if single occupancy or sharing a bed. Higher rates on holidays.	
	US $10-$20
$	US $21-$40
$$	US $41-$60
$$$	US $61-$80
$$$$	US $81-$125
$$$$$	Over US $125

La Mansion del General Hotel Inn, ☎ 833-212-2873, at 813 Emilio Carranza Ote, is about seven blocks east of the Plaza de Armas. They have inexpensive, clean, air-conditioned rooms. $

Within a block of the bus station, the small, newly opened **Tampico Garden Hotel**, at 104 Ave. Rosalio Bustamant, boasts six brand new rooms that include air-conditioning, color TV, carpeting, king-size beds, and parking. The newness of the hotel makes it an appealing choice if you find yourself staying near the bus station, as other hotels in this area are often old and rundown. Reservations and credit cards are not accepted. They do not yet have a phone number. $$$

Hotel Inglaterra, ☎ 833-219-2857 or 0800-71-57123 (MX), is on the Plaza de Armas, 116 S. Diaz Mirón Ote. It's a bit pricey for a member of the Best Western chain, but it does offer much more than any Best Western I have seen, and has more amenities than many of the hotels in Tampico. Facilities include meeting rooms, swimming pool, sauna, parking, restaurant and even a heliport! Rooms are nicely maintained, air-conditioned, and conveniently located. They offer transportation to and from the airport, which adds to the convenience. $$$$

In the Plaza de la Libertad, is **El Gran Hotel Sevilla**, ☎ 833-214-3833 or 01-833-2143833 (MX), www.granhotelsvilla.com.mx, 304 Héroes del Cañonero. This is a good choice for those who want an upgrade in comfort. Like most of the higher-priced hotels in Tampico, it seems to target the many business travelers that frequent the city. The hotel offers room service, good views of the park, and a restaurant and bar – as well as event rooms for the business travelers. $$$$

Hotel Monte Carlo, ☎ 833-214-1093, at 10 César López de Lara Nte, is only three blocks east of the Plaza de Armas; it's a huge hotel with a formal restaurant, parking, a bar open until 1 am, and standard rooms as well as suites. Rooms are comfortable, clean, air-conditioned, and have cable TV and room service. $$

Next to the Plaza de la Libertad, the **Hotel Plaza**, ☎ 833-214-3757 at 204 Madero Ote, has comfortable budget air-conditioned rooms, and parking. $$

It's a little bit far out, but the **Hotel Camino Real Tampico**, ☎ 833-213-8811, is one of the nicer hotels in Tampico. You'll find all the amenities (parking, room service, restaurant) plus a handsome landscaped pool, and large air-conditioned rooms with minibars. If you really feel like splurging, take the presidential suite. $$$$$

If you find yourself on the edge of town and don't want to deal with the hassle of town, stop by the Camino Real's associated hotel, the **Hotel Mansión Real Altamira**, ☎ 833-229-3400 (Km 16 on Highway Tampico-Mante), which is just as nice, offering minibars and air-conditioned rooms. The reservations desk can arrange tours for you, or set you up for tennis, golf, or fishing. $$$$$

Hotel Doña Juana Cecilia, ☎ 833-229-1410, Blvd. Costero Playa Miramar, has good views of the beach, spacious rooms with air-conditioning and cable TV, a large clean pool, and a restaurant. You pay a little bit less if you stay in the swimming pool section. The Master Suites are especially generous. $$$-$$$$

Club Maeva, ☎ 833-230-0202 or 1-888-739-0113 (US), Blvd. Costero Playa Miramar, is a large, popular (but quite expensive) all-inclusive resort. You get an air-conditioned room, meals, and access to activities such as kayaking, windsurfing, horseback riding, golf, bicycling, and volleyball. $$$$$

Two blocks from the Plaza de Armas at 202 Juárez, **Hotel Capri**, ☎ 833-212-2680, has a sign and narrow entrance you'll hardly notice. At the top of the entrance stairwell, you check in at the hotel clerk's booth, and then go to your room, past an old but very charming balconied interior courtyard. The rooms themselves are old, small, and basic, but very clean; they come with a fan and, for a little bit extra, you can upgrade to air-conditioning. The bathrooms are small and on the verge of being too old, but they too are very clean and, at these prices, in this location, it's hard to complain.

Hotel Tampico, ☎ 833-219-0057, four blocks east of the Plaza de Armas, has comfortable old rooms, a restaurant, and parking. $

Hotel Posada de Tampico, ☎ 833-230-1010 or 0800-570-4400, at 5300 Ave. Hidalgo, is a little out of the downtown area, but two of its rooms are handicap-accessible. Rooms are pleasant and clean, with cable TV and air-conditioning. The hotel also has a swimming pool, gym, tennis court, parking, and an airport and local shuttle. $$$

■ Where to Eat

In the middle of the Plaza de Armas, **El Globito** is a good place to stop and grab lunch; they sell fast items, such as *tortas* and *tacos*, as well as different types of fruit drinks and sodas. $

DINING PRICE CHART	
Price per person for an entrée, not including beverage or tip.	
$	Under US $5
$$	US $5-$10
$$$	US $10+

A charming place to have dinner is in the dark wooden interior of the **Salón Palacio**, on the Plaza de la Libertad at Aduana on the corner of H. del Cañonero. It has a great wooden bar, upstairs interior balcony seating, old photographs of México on its walls, and live music in the evenings. There's a huge selection of wines (by glass or bottle), and the food is good as well. Traditional entrées are made tampiqueña-style, including tacos, shrimp, crab and fondues. $$-$$$

Up the street a little, **Restaurante Marios** at 420 Juárez Nte is a very clean spot, and a good place to get a budget meal. It's a cafeteria-style buffet, serving *tortas*, *tacos*, and sodas. $

The chain food restaurant **VIPS** (on the Plaza de la Libertad) is always a good safe spot for an uncomplicated meal. They serve burgers, salads, and sandwiches, as well as some Mexican specialties. $$

Right off the Plaza de la Libertad at the Hotel Posada del Rey, 218 Madero, is **La Troya**, a Spanish restaurant, often popular at night as diners sit at balconies overlooking the Plaza. $$

You'll also find a couple of nice restaurants out of the city center, up Ave. Hidalgo, including the pricey **Jardín Corona** at 1915 Ave. Hidalgo, which specializes in meat and seafood. $$$

Another is the **Restaurant/Bar El Porvenir** at 1403 Ave. Hidalgo, a good restaurant specializing in seafood. $$$

If you're in Altamira, you can get a good "natural" buffet lunch at **Restaurant Javier**, 5 Calle Iturbide. They specialize in low-fat natural foods and lots of juices; there is a special discounted rate for children. $

Veracruz

State Capital: Xalapa

When you go to Veracruz, be aware of three things: there is no such thing as too much film; even in the most populated of cities, a traveler's check is sometimes no more than a fancy piece of paper; and accept that you just might have to come back for another visit. After that, it's just a matter of

5 PLACES NOT TO MISS	
Xalapa (culture)	191
El Tajín (archaeology)	144
Xico (beauty)	220
Puerto de Veracruz (partying)	165
Tlacotalpan (relaxation)	187

choosing what you would like to do. For the energetic, there's hiking in the mountains around Orizaba; for the intellectuals, there's drinking coffee and going to museums in Xalapa; for the adventurous, there's rafting the rivers of the Filobobos; for the revelers, there's Carnaval in the Puerto de Veracruz; for the curious, there's cigar making at San Andres Tuxtla.... well, you get the idea.

The state has some highly important historical sites as well. It was here that Hernán Cortés established the first Spanish colony, and where he planned his moves against the Aztec empire, marching across the countryside (from Cempoala to Xalapa and on between the mountains of Cofre de Perote and the Pico de Orizaba), leading eventually to the fall of Tenochtitlan, the Aztec capital.

Today, the state, especially the coast, is well-connected by bus and highway, and you won't have to hike as Cortés once did – unless you really want to (some adventurous tourists *do* hike Cortés' first march). It is a major tourist destination for Mexicans, particularly during holidays, when hotels and buses to the coast are booked solid. And, with its geography extending over most of the Gulf Coast (it takes around 12 hours to drive from one end to another), there's something to please just about everyone – rivers, lagoons, waterfalls, mountains, hills, marshes, estuaries and caves.

Though you will find large, busy cosmopolitan cities with four-star hotels and a well-planned listing of events, for the most part, the tourism infrastructure remains woefully underdeveloped. If you're visiting a village, adjust your expectations accordingly. Street signs may not always be there, roads to the most beautiful of places may not be well-paved, and public transportation might well be an ancient school bus. But I assure you, down those windy, bumpy roads, there's always someone with a new food, a new smile, and a lead on a new discovery that will keep you moving ahead.

Northern Veracruz

There isn't a lot on the roads heading south from Tampico to Tuxpan. For the most part, your cross-over into the state of Veracruz will be with little fanfare. The scenery is mostly savannah coastlands, and for many miles

IN THIS CHAPTER	
■ The Road to Tuxpan	41
■ Tuxpan	57
■ Poza Rica	67

there is little to see. It becomes more promising as the surrounding vegetation gets greener and more lush the farther south you travel. The few villages in this northern section are small and, in some cases, quite poor. A drive through one of them will give you a quick idea of what the rest are like – houses, rocky dirt roads, and almost always dogs and chickens who refuse to get out of your car's way. During the hurricane season, it's not uncommon for the lowlands here to be in the path of storms, and with Highway 180 running so close to the coast, you'll want to keep an eye on things. Roads can quickly flood and become impassable, forcing you onto a roundabout inland route, away from 180.

The area is part of the Huasteca region, which continues north into southern Tamaulipas and west into parts of San Luis Potosi and Hidalgo. In many places, locals still speak the indigenous language (similar to Mayan), practice cultural dances, and wear traditional clothing. If you get a chance, try some of the regional dishes such as the *sacahuil* (an enormous tamale), *enchiladas huasteca* (a spicy red enchilada dish), and *atole* (a thick, warm corn drink). The larger towns of Pánuco and Tantoyuca are good choices for lunch.

Who's Who?

The Huastecs (or Huaxtecs): An indigenous group numbering today around 80,000, living in southern Tamaulipas, northern Veracruz, and parts of San Luis Potosi and Hidalgo states. The Huastecs flourished during the Postclassic period (900-1200 AD).

Above: Tlacotalpan, Veracruz (see pages 188-89)
Below: Tlacotalpan

Above: Olmec head, Tabasco (see pages 275-76)

Below: Market in Oaxaca

Above: El Tajín (Joanie Sánchez - see pages 144-49)

Below: El Tajín, with the Pyramid of the Niches in the background (Joanie Sánchez)

Above: Semana Santa festival in Papantla, Veracruz (Joanie Sánchez - see page 14)
Below: Boat tour of Tlacotalpan (Joanie Sánchez - see page 190)

The Totonacs: An indigenous group who lived in Veracruz, and are often associated with El Tajín. A Totonac ruler joined forces with the Spanish against the Aztecs. The Totonacs flourished during the Postclassic period (900-1200 AD).

The Olmecs: A Gulf Coast civilization that was probably the granddaddy of all Mesoamerican cultures. They flourished during the Middle Preclassic period (1200-600 BC).

The Aztecs: A civilization that became a huge dazzling warlike empire, controlling huge amounts of land and wealth. Known for their ferociousness, they flourished during the late Postclassic period (1200-1520 AD).

The Road To Tuxpan

Heading south from Tampico toward Tuxpan, you can take either Highway 70 south to Highway 105 (which leads you slightly inland) or ride on Highway 180, which pretty much follows the coast, though you can't see it. The first route takes you past the town of **Pánuco**, a port on the banks of Río Pánuco about 43 miles/69 km southwest of Tampico. It's a good spot to stop for some tasty Huastec specialties, including the *sacahuil* – a huge banana-leaf-covered tamale, traditionally made up to a yard long and shared among several dozen people. There is a waterfront where you can look onto the flat, shrubby, river, and it's a place known for its *huapango*, a regional dance performed to the music of a violin and *jarana* (similar to a guitar).

Continuing south on Highway 150, just outside Pánuco, in the middle of the road, is a huge Olmec head. As you continue, just after passing through the town of Tempoal, the highway splits. Highway 105 continues south into the state of Hidalgo, while Highway 127 goes southeast into Veracruz and back towards Tuxpan. Follow 127 and you'll reach the town of **Tantoyuca** – another good spot to stop for lunch. Huastec dishes here are everyday fare.

Alternatively, if you follow Highway 180 from Tampico, you'll mostly pass through industrial oil towns. As you head south, you run alongside the huge **Laguna de Tamiahua** (see *Tuxpan – On Water*, page 134) for many miles before hitting the first big town of **Naranjos**, which, though it has a promising name (naranjo = orange), doesn't quite live up to it's promise of pretty orange orchards. The town was named after the wild orange trees that grow in the area, but it makes its living from the oil industry. There's a museum dedicated to the Huastecas downtown. Another archaeological remnant is just a few miles away, a prehispanic sculpture called El Sol Poniente. The museum can give you directions to its location.

Back on the Highway, Cerro Azul is another (unattractive) oil town you won't want to stop at. Just keep going south to the town of **Alamo**, where, if you need to kill time, you can get directions to a prehispanic figural sculpture in nearby Cinco Poblados.

Tuxpan (or Tuxpam)

There were two Americans, a Frenchman and a German. No, not the beginning of a joke, but the makeup of the check-in line at my hotel. Many people find Tuxpan (pronounced TOOKS-pahn) a convenient spot to spend the night on their way elsewhere. If you're coming down the coast of Veracruz heading south, Tuxpan, situated on the Río Tuxpan (which empties into the Gulf seven miles down), will be the first major port that you hit. It's a pretty spot, with a palm-lined boulevard following the river and bordering the downtown, where you'll find a zig-zag of busy streets and happy buildings. It is a working port, with oil rigs and large ships occasionally seen chugging back and forth along the river, though you don't see very many of them. And at night the riverfront can be quite calm and peaceful. The downtown is pretty busy during the day – but pleasingly so. The buildings might be crowded in, and the streets narrow, but the people are friendly. Even a police officer, standing in the middle of a busy intersection, happily and patiently gave directions, not minding at all the slow-down in the traffic.

■ Orientation & Practicalities

Tuxpan is off Highway 180, about an hour's drive from Papantla. In town, the main drag is the **Blvd. Heroles**, which follows Río Tuxpan on the south side of town; the ocean is seven miles to the west. The main square, or *zócalo*, **Parque Reforma**, is one block north of the river on Juárez. Strangely enough, the **Palacio Municipal** is not on the *zócalo*, but instead is in front of Parque Cano on Juárez, about five blocks east.

Exchanging Money: There are a number of banks on Juárez near the *zócalo*.

Post Office: The *correo* is two blocks away from the main park on Mina.

Tourist Information: A tourist information office is on the first floor of the Palacio Municipal.

Getting There & Around

The UNO/ADO bus station is about a 10-minute walk from the Parque Reforma on Rodriguez, between Blvd. Heroles and Juárez. To get there from Parque Reforma, head east down Juárez until you reach Rodriguez. Turn right onto Rodriguez, toward the river. The bus station is about half a block down.

Destination	Bus Line	Fare	Time
Matamoros	ADO	388 pesos	10 hours 20 minutes
México (Norte)	UNO	277 pesos	6 hours
	ADO GL	200 pesos	6 hours
	ADO	168 pesos	5 hours 10 minutes
Tampico	ADO	122 pesos	3 hours 40 minutes
Papantla	ADO	36 pesos	55 minutes
Poza Rica	ADO GL	34 pesos	45 minutes
	ADO	28 pesos	50 minutes
Reynosa	ADO	390 pesos	10 hours 30 minutes
Veracruz	ADO	156 pesos	4 hours 25 minutes

Sightseeing

There are two museums. **Museo Arqueológico** (on Morelos next to the Parque Reforma) has a display of regional archaeological fragments (9 am-6 pm, daily; free). Slightly more interesting is **Museo de la Amistad México-Cuba** – Museum of Mexican-Cuban Friendship. The building that houses the museum served as the home of Fidel Castro in 1956 before he sailed back with revolutionary Che Guevara (and more than 80 others) to begin the Cuban Revolution. To get to the museum, take a motorboat over to the south side of the river. You can find boats at a number of places along Blvd. Heroles (they pretty much go back and forth all day). From here, it's a short walk to Obregón, where you'll eventually see the museum entrance.

■ Adventures

On Water

The brown sandy beach near Tuxpan, called **Playa Norte**, is a nice spot for walking down the coast and admiring the coconut trees and the dark ocean waters, while the Gulf sea breeze blows through your hair and dries the sweat that has probably become a permanent fixture on you forehead. It's also an ideal spot to find a little restaurant and relax under a *palapa* with some fresh seafood and an ice cold beer. You can swim here as well, though the surf can get a bit rough at times. The beach is a bit far from town to walk, so you can pick up a local bus marked *Playa Norte* a little past the ADO bus station. Buses will be heading east along Blvd. Heroles (about 10 pesos).

Laguna Tamiahua (tahm-ee-AH-wah) is a huge lagoon starting just south of Tampico, and continuing down more than 60 miles to the town of Tamiahua itself (about 25 miles to the north of Tuxpan). Besides the sand barrier, known as Cabo Rojo, which separates it from the ocean, there are a number of islands, including Isla Lobos (in the ocean just past the sandbar), and Isla El Idolo (inside the lagoon). Though there are few tourists here, you can find boats to take you out into the lagoon and around some of the islands, or you can sign up for a diving trip to the islands by stopping in at the dive shop **AquaSport** (about four miles/6.4 km out on the road to Playa Norte). At the lagoon, you'll find a couple of restaurants; try a fresh *ceviche* (a mixture of octopus, fish, oysters, onions, and tomatoes) while you're there.

To get here, pick up a bus heading east along Blvd. Heroles marked Tamiahua (follow directions to Playa Norte above).

If you're a sailor, you might be interested in checking out the **Regatta de Amigos**, sponsored by the US-based Galveston Bay Cruising Association and the Lakewood Yacht Club. Each year during June, sailors make a 630-mile/1,008-km journey down the Gulf Coast to the Puerto de Veracruz, stopping at Tuxpan. On the return journey, many take a break for snorkeling around the islands in the Laguna Tamiahua. For more information, visit their website at www.gbca.org or ☎ 281-291-0360.

Archaeological Discoveries

The **Castillo de Teayo** is not really a castle (*castillo*) at all, but a pyramid, dating back more than 1,000 years. It's in a site with Huasteca origins that was subsequently inhabited by the Toltecs, and later the Aztecs. Today it sits strangely out of place on one side of the main square in the middle of a village, the original settlers having decided to build their own town around it. It's an unadorned pyramid with a steep staircase up one side, leading to an altar at its top. A number of artifacts found in the vicinity are on display in the village's small museum. To get to  the village of Castillo de Teayo, head south on free Highway 180 towards Poza Rica; about three miles after it merges with Highway 127, you'll see a small turnoff to the west (your right) heading towards Castillo de Teayo (the third village down). As for sites and services, the village doesn't have much more to offer other than the pyramid, so go prepared.

■ Festivals & Events

If you're around on the days surrounding August 15th, you can celebrate along with the town as residents honor their patron saint with parades, fireworks, cockfights, and bullfights during the **Dia de la Asunción**.

■ Where to Stay & Eat

One of the first hotels you see as you drive into town, right on the riverfront, is **Hotel Riviera**, ☎ 783-834-5349, at 17 Blvd. Heróles, which offers an interior garage, and clean rooms, some with good views of the river. Rooms are a little stuffy, and the a/c doesn't work too well, but it's one of the cheaper hotels on the waterfront. $

HOTEL PRICE CHART	
Rates are per room based on double occupancy. Rates lower if single occupancy or sharing a bed. Higher rates on holidays.	
	US $10-$20
$	US $21-$40
$$	US $41-$60
$$$	US $61-$80
$$$$	US $81-$125
$$$$$	Over US $125

Right in the center, the **Hotel El Huasteco**, ☎ 783-834-1859, at 41 Morelos, has clean rooms with fan or a/c and TV at very good prices, although the street can be a bit dark at night. There is no on-site parking, but there is a parking lot about a block away. $

Hotel Plaza, ☎ 783-834-0738, at 39 Ave. Juárez, is conveniently located, and has a restaurant, parking, and clean rooms with a/c and color TV. $$

Hotel Reforma, 25 Ave. Juárez, ☎ 783-834-0210, is about three blocks away from Parque Reforma, and offers rooms with a/c and cable TV that are a little bit more expensive, but also a little bit nicer. $$

Hotel May Palace, ☎ 783-834-8881, at 44 Juárez, sits facing the main park, and has a spacious air-conditioned lobby, and clean rooms. $$$

There are a couple of places to eat in the *zócalo*, for the most part serving cheap and tasty *comida corridas*. You'll be mixing and mingling with the locals, listening to the kids in the park playing marbles and popping fire crackers, and watching the vendors sell ice cream... basically just another night in the park. The most popular spot seems to be at the northwest corner in an eaterie simply marked *Restaurant*.

Poza Rica

Poza Rica is crowded, congested, and unpleasant. It has nothing that would make you want to stay there long. If you are driving, you will be frustrated from the start – bumper-to-bumper traffic that crawls along inch-by-inch during rush hour. Basically, it's a huge industrial city, which serves as the commercial center for the state. There are a number of hotels around, which cater to the businesspeople and weekend tourists, who use them as a base for nearby El Tajín and Papantla. Try to stop at nearby Tuxpan (to the north) or Papantla (to the south) if your drive requires a stay in the vicinity. Sometimes, however, you have no choice.

■ Orientation & Practicalities

Poza Rica's nearby **El Tajín airport** is serviced by **Aeromar**, ☎ 800-531-7921 or 0800-237-6627 (MX), www.aeromar.com.mx, which flies to México City and Reynosa.

Banks are around the *zócalo*, and there's an **American Express** office (Viajes Lorimar), ☎ 782-824-3291, at 1202 Blvd. Ruiz Cortines. It's open Mon.-Fri., 9 am-5 pm.

■ Getting There & Out

There is a big first-class bus station serviced by UNO and ADO, on Calle Puebla.

TYPICAL BUS FARES

Destination	Bus Line	Fare	Trip Time
Costa Esmeralda	ADO	40 pesos	1 hour 20 minutes
Matamoros	UNO	617 pesos	10 hours
	ADO	416 pesos	10 hours 50 minutes
México City	ADO	140 pesos	4 hours 55 minutes
Oaxaca	ADO	394 pesos	10 hours 10 minutes
Orizaba	ADO	203 pesos	5 hours 40 minutes
Papantla	ADO	11 pesos	30 minutes
Reynosa	UNO	620 pesos	8 hours
	ADO	420 pesos	11 hours 30 minutes
San Andres Tuxtla	ADO	264 pesos	5 hours 45 minutes
Veracruz	UNO	225 pesos	3 hours
	ADO GL	160 pesos	3 hours
	ADO	126 pesos	4 hours 10 minutes
Villahermosa	ADO GL	496 pesos	10 hours 30 minutes
	ADO	419 pesos	9 hours 45 minutes
Xalapa	ADO GL	160 pesos	4 hours 15 minutes
	ADO	138 pesos	4 hours 15 minutes

■ Where to Stay

There are a few cheap places by the bus station, but you'll want to check them out carefully before deciding on a room. One option is the **Hotel Fenix**, ☎ 782-822-1816, at 106 6 Norte. $$

The **Best Western Hotel Poza Rica** (corner of 2 Nte and 10 Ote) is a modern hotel in the downtown area that's clean and reliable. $$$$

Hotel Victoria, ☎ 782-826-2600, at 1306 Blvd. Ruiz Cortinez, is a little pricier, but sets you up in comfort with a pool, restaurant, and suites. $$$$

Central Veracruz

Central Veracruz splinters up into so many pieces it's challenging to remember that it's all the same state. Coming out of northern Veracruz, before you get to the true central portion of the state, is a region that includes the ruins of El Tajín and Papantla – an area with a deep Totonaca culture. Continuing south, you pass the Costa Esmeralda – the closest thing to a beach resort on the Gulf Coast, where the heat can be stifling and humid. A bit farther south and to the west, you'll find towns high in the mountains of the Sierra Madre Oriental, where you

IN THIS CHAPTER	
■ Papantla	139
■ Costa Esmeralda	153
■ Tlapacoyan	158
■ Villa Rica to Cardel	161
■ Veracruz	165
■ Tlacotalpan	187
■ Xalapa	191
■ Perote	215
■ Coatepec	218
■ Xico	220
■ Jalcomulco	227
■ Orizaba	233
■ Fortín de las Flores	245
■ Córdoba	249

have to don a sweater in the mornings to protect yourself from the chilled air. South again, and you've reached the highest mountain in México, while at sea level to the west, is the site of the first Spanish settlement. Confused? Well, there is help. Most adventure agencies either have a base here or do excursion trips to the area, and many are affordable, offering the opportunity to do everything from rafting a mountain stream past ancient ruins to bird watching along the coast.

Who's Who?

Juan de Grijalva: In the early 1500s he was sent from Cuba to investigate findings of gold and jewels on the unexplored Yucatán. He sailed down the coast as far as today's Puerto de Veracruz, discovering that the peninsula was in fact a continent, which he dubbed New Spain. Veracruz' Río Grijalva is named after him.

Hernan Cortés: This Spanish conquistador set out in 1519 as the leader of an expedition into "New Spain" to investigate, seek gold and jewels, and to spread Christianity.

Moctezuma II: Aztec emperor from 1502-20, his huge empire controlled the territory and wealth of the Gulf Coast.

Chicomeácatl Quauhtlaebana: Totonac leader of Cempoala, known as being incredibly obese. He joined forces with Hernan Cortés against the Aztecs.

Papantla

Nineteen km/12 miles south of Poza Rica, just as the land starts to wrinkle up in the foothills of the nearby Sierra Madre Oriente, and just before Highway 180 takes a turn for the coast, you hit the village of Papantla. Though unfamiliar to English-speakers, the village is well-known in Veracruz, mainly due to the nearby Totonac ruins of **El Tajín**. These are the most important archaeological remains in the Gulf Coast region, and a must-see on any traveler's agenda.

Papantla is the place to base yourself for Tajín, but it is more than just a convenient spot to bed down. In fact, it's difficult not to become enchanted with the village. Visually it's charming, with houses built into the hills, and narrow, steep, winding streets... thoughts of your car losing its brakes on one of them will keep you preoccupied for hours. Culturally, its charm goes even deeper – festivals and events are marked by the unforgettable dances with women and men in full native costume. The Totonac heritage is proudly displayed in a huge mural that spreads across one side of the downtown church and, more famously, in its unique Voladores performance, an impressive ritual (similar to a bunjee-jump) performed from atop tall poles.

Papantla is also a major producer of vanilla. Can you imagine a more unusual souvenir than a vanilla bean sculpture?

■ Orientation & Practicalities

Emergency Services: Hospital, ☎ 784-842-0094. Red Cross, ☎ 784-842-0126.

Exchanging Money: There are a number of banks on Ave. Enriquez, across the street from the *zócalo*, including a Santander Serfin, open Mon.-Fri., 9 am-4 pm and Sat., 10 am-2 pm, and a Bancomer, open Mon.-Fri., 8:30 am-4 pm. A Banamex, Bancrecer, and a Banrural are a block farther down Ave. Enriquez, towards Ave. Pino Suarez.

Internet Cafés: Right next door to the Hotel El Tajín, a shop marked simply **Internet**, has a friendly staff and reasonable prices of 10 pesos per hour, though at times the connection is a bit slow. Another option is **Tote.com 2**, next to Mercado Hidalgo. They too charge 10 pesos per hour, or 3 pesos for 15 minutes.

Post Office: The post office is a bit out of the way, on Olivo, between Calle Azueta and Ave. 20 de Noviembre.

Tourist Information: The tourist information office is only steps away from the *zócalo* on Calle Artes (almost at the corner of Calle Reforma and Calle Artes), but resides in an unmarked building that renders it almost invisible unless you are looking for it (keep your eye out for a sign inside the building saying *Turismo*). The lobby is a museum with a couple of glass cases displaying artifacts from the area: clay faces, figurines, and some little statues, most of them on loan from private owners. They also have a number of well-researched pamphlets covering vanilla, the Voladore monument, and Tajín, as well as maps of the village; everything, however, is in Spanish, and the staff doesn't speak English.

■ Getting There

By Car

Papantla is just south of Poza Rica, on Highway 180.

To El Tajín: To get to El Tajín from the center of Papantla, take Ave. 16 de Septiembre east, follow it heading out of town (towards El Chote) until it intersects with Highway 130. Turn right onto the Highway, heading north, following the signs to El Tajín. From downtown, it is approximately 10 miles/16 kilometers, a 20-minute ride, to the site.

By Bus

The cute little bus station is fairly close to downtown, and if you don't have a lot of luggage (it's practically all uphill to get to the *zócalo*), the short walk can be enjoyable. ADO services the station.

TYPICAL BUS FARES			
Destination	Bus Line	Fare	Trip Time
Catemaco	ADO	256 pesos	5 hours 10 minutes
Costa Esmeralda	ADO	29 pesos	50 minutes
Nautla	ADO	48 pesos	1 hour 5 minutes
Poza Rica	ADO	11 pesos	30 minutes
Tampico	ADO	164 pesos	6 hours 15 minutes
Tecolutla	ADO	19 pesos	45 minutes
Tuxpan	ADO	36 pesos	50 minutes
Veracruz	ADO	118 pesos	3 hours 15 minutes
Villahermosa	ADO	408 pesos	9 hours 20 minutes

Getting There ■ 141

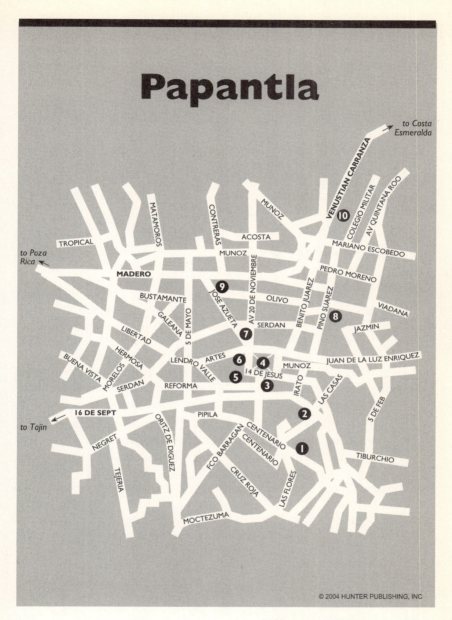

1. Monumento al Volador
2. Bus to Tajin
3. Catedral de la Asunción
4. Zocalo
5. Mercado Juárez
6. Palacio Municipal (Town Hall)
7. Mercado Hidalgo
8. Casa de la Cultura
9. Post Office
10. ADO Bus Station

To get to the towncenter, take a left as you exit the station onto Ave. Venustiano Carranza; it'll merge with Ave. Madero, at which point you should take another left onto 20 de Noviembre. Follow the road three short blocks to the *zócalo*.

To El Tajín: Local buses run frequently to El Tajín, and can be picked up at the corner of Obispo de la Casas and 16 de Septiembre, a block or so south of the *zócalo*. Get on the bus marked *Tajín/Poza Rica*. The ride will take you up and down some steep side streets, past the Museo de Cultura, and on to El Tajín. The bus will drive right up to the entrance, marked by a huge statue of a Voladore. Pick up the return bus marked *Papantla* in the same spot. The trip takes around 30 minutes, and costs 8.50 pesos.

■ Adventures

On Foot

From just about anyplace in the city, you can easily pick out one of the main symbols of Papantla – the **Monumento al Volador**, a huge monument perched on a hill overlooking the city. A hike to its feet will reward you with a breathtaking view of the town and nearby countryside. The road to the monument is not long (it'll take only 15 minutes), but it is pretty steep. Don't forget to bring your camera and binoculars.

To get up the hill, known as the **Cerro del Campanario**, starting at Calle H. de Jesus in the *zócalo* (which runs right past the church), take a left onto the unmarked street, Calle Centenario, that heads uphill past the front of the church. The street curves up and to the left into a residential area where you'll probably see your fair share of chickens roaming around. It opens into a cleared lot at the monument's base, marked with inscriptions describing the significance of the monument and of the related *Danza del Volador*. Climb a couple of steps up to the lookout at the Volador's feet, and you have a bird's-eye view of the city.

Some 32 km (20 miles) from Papantla, **Cuyuxquihui** (1250 AD) is a rarely visited Totonac site – possibly because it is so small, and more probably because it is a bit of a hike to get to (most maps don't even have it marked). With about half a dozen excavated structures set on a hill near the Tecolutla river, and inaccessible by car, the site is a bit more suitable for hikers than the everyday tourist.

From the village of Paso del Correo, you'll have to leave the car and take a two-km walk (a little more than a mile) to Cuyuxquihui. Paso del Correo is located south off Highway 130, towards the village of Joloapan. The site is open daily, 9 am-5 pm.

Cultural & Eco-Travel Excursions

 One of the most unusual dances that you are likely to see performed anywhere is the **Danza del Volador,** a prehispanic religious rite practiced by the Totonacs, and today still performed regularly in Papantla. The performances, re-creations of ancient rituals, are stomach-turning jumps from several stories up – seemingly death-defying feats, especially when considering that there are no safety harnesses or nets beneath the dancers. Performances are held on Sundays in front of the church in Papantla, as well as daily at the ruins of Tajín and are free (donations solicited). You're likely to catch a performance in the afternoon, though there is no schedule – keep your ears open for the music and your eyes peeled for the gathering crowds. You probably won't see anything like it again.

The attempt to preserve the history and culture of Papantla is evident everywhere in the village. The **Mural de la Cultura Totonaca**, on the south side of the *zócalo*, decorates one huge wall in front of the Franciscan-styled Catedral de la Asunción. The relief is stunning, a huge representation of the divine god Quetzalcoátl, sometimes referred to as "The Feathered Serpent." It stretches the full block, from one end of the wall to the other, outdone only by an eye-catching centerpiece showcasing a beautiful image of El Tajín. Look closely and you'll see that the mural has many images representing all aspects of the Totonac culture, from its beginnings and beliefs, to the ball game and Tajín, to its religious dances. Other sites to investigate include the ceiling of the **kiosk** in the center of the *zócalo* (where you'll find another mural, this one meant to depict the world's creation), as well as the outside wall of the front entrance to the *zócalo*, which has two interesting paintings – on the left, an old image of the village, on the right, a more recent depiction.

Danza del Volador

 This spectacular religious rite was performed by the Totonacs every 52 years at the beginning of a new century in the ancient Náhuatl calendar. The ritual involves five dancers, and begins as the one known as the *caporal*, who stands atop a 56-foot/20-m wooden pole (on a wooden platform a mere 12 inches/30 cm wide), plays a flute and beats a drum while bending, balancing, and jumping (untethered) from foot to foot, as he turns toward each of the cardinal points – north,

south, east, and west. The other four dancers are the flyers who, at the appointed time, throw themselves off the top of the pole, descending to the ground in a spiral swing, arms spread wide, with nothing but a cord tied around their waists. The cords are made to the specific length required so that the flyers rotate around the pole (and thus wrap the cord around it) exactly 13 times. When multiplied by the number of flyers (four), that produces the number of years in the Totonac century – 52.

Symbolically, the *caporal* represents the *Dios Sol* (or Sun God), while the four flyers symbolize the sun's rays, projecting down to fertilize the Earth. It is believed that the Goddess Earth, which represents water, and the sun's rays, which represent fire, join together to produce fertility.

El Tajín Archaeological Site

It is hard to forget El Tajín if you visit early in the morning before the misty fog has burned away. It is lonely and empty at this time, with the exception of the iguanas and the colorful birds, whose beautiful chirps and whistles soon fade into the background, they are so common. This will be your memory – sitting on top of a ruin, the vegetation of the surrounding hills, so tropical and lush... so *alive*, you wonder at how it hasn't already reclaimed the site. And how are you going to manage with only one roll of film?

By far the best time to visit El Tajín is in the mornings, when there are fewer visitors. The Mexican tourists, who make up the bulk of the sightseers, for the most part, won't arrive until the afternoon. Even then, don't expect crowds, just clusters of people. Tajín is far less visited than you would expect, considering its historical importance. Also, an early start will help you avoid the humidity that sets in later. The morning mist will turn the jungle into a soupy haze as the day wears on.

The excavated portion of the site is not that big, and fairly compact, so you can probably get away with a visit of two hours; however, if you want to enjoy yourself more (and Tajín does elicit a tingle in the explorer's heart), allot around three hours. The site has parking, a museum at the entrance, and an overpriced souvenir shop. In addition, vendors set up stalls in front of the entrance, selling Totonac paraphernalia (bows, arrow, rattles, drums, clothing).

Here, as at most other archaeological sites, there are no free pamphlets or maps. There *are* a few plaques with informational descriptions. Some are just in Spanish, while others are in Spanish, English, and French. Somehow, though, the staff failed to mark any of the structures, so that when you finally find something in your language, it could refer to any number of buildings. You're left to guess which is which. In short, be sure to bring your guidebook with you or, alternatively, buy a book on Tajín in the market at Papantla. One last note. Many of the buildings have been roped off for conservation purposes. Don't be too bummed out, however; there are some structures that have been left open (if there isn't a rope or sign marking it off, you are free to climb it). Enjoy.

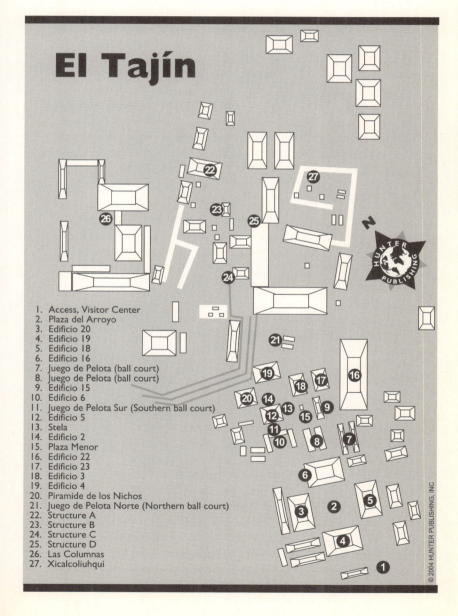

El Tajín

1. Access, Visitor Center
2. Plaza del Arroyo
3. Edificio 20
4. Edificio 19
5. Edificio 18
6. Edificio 16
7. Juego de Pelota (ball court)
8. Juego de Pelota (ball court)
9. Edificio 15
10. Edificio 6
11. Juego de Pelota Sur (Southern ball court)
12. Edificio 5
13. Stela
14. Edificio 2
15. Plaza Menor
16. Edificio 22
17. Edificio 23
18. Edificio 3
19. Edificio 4
20. Piramide de los Nichos
21. Juego de Pelota Norte (Northern ball court)
22. Structure A
23. Structure B
24. Structure C
25. Structure D
26. Las Columnas
27. Xicalcoliuhqui

Admission costs 37 pesos, with the exception of those under 13 and over 60, for whom admission is free; Sundays are free for Mexican citizens only. Hours are 9 am-6 pm daily.

El Tajín: Who & When?

Exactly who built El Tajín remains a mystery. It has been, and is, often associated with the Totonacs simply because of the centuries in which they have lived in the region and established a certain history with the site themselves – even having named the site. Whether or not it was constructed by them, the Huastecs (another popular belief), or some other culture altogether, is anyone's guess. In any event, Totonac legend holds that El Tajín is inhabited by "The Tajín," 12 old men who rule the thunderstorms (in Totonaca, Tajín translates to "thunder" – hence the name).

Regardless of *who* built the site, the *when* is a little bit clearer. El Tajín has been dated from the Early Classic period (300-600 AD), reaching its height in the Late Classic period (600-900 AD), and dying out (it was burned) in the Early Postclassic period, around 1200 AD.

Fast forward to recordable memory, Tajín was rediscovered by the outside world on July 12, 1785 when a Mexican newspaper published the findings of Engineer Diego Ruiz. For almost 600 years prior, it had remained relatively abandoned, covered in jungle, and lost to the memory of all save some of the local people. A few visits to the site were made in subsequent years, but it was not until around 1938 that excavations started in earnest, continuing off and on to the present day. Restoration activities continue by anthropologists from Veracruz University and the Institute of Anthropology and History. Few of the buildings here have actually been named, most simply marked by a number or letter designation.

As you enter the site, you come upon the **Plaza del Arroyo** ("Plaza of the Stream" – named after the stream that flows nearby). This simple plaza is surrounded by four buildings constructed in a much more rudimentary style than the rest of the site. The plaza was possibly used as a marketplace. Exiting the plaza by the right (east) side of Edificio 16, you come upon the first two of the 17 **ball courts** that have been discovered at Tajín. The courts are formed by two low structures that create the alley of the court. Glyphs found here seem to associate them with Venus, and thus possibly with Quetzalcoátl, a divine figure often linked with that planet. Turn left (west) to see the **Southern Ball Court**, formed by buildings 5 and 6, fascinating in that it has six relief panels (one at each corner of the court and two at its center). The reliefs are of excellent quality, showing in elaborate detail some of the ritualistic ceremonies of the game. Perhaps the most gruesome image, the **northeast panel**, shows one player seated, while other players surround him – one holding him, while another thrusts a knife into his heart. To the right, what appears to be a ruler watches the scene unfold, while to the left, the upper body of the Death God can be seen emerging from a jar (look for a skeletal face with a beak-like mouth). A second Death God can be seen descending straight down atop the victim. The scene is thought to represent the destiny of the captain of the losing ball team. If the northeast panel is gruesome, the **south center panel** is perhaps the most scandalous. The panel shows the rain god in a crouched position, performing an act of genital blood letting. The blood is shown leaving the genitals in a thick flow, spraying onto the head of a human (wearing a fish mask) sitting in a pool of water.

The **southwest panel** shows an eagle (or possibly a priest dressed as an eagle) resting on top of a human figure lying on his back. The two figures to each side are performers – a drum player and a person shaking a rattle. On the left, another Death God can be seen.

THE BALLGAME: A GAME OF LIFE & DEATH

The object of the ball game was to hit a hard rubber ball (similar to a bowling ball) through a ring that was attached high upon one of the court's side walls. To make a difficult task almost impossible, players were not allowed to use their hands or feet – hips, torsos, and knees were used instead (thick padding was worn on the knees and hips for protection). The grand finale: the captain of the losing team was apparently sacrificed, making it a game to the death.

Exiting the west (left) side of the ball court, turn right (north), towards one of the last buildings constructed at Tajín. Built during the

sixth century, the **Pyramid of the Niches**, shown at left, is visually the most unusual structure at Tajín, and the building long-used to represent the site. It is stunning. Though not very tall (a mere 60 feet/20 m), the building still seems majestic. Flying cornices, and 365 niches, one against another, decorate its four sides, catching the sun in an interplay of light and shadow that is fascinating (and makes for great pictures!). There is one niche for each day of the solar year. Originally, the pyramid would have had a sanctuary at its top, and would have been painted red. It also appears that its single staircase was not included in the original design, and was added at a later date. If you look at the staircase, you can see that it is not centered, and truly appears to almost be plastered on top of the building. In fact, archaeologists have discovered that the façade's design continues unbroken beneath the staircase.

FLYING CORNICES

These are used on a lot of the buildings at Tajín, and they're what makes many of the buildings look as though they belong in the Orient. The cornice is that horizontal molding along the top of some buildings; at Tajín, you will see that there is more than one stacked on top of another, each coming out a little farther than the last. The Pyramid of the Niches exhibits this architectural feature beautifully – each row of niches is topped by a flying cornice.

On the right (south) side of the plaza (if facing away from the front of the Pyramid of the Niches), are Buildings 2 and 5 – the former having been built into the latter. **Building 5**, a pyramid in the platform of Building 2, is interesting in that on its front (eastern side), before the final staircase to the top, sits a monument – **Stela**, which is a beautifully carved stone possibly depicting the God Tajín. The plaza which the god faces is called the **Plaza Menor** (Minor Plaza), and was probably used for religious ceremonies.

Heading through the Plaza Menor (east) away from Building 5, you pass by **Building 3**, a pyramid with a staircase similar to the Pyramid of the Niches. It is adorned by six platforms, whose use is not clear – possibly altars or seating areas for the Plaza Menor. Continuing east, you head past another pyramid, Building 23, before encountering the somewhat ruined remains of **Building 22**, a long structure, still climbable, offering a great vantage point of the Zona Central (Central Zone) and a nice spot to take a breather.

At this point you've seen the most-visited portion of the site, and if you're out of steam, you can leave without regrets. For those remaining, the last two must-see sections are to the north, uphill just behind the Pyramid of the Niches. From Building 22, head to the northwest, through the **Northern Ball Court** (dated around AD 600, much earlier than the Southern Court. It is much shorter than full size, calling into question whether or not it was actually used. As in the Southern Ball Court, here there are detailed reliefs visible at each corner, as well as one on each side in the court's center.

As you continue uphill and to the right (north), you'll pass other ruins, and quickly come to the upper (somewhat secluded) terrace known as **El Tajín Chico** (the Small Tajín). Most of the buildings here were used as housing quarters for the upper class, many were painted, and some rooms at one time had murals. The structures are very interesting architecturally. Surprisingly, a mixture closely resembling a lightweight version of modern-day concrete seems to have been used in the construction of many of the ceilings, allowing for huge slabs of concrete (as in **Structure C**, AD 800), a technique not seen in many other sites. **Structure D** in the complex has a tunnel that heads back downhill into the section known as **La Gran Xicalcoliuhqui**, a walled plaza associated with the divine figure Quetzalcóatl, containing two ball courts.

Continuing uphill and to the west of El Tajín Chico, you'll come upon the highest section at the site, dominated by the huge (somewhat ruined) complex of **Las Columnas** (The Building of the Columns). Its namesake, the huge columns flanking the main stairway, are covered with reliefs depicting gods, rituals, and people (specifically, the deified ruler 13 Rabbit, often seen as the embodiment of Quetzalcóatl). If you don't have a chance to make it here in person, you can view some pieces of the columns in the museum at the entrance to the site. They were moved to protect them from vandalism.

■ Festivals & Events

If you want a real taste of culture, schedule your visit during Papantla's annual (religiously-based) **Corpus Christi Festival**. For a little more than a week around the end of May and beginning of June, the village is in action and in full decorated regalia. Food, drinks, music, parades, dances, and performances of all types fill the streets. During the same time, the village celebrates the **Festival de Vainilla**, an aromatic event honoring the town's famous, beloved pod. This region is one of a few places in the world where it grows naturally. Entertainment during festivities focuses mainly around the *zócalo*.

The Dances

During festivities or special events, you're likely to see elaborately costumed local dances – an experience that will give you a real sense of where you are. Besides the **Danza del Volador**, there are others that are often performed.

LA DANZA DE LOS NEGRITOS. The dance of the little black ones is believed to have been adapted from magic rituals of black slaves brought to México by the Spanish. It is believed that the Totonacs, observing the African ritual (which was supposedly meant to cure a boy who had been bitten by a snake) learned and then imitated it, adding their own cultural touches. The result is a beautiful dance, today performed mainly in the states of Veracruz, Oaxaca, and Puebla. A man dressed as a woman (the *maringuilla*), with a group of dancers (all in colorfully decorated black pants and hats paired with white shirts), performs a series of steps and shouts to the accompaniment of a violin and a guitar.

LA DANZA DE LOS MOROS Y CRISTIANOS. After the expulsion of the Moors from the Iberian Peninsula, the Spanish set about teaching others of their triumph over the infidels – as much to honor their victory as to spread Christianity. The dance of the Moors and the Christians was one outcome – a reenactment of the Christian victory. Once again, the Totonacs observed and imitated the dance, making it their own, to the great pleasure of the Spanish.

SANTIAGUEROS. Yet another reminder for the indigenous groups that they dare not separate from the new religion the Spanish were bringing in, was the *santiagueros*, a variation of the Dance of the Moors and the Christians. This dance, however, features the patron saint of the soldiers of Cortés – the apostle Santiago, who fights and defeats the Moors, converting them to Christianity.

LOS GUAGUAS. The prehispanic dance of the *guaguas* (which in the Totonac language means *guacamaya* (macaw), is a beautiful fertility ritual by several dancers dressed in vivid costumes complete with plumes, to the accompaniment of a reed flute and a drum.

■ Shopping

Looking for that souvenir for those you left at home? Papantla is the place to buy all things vanilla – the Totonacs harvested vanilla for a long time before it was discovered by Spanish Conquistador Hernán Cortés, who introduced it to the rest of the world. At **Mercado Hidalgo** on the northeast corner of the *zócalo* (opposite the church), you'll find everything from pure vanilla (90 pesos for one liter, 60 pesos for a half-liter), to figurines made out of vanilla beans, vanilla pods, and vanilla liqueur.

If you don't know much about vanilla, you may be somewhat surprised to find out that it actually comes from a type of orchid. The market vendors sell the orchid's seedpods, which have have been heated and dried for several months, turning them into the long, dark brown, thin beans that you see in the stalls. Toss out the idea of buying and saving the pods to grow the plant later. Apparently, orchids are notoriously difficult to grow from seed. Without the curing process, it lacks the vanilla odor and flavor completely. Surprised at the price of those pods? Vanilla is the second most expensive spice in the world (behind saffron) – but worth it (my pods still have my drawers smelling wonderful).

The market also has other must-buy items, such as beautiful handmade regional clothing, postcards, and hats. **Mercado Juárez**, next to the church, is more of a food market, but comes alive at night with vendors selling knick-knacks such as bracelets and necklaces.

■ Nightlife

Small village nightlife, here as anywhere, mainly involves heading down to the *zócalo* for a stroll, people watching, and eating some ice cream. Here, the backdrop for such a thing is beautiful – the church is lit up at night, the kiosk is filled with the sounds of people having a good time, and on a cloudless night, stars fill the sky.

■ Where to Stay

The best-priced rooms are likely to disappear fast during holidays and festivals; plan your trip so you can stop by the hotel early to get your pick of rooms.

On the *zócalo*, **Hotel Tajín**, ☎ 784-842-1623, 104 José de J. Nuñez, literally only a few steps away from the cathedral, is surprisingly low-priced considering the quality of the rooms, level of service, and friendliness of the staff. They have very clean rooms with cable TV, ceiling fans, and even a little bit of character. Add about 100 pesos to the room price for air-conditioning. In the mornings, the soft chime of church bells combined with the chirping of hundreds of birds welcoming the daylight add a country charm to the stay. In some of the back rooms, you might even be able to turn off your alarm and rise to the crows of the neighbor's rooster. $

The fairly new **Hotel Provincia Express**, ☎ 784-842-1645 (103 Enriquez) is on the north side of the zócalo (across from the church), and offers good service, and clean rooms with cable TV and air-conditioning. $$

HOTEL PRICE CHART	
Rates are per room based on double occupancy. Rates lower if single occupancy or sharing a bed. Higher rates on holidays.	
$	US $10-$20
$$	US $21-$40
$$$	US $41-$60
$$$$	US $61-$80
$$$$$	US $81-$125
	Over US $125

At the corner of 20 de Noviembre and Oliva, two lo-o-o-ong blocks from the zócalo (the uphill walk makes a normal block seem to go on forever), **Hotel Totonacapan**, ☎ 784-842-1220, offers nice rooms, though rather steeply priced compared to other nearby hotels. Though lacking character, rooms are clean, air-conditioned, and include cable TV. $$$

■ Where to Eat

During the evening hours, the locals pack **Restaurante Sorrado**, a café-style restaurant right in the zócalo on Ave. Enriquez. The restaurant serves traditional Mexican food as well as some regional specialties, including mariscos (shellfish), pescados (fish), and acamayas (a type of crawfish). $

DINING PRICE CHART	
Price per person for an entrée, not including beverage or tip.	
$	Under US $5
$$	US $5-$10
$$$	US $10+

Next to Restaurante Sorrado on Ave. Enriquez, and a bit more upscale, is the **Plaza Pardo**. The restaurant/bar has a much more romantic mood, with tables on a second floor balcony overlooking the zócalo, dim lighting, and a huge menu. Options seem unlimited, with everything from tacos to seafood to burgers or sandwiches, and prices are reasonable, with a filet mignon running around 65 pesos, and beef and fowl dishes between 35 and 60 pesos. $

Though I don't recommend it all the time, one option if you are in the mood for something different, is to go to the market – **Mercado Hidalgo** (at the corner of Reforma and Jose Azueta on the zócalo). Mornings and nights you can find the local women selling tamales,

The *tamale de pulacle* is a tasty regional specialty that may be easier on your stomach as it contains no meat. It's made with different vegetables, including onions, tomatoes, and beans.

Costa Esmeralda

There is no mistaking it. When you hit the jewel of the Gulf Coast, the more than 19 miles/30 km of coastline that make up the Costa Esmeralda, you will know it in an instant. Even if you didn't notice that the highway had crept out to the ocean, delivering gorgeous views of blue water and miles of sand, with intoxicating smells of salt and sun, and refreshing sea breezes blowing through your car window, there is no escaping the rows of huge palm trees that suddenly spring up alongside the road, marking your entrance into this "Emerald Coast."

This stretch of highway is marked by a number of villages filled with local seafood restaurants, vendors plying their ocean-oriented wares, and entrepreneurial kids selling local fruits. Between villages, one side of the road is marked by fields, cow pastures, palm trees, and the occasional hotel, while the other side boasts an endlessv stream of accommodations, all with oceanfront views and direct beach access. And, to the great delight of campers and RVers everywhere, there is a bigger selection of camping sites in these few miles than anywhere else in the Gulf region.

Except in the summer, things here stay relatively quiet and empty, and you can find yourself enjoying long expanses of beach in solitude, with your pick of trees to hang your hammock. Be sure, however, to plan your visit in advance during holidays, as just about everything fills up fast then. Even the buses can be sold out days in advance.

■ Getting There

By Car

The Costa Esmeralda, about 19 miles/30 km southeast of Papantla, extends from the mouth of the Río Tecolutla down to the seaside village of Nautla, on a narrow strip of Highway 180. There is a toll bridge at the Barra de Tecolutla (22 pesos), as you enter, and another at Nautla (17 pesos) as you leave. **Tecolutla** is on the north bank of the Río Tecolutla, where it pours into the sea. The town can be reached by heading east off Highway 180 at Gutiérrez Zamora (approximately 11 km/seven miles).

By Bus

There is an ADO bus station a little after the start of the Costa Esmeralda with a variety of hotel options next door or across the street (beachfront). All the buses here are *de paso*, meaning that they originate elsewhere and are only passing through this particular stop. So keep in mind that, especially during holiday-time, buses are likely to fill up quickly.

Adventures

On Water

Fishing

Ready to catch that hundred-pounder? Tecolulta's waters are filled with huge *sábalo* (aka tarpon or silver king), a fact that locals and outsiders alike rejoice in with the village's annual **International Sábalo Fishing Tournament**. If you're interested in trying your hand at catching the biggest, heaviest fish (most weigh at least 130 pounds, with winners around 190 pounds), the fishing club can direct you to boats and equipment available for rent (1,350 pesos to 1,800 pesos for a full day). If you come with your *own* boat, the club does have facilities to accommodate boats up to 40 feet. The event usually takes place in May, and hosts around 200 participants. For more information, contact the **Club de Pesca Deportiva El Sábalo, A.C.**, at Km 7½ on the Gtz-Zamora/Tecolutla Highway; www.sabalo.com.mx.

If you're more into a relaxed version of fishing – such as just dropping a pole in the water, without pressure (fishing as it *should* be), Tecolutla's waterfront has plenty of launches (many of them belonging to fishermen) that will take you to the best fishy waters for a rental fee.

Boat Launches

At **Tecolutla** you can find boats ready to take you out on guided tours of the local *manglares* (mangroves) and marshlands of the Río Tecolutla, giving you a chance to take in the local flora and wildlife. For the most part you'll see a variety of birds (Tecolutla actually means "place of the owls" in Náhuatl, the Aztec language, so don't be surprised if you see a few), crabs, turtles, and possibly even a crocodile or two. You can also find some launches in the village of **Casitas**, at the southern end of the Costa Esmeralda. Many boats ply the river, passing through town and out to the ocean. Boats there will take you into the marshlands of La Ciénaga del Fuerte, from where you'll have a chance to see the local flora and wildlife (mainly birds… and fishermen).

Beaches

What has made this section of coastline so popular to holiday-goers are the miles of sand and ocean – not overdeveloped and easily accessible. The beach is pretty, with soft brownish sand, tons of coconut and palm trees, and attractive bluish-green waters, which can get somewhat rough with strong winds, but on a calm day are gentle enough to bathe in. If you're not staying the night, there are a few public access points that are easy to spot; one is between Km 84 and 85. You'll definitely want to walk for a bit, and there is plenty of beach for that, so be sure to bring a hat and sunscreen, as there is not much shade.

It's not hard to miss the next most popular activity here – relaxing. String up a hammock between a couple of palms, and slow down to the Mexican pace. Of course, between siestas, the ocean awaits; if you don't have floats or watertoys for the kids, stop by the village of Casitas to pick something up. You'll be shoulder-to-shoulder with families during holidays, but off-season the noise dies down, the beaches clear, and hammock space is abundant.

Archaeological Discoveries

To the southwest of Nautla, right outside the village of Misantla, lie the remains of a place half-shrouded by time and jungle – the Totonaca city of **Paxil**. The *Popol Vuh* (the sacred book describing the creation story) mentions a location called Paxil-Tlalocan in relation to maize – quite possibly this site. Although there are only a few buildings that have been recovered so far, what can be seen is remarkably beautiful: stone ruins sit forgotten amid lush green foliage that seems barely kept at bay. You'll feel as though you're the first person to have discovered the site and, indeed, you'll be one of few who have been here. Only a few excavation and conservation efforts have been undertaken, and visitors are few and far between. The site has a couple of small pyramids (one whose platform and staircase is accessible through an interior tunnel), many vegetation-covered mounds that are, in fact, ruins overtaken by nature, and two ball courts. The city was occupied between 450 and 1500 AD and was at its height during the Postclassic period.

The ruins are right outside the village of Misantla. Ask in the village for walking directions. To get to Misantla from Highway 180 and the Costa Esmeralda, take a right onto Highway 129 right after the village of Casitas. At Martinez de la Torre (about 30 km/18.6 miles down), turn onto a smaller road heading southeast another 30 km towards Misantla.

About 18 miles south of Nautla on Highway 180, right past the town of Vega de Alatorre, is **Las Higueras**, a small archaeological site famous for its murals. The one pyramid from which the murals were recovered is being restored, but is still not much to look at. Other than that, there are a few tree-covered mounds, and some displays in the site's museum. The larger sections of the mural are in Xalapa's Museo de Antropología (see page **).

Cultural & Eco-Travel Excursions

Turtle Preserve

The only place in the world where you can find the nesting ground of the endangered tortuga-lora (*Lepidochelys kempi*) is in a portion of México's Gulf Coast. Tecolutla sits at the end of that zone. There is an effort to try to get a marine conservation center set up here; in the meantime, a local ecologist has dedicated himself to their protection – patrolling the grounds and educating others.

■ Festivals & Events

What would compel you to make the largest candy that you possibly could? And then, what would it taste like? Well, you can find out at the annual **Coconut Festival** held in Tecolutla each February, when villagers get together in a celebration which, oddly enough, centers around the making of one huge piece of coconut candy. Word has it that the candy has even won a place in the *Guinness Book of Records*. It's called a *cocada,* made mainly from coconut and sugar, but normally *not* in this gigantic size.

■ Where to Stay

There are a wide range of options to choose from, starting in Tecolutla, which has a huge number of hotels ranging from lower to higher budget. Along the Costa Esmeralda, hotels line the oceanfront side of the road (be sure to check the rooms, as during peak weeks upkeep in some places can sometimes slide). Farther down, you'll start to see a variety of options for campers – at least a dozen

HOTEL PRICE CHART	
Rates are per room based on double occupancy. Rates lower if single occupancy or sharing a bed. Higher rates on holidays.	
	US $10-$20
$	US $21-$40
$$	US $41-$60
$$$	US $61-$80
$$$$	US $81-$125
$$$$$	Over US $125

camping and RV spots have sprung up, mostly on the southern end of the coastal strip.

Right before La Guadalupe, where Highway 180 hits the beginning of the Emerald Coast, is **Hotel Playa Riachuelos**, ☎ 784-888-6476, situated on the oceanfront, a you catch your first glimpse of the coast's palm trees. It has a number of small, simple, but clean rooms with hot water and fan, as well as a pretty site for tent camping. Boat launches and fishing excursions can be found here as well. $

In Tecolutla, in front of the beach on Calle Murillo Vidal esq. Orquidea s/n, is **Hotel Aldana**, ☎ 766-846-0302, a nice hotel offering clean rooms with a/c, color TV, and guest parking. $

Where an address is listed as s/n, that means sin numero; in other words, there is no street number.

The **Bungalows Mar Bella**, ☎ 232-321-0014 at Km 85 on Highway 180, offers some clean villas with kitchens and a/c. They also have a pool and are by the ocean. $

One of the best hotels in Tecolutla, the large **Hotel Balneario Tecolutla**, ☎ 766-846-0011, on Calle Matamoros s/n, offers good rooms (some with views), parking, a restaurant, and two pools fronted by a row of palm trees (on the other side of which the ocean beckons). Standard rooms have fans; air-conditioning costs about 120 pesos extra. $$$

Camping & RV Sites

On the oceanfront side of Highway 130 at Km 86 is **Hotel Playa Paraiso**, ☎ 232-321-0044, which has lots of RV spaces and hookups, as well as spots for tent campers. Though a little bit higher-priced than other campsites, it offers a wider range of amenities than elsewhere, including tennis courts, pools, and a restaurant.

Farther south down Highway 130, between Km 82 and 83 on the oceanfront side of the road, is **El Corsario Trailer Park/RV Center**, ☎ 232-321-0001, catering mainly to RVs. It has full hookups, a pool, and offers some of the cheaper prices in the area. Right next door is **Playa Oriente El Pino Trailer Park**, ☎ 232-321-0016, which has pleasant open grassy areas perfect for camping, some with electricity. The site also includes a few full hookup spaces for RVs.

Almost at the end of the Costa Esmeralda is the **Trailer Park Neptuno**, ☎ 232-321-0102, a popular spot between Km 86 and 87. It's a very pretty site on the oceanfront side, with a couple of pools shaded by *palapas*. It caters mainly to RVs, with a number of full hookups.

For Under US $10

On the oceanfront side, between Km 88 and 89 (almost at the village of Casitas), is the **Casitas del Tajín** (no phone), a small site, which in addition to renting cabanas, has a pool and camping spaces, some of which have full hookups for RVs. Next door, the **Hotel CocoLoco**, ☎ 232-321-0127, is a small site with a tiny pool and some spaces dotted with coconut trees to set up camp. It caters mainly to campers.

■ Where to Eat

As you drive along this portion of Highway 180, it will quickly become clear that the specialty of the restaurants is seafood, most of which you can bet has been caught by the local fishermen. The most popular seems to be shrimp (especially the *acamaya*, or river shrimp), *robalo* (sea bass), and crab's claws (you'll see stands set up along the road with hundreds of the little arms). In Tecolutla, don't miss the local shrimp soup (*huatape*), or the fish *tamales*.

Tlapacoyan

The pictures you might see of Veracruz, showcasing rafters in deep canyons paddling through bright shafts of sunlight and crystal-calm waters, are taken on the Río Filobobos near Tlapacoyan (Tlah-pah-KO-yahn). It's a town surrounded by rivers, a couple of local adventure outfitters, and a pretty church. There are also two waterfalls and two archaeological zones nearby. All are probably better seen by raft. (That's right, I did say *all*!)

THE FILOBOBOS RIVER

Upper Filobobos (Alto Filo): A fast-moving deep section of the river that starts up high, runs from Cuetzapotitlan to the El Filo bridge. Class IV to V.

Middle Filobobos (Filo – El Encanto): This is the section that goes past the ruins of Cuajilote and Vega de la Peña. Class II to Class III.

Lower Filobobos (El Encanto-Palmilla): This is the section to visit the El Encanto waterfalls. Class II to Class III.

Remember, class levels change, usually becoming more difficult during the rainy season.

■ Adventures

Rafting

If you were to go rafting anywhere, this is the place to do it – the scenery is beautiful, the weather is great, and there are plenty of adventure outfitters who run the rivers. In the Nautla river, on the Bobos section (just south of Tlapacoyan), you'll find an opportunity you're unlikely to find elsewhere – a chance to raft right past ancient ruins. A raft trip through the Filobobos River here takes you to the sites of **El Cuajilote** and **Vega de la Peña** (see below). Depending on the guide and kind of trip you sign up for, you can raft, get out and explore, and get transportation back to your base city in one day. Or you can make it a longer affair, check out the ruins, camp on the banks of the river, and spend Day Two exploring the beautiful nearby canyons and waterfalls.

As for those waterfalls, they can be a trip of their own. The **El Encanto Falls** can only be reached by water. When you get there, you find a spectacular canyon known as El Encanto, with a 50-m (164-foot) waterfall. Nearby, another section of the river contains the **Tomata Falls**, 30 m (98.4 feet) high.

Trips are fairly affordable. Basic day trips start out under US $50 per person, and most outfitters have a wide selection of packages to choose from, including cabin stays or camping, and single-day to multi-day trips. Most of the runs here go from Class II to Class IV; find out from your guide which is most appropriate for you.

Outfitters

You can find some outfitters in the town of Tlapacoyan itself, as well as a number of others who do day trips. To start, you can check with:

Adventurec

They offer a number of options for rafting, including single-day to three-day trips, the waterfalls, and the ruins; they also have horseback riding trips. The campsite is four km (2½ miles) from Tlapacoyan on the highway towards Martínez de la Torre. Their offices are in Puebla, and can be reached at ☎ 222-231-2725, www.aventurec.com.

Selvazul

Offers a range of rafting trips, to the ruins and falls, and on other rivers as well (Class II to Class V trips). Camp on the highway between Tlapacoyan and Martínez de la Torre. Offices are in Puebla, ☎ 222-237-4887, www.selvazul.com.

Exciting México

Has longer trips that leave on set schedules, and can arrange everything, including transportation from the airport (based in México City, Félix Cuevas 224-B, Col del Valle). Take a look at their website to contact them and see what's next. www.excitingMéxico.com.

Veraventuras

Offers trips down the Filobobos to the ruins and falls, as well as trips on other rivers. You can pick a single-day outing, or a multi-day package that includes meals and trips on different rivers. They prefer an advance reservation of two weeks. Based in Xalapa at Santos Degollado 81 Int. 8. Contact them at ☎ 0800-712-6572 or 228-818-9779; www.veraventuras.com.mx.

WHITEWATER RAFTING CLASSES

Class I: Easy. Slow-moving waters, no rocks to negotiate – could you hold my paddle while I write in my journal?

Class II: Novice. A little bit of movement, some waves, maybe you'll even see a rock in the wide river that you'll have to avoid.

Class III: Intermediate. *Now* we're talking! There's turning and weaving and moving – and you'll probably even get wet! Can you swim? What an adventure to tell everyone at home!

Class IV: Advanced. Don't fall in, you'll probably get hurt! Fast, obstructed, powerful – I hope you know what you're doing!

Class V: Expert. Can a raft *really* go down there?

Class VI: Off-the-charts. Turn around and walk the other way! Even the experts don't try them.

Archaeological Discoveries

Right next to the Filobobos River, half shrouded in jungle, you'll find the iguana-overrun ruins of **El Cuajilote** (200-900 AD), a site more frequented by rafters than hikers because of its remote location. There are a number of buildings here, including a ball-court, a huge plaza surrounded by buildings (where phallic clay figures were recovered), and a smaller plaza, where archaeologists identified, then re-buried, a *temazcal* (steambath)). It was inhabited at different times by different groups, but it's not known who originally founded the site, although it was apparently dedicated to fertility rituals. You can get here (with some difficulty) on foot, but be careful not to get lost. From Tlapacoyan, head down the road south to the village of Santiago, where you should ask directions. The site is a few km south along the river.

A little farther downstream is **Vega de la Peña**, another site easily accessed by river. The tree-covered mounds include a palace and the Temple de la Grecas, also known as Xicalcoliuhqui, in reference to its architectural design. The site flourished between 900 and 1500 AD, and is believed to have been a tributary of the Aztecs.

*So much rafting! The most popular rivers to raft in Veracruz are the **Pescados River** (Jalcomulco vicinity), **Actopan River** (Actopan vicinity), and the **Filobobos River** (Tlapacoyan vicinity). Check with an adventure outfitter!*

Along the Coast: Villa Rica to Cardel

■ Ruins of Quiahuiztlan

If the weather is nice, head to the ancient Totonaca burial ground near the coast known as Quiahuiztlan. To get there, take Highway 180 north from the Puerto de Veracruz about 62 km (38.4 miles); right after the village of El Farallón, on the left you'll see a dirt road heading towards a hill known as the Cerro de Metates. There you'll find Quiahuiztlan. There are great views from the top and, though dozens of tombs were discovered here, don't worry about being bothered by unsettled spiritual energy – many of the tombs that were found had holes drilled into them to allow the soul to leave. It's a gorgeous spot. Open Tues.-Sun., 9 am-5 pm.

■ Spanish Settlements

When the Spanish first established a settlement in México on Good Friday, 1519, it was actually in an area slightly north of the port of

Veracruz in a spot whose name leaves little doubt as to its founders – **La Villa Rica de la Vera Cruz** (The Rich Town of the True Cross). The only evidence left of that long-ago arrival in the village is the ruinous remains of a church, still decaying by the ocean. La Villa Rica sits just west of Quiahuiztlan.

In an attempt to improve their settlement (the first location was strategically horrible), the Spanish moved the settlement of La Villa Rica de la Vera Cruz from it's original spot to the mouth of the Río Huitzilapan; today, it's the village known as **La Antigua**. What is left of this second settlement is open to visitors, and is an interesting step back in time – specifically with a visit to the old Spanish *Aduana*, referred to as the *Casa de Cortés*. It still stands thanks to a thick network of roots and vines that have become part of the structure. Nearby you'll also find the ruins of *La Ermita del Rosario* (a church), and the *Ceiba de la Noche Feliz,* a large tree Cortés is said to have tied his boats to. The Spanish settlement of Villa Rica left this location and moved a third time in the year 1600. La Antigua is about 28 km (17.4 miles) north of the Puerto de Veracruz, and can be reached from downtown by 2nd class bus (ask the driver where you should get out – you will have to walk a little), by taxi, or on Highway 180 heading north.

■ Sulfur Springs of Tinajitas

On Highway 180 just after you pass La Mancha (if heading north from Veracruz), is the town of Farallón don Carlos, where you will find a lagoon. From here, if you want to get *way* off the beaten track, you can turn left (west) away from the coast, and head a short way up the mountains towards Tinajitas, where you will find a natural hot sulfur spring.

■ Birding in La Mancha

There is a coastal research center, known as the Centro de Investigaciones Costeras La Mancha (CICOLMA) at the edge of the Laguna La Mancha, a signal that this is a protected ecological area. **Bird watching** here is excellent during migratory season, though you'll have to put up with few services to do so, so come prepared. To get to La Mancha, from the Puerto de Veracruz, head north along Highway 180, past Cardel. Just past San Isidro on the right, you'll see the Laguna La Mancha and a road heading right (east) towards the ocean and CICOLMA.

Ruins of Zempoala (Cempoala)

This archaeological site is unforgetable, not for its setting (though it *is* nice), but for the huge role it played in its own – and México's history. The Totonaca ruler of Zempoala, Chicomeácatl Quauhtlaebana, invited Hernan Cortés to his (this) city, where the two hit it off, discussing, for the most part, politics. Cortés, taking advantage of the ruler's dislike of Moctezuma, formed an alliance with the Totonac leader, enlisting his aid (including a donation of hundreds of warriors) in a march against the Aztecs. Eventually, the Spaniards moved against, and defeated, the Totonac Indians as well. Today, there are empty ruins left of what was a flourishing city (postclassic period) of 30,000 people. The buildings are unique, having been constructed from river-rocks collected from the many nearby rivers.

The **Templo Mayor** (Major Temple) is straight ahead and at the very back away from the entrance (at the far north of the site). It's a long structure of 13 platforms constructed during three or four different periods, the oldest part of which dates back to the late 13th century; originally, it would have been brightly painted. A 90-foot staircase leads up the platforms, but access has been roped of for conservation purposes. At the top, there is a three-room structure, probably used for religious purposes.

The **Templo de las Chimeneas** (Temple of the Chimneys) is a seven-platform structure just to the west of the Templo Mayor, easily identified by a number of hollow columns at its base, which were at one time believed to be chimneys. Stairways lead to the top, where at one time there was a temple. It is believed that when the Totonac ruler invited Cortés to Zempoala, this is where they joined forces.

The **Gran Pirámide** (Great Pyramid) is at the far west side of the site, is a structure dedicated to the God of the Sun.. On its eastern front, two staircases rise to the top, a signature style of the time. Adjacent to the north, you'll see the remains of the **Templo de la Luna**.

When you leave the zone, don't miss the **Edificio de "Las Caritas"** (Building of the Little Faces) just outside of the site itself, on the eastern boundary; the building at one point had stucco skulls. Then head into the *town* of Zempoala (across the road from the site), and you will find the circular remains of the **Edificio del Dios Viento** (Building of the God of the Wind), shown above.

To get to Zempoala, about 40 km (24.8 miles) north of the Puerto de Veracruz, you'll want head north on Highway 180. Just past Cardel after the village of El Arenal, you'll see a gas station on your right, here turn east off the Highway onto a smaller road heading towards the *town* of Zempoala, where you'll find the archaeological site of Zempoala. Open daily, 9 am-5:30 pm).

■ Dunes in Chachalacas

Say it three times fast – Chachalacas, Chachalacas, Chachalacas. Yep, it's a tongue-twister all right. It's also a spot that has gained some popularity thanks to its huge brown sand dunes from which fun-seekers can jump, speed, and roar over to their heart's content. The beach is right in front of the town of Chachalacas, a place that has some accommodations, and a number of restaurants, but thankfully, not too very many tourists. Most restaurants are right in front of the ocean, and serve a delicious river fish called mojarra, caught in the nearby Río Actopan. A little up the coast to the north are the aforementioned dunes. Here you can find vendors renting **motorbuggies** for speeding around the dunes, **paraglides** to sail over them, and **boats** to take you out onto the river. To get to Chachalacas – the beach and the town, head north of the Puerto de Veracruz on Highway 180 until you reach Cardel, from which you'll take the short road past Ursulo Galván to the coast.

> *Veracruz is one of the world's premier spots for birdwatching! During the migratory season (September to November) you'll see millions of raptors flying through the coastal wetlands near the Puerto de Veracruz.*

■ Birdwatching in Cardel

In some months, the trees along the coast are filled with noise and feathers as millions of migrating birds settle for a brief rest. The town of Cardel sits right in the middle of the route, so you will see the skies filled with movement – most of which are **birds of prey** (hawks, eagles, and falcons). So many pass by each day that the migration is called a "River of Raptors," so many birds that you can't count them – or can you? During the peak migrating season between September and November, experts from Pronatura, trained in identification and counting methods, perch on the rooftop of the Hotel Bienvenido and commence counting the birds during Pronatura's annual registry. The Hotel Bienvenido, ☎ 296-962-0777, is at 1 José Cardel Sur, in the center of Cardel. Cardel is 35 km (21.7 miles) north of Veracruz on Highway 180 (just where the tollway ends).

Veracruz

Veracruz, like New Orleans, is renowned for its festive atmosphere, infused with music, dancing, and food. An evening walk through the *zócalo* is an assault on the senses: a wild cacophony of intermingled sounds as instruments are played into the night for restaurant goers. Street performers compete with each other for your attention, and locals pair off to join in on the sexy, Cuban-influenced *danzón*. In the daytime, you relax in an outdoor café, sipping the local coffee, or head to the beach for sun, laughing and food. And Veracruz has its own hedonistic over-the-top celebration – Carnaval, the largest, most outrageous in all of México.

The locals are slightly darker-skinned than elsewhere in México due to a mixture of African blood dating to the arrival of Spanish slave ships from Africa. The people are laid-back and fun-loving.

The Spanish Conquistador Hernan Córtes landed here with Spain's first major expedition, some remnants of which still survive. Divers can explore old Spanish galleon wrecks, the curious can visit Córtes' actual landing spot, and the imaginative will envision the old fortress defending the city from the pirate attacks that long plagued it.

The port has great music, an interesting history, and good museums to explore. If you really want to enjoy Veracruz however, take some time to follow your ears and nose wherever they lead you – you'll find that the best experiences here are found simply by wandering about.

■ Orientation & Practicalities

Follow the mountains to their base, and keep going until you reach the ocean – that's where you'll find the "City of the Dead" (as the Aztecs affectionately dubbed it), though I can't think of a city that's more living and breathing than this one. Today, the city sits on the Gulf, nestled against La Antigua to the north, and Alvarado to the south, pulsing with music and merriment.

Emergency Services: Hospital, ☎ 222-931-1212; Red Cross – Veracruz, ☎ 229-937-5500, Boca del Río, ☎ 229-986-0027.

Exchanging Money: Once you arrive, you can change or withdraw money at any of the many banks or money exchange offices found throughout the *zócalo* and *malecón*; exchange rates are all pretty comparable. If you arrive late in the day and nothing is open, many hotels will exchange money, although you're likely to lose a few dollars in the exchange. The American Express office (American Express Reptur) is at Aquiles Serdán 690-B, ☎ 229-931-0838; they're open Mon.-Fri., 9 am-5 pm.

Internet Cafés: There are a number of easy-to-spot Internet cafés scattered throughout the *zócalo*, Plaza de la República, and Boca del Río. Most charge about a dollar for an hour's worth of high-speed access, are air-conditioned, have printers, and are open late on weekends.

Post Office: Drop off your postcard at the Correos y Telégrafos in the northern part of downtown on Ave. Marina Mercante. To get here from the *zócalo*, go down Miguel Lerdo de Tejada towards the harbor, and take a left at its end; the post office is next to the Aduana Maritima.

Tourist Information: The tourist office is in the *zócalo* under the archways of the Palacio Municipal. Although the staff here speaks little English, they are quite helpful and friendly, and will give you the scoop on any seasonal or temporary events happening around the city, along with a decent map, and a little booklet of information on Boca del Río.

> *There is not an American Consulate in Veracruz! In case you have an emergency, and you need their assistance, the closest is in México City, at Paseo de la Reforma, 305 Col. Cuauhtoc, ☎ 01-55-5080-2000.*

■ Getting There

By Air

Veracruz' international airport, Aeropuerto Internacional Heriberto Jara, is only about seven miles (11 km) to the west of the city's center, and offers daily nonstop flights from the United States (directly through Houston on Continental Airlines), as well as service to and from many Mexican cities (including Monterrey, Merida, and México City) on Aeroliteral, Aerocaribe, Aerocalifornia, and Aeroméxico. If you're like me and hate finding out you have a connection, take heart! The flight from México City, one of the most frequent connections, is a pleasantly short 45 minute.

By Bus

If you play your cards right, traveling by bus to Veracruz, can be a relaxing ride of luxury in a deluxe bus, since the better-than-first-class busline UNO services the city. Though the ride can be a bit long in some cases (from México City, it takes about five hours), you might just never get on a plane again if UNO has its way. The station itself is quite the opposite, and you'll want to get out of there as quickly as possible, though there is luggage storage for 18 pesos if you agree to come back within 24 hours. It's actually comprised of two adjoined hectic, hot, stressful bus terminals serviced by ADO, ADO GL, Cristóbal Colón, AU, and UNO, offering service just about anywhere you want to go. Be wary during holidays (both national and school). I learned the hard way that seats do fill fast, so make sure you've booked your reservations well in advance if your vacation falls during this time.

The terminal is a bit far from the *zócalo* (about a 20-minute walk). To get there, turn right onto Salvador Díaz Mirón as you leave the bus station; it will eventually join with Ave. Independencia, which takes you right into the heart of downtown. An easier option is to pick up a taxi or local bus heading downtown right outside the bus terminal on Salvador Díaz Mirón.

BUS TRIPS			
Destination	Bus Line	Fare	Time
Alvarado	AU	31 pesos	1 hour 5 minutes
	ADO	33 pesos	
Catemaco	AU	69 pesos	2 hours 50 minutes
	ADO	78 pesos	
Córdoba	AU	60 pesos	3 hours 40 minutes
	ADO	65 pesos	1 hour 35 minutes
Costa Esmeralda	ADO	87 pesos	2 hours 30 minutes
Matamoros	UNO	779 pesos	13 hours
	ADO	541 pesos	16 hours 10 minutes
Merida	ADO GL	621 pesos	15 hours
	ADO	543 pesos	16 hours 25 minutes
México City (TAPO)	UNO	368 pesos	5 hours 30 minutes
	ADO GL	269 pesos	5 hours 30 minutes
	ADO	232 pesos	5 hours 45 minutes
	AU	192 pesos	5 hours 45 minutes

Nautla	AU	68 pesos	2 hour 10 minutes
	ADO	78 pesos	
Oaxaca	ADO	267 pesos	6 hours 10 minutes
	AU	217 pesos	8 hours 35 minutes
	Cuenca	175 pesos	9 hours 30 minutes
Orizaba	ADO	76 pesos	2 hours 5 minutes
	AU	71 pesos	2 hours
Papantla	ADO	116 pesos	3 hours 15 minutes
Perote	AU	71 pesos	2 hours 50 minutes
Poza Rica	UNO	225 pesos	4 hours
	ADO	126 pesos	3 hours 40 minutes
	AU	113 pesos	4 hours 10 minutes
Reynosa	UNO	775 pesos	15 hours
	ADO	545 pesos	17 hours 25 minutes
San Andres Tuxtla	ADO	72 pesos	2 hours 20 minutes
San Cristóbal de las Casas	Altos	351 pesos	13 hours 45 minutes
Santiago Tuxtla	AU	58 pesos	2 hours 5 minutes
	ADO	66 pesos	
Tampico	UNO	470 pesos	8 hours
	ADO	265 pesos	8 hours 50 minutes
Tlacotalpan	ADO	51 pesos	1 hours 30 minutes
Tuxtepec	Cuenca	70 pesos	3 hours 30 minutes
	ADO	78 pesos	2 hours 20 minutes
	AU	71 pesos	2 hours 20 minutes
Tuxtla Gutiérrez	Altos	330 pesos	11 hours 45 minutes
	Maya de Oro	443 pesos	11 hours 15 minutes
Villahermosa	UNO	387 pesos	7 hours
	ADO GL	279 pesos	7 hours
	ADO	244 pesos	6 hours 10 minutes
Xalapa	ADO	55 pesos	1 hours 55 minutes
	AU	49 pesos	1 hours 55 minutes
	ADO GL	64 pesos	2 hours

By Train

The station is still there (nice for those of us who appreciate a beautiful building) but the train service is not. The downtown station until recently used to provide twice daily rides between México City and Veracruz, but unfortunately there are no current plans to resume service.

By Car

The drive from México City goes very quickly, especially now that toll roads pave much of the way, bypassing many of the local villages you previously had to stop for. Though you may raise an eyebrow at having to spend a few dollars on the 4½-hour trip, stay on the toll roads, they're worth it. From México City and points west follow toll Highway 150D east, past Puebla and Orizaba, and on up into the Puerto de Veracruz. From points along the coast, simply follow coastal toll Highway 180 towards Veracruz, or from Xalapa, follow Highway 140 south.

■ Getting Around

Car Rentals

It's very easy to get around Veracruz without renting a car – buses, taxis, and your good old feet will take you to all the nearby sights and allow you to get a feel for the atmosphere of the city. Renting a car, however, does have its advantages, especially if you plan on traveling around the region a bit, and want the freedom and flexibility you can't find on bus schedules. Many car rental agencies have offices here, including:

Avis (with counter at airport)	☎ 229-932-6032
Alamo	☎ 229-989-0531
Dollar	☎ 229-935-8808
National	☎ 229-932-8950
Hertz	☎ 229-937-4776
Europcar	☎ 229-935-2329
Lone Star Rental	☎ 229-927-0292
Powerfull Auto Rent	☎ 229-932-8573
Today's	☎ 229-935-7015

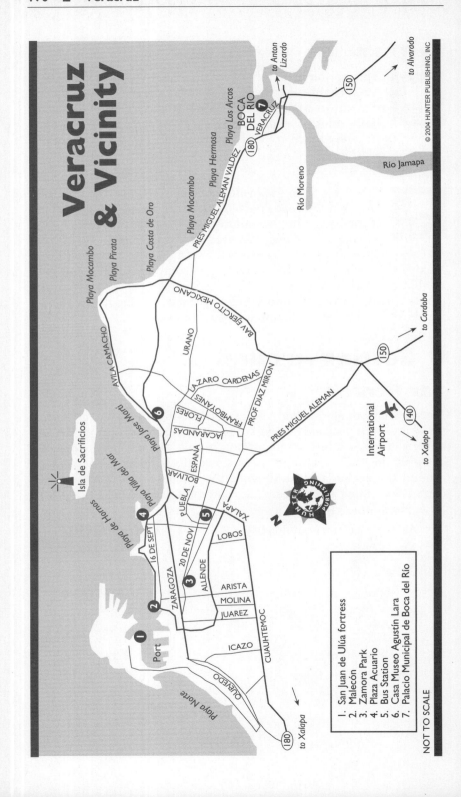

Local Transit

The local city bus is very easy to pick up, and stops just about anywhere you want to go; look at the bus windshield for your destination. For a few dollars more, you can hail any of the taxis roaming the street. Just be sure to agree on a price before yo set off.

To San Juan de Ulúa & Boca del Río

Pick up a bus to either one right in front of the long yellow building next to the Post Office. Again, check destination on window. Fare is 4.50 pesos. Trips to Boca del Río are about 25 minutes. Buses go down Zaragoza, and actually can be picked up anywhere along this street, before continuing on up Blvd. Ávila Camacho. Trips to the fortress at San Juan de Ulúa are about 10 minutes.

To Mandinga

The AU bus stops in Mandinga, as does the local bus (7.50 pesos).

■ Sightseeing

I won't deny that *Romancing the Stone* is one of my favorite movies, so when I heard that the fort scenes at the end were filmed in the **San Juan de Ulúa** fortress at the entrance to Veracruz' inner harbor, I liked the place, even before I went there. All bias aside, if you only have a limited amount of time in the city, make this old stone fortress one of your must-sees. For a few dollars, you can walk the ramparts, cross the drawbridges, climb to the rooftops, and tour the grounds on your own; or pay an extra 10 pesos for a tour guide who will give you a bit of the captivating history. It was built by the Spaniards in the 1500s to protect the harbor from pirates, then transformed into a death-trap of a prison until 1915. Tours leave when there's a full group (about every 30 minutes), and are conducted in English only if you have a large enough party.

Inside the fortress you'll find a museum with, among other things, displays of guns, a canon circa 1734, and a sample of what the fort is made out of – coral (another great spot to see this clearly is on the roof). Since there wasn't enough stone in the area, coral was collected from the ocean reefs and bound with a mixture known as *cal*. This construction material absorbs water, which explains the moisture in the chambers, which has caused stalactites to grow from many of the ceilings. Another amazing featureh is that the fortress walls range from 4½ to as much as 15 feet in some places.

Veracruz

1. Train Station
2. Telegraf Office
3. Post Office
4. Clavijero Theater
5. Palacio Municipal (Town Hall)
6. Zocalo, Plaza de Armas
7. Catedral de la Asunción
8. Mercado de Artesanías
9. Faro Venustiano Carranza (Lighthouse)
10. Casa Salvador Díaz Mirón
11. Historical Library & Archives
12. Museum of Naval History
13. Museo de la Ciudad (Town Museum)
14. Cultural Institute
15. Baluarte de Santiago fort
16. Iglesia del Cristo del Buen Viaje
17. Bus Station
18. El Acuario (Aquarium)
19. San Juan de Ulúa fortress
20. Pemex

NOT TO SCALE

So, you've heard about robbing from the rich to give to the poor? In this case, it's not Robin Hood, but one of México's legendary bandits, who was held prisoner here for many years. Jesus Arriaga, aka Chucho el Roto, was captured and moved to different prisons before ending up here. In a bizarre turn, his friend Simón Palomo helped him escape to freedom in a boat. He was free for nine years before being caught once again, at which point, the wily bandit tried another escape. This time he was caught and, in retaliation, literally beaten to death. In the front section facing the harbor, you can see the tiny coffin-like dungeon where he was kept. Prisoners at the fortress were kept in horrible dark cells with no bathrooms, and used as forced labor during the days. Many died quickly of tuberculosis and yellow fever.

Admission for students and teachers is free. This generally applies to Mexicans, but if you have credentials you might be able to talk yourself into the discount. Otherwise, it's 35 pesos for everyone else. Open Tues.-Sun., 9:30 am-5 pm. You can pick up a local bus downtown (see *Getting Around – Local Transit*).

The Veracruz coat of arms, at left, features the fortress. In addition to defending the city from pirates searching for gold, the fortress was the site of a battle against the Spanish in 1823, after Spain's refusal to accept México's declaration of independence; against the French in 1838 (the Pastry War – instigated in part by a French cook who claimed his pies were stolen); and twice against the Americans (the Mexican-American War in 1847 and an American occupation during the Mexican Revolution in 1914). Monuments throughout Veracruz commemorate these battles and refer to the port as the "Four Times Heroic City of México."

El Acuario, built in 1992, is a big attraction for Mexican tourists, as it is said to be one of the largest aquariums in México, and one of the best in all of Latin America. This is a great place to come and see what's in that dark Gulf water. The aquarium houses innumerable species native to the Gulf, including endangered sea turtles, huge sharks, colorful corals, barracuda, and teams of exotic fish. The building's centerpiece is a huge saltwater tank holding 330,000 gallons of water, where you can check out the bigger species not found in the smaller salt and fresh-water tanks. Expect to spend a couple of hours here – more like half a day if you have kids. It's in the Plaza Acuarío (shopping mall) on Blvd M. Ávila Camacho off the *malecón*. Open Mon.-Fri., 10 am-7 pm, Sat. & Sun., 9 am-7 pm; adults, 50 pesos, children, 25 pesos.

Mandinga: Time moves like molasses in this village on the edge of the lagoon of the same name. From the shore, you'll see the fishermen standing in their *cayukos* (similar to canoes), pushing themselves slowly through the water with long poles. They wear broad-rimmed hats to shield themselves from the sun, most have their shirts rolled up around their elbows, and when they finally meander over to shore, you'll see that many have bags filled with oysters. They unpack them quietly, without fanfare; that's life in Mandinga – quiet waters crowded with trees, fishermen silently maneuvering through mangroves, and a couple of restaurants serving up *really* fresh seafood. It's a great spot to go for lunch or for a boat tour, and only about 17 km (10½ miles) south of Veracruz.

Boca del Río: If you find the port a little overwhelming – too busy, too loud, too brash – then Boca del Río (Mouth of the River) is probably the place to go. A community at the south side of town on the banks of the Jamapa River, today it is basically considered a part of the port, distinguished only by the fact that you'll see the crowds thinning and the beaches becoming nicer as you head toward it. The downtown is very small, with a spotless *zócalo*, on which you'll find the Palacio Municipal and, to the west, the **Iglesia de Santa Ana**, a Colonial church built in 1776. It's a nice alternative if you want to escape the hedonism of the city; there are a few hotels here, and lots of seafood restaurants.

■ Adventures

On Foot

Town Walks

The *malecón* (boardwalk), is the place to take in the city. It extends along most of the harbor, starting at the northern end at the corner of Insurgentes, directly across the harbor from San Juan de Ulúa, and continuing a couple of miles southeast to the Playa Costa de Oro. In the daytime, a walk along its pathway rewards you with excellent photos of the fortress across the harbor, views of the port's industrial side in action as boats chug back and forth, and a chance to intermingle with locals, vendors, and tourists. The northern end is a little bit more formal, lined with public and private buildings, including the spot where the Mexican Constitution was drafted, the **Faro Venustiano Carranza** (a lighthouse). A huge statue stands outside this one-time residence of former Mexican president (1915-1920) and general, Venustiano Carranza. The building is closed to visitors. If you were wondering about the intimidating uniformed men out front, it currently is headquarters for the Tercera Zona Militar. More information on Carranza can be found in the Museo Histórico Naval. The farther you walk along the *malecón*, the more markets, plazas, hotels, restaurants, beaches, and vendors multiply. If you keep walking through this mess, you'll eventually come upon the **Plaza Acuarío** (a shopping mall where you'll find a food court, shops, and the aquarium – *see Sightseeing* above).

The next beach is the Playa Villa del Mar, followed by the Playa José Marti, where you'll find the **Casa Museo Agustín Lara** (10 am-7 pm, Tues.-Sun., 15 pesos). Continuing down the *malecón*, you eventually reach the Punta Mocambo, then, right around the bend, the Playa Costa de Oro.

In the evenings, the *malecón* becomes a popular spot to enjoy the sea breeze and sunset; a perfect place to unwind before the festivities of the night.

As for the heartbeat of the city, you can start your walk downtown in the *zócalo* – the **Plaza de Armas** (sometimes also referred to as the Plaza de la Constitución), on Ave. Independencia between Lerdo and Zamora. The square is surrounded by arcades, under which cafés and restaurants have set up tables for the locals and tourists. They come in the daytime to relax and sip coffee, and then return at night, when it becomes a hotbed of activity, with street entertainers, musicians, and food vendors. On one side is the arched façade of the **Palacio Municipal** (City Hall) dating to 1608, while facing the *zócalo* on Zamora is the **Catedral de Nuestra Señora de la Asunción** (Cathedral of Our Lady of the Assumption), a beautiful cathedral built in 1721, with a very simple interior.

From here, head out to investigate some of the most important historical sites in the city, including, about three blocks from the *zócalo*, the **Casa Museo Salvador Díaz Mirón** (322 Ave. Ignacio Zaragoza, Mon.-Fri., 10 am-8 pm, Sat.,10 am-6 pm, free). This is the former home of poet Salvador Díaz Mirón (born in 1853), which today serves as a base for cultural workshops, as well as a museum with some period-furnished rooms. A little bit farther down Zaragoza, the **Museo de la Ciudad** (Museum of the City, 397 Zaragoza, Wed.-Mon., 10 am-6 pm) has displays on the city's culture and history.

From Zargoza, turn right onto E. Morales, and then left onto Landero y Coss, to find the **Museo Histórico Naval** in the large building at 418 Ave. M. Arista on the corner of Landero y Coss (Tues.-Sun., 10 am-5 pm, free). The naval museum (in a building that formerly housed the naval military school) has great exhibits on the naval history and defense of the city, as well as on former Mexican president/general Venustiano Carranza. Finally, leaving the naval museum, take a right turn onto M. Arista, and a right onto 16 de Septiembre to get to the **Baluarte de Santiago** at the intersection of Ave. Francisco Canal and Gómez Farías (Tues.-Sun., 10 am-4:30 pm, museum 30 pesos). This is the only one left of the nine original forts constructed in the 1700s as part of a defensive fortification of the city. You can climb up the ramp to its roof free of charge, where you'll find canons and lookouts. There is a museum inside with a display of ancient Aztec jewels recovered from a Spanish captain.

A WORD TO THE WISE

On my most recent visit here in 2003, many of the buildings in the zócalo were undergoing facelifts and have scaffolding covering their facades (including part of the Palacio Municipal, and a section housing some cafés). As a consequence, much of the action during the daytime has moved to the malecón.

Golf

For those of you who love to swing that club (as opposed to swinging *in* clubs, for which you should see *Nightlife* below), there is a beautiful nine-hole golf course here that rents equipment, offers lessons, and has caddies. **Golf Villa Rica** is near Boca del Río at Km 1.5 Antón Lizardo Highway, ☎ 229-986-0901.

On Wheels

Bus Tour

The streets of Veracruz had electric trolleys as public transportation up into the '80s. When they were retired, a modern replica was built and put on the streets as a tour bus. The trolleys take you around the historic center, past the Baluarte de Santiago, the Parque Zamora, and the Teatro Clavijero, on a 45-minute narrated ride – conducted completely in Spanish. There is a ticket booth in the *zócalo*; daily 11 am-9 pm; adults, 30 pesos, students 25 pesos, children, 15 pesos.

Bike Rentals

In front of Playa Villa del Mar, next to the frozen ice vendors (try the guanabana!), is a bike rental vendor, offering short rentals of 30 minutes for about 25 pesos, a little pricey, but no less popular for the kids.

Coastal Drive

The section of Highway 180 heading **north** away from the Puerto de Veracruz has a number of off-the-beaten-track places to stop by on a cruise of the coast. During the fall season, at Cardel and La Mancha, you can find world-class **birdwatching**. Year-round, at Chachalacas, you can find huge sand dunes to run down. And for centuries, the ruins of Cempoala and Quiahuiztlan, as well as the first Spanish settlements of La Villa Rica de la Vera Cruz and La Antigua have been waiting for your visit. (See *Along the Coast: Villa Rica to Cardel, page 161.*)

As you head **south** on Highway 180, you'll continue to spot plenty of birds. Eventually, 80 km (50 miles) down, you'll reach the fishing port of **Alvarado**. The port is a smelly, crowded, noisy place; even the waterfront hasn't escaped its harshness – abandoned unseaworthy fishing vessels sit ignored, left to rust and sink halfway into the ocean. Ugly, but strangely worth a picture. The *zócalo*, on the other hand, is spotlessly clean – but strangely deserted.

The people of Alvarado are known nation-wide for their cursing! But the profanity is used more in fun than as a serious matter.

On Water

Beaches & Lagoons

The beaches here are not great – the water is murky, the sand is brown, waves can be rough, and some beaches are both polluted and crowded. Even if you see people lounging about, you'll want to avoid the Playa Norte altogether. If you want to get in the waves, I recommend some of the other water excursions listed below; or just use the beach to get some sun, play volleyball, or go for food.

The beaches south of Punta Mocambo until Boca del Río are pretty clean, though they can be a bit rough. Here you'll find the **Playa Costa de Oro**, followed by the pretty beaches at **Playa Mocambo**, and, in Boca del Río, the **Playa Los Arcos**, where you'll see speed boats and banana boats zooming past. Close to downtown, **Playa Villa del Mar** and **Playa José Marti** are popular with families on vacation, though most stay on the sand rather than in the water. Chairs, tables, and tents are spread out on the wide expanse of sand, while music blares.

A WORD TO THE WISE
Many hotels will let you use their bathrooms, showers, and pools for a fee (10-20 pesos) even if you are not staying there.

Boat Tours

In Veracruz: From the *malecón*, boats depart in true Mexican fashion (as soon as there are enough people signed up) for hour-long tours of the harbor. For about seven pesos a person the tour takes you out around the harbor, past the fortress San Juan de Ulúa (see *Sightseeing*), and by the Isla de los Sacrificios, where inhabitants in the 1500s performed religious sacrifices. Bodies have been found buried beneath the sand's surface. Guides give you a bit of commentary, but once again everything is in Spanish. Take the trip even if you can't understand them – it's a great chance to get out on the water and see the port in action.

> When the Spanish made their first explorations of Veracruz, they landed on the Isla de Sacrificios, where they discovered that the inhabitants sacrificed – and then ate – their captives.

In Boca del Río: A man rode up to me on a bicycle while I was at the Palacio Muncipal in Boca del Río, shirt billowing away from his body, sweat beaded on his forehead – he looked as though he had worked hard to get to me. He smiled, and rode next to me, talking as he slowly pedaled along; he had a boat, he said, and for a price could take me out on the river and through the mangroves, or river fishing if that was more my speed. Or perhaps I'd like to go and pick up oysters? Had I yet seen the ruins of the building La Condesa?

You don't have to worry about finding a boat launch here – they'll find you. My friend wanted to ensure that he was first on the list, as I soon found out that he was a member of the Sociedad Cooperativa de Lancheros, many of whom are fishermen themselves, and have a kiosk set up right on the river waterfront of Boca del Río, on M. Ávila Camacho. You'll see a slew of motor boats docked up and eager guides waiting to take you on a customized trip; depending on what you'd like to do, boats go to sites along the river, and rent for about 200 pesos for a couple of hours.

In Mandinga: It's easy to spot the boats tied up at the dock, and the fishermen who will take you out. If someone doesn't approach, ask around – guides take you on a pretty route into the mangroves and adjacent lagoon, giving you a great chance to see more than you could onshore.

Cafés in the zocalo of the Puerto de Veracruz (Joanie Sánchez - see page 174)

Mandinga, Veracruz (Joanie Sánchez - see page 174)

Above: The colorful streets of Xalapa, Veracruz (Joanie Sánchez - see page 198)

Below: La Parroquia de Santa María Magdalena, Xico (Joanie Sánchez - see page 222)

One of the winding alleys of Xalapa (Joanie Sánchez - see page 198)

Diving

Diving trips head south of the city to Antón Lizardo, a village close to the Sistema Arrecifal Veracruzano, a system of 22 coral reefs about 20 km (12.4 miles) from the port itself. I've heard that there aren't a lot of fish in this National Marine Park because of overfishing and all the human activity in the area, but that the old Spanish underwater shipwrecks are interesting and make an excursion worthwhile. There are several diveshops in the area that will rent you gear and take you out on an organized trip, including:

- **Tridente**, ☎ 229-931-7924, 165-A Blvd M. Ávila Camacho
- **Dorado Buceo**, ☎ 229-229-931-4305, 865 Blvd. M. Ávila Camacho
- **Adventure**, ☎ 229-931-4305, 1269 Blvd. M. Ávila Camacho
- **Scubaver**, ☎ 229-932-3994, 563 Hernández y Hernández

Fishing

The boat tours in Boca del Río and Mandinga (see above) are in many cases operated by fishermen, who with little cajoling, will take you out into the mangroves or river for a few hours and supply the necessary equipment for you to fish to your heart's content. Prices depend on number of people, and amount of time you want to spend – typically starting at a few hundred pesos.

Sailing

The **Regatta de Amigos**, sponsored by the US-based Galveston Bay Cruising Association and the Lakewood Yacht Club, is a chance for sailors to get together and make the 630-mile trip from Galveston to the Puerto de Veracruz (stopping in Tuxpan along the way). The event takes place in June. See www.veracruzregatta.com for further information.

Kayaking/Rafting

You can get a guided kayak trip to Antón Lizardo or the Isla de Sacrificios, which on a nice day makes for a three-hour workout. Contact **Fiesta Viajes** at ☎ 229-980-6762. They have an information booth in the lobby of the Hotel Imperial, and their office is in Boca del Río at 7 Ávila Camacho; they offer rafting, diving, and fishing trips as well.

Another local agency offering diving, fishing, and rafting trips is **VIP Tours**, ☎ 229-922-1918 at 1111 Blvd. Ruiz Cortines.

If you're really interested in rafting, see *Jalcomulco* and *Tlapacoyan* (pages 227 and 158) for more adventure outfitters; some may even provide transportation, picking you up and dropping you off at your hotel in Veracruz.

By Air

You can do just about anything in Veracruz, including chartering a helicopter. Contact **Helitafe**, ☎ 229-931-1835, 249 Serdán.

Archaeological Discoveries

El Zapotal

Although it has yielded a number of significant finds, they have almost all been moved elsewhere. The most significant find here was unearthed in 1972 – nine stairs (representing the nine worlds of the underworld) leading down to a sculpture of Mictlantecuhtli – the Lord of the Dead, a fearsome seated skeletal figure guarding the underworld. Other findings here included the Mocihuaquetzque or brave women – a number of life-size sculptures of women who died during childbirth. Many artifacts that were found here now reside in Xalapa's Museo de Antropología, although there are a few onsite. The two hills of El Zapotal – the Cerro de la Gallina (Hill of the Hen) and the Cerro del Gallo (Hill of the Rooster) have also yielded human remains, offerings, and figurines, but there isn't much to see now. To get here, take Highway 180 south from Veracruz; right after the town of La Laguna (about 10 km past Highway 150), turn right (west) onto a road heading towards Tlalixcoyan. A little past Tlalixcoyan you'll find El Zapotal, a total of about 60 km (37 miles) from the port.

■ Festivals & Events

Carnaval

The biggest, and most famous event here is Carnaval which takes place nine days before Ash Wednesday (late February/early March). It is the biggest Carnaval celebration in all of México, and is said to rival Río in scope (think Mardi Gras times 10). Processions start with the *comparsas* (congos, drums, and dancers moving to Afro-Cuban music), followed by parades of floats... you can't help but be drawn by the rhythm and excitement as they pass by. Everybody gets in on the action – miles of parades wind up and down every street, and hoards of people cheer them on. For days there is music, food, dancing, handicrafts, and fireworks. Rest up, because there is something happening every minute of the day during Carnaval.

Festival Internacional Afrocaribeño

During the month of July, the fairly new Festival Internacional Afrocaribeño (Afro-Caribbean Festival) livens the streets with different styles of Caribbean dance, music, art, and film. The festival is organized by the Veracruz Institute of Culture, who invites all the Caribbean countries to participate, as well as to send along the best Caribbean musicians to fill the streets with meringue, samba, rumba, son jarocho, son montuno, cumbia, and candombole.

School Holidays

Veracruz is high up on many local tourists' lists as a vacation destination. Just a reminder that the peak travel time is the winter (December to New Year's), Easter, and summer school holidays (June to September). Hotels and buses fill up fast, so be sure you've made reservations in advance.

The Fiesta de Santa Ana

On July 26 each year in Boca del Río, this is celebrated with the making of a huge *filete relleno de mariscos* (fillet stuffed with seafood). Is it tasty? I don't know, but it's huge – and it even got a Guinness Record. Many restaurants collaborate on its making, and in Boca del Río you can find the certificate.

■ Shopping

Local shops around the tourist areas are likely to be a bit overpriced, but if you stay away from the Plazas and look around, you'll be able to find some good deals. You can always stop by the huge busy, maze-like **Mercado Hidalgo** (a block west of Parque Zamora on Madero between J. Soto and H. Córtes). Here you can pick up just about anything (Mexican ceramics, hand decorated glassware, shell jewelry, regional clothing, food) at an affordable price. Another good option is the **Plaza de las Artesenias**, on the *malecón*. It has a number of stalls and shops selling locally made ocean-themed souvenirs (shell necklaces, earrings, bracelets, boxes), ocean-front necessities (sunglasses, hats, T-shirts,

■ Nightlife

It seems that as darkness approaches, people start gathering, music and laughter get louder, and entertainers multiply. The *zócalo* is the main place to be at night. Here you'll find everything from temporary events such as folk dancing, comedians, and bands, to the more informal entertainment of street performers, vendors, and party-goers. Musicians playing violins and guitars wander through the arcades and every now and then a couple joins them in dance. Many years ago, the *zócalo* was (among local teenagers) the place to meet a date. Girls would arrive as darkness fell and stroll in one direction around the square, while the young men would arrive and stroll in the opposite direction. When a young man found a girl he was interested in, he would join her as she walked, and hopefully strike a rapport that would lead to a date for the evening. Today, the tradition has faded, but you can still see plenty of young Navy men here hoping to meet local girls.

Dancing

Many evenings around 8 pm at the Palacio Municipal in the *zócalo*, a band strikes up, locals start gathering, and couples appear to dance the *danzón*, a traditional dance supposedly brought to México by Cuban refugees. If you're here on an off-night, try the Plazuela de la Campaña (Square of the Bell) about three blocks south of the *zócalo* between Ave. Independencia and Zaragoza. The simple dance has a couple of basic steps that are not difficult to learn, though the musical interludes where partners stop for a few minutes before resuming, are sometimes hard to foretell. If you love to dance, grab a partner and join in. It's a lot of fun. There are people here of all levels. Just stop when others do and resume with them.

You might also want check in with the tourism office for any scheduled happenings around town. If you *still* can't get enough, or want to make sure your partner can take his skills home, the dance school **El Cason**, ☎ 229-932-2992, 622, 1 de Mayo at the corner of Díaz Aragón, might be able to help you out. They are open Mon.-Fri., 5-8 pm, and Sat., 10 am-noon).

Nightclubs

If you're interesting in discos and bars, there are plenty around, including those that charge a cover, and those that don't. Many clubs really start grooving around midnight and continue partying until daybreak. Many are right by the ocean at the intersection of Blvd. Ávila Camacho and Blvd Adolfo Ruiz Cortinez. Just walk around until you find the crowd that you like. In Boca del Río, popular salsa spots are **Kachimba**, a "salsoteca" on Blvd. Ávila Camacho at the corner of Médico Militar, and **Carioca**, 10 Calz. Ruiz Cortinez.

Taaaxxxiiii!!!

Radio Serta Caver.	☎ 229-935-9888
Radio Taxi GL	☎ 229-938-5424
Taxi de Lujo y Confort.	☎ 229-937-6715

■ Where to Stay

There are lots of places to stay in Veracruz and, unless you will be there around the time of a festival, you don't need to worry about booking too far in advance. Room prices run the gamut from cheap to super-expensive, so take a look at your budget and go with that – there are decent hotels in all categories. Rates shoot up drastically during high seasons, while summer prices are typically between the low and high rates.

HOTEL PRICE CHART	
Rates are per room based on double occupancy. Rates lower if single occupancy or sharing a bed. Higher rates on holidays.	
	US $10-$20
$	US $21-$40
$$	US $41-$60
$$$	US $61-$80
$$$$	US $81-$125
$$$$$	Over US $125

Near the bus station, the **Hotel Azteca**, ☎ 229-937-4241 (218 22 de Marzo at the corner of Orizaba), has acceptable air-conditioned rooms. $$

Nearby, the **Hotel Rosa Mar**, ☎ 229-937-0747 (1100 Ave. La Fragua, between Orizaba and Tuero Molina), is a decent choice for this area, although I will never, *never* understand why the bathrooms are designed so poorly. My bathroom, though very clean, had no shower curtain and an unadjustable shower head which shot water straight across the room, missing me, but bathing the toilet thoroughly! Add $3 US for a/c. $

A little bit higher priced, the **Hotel Central**, ☎ 229-937-2254 (1612 Ave. Díaz Mirón at the corner of M. Tuero Molina), with fan or, for 30% more, a/c. The pleasant **Hotel Arrecife**, ☎ 229-980-2200 (883 Xalapa at the corner of M. Alemán), is a nice clean spot with fans or a/c and about a block and a half from the bus station (across the busy street). $

If you don't mind walking to get around, the budget **Hotel Acapulco**, ☎ 229-932-3492 (1327 Uribe off Ave. Díaz Mirón), is a little inconvenient (halfway between the bus station and downtown), but has clean rooms with great prices, and is a block from the Chedraui supermarket. Rooms come without a TV (add about $5 US for that). $

The **Hotel El Faro**, ☎ 229-931-6176 (223 16 de Septiembre), is a good centrally located choice, with a friendly staff, and clean rooms. $$

The **Isla Sacrificios**, ☎ 229-932-1803 (1 de Mayo 1592), is right in downtown, and has 32 pleasant rooms with TV and a/c. Credit cards not accepted. $$

The **Hostal Don Antonio**, ☎ 229-932-9143 (1720 16 de Septiembre), is in the pink building about two blocks inland from the Acuario (from Blvd. M. Avila Camacho, turn left onto Mina or Perez), and has clean rooms with a/c and cable TV. $$

The **Gran Hotel Boulevard**, ☎ 229-986-0108 (304 Zamora, between Ave. Veracruz and Ave. Xalapa), is near the center of Boca del Río and has a tropical, laid-back vibe. Roooms with TV and a/c. $$

You might want to visit the **Hotel Imperial**, ☎ 229-932-9718, www.hotelimperial-veracruz.com (on 153 Lerdo between Independencia and Zaragoza, hidden away near the *zócalo*), even if you're not staying there! It has a gorgeous, elegant lobby showcasing a century-old Swiss grilled elevator identical to one at Chapultepec Castle in México City. The wide, curving staircase behind it is made of Italian marble, a feature you'll find in some of the rooms, and the building itself was originally made entirely of coral from the surrounding reefs (like the San Juan de Ulúa). Rooms here are good, if not the most modern you will find. They accept credit cards. $$-$$$

If you're willing to walk a little bit for a cheaper room, the **Hotel Polanco**, ☎ 229-931-2856 (391 C. Serdan), is halfway between the bus station and the ocean, about seven blocks from the Acuario. From Blvd M. Ávila Camacho, take a right turn down M.F. Altamirano until you reach Serdan. Rooms are clean, have nearby parking, and are good bargains for one person. $$-$$$

Right on the *zócalo*, the **Hotel Colónial**, ☎ 229-932-0193 (117 Lerdo), is a large central hotel with some higher-priced balconied rooms overlooking the nightly action of the square. $$-$$$

Three blocks from the bus station, the large **Hotel Veracruz Plaza**, ☎ 229-989-7100 (766 Ave. Díaz Mirón between Iturbide and Azueta), is a good choice in this area, catering to a lot of business people, and offering a/c, cable TV, parking, a restaurant, suites, and room service. $$$

With a view of Playa Villa del Mar, the **Hostal de Cortés**, ☎ 229-923-1200 or 0800-112-9800, www.hostaldecortes.com.mx (Blvd. Avila Camacho s/n at the corner of Bartolomé de los Casas), is a good modern choice, and has all the amenities – parking, lounges, a pool, a lobby bar. Comfortable rooms come with a/c and cable TV; suites are also available. $$$$

The pretty **Hotel Villa del Mar**, ☎ 229-989-6500 or 0800-322-1212, www.hotel-villadelmar.com (Blvd. M. Avila Camacho s/n), is a good chioce if you want to be near the oceanfront, and it has a Jacuzzi and pool in case you're not up for the beach. The hotel has standard rooms with cable TV and a/c, but also has suites and bungalows. $$$$

The **Hawaii Hotel**, ☎ 229-938-0088 (458 Paseo del Malecón), right on the *malecón* offers clean rooms at prices about what you'll find for a hotel on the *malecón* close to the center. $$$$

The huge **Hotel Fiesta Americana**, ☎ 229-989-8989 (Blvd. Avila Camacho s/n), in Boca del Río, is a modern hotel that has every luxury you could hope for – parking, room service, minibars, Jacuzzi, gym. $$$$$

The **Hotel Mocambo**, ☎ 229-922-0200 (4000 Blvd. Cortines, next to Playa Mocambo), is a huge luxury hotel that's a little bit older and a little bit classier than the rest. $$$$$

The five-star **Hotel Emporio**, ☎ 229-932-0020 (244 Paseo del Malecón), is in a great location, right on the *malecón* downtown. $$$$$

■ Where to Eat

Wherever you go, whatever you get, just be sure to try something *"a la veracruzana"* – one of the most popular ways of cooking fish in México. It comes with a sauce made out of tomatoes, onions, capers, olives, and bell peppers. Also try *jaiba* (crab). *Jaiba chilpachole* means deviled crab and *jaiba rellenas* means stuffed. Enjoy.

DINING PRICE CHART	
Price per person for an entrée, not including beverage or tip.	
$	Under US $5
$$	US $5-$10
$$$	US $10+

In the *zócalo* you have a number of choices – cafés line the *portales* with outdoor tables, enticing passersby with the aroma of fresh coffee. One is as good as the next, and all serve food. The walkway between Independencia and Zaragoza has the **Restaurant Flamingo**, which serves basic fare – tortas, soups, desserts, as well as some heavier dishes, including fajitas (55-105 pesos) and seafood (78-159 pesos). $$

Next door is the **Restaurant Colónial**, part of the Hotel Colónial, offering a little pricier, similar dishes. $$$

For something a little different, try **El Rincón del Negro** (2118 Arista), which serves up Cuban specialties along with live music (open Fri.-Sun., 1-8 pm). $$

One of the most popular places to go off the *zócalo* has always been the **Gran Café del Portal** (1187 Independencia), a large café often busy with musicians out front playing upbeat tunes. $$

The **Gran Café de la Parroquia** near the waterfront (34 Gómez Farías) is the other Veracruz institution. This huge café is full of people almost any time of the day or night; most are listening to the live music, and ordering the popular *lechero* (coffee with milk), a Veracruz tradition. A tap on the glass, and a waiter fills your coffee up with milk. $$

Seafood

You're at the ocean in the midst of fishermen, so don't miss some of the seafood restaurants – in many cases the fish's eyes have barely glazed over before they are scaled and served up. Some of the tastiest options are in Boca del Río (see below), and nearby Mandinga (oysters, clams, and prawns). Mandinga is small; just walk to the water and you'll find a few restaurants. You can, of course, find some places on the waterfront of the port itself, most of which focus more upon entertainment, with live music and a festive atmosphere, than on the food itself. There are some fun seafood choices facing the beach in front of the Playa Villa del Mar. Look for live entertainment on Saturdays and Sundays.

Boca del Río

At 101 Blvd. M. Avila Camacho, across the street from the riverfront, is **Restaurant Bar Miguel**. In 1992 it won the Guinness record for the largest *filete relleno* (stuffed filet), which measured in at 154.5 meters (616.4 feet)! The restaurant has Guiness Certificates framed on its walls, as well as pictures of the event. Oh yeah, you can get good seafood here too. $$

Across the street overlooking the water, at 102 Blvd. M. Avila Camacho, is **Boulevard Restaurante**, which you'll find full most of the time, with people enjoying the live music (often harp and guitar players) and fresh seafood.

A little farther down, at the corner of Zamora and Orizaba, is **El Varadero**, another seafood restaurant with plenty of live music, and a palapa with outdoor seating. $$

Well-known **Paradiños**, at 40 Zamora right near the *zócalo*, offers a more elegant dining experience, with stuffed crab and shrimp, robalo (a type of fish), as well as some chicken dishes. Prices range from around 45 pesos for an appetizer to 140 pesos for some of the seafood entrées. $$$

A Taste of Home

If all this is a little bit much for your stomach, inside the Plaza Acuario is a **VIPS**, part of a chain offering standard international snacks and meals. $$

There's also a **Bennigan's** at Blvd. Avila Camacho at the corner of Tortugas. $$

And there's a **Sanborn's** in Boca del Río (in the Plaza Las Americas). $$

Tlacotalpan

The day of my arrival in Tlacotalpan, there was a handwritten sign posted on the doorway of a bright blue house in the center of town – a sign, but easily the first thing you saw. It stood out in the rows of spotless houses and streets: *Extras Wanted for the movie – "La Novia del Mar."* Once you visit Tlacotalpan, you won't be surprised that it would attract the eye of a production company. The wide streets are lined with picture-perfect houses, many with *portales*, all painted vibrant shades of blue, yellow, red and orange. It's peaceful. Sitting at the edge of the Papaloapan River, listening to the slap of water against fishing boats, the cries of seagulls chiming in, you relax completely. The downtown as well, just steps away, is quiet and pleasantly empty. It's beautiful too – the buildings, the river, the birds, the boats. It all adds up. People generally seem to come on a day's outing from San Andres Tuxtla or Veracruz, but you'd probably be just as happy staying the night, taking your time picking around the streets, having a quiet dinner on the waterfront, listening to the regional music, and heading to the river in the morning for the sunrise.

Orientation & Practicalities

Tlacotalpan is on Highway 175, almost at its juncture with Highway 180, on the banks of the Río Papaloapan. The downtown is small, with restaurants, hotels, and the *zócalo* a block or two from the river at the end of Alegre.

Money: There's an ATM on Carranza, two blocks from the riverfront.

Post Office: The post office is a block from the river at the end of Benito Juárez.

Getting There & Around

The ADO/AU bus station is at 26 Calle Beltrán, between Aldama and Ocampo, about three blocks from the main square.

BUS TRIPS			
Destination	Bus Line	Fare	Time
Alvarado	ADO	19 pesos	30 minutes
México City (TAPO)	ADO	290 pesos	7 hours 25 minutes
San Andres Tuxtla	Cuenca	35 pesos	1 hour 40 minutes
Santiago Tuxtla	Cuenca	28 pesos	1 hour 20 minutes
Tuxtepec	Cuenca	41 pesos	10 minutes
Veracruz	ADO	51 pesos	1 hour 30 minutes
Xalapa	ADO	106 pesos	3 hours 35 minutes

Sightseeing

The downtown is like something out of the pages of a storybook. It's spotlessly clean, as if each house was in a competition with the next. Though there's not a lot to see, it's a pleasure to walk the streets here.

Make sure you visit the quiet *zócalo*, also known as **Plaza Zaragoza**, a block away from the river on Benito Juárez between Enriquez and Chazaro. Its beautiful white benches and bright white-and-green kiosk sit in the middle of a meticulously maintained square set amid artisan shops. Occasionally a shop owner will walk by, but the rest of the time, you pretty much have the place to yourself. Many of the surrounding buildings have plaques, written in both Spanish and English, describing their historical importance.

On one side, the Neoclassical **Palacio Municipal**, a long green building lined with *portales*, adds its own touch of class. It was built in 1849, and originally served as a station for people arriving at the port (the riverfront is directly behind it). On the opposite side of the *zócalo*, the **Iglesia de la Virgen de la Candelaría** was built in 1779, and has an interior completely at odds with its exterior – surprisingly festive, happy, and colorful (bright blues and yellows), perfectly reflective of the town.

Nearby, the huge, classical **Iglesia San Cristobál**, at the corner of Benito Juárez and Chazaro (on the *zócalo*), is historically the more important of the two, built in 1812 under the Vice Regal Administration. Its interior is much more somber and ceremonious, with muted colors, and a picture of La Guadalupe at the altar.

Adjoining the *zócalo* is another smaller, quieter park, **Plaza Hidalgo**, which has some benches with pictures of the town square on them, but not a whole lot else; facing it is the **Museo Salvador Ferrando**, which has some historical items on display.

One of the town sources of pride is that **Augustin Lara**, a famous songwriter (producing many of his most important works in the late '20s and early '30s) was born here. Downtown is a museum dedicated to him, the **Casa de la Cultura Agustin Lara** (marked simiply with a sign saying *Museo*). Inside are pictures, furniture, and regional clothing of the 19th century, as well as information on Lara (6 Alegre, daily, 10 am-5 pm). Right off Enriquez, behind the Iglesia La Candelaría, is the **Plazuela Augustin Lara**, which has a statue of the songwriter.

Finally, if you head all the way down to 25 Carranza (about a 15-minute walk), you'll get to the **Mini-Zoológico Museo**, a museum with a modest animal exhibit (crocodiles), as well as a few historical items.

■ Shopping

You won't want to miss the artisan shops here, which have some surprisingly good locally crafted items. Right next to the Palacio, a thick-walled building that was once a jail today houses the **Casa Artesanal**; inside there are gorgeous blouses, scarves, straw hats, and guitars for sale.

■ Adventures

On Water

From the **Río Papaloapan**, you can get a whole different view of the town. Rides take you on the river for 30- to 45-minute tours, heading out past the town so you can get a good look at it from afar – cuddled cozily up on one bank with the church tops barely visible behind the waterfront buildings. These quickly disappear, replaced by huge houses (some even with tennis courts) lining the waterfront. On the other side, you'll see some wide ranches, and a few more large summer houses owned by wealthy figures who leave them empty most of the year – one of the houses belongs to the head honcho of the super-popular Holanda ice cream line.

Tisniche

If you're here during April, you might be able to see fishermen standing in the shallow waters on the far side of the river, combing the area with huge nets. They're catching tiny fish (about half the width of a grain of rice) known as *tisniche*. The fish are fried and made into patties – a tasty treat available only during this time of the year (the fish are seasonal). The fishermen stay in the water with their nets for hours. It takes around a thousand fish to make one pound of patties. You might also notice some plastic bottles tossed in the water – the first sign of litter that you will have seen here. In fact, the fishermen put them there to mark the location of their crab traps. Unfortunately for the fishing town, the fish that used to be abundant are starting to disappear thanks to a nearby sugarcane factory, which is polluting the water.

Boats head into the river from sunrise to sunset. They go out from the dock at the end of Alegre and cost 20 pesos per adult; or you can rent the whole boat for about 100 pesos.

■ Festivals & Events

La Candelaría (Candlemas Day), a festival starting at the end of January and running until the Virgen de la Candelaría's birthday at the beginning of February, attracts lots of merrymakers. For days, booths, and floats fill the streets, and people from throughout the region fill the town with their own styles of music. As the festival comes to an end, the parades give way to a wilder aspect of the celebration – the running of the bulls. A huge bull is actually driven through the narrow streets of the town. As the festival draws to a close, be sure to get a spot by the waterfront to see the last parade go down the river, headed by an image of the Virgin, in whose honor the festival is held.

■ Where to Stay

The charming **Hotel Tlactoalpan**, ☎ 288-884-2063, is at 35 Ave. Beltrán (the bus station is across the street). The hotel is inside a pretty bright blue Colonial building; its sunny courtyard has a restaurant on one side. The rooms are comfortable. No credit cards accepted. $$

About one block down from the bus station on Beltrán (two blocks from the *zócalo*), are the huge mahogany doors of the pink-pillared building known as **Hotel Candelaría**, ☎ 288-884-3192. There's an elegant chandeliered lobby and nice rooms with a/c and TV. No credit cards accepted. $$

The **Doña Lala**, ☎ 288-884-2580, is across the street from the waterfront at 11 Ave. Venustiano Carranza. They have a large hotel with pool, restaurant, and pleasant rooms. $$

■ Where to Eat

Most of the restaurants are on the dock behind the *zócalo*, with covered outdoor tables and serving fresh seafood. On my last visit, tables were full of actors and production staff chatting and laughing, while waiting for their crab and fish dishes to arrive. Most days, you'll find it cheery but peaceful, with only a few tourists sampling the food. Try **El Pescador** for a good decently priced breakfast (15-28 pesos) right on Ribera (at the riverfront behind the Palacio) $.

Or go a little farther down to **Restaurante Las Brisas del Papaloapan** for a *caldo de jaiba* (crab soup) or the popular *filete relleno de marisco* (stuffed filet of seafood). $

Xalapa

The beautiful hilly city of Xalapa (pronounced ha-LA-pa and sometimes spelled Jalapa) sits at the top of the must-visit list in the Gulf Coast region. For some, it's the fact that it has one of the best archaeological museums in the country. The Museo de Antropología, with its huge Olmec heads and hundreds of Maya artifacts, will keep you enthralled for at least half a day. For others, it's the seemingly endless number of art galleries. You could spend hours wandering from gallery to gallery without touching your wallet – almost all are free. For me, it has something to do with the numerous alleys, each with its own ghostly legend, the romantic beauty of the parks and lakes (every tree seems to bloom with flowers in lavenders, blues,  pinks, and whites), and the magnificent weather. Mornings are brisk due to the mountain setting, afternoons are sunny and not too humid, and mysterious fogs sometimes obscure the streets. Perhaps its nicknames will give you a better sense of the place: "The Veracruzan Athens," "The City of Fairs," "The City of Hot Peppers," and, most recently, "The City of Flowers."

And yet, Xalapa suffers by being too close to México City (which could very well work to your advantage). Curiously, though it is the state capital of Veracruz, it has only a tiny local airport – relying instead mainly upon tourists from México City to take the bus or drive its way. But, in fact, many tourists are taken in by the cosmopolitan life of México City and never see Xalapa. As a result, Xalapa has a remote feel about it, with few tourists for a city which, for all its offerings, deserves far more. And, as a university town, home to the Universidad Veracruzana, Xalapa has a fresh, young feel about it.

Your best bet is to spend a couple of days here taking it all in, and a few more days using Xalapa as a base to visit the surrounding villages and natural attractions – there are waterfalls, rivers, coffee plantations, and mountains all within a 20-mile/32-km radius.

■ Orientation & Practicalities

 Everything centers around the *zócalo*, also known as Parque Juárez. To the north is the Cerro de Macuiltepetl, and to the south you'll find the road to Coatepec.

Emergency Services: Cruz Roja/Red Cross, ☎ 228-817-3431; Hospital, ☎ 228-818-4400

Exchanging Money: A number of banks with ATMs fill the downtown, including an Inverlat (Enriquez 36, Mon.-Fri., 9 am-4 pm, Sat., 10 am-2 pm), a Serfin (Enriquez 24, Mon.-Fri., 9 am-4 pm), and a

Orientation & Practicalities ■ 193

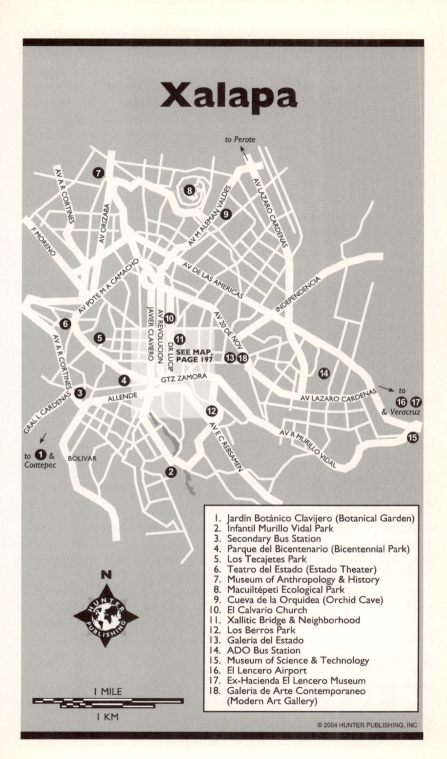

Xalapa

1. Jardín Botánico Clavijero (Botanical Garden)
2. Infantil Murillo Vidal Park
3. Secondary Bus Station
4. Parque del Bicentenario (Bicentennial Park)
5. Los Tecajetes Park
6. Teatro del Estado (Estado Theater)
7. Museum of Anthropology & History
8. Macuiltépeti Ecological Park
9. Cueva de la Orquidea (Orchid Cave)
10. El Calvario Church
11. Xallitic Bridge & Neighborhood
12. Los Berros Park
13. Galeria del Estado
14. ADO Bus Station
15. Museum of Science & Technology
16. El Lencero Airport
17. Ex-Hacienda El Lencero Museum
18. Galeria de Arte Contemporaneo (Modern Art Gallery)

© 2004 HUNTER PUBLISHING, INC

Banamex on Xalapeños Ilustres (Mon.-Fri., 9 am-4 pm). You can find ATMs in the Plaza Crystal, Plaza Museo, and Plaza Animas as well.

Internet Cafés: A charming Internet café is at Callejón del Diamente 17 (when you go up the alley, you'll see a sign marked simply "Internet," with an arrow directing you in). The owner and his young assistants are very friendly and helpful, and have a cute knook with a few computers that are almost always available. Open 9 am-11 pm, daily; 8 pesos per hour. Uphill behind Parque Juárez on Calle Milan 24 (right at the bottom of the short hilly street) is the Internet café **Planet**, open Mon.-Sat., 9:30 am-11 pm; 7.50 pesos per hour.

Post Office: The Post and Telegraphs Building is in the Palacio Federal, inconveniently at the corner of Gutiérrez Zamora (Enriquez turns into Zamora) and Diego Leño, about four blocks from Parque Juárez.

Tourist Information: In the lobby of the Palacio Municipal (right in front of Parque Juárez on Enriquez) is a tourist information booth where you can get a map of the city, as well as recommendations on local hotels and restaurants; open weekdays 9 am-4 pm (usually closed for lunch).

The state tourist office is a bit of a ride away at the Torre Animas, but unless you need specific information about someplace in Veracruz (they have a wide variety of pamphlets and maps), don't bother, as there is not much else out there. If you do need to get there, catch a bus marked "Torre Animas" across from the Banorte, to the right of the Palacio Municipal. It's a 20-minute (4-peso) ride. The bus will drop you off in front of a modern multi-storied building in which you'll find the office on the first floor at the back of the building.

■ Getting There

By Air

Xalapa's tiny airport, **Aeropuerto El Lencero**, is about seven miles/11 km from downtown, at Km 13.5 of the Veracruz-Xalapa Highway. It has one daily flight to and from México City on **Aeromar** (☎ 800-531-7921 or 0800-237-6627 (MX); www.aeromar.com.mxl). The 20-minute flight costs around 2,000 pesos round-trip. From there, you can take a taxi to downtown for about 150 pesos. Another option, is to fly into the Puerto de Veracruz (about 60 miles/96 km away) and drive to Xalapa.

By Car

To get here from the west (México City), take Tollway 150, and turn left onto Highway 140 (heading northeast) towards Xalapa. The road becomes narrow, twisting and mountainous (but beautiful) around Perote, so care should be taken. From México City, the trip takes around 4½ hours (301 km/187 miles). From the northeast and southeast (Papantla or Veracruz), follow the coast on Highway 180 before turning left (west) at Cardel onto Highway 140.

By Bus

The large **Central de Autobuses**, aka CAXA (bus station), is off Ave. 20 de Noviembre a little more than a mile east of downtown. It services all first-class lines (UNO, ADO GL, and ADO), as well as the second-class AU line. It has luggage lockers (30 pesos for 24 hours), shops out front selling scarves, hats, mittens, and coffee, plus taxis to take you downtown (around 20 pesos). Or it's a pleasant 30-minute stroll downtown from the station. Turn right (west) as you exit the station and follow Ave. 20 de Noviembre a few blocks until it turns into Xalapeños Ilustres, which turns into Enriquez, which terminates at Parque Juárez. Take a cab if you arrive in the evening – the street becomes a little deserted in some sections and is not completely lit with street lamps.

BUS TRIPS			
Destination	Bus Line	Fare	Time
Coatepec	ADO	6 pesos	30 minutes
Coatzacoalcos	UNO	343 pesos	5 hours
	ADO GL	248 pesos	5 hours
Córdoba	ADO	90 pesos	3 hours 5 minutes
México City (TAPO)	UNO	263 pesos	4 hours 30 minutes
	ADO GL	189 pesos	4 hours 30 minutes
Orizaba	ADO	101 pesos	3 hours 10 minutes
Papantla	ADO	126 pesos	3 hours 45 minutes
Perote	ADO	26 pesos	1 hour 10 minutes
	AU	23 pesos	1 hour 10 minutes
Puebla	ADO	93 pesos	3 hours
	AU	82 pesos	3 hours
Tampico	ADO	278 pesos	8 hours
Veracruz	ADO GL	64 pesos	2 hours
	ADO	55 pesos	1 hour 50 minutes
	AU	49 pesos	1 hour 50 minutes
Villahermosa	UNO	456 pesos	7 hours
	ADO GL	323 pesos	7 hours
	ADO	298 pesos	7 hours 40 minutes

Coming from México City, you'll have to go to the Terminal de Autobuses de Pasajeros de Oriente (TAPO) to get a bus to Xalapa. If you are at the airport, take a bus to Puebla's central bus terminal and connect to a bus going to Xalapa – the trip will take you about the same amount of time as from México City.

■ Getting Around

Put on your walking shoes, because this is a town that begs to be explored on foot. For the few out-of-the-way places, you can take a local bus (the station is at the corner of Calle Allende and E. Galeana), or call a cab. If, however, you're interested in renting a car, you can contact **Kanguro**, ☎ 228-817-7878 (1350 Av. Ávila Camacho), or **Spacios Rent-Car**, ☎ 228-810-3475 (23 Ignacio de la Llave).

To Coatepec & Xico

Head to the local bus station at the corner of Calle Allende and E. Galeana. To get there, walk about 10 minutes west to the end of Calle Allende until you see a rotary with a park and statue in the middle of it. On the right, you'll see a bunch of buses lined up; you want the bus marked *Xico*. The ride takes approximately 30 minutes, passing first through Coatepec, then through hills, over creeks, around windy roads with views of lush mist-covered vegetation, before reaching Xico. Get off at the *zócalo* several stops into Xico. The bus will drop you off right in front of the pretty white and peach trimmed church. The fare is 10 pesos per person; as on many buses, the driver's assistant will come around once the bus is moving to collect the fare.

To Jalcomulco

You can make it to Jalcomulco by local bus, with time, patience, and a couple of bus changes. Pick up the bus marked *Xico*. Follow directions above, and get off at Coatepec (about 10 minutes and 5 pesos). From Coatepec, get on a local bus marked *Jalcomulco*. You can catch the bus in various places; one sure spot is at the corner of Juárez and Cuauhtemoc. Buses run approximately every hour, cost 12.50 pesos, and take about 50 minutes for the really scenic ride through mango trees, mountains, and canyons.

To Perote

See ADO & AU bus times and prices in the chart above. Buses leave approximately every hour, all day from 4 am until 11 pm.

Getting Around ■ 197

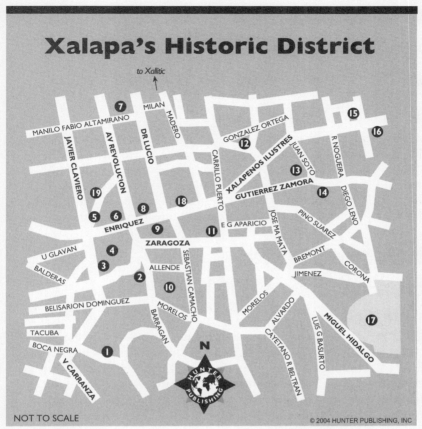

1. Casa de Artesanias
2. Paseo del Ayuntamiento
3. Agora de la Ciudad
4. Juaréz Park
5. Historical Archive
6. Palacio Municipal (Town Hall)
7. Jáuaregui Market
8. Cathedral
9. Palacio de Gobierno (Government Palace)
10. Paseo Los Lagos (park)
11. Iglesia del Beaterio (church)
12. Recreation Center
13. Galería de Arte Ramón Alva de la Canal (art gallery)
14. Palacio Federal (Federal Palace), Post Office
15. Iglesia de San José (church)
16. Callejon de Jesús Te Ampare (alley)
17. Los Berros Park
18. Callejon del Diamante (alley)
19. Callejon de Rojas (alley)

Sightseeing

Museum

For some of you, looking at a car might be more fun than being in a car. At the **Museo de Ciencia y Tecnología** (Science and Technology Museum), you can do just that in its transportation gallery, where you'll find plenty of planes, trains, and automobiles. The museum also has exhibits on life, space, the earth, science, water, ecology, as well as an IMAX theater and planetarium. It's not your typical Mexican tourist destination, but sure fun for the kids. The museum is on Ave. Rafael Murillo Vidal s/n, and costs 50 pesos for adults, 35 pesos for children (open Tues.-Fri., 9 am-6 pm, Sat. and Sun., 10 am-7 pm).

Adventures

On Foot

Town Walk

The city has not been dubbed "Ciudad de las Flores" (City of the Flowers) for nothing. The cool misty environment combined with the city's dedication to ecology has produced lovely backdrops of color and peace. One of the most beautiful spots, the **Paseo de Los Lagos**, is a gorgeous retreat in the middle of the city where you can find people biking, walking, and jogging along a footpath that winds its way around a series of three interconnected lakes. It's an ideal spot for a morning jog or an afternoon stroll, and is nicely kept up, with manicured lawns, ducks, stone benches, bridges, a playground, and rows of gorgeous flowering trees in blues, reds, purples, and whites.

The area actually began with the construction of a dam to catch the waters of the Tlalmecapan spring, in order to generate power for the area. In the early '70s, under governor Rafael Murillo Vidal, the landscape was widened, cleaned, and made into the recreation spot it is today. To get there from Parque Juárez (only a few downhill blocks), walk down Ignacio Allende, turn left onto J.J. Herrera, take a right onto B. Dominguez, and a quick left onto Calle del Dique. The entrance is about one block down on the left, and is marked by the Plaza V. Centenaria 1492-1992.

The city's main square is **Parque Juárez**, a large plaza filled with flowering trees, benches, and pathways. It sits atop a terrace, with one side offering a lookout to the city's rolling hills below. Most evenings the park is filled with entertainers (clowns are a favorite), vendors selling *churros*, popcorn, and ice creams, and plenty of people who lounge under the trees, walk about (on their way to and from the surrounding coffee shops and galleries) and enjoy the view.

Be sure to stop by the cultural center **Ágora de la Ciudad** (open Tues.-Sun., 9 am-9 pm; free), inside the park, and enjoy its gallery and a cup of coffee in its cafeteria-with-a-view. From the southeast side of the park, you can see the **Paseo del Ayuntamiento** on the street below, four statues sitting on a terrace, surrounded by flowering trees. The statues represent the four virtues – strength (a woman holding a mallet, and standing in front of the head of a lion), prudence (a woman holding the ear of a creature representing disorder), justice (a woman with a sword and chain), and temperance (represented by a man). Originally meant for México City's Palacio de Relaciones Exteriores, three of the these statues were never used and were subsequently donated to Xalapa, while the fourth (Temperance), is only a replica. The original remains in México City's Chapultepec Park.

Parque Juárez was inaugurated on September 16, 1892. On its site was the second convent ever constructed in México (the Convent of San Francisco). Sadly, after being partially destroyed by an earthquake, it was torn down in 1886 under governor Juan de la Luz Enríquez, to make way for the future park. The park sits at the end of Enriquez, across the street from the Palacio Municipal, and is bordered on the east by the neoclassic **Palacio de Gobierno** (the state government building). You can enter the building (the front desk will have you sign in and give you a visitor's pass) to view its arched courtyard with a fountain and the state emblem at its center.

Follow an inconspicuous and unmarked pathway (which looks almost like an the entrance to a hotel), climb some stairs and go down a short path to the **Parque del Bicentenario** (Bicentennial Park), inaugurated as such at Xalapa's bicentennial in 1991. This is the place to take your beloved – it's a romantic setting with four fountains, old metal benches set among tall green trees, and a peace broken only by the calls of a few birds. Cuddled up on many of the benches you'll find young lovers holding hands and planning where to go for dinner. The back entrance is the unmarked pathway described above, right off Ursulo Galván, across the street from the Hotel Posada Santiago; the front entrance is around the corner from Parque Juárez on Ave. Manuel Ávila Camacho (walk about a block down Enriquez until you see the purple wall marking the entrance).

A popular local spot on Sundays is the **Parque de Los Berros** or Park of the Watercress (so named because of the way the plant grew at one time in great abundance close to a nearby pool). The park draws families, ice cream vendors, and people just out to enjoy the day. It's a large circular area filled with tall trees, a kiosk in its center, and a few statues, including one of Miguel Hidalgo y Costilla (you will sometimes hear the locals refer to this park as Hidalgo Park). The park is a few blocks southeast of downtown, on Miguel Hidalgo.

If you want a look at the talent of Mexican sculptors, the **Jardín de las Esculturas** (Sculpture Garden) hosts national and international outdoor exhibits, both temporary and permanent. The garden is on Ave. Murillo Vidal s/n, open Tues.-Sun., 10 am to 6 pm.

About a mile and a half outside downtown is **Parque El Haya**, set aside for enjoyment of nature. The site includes some trails and a playground. Open Tues.-Sun., 9 am to 5 pm, on the old road to Coatepec (follow Ave. Lázaro Cárdendas west out of town).

On the same road, at Km 2.5, is the **Jardín Botánico Clavijero** (Botanical Garden of Clavijero), a nature center with acres of local plants. The main sections – the forest, with unique palms, the formal garden, with many ornamental plants, and the aquatic zone – are criss-crossed by paths. They have a section with plants for sale as well. It can be tempting, but don't forget about Customs restrictions on bringing plants home. Open Tues.-Sun., 9 am to 5 pm. To get to either, take a bus marked *El Haya* from in front of the Palacio Municipal.

Hikes

There is an old dormant volcano some blocks northeast of Xalapa's main square that has been turned into a one-of-a-kind nature sanctuary known as the **Macuiltépetl Ecological Park**. The park has trails that wind up to its peak where, at the end of your hike, you come to the volcano's crater (thankfully long dormant), and a fine view. Keep an eye out for butterflies and birds, including hawks, eagles, and owls. If you don't see them in the wild, you can stop at the volcano's **Museo de la Fauna** (Fauna Museum). The Museum is open Tues.-Fri., 11 am-5 pm; the park is open daily, 6 am-6 pm. It's at Calle Tepic and Calle Toluca, about a 20-minute walk from downtown (follow Ave. Revolución north and it turns into Ave. Miguel Alemán; you'll see the park rising up on the left). Or, more simply, take a cab. While you're here, you might also want to go across the street and see the **Cueva de la Orquidea**, a cave virtually in the middle of the city (Ave. Miguel Alemán in front of the park; open daily 7 am-7 pm).

WORD TO THE WISE

Adventure outfitters have taken advantage of Xalapa's natural surroundings, and offer a limitless array of activities – all quite affordable. **Veraventuras**, ☎ *0800-712-6572 or 228-818-9579, and* **Amigos del Río**, ☎ *228-815-8817, have offices in Xalapa. See* Jalcomulco, *page 229, for more outfitters.*

Tour the Churches

If you get lost, don't use the distant belltowers of a church as a familiar landmark, or you may just end up getting a complete tour of the entire city in one day... Xalapa is filled with churches! For those of you who seek out those towers as destinations in themselves, however, start by visiting **La Catedral**, Xalapa's main church, just to the east of Parque Juárez on Enriquez. Dedicated to Xalapa's patron saint, la Señora de la Inmaculada Concepción, the church plays an important role in the city, reflected in its quiet elegance. The current building is over 200 years old (the original church, built in 1641, was reconstructed in 1773) and is an interesting combination of neogothic and neoclassic styles. The inside is large and welcoming, housing the remains of Veracruz' fifth bishop, Rafael Guízar y Valencia, as well as a striking painting by Mexican painter Miguel Cabrera.

The Legend of Iglesia de los Corazónes

The sad legend of the Iglesia de los Corazónes (Church of the Hearts), goes something like this. A young man fell in love with the daughter of a Spanish immigrant and asked her father for the girl's hand in marriage. The father, seeing that the boy was poor, refused the request, and sent the boy away. In desperate love, the boy set out to make his fortune so that he and his love could be together. Time passed, and the girl, with no word from her beloved, died of a broken heart. She vowed that their hearts would never be separated. The father, now heart-broken himself for having caused his daughter's death, received comfort and advice from a priest who told him that, in a dream, he had seen the father making peace with himself once he built a church. A butterfly would lead him to the place. Leaving the priest, the Spaniard saw the butterfly, followed it, and watched it land. He built the church that you see today, a few blocks northwest of downtown on Altamirano 121.

Ready for more? Xalapa won't disappoint. A few blocks north of the city center on Ave. Revolución and P. Moreno, sits the pale yellow building of the old **Iglesia del Calvario**. The church has a gated wall enclosing a plaza, two towers, and a clock imported from London in 1765. For a really old one, swing by the **Iglesia de San José** on Xalapeños Ilustres at the end of Callejón Jesús te Ampare, which has origins dating back to around 1555. For a colonial-styled one, stop for services at the **Iglesia La Piedad** on Ave. Revolución, or, if neoclassical is more to your liking, the **Iglesia de Santiago** at 110 Ursulo Galvan. Or maybe you just want to stay close to Parque Juárez? Two blocks west you can check out the 18th-century **Iglesia del Beatrio**.

Wandering the Alleys

One of the most enchanting aspects of Xalapa are its alleys (*callejóns*) – narrow, cobblestoned, and hilly, they are unmistakable. Walking down them when the fog rolls in, you feel as if you're on the set of an old movie. Adding to the mystique, grisly legends are associated with many of them. The alley between Xalapeños Ilustres and Gutiérrez Zamora, **Callejón de Jesús te Ampare**, is incredibly picturesque. It's a long narrow pathway covered with square cobblestones and lined with small, single-story, tile-roofed houses painted red and yellow. On some of the houses you'll notice metal grates covering the windows. An old legend says that a young man by the name of Cosme de Taboada was so enamored by his beloved, that he would come to this alley each night to visit and talk to her through the grates of her house. One night, a drunk man (possibly jealous of their love), saw Cosme, and viciously stabbed him to death. His beloved, seeing this, shouted "Cosme, Jesús te Ampare!" (May Jesus Protect You!). Thus the alley was named.

A block away from the Parque Juárez, off Enríquez, you'll find a little alley squeezed in among the buildings. The *callejón* is a cute place to browse around; it winds its way up a hill, leaving behind a trail of restaurants, galleries, and artists. Tables are set out and filled with handmade bracelets, rings, and necklaces, paintings, and carved objects. This is **Callejón del Diamante** – Diamond Alley.

As one legend goes, there once was a beautiful young woman, engaged to a handsome young man who gave her an enchanted black diamond ring, which supposedly would tell if his future wife ever became unfaithful. Time passed, and one day, while her husband was away, the wife went to the house of her lover and took off her ring. (She had fallen in love with a close friend of her husband.) The husband stopped by his friend's house on the way home and spotted the ring on the nightstand. Distraught and heartbroken, he went home and stabbed his wife to death.

The Callejón del Diamante is actually crossed by another alleyway to explore, the **Callejón de las Flores** (connecting the streets of Lucio and Carrillo Puerto).

If you aren't already, by the time you get to the **Callejón de la Calavera** (Alley of the Skull), you'll definitely have your guard up against getting to know the locals (the risk just may be a little too great).

Legend says that a woman living on this street was married to a man who loved to drink. Fed up with the whole business, one day when he stumbled home, she gave him a sleeping draught, then chopped off his head. To clean up the evidence, she buried the body under the floorboards of her house, but the head she stowed under her bed in a box. A short time passed, and concerned neighbors reported the husband missing. The police discovered the head under the bed. Callejón de la Calavera is north of Puente Xallitic, off Madero.

The most famous of the *callejóns* of Xalapa are mentioned above, but another of my favorites, right across the street from Parque Juárez (the alley connects to both Enriquez and Revolución), is **Callejón de Rojas**, a charming narrow cobblestoned street, lined with street lamps and colorful houses. It's perfect for an evening stroll.

A Daytime Stroll

Here is a spot whose loveliness suddenly appears from nowhere. One minute, you're in the middle of street vendors, approaching an unremarkable bridge. The next, you're on the bridge and, if you look down, you'll blink twice before you believe what you see. An enchanting narrow street, lined with colorful houses and gorgeous, brilliantly flowering trees, winds its way under the bridge, up a hill, and out of view. This is **Puente Xallitic** – one of the four original neighborhoods that formed what would become Xalapa. Go on a sunny day, when you can enjoy wandering around the neighborhood to its fullest. To get there, from Parque Juárez, simply turn from Enriquez onto Dr. Lucio, and follow it uphill and out of the immediate downtown area for a few blocks, until you reach the Lucio Street Bridge.

Take the stairs down the right (east) side of the bridge, where you'll find an old arched open-air red building, which houses an unexpected laundry spot – **los lavaderos**. The long building has 13 adjacent wash spots on each side; clothes are put into the waist-high sink bowl, which has a rough rock on the bottom for abrasion when scrubbing. You may see a woman hard at work while you're there. You can wander under the bridge, and up the street to enjoy the rest of the neighborhood.

Lavaderos (something like wash-board-sinks – an early one is shown at left) have long been the main means to do laundry, since many Mexicans do not have washers and dryers. Even today, in larger cities where laundromats and washers are becoming more common, new houses and condos are still being built with a lavadero on the back porch.

Sports

A few blocks to the west of downtown, at the corner of Ave. M. Ávila Camacho and Calle Victoria, is the **Parque Los Tecajetes**, an ecological area meant to protect and display the local flora, as well as provide a space for activities. The site offers a track for **runners, basketball courts**, space to play **soccer**, and a **playground** for children, all in a natural setting, complete with ponds and streams (open 9 am-6 pm daily).

On Wheels

DID YOU KNOW?

In the Anthropology Museum (see below), there is an ancient Indian child's toy that has wheels and is meant to be pulled. It is believed, however, that the wheel was not used by the Indians in their everyday worklife – possibly because they had no beasts of burden to make suitable use of it.

Bus Tour

 A great way to see the city is on the open-air trolley **El Piojito**, which gives 60-minute tours of the most important parts of the Centro Histórico (historical center) and includes a narration (everything, of course, in Spanish) on the history and legends of the streets and buildings. You can find the trolleys in front of the Bank Serfin on Enriquez. Buses run from 10:30 am to 8 pm, and charge 30 pesos for adults, and 25 for children and students.

Drives

 It's always fun to drive around and explore spontaneously. Some spots that offer possibilities follow. About 24 miles/39 km from Xalapa is the **Valle Allegre** (or Happy Valley), an animal/ecological reserve where you can get out of the car and do some horseback riding as well. To get there, head west from Xalapa on Highway 140 and right after Las Vigas take the unpaved road south (left).

Stop by Las Vigas (west on Highway 140 from Xalapa), and ask about a huge system of caves in a nearby area known as **El Volcancillo** (some outfitters, including Veracruz-based **Amphibian**, ☎ 229-931-0997, offer outings here). While you're there, ask for directions to **El Bordo** as well (a mile or two away in the direction of the village Tatatila), which is a good vantage point to view the **Cascada Tenexpanoya** (waterfalls), after which you might want to check out the village of **Tatatila** itself (north on a road from Las Vigas).

The town of **Las Minas** (west on Highway 140 from Xalapa, then north onto a road after Las Vigas) has some streets made of cast-off marble mined from the nearby mountains.

Be aware that, once you get of the main highway, roads become smaller, and driving gets slower. If you don't mind driving down the windy road to get there (it'll take you 45 minutes to an hour), the village of **Naolinco** has a pretty waterfall right at the edge of town. From Highway 140, exit north at Banderilla, continue down the road, crossing the Río Actopan and passing Coacoatzintla. Naolinco will be your next stop. The waterfalls are down a short path at the edge of town (ask around).

On Water

 The hot sulfur springs of **El Carrizal** might have some curative properties for your ailments. They're about half an hour's drive away (head toward Veracruz on Highway 140). At Km 36, right after the village of Plan del Río, you should see a smaller road off to the right heading toward

Carrizal. The springs are next to a river, near a restaurant and some pools.

Archaeological Discoveries

One of the best archeological museums in México, the **Museo de Antropología**, attracts many visitors to Xalapa just for the chance to browse through its remarkable collection. The gallery is divided into five main halls, displaying around 3,000 pieces, taking you through the Gulf Coast cultures – the Huastec, the Totonac, and the Olmecs. One of the first pieces that you will see, right at the entrance, is a colossal head created by the Olmecs. The museum has 10 of these larger-than-life creations throughout its halls, seven of which come from the site of San Lorenzo Tenochtitlan, and are fascinating not just for their expressions (straight-faced, grimaces – one is even smiling), but also in that the features themselves have a somewhat Negroid appearance, clearly raising many anthropological questions. The museum is organized geographically and chronologically, starting with pieces from the preclassic period (1300-900 BC) and ending with the 'modern' postclassic (1250-1521 AD) pieces. Representative pieces in the collection include the Caritas Sonrientes (smiling faces) – ceramic faces wearing an exaggerated comical expression of mirth. You will have a hard time believing that they aren't modern. Then there are the Cihuateotl – sculpted life-size figures of women who died while giving birth, recovered from the site of El Zapotal. There is a riveting sculpture of Mictlantecuhtli, the Lord of the Dead, an unmistakable, fearful, seated skeletal figure. And you will see the murals of Las Higueras – coloful layered paintings (new ones covering older ones), parts of which date back as early as the birth of Christ.

In addition, there is an intriguing display case in the main hall showing the indigenous custom of binding women's skulls to reshape them into a more beautiful conical shape.

The museum does not supply any pamphlets, brochures, or maps with your paid admission. It does, however, have explanatory wall panels with timelines, geography, and descriptions of the different cultures – everything is in Spanish. Most of the exhibits themselves are labeled, and for those of you who aren't fluent in Spanish, there are some great laminated guides that you can pick up at the entrance to each room. They come in English and direct you to the more important pieces in that section; unfortunately, there is only one guide available for each room (and you have to return it to its holder before you move on). But not everyone seems to see these guides, so chances you can grab one are pretty good.

To get to the museum (Ave. Xalapa s/n), catch a bus on Enriquez in front of the Palacio Municipal marked *Museo*. The museum is a large modern building surrounded by gardens (on the left side of the bus – just tell the bus driver where you're going if in doubt). To get back, take a bus from in front of the museum marked *Centro*.

General admission is 40 pesos; children ages 12 and under are admitted for free. There is an extra fee to take photos or use a video camera – and, yes, the guards patrol the galleries and will ask you for your ticket if they see you taking pictures. Open 9 am-5 pm, Tues. to Sat.

What is on exhibit at the Museo de Antropología is only a fraction of the museum's entire collection – there are actually around 24,000 more artifacts not on display!

■ Cultural & Eco-Travel Excursions

Art Galleries

I met a tourist in Xalapa. She had her walking shoes on, a cup of coffee in one hand, a crinkled map in the other, and a huge smile on her face. She was standing at a corner and, as I walked by, she motioned me close and in an excited speech – clearly high on culture and java – asked me if I had been to this spot, that I needed to go to that spot, and by the way, did I know where she could find this other spot? She had already been to half a dozen galleries. She left me, on the way to another one. Are *you* ready?

Grab a cup of coffee and start in Parque Juárez at the **Ágora de la Ciudad** (Tues.-Sun., 9 am-11 pm; free), a gallery with displays showing off the local culture. From here, it's a short walk to the **Pinacoteca Diego Rivera** (J.J. Herrera 5, Mon.-Sat., 8 am-6 pm; free) on the west side of Parque Juárez, under it's terrace, where you'll find a permanent exhibit of paintings by Diego Rivera (as the husband of Frida Kahlo, he recently became something of a household name among moviegoers after release of the movie *Frida*).

The **Galería de Arte Ramón Alva de la Canal**, on Gutiérrez Zamora 27 (Mon.-Fri., 9 am-2 pm and 5-8 pm; free), is a two-floor gallery with several different rooms that hosts temporary exhibits.

When I was last there, a beautiful exhibit of the lithographs of José Luis Cuevas was on display.

Galería de Arte Contemporáneo de Xalapa is a short walk east of downtown at Xalapeños Ilustres 135 (Tues.-Sun., 10 am-3 pm, 6-9 pm; free). It is a state gallery, and has contemporary art filling its main room, as well as a smaller side room. Close to downtown on Alfaro 10 (north off Gutiérrez Zamora) the **Galería Marie-Louise Ferrari** (Mon.-Sat., 4-8 pm), is in a colonial house, part of which has been transformed into a gallery of both temporary and permanent exhibits. The **Centro Cultural los Lagos** (formerly known as the Casa de Artesanías), in the Paseo de los Lagos, has some temporary exhibits, and is worth a quick stop on your morning stroll to see what cultural events might be planned during your stay (Mon.-Fri., 9 am-3 pm and 6-9 pm; Sat., 10 am-2 pm).

Other options include the **Galería de Artes Plásticas** (Fine Art Gallery) on Belsario Domínguez 25 (Mon.-Sat., 8 am-3 pm), the **Galería Alberto Beltrán** on Juárez 79 (Mon.-Fri., 10 am-2 pm and 6-8 pm), and the **Galería del Centro Recreativo**, at the corner of Insurgentes and Xalapeños Ilustres (daily, 9 am-2 pm, 4-7pm).

Visit a Hacienda

About a 15-minute drive south of Xalapa is the former residence of past Mexican president General António López de Santa Anna (1794-1876). The estate, known as the **Museo Ex Hacienda El Lencero**, has also been both an inn and a farm. It has now been converted to a museum, offering visitors the chance to step back into the 1800s as they tour the hacienda and the surrounding gardens. The museum is on the Highway 140, Km 10, and open Tues.-Fri., 10 am-5 pm; 40 pesos.

With so much of the beautiful area from Xalapa to Xico and Coatepec dedicated to coffee plantations, Veracruz' tourism department has developed the "Coffee Route" (also see *Xico*) – a tour of plantations, hotels, and haciendas in the area. In Xalapa, the **Hacienda Lucas Martín**, ☎ 228-818-1122, on the outskirts of town (on Calle San Luis de la Paz s/n, a turnoff from Highway 140 heading west towards Banderilla), should be contacted beforehand to make arrangements for a plantation tour. Another, the Hacienda de Nuestra Señora de los Remedios (also known as the **Hacienda de Pacho**), is a 17th-century New Orleans-styled building that can be visited by prior arrangement; ☎ 228-817-2385. They are a short distance west from the village of Estanzuela off Highway 140.

Learn the Lost Art of Goldsmithing

In the building adjoining the Galleria Artesins, at 38 Gutiérrez Zamora, is the **Taller Escuela de Orfebreria**, where a third-generation goldsmith is trying to rescue the prehispanic goldsmith culture. Maestro José Luis Gomez Lima, Master Goldsmith, gives workshops, where he teaches his students the fascinating, ancient lost-wax technique. Courses range from novice-level introductory workshops, to more advanced techniques, most of which he tries to do in conjunction with the School for Foreign Students (see *Study Abroad* below). Examples of pieces he and his students have made include beautiful hairpieces, necklaces, pins, charms, and bracelets. His classes are small – 12-14 people – and course length and price vary, depending on skill level. An introductory course, for example, lasts about two months. He is willing to tailor courses to a shorter time period, such as two or three weeks, especially for groups. This is a relatively new endeavor for Maestro Luis Gomez, whose project is supported by him as well as the Government of Veracruz, Cultural Foundation of Bancomer. He is midway through a two-year commitment, and hopes to continue if there is enough interest. For more information, you can contact Maestro Luis Gomez at ☎ (228) 841-1202, or email ceraperdida@yahoo.com.mx or bancodeideas@.com.

LOST WAX

The art of lost wax has been used for thousands of years to make jewelry. The technique involves creating an exact, detailed, wax model of the object that you wish to create, which is then covered in a fire-proof mold (some casters use plaster of Paris). The hardened mold (which now has the wax model inside), is heated until the wax melts out, or is "lost" (commonly it melts out of a small hole in the base). Molten metal is then poured into the hollow cast. When cooled, the result is an exact duplicate of the original wax mold.

Theaters

To hear a little bit of local culture, stop by one of the theaters to see what's going on while you're in town. The **Teatro del Estado** (State Theater) on Ave. Ignacio de la Llave is one of the best choices. On many Friday evenings, they host Xalapa's Symphony Orchestra (Orquesta Sinfónica de Xalapa; ☎ 228-818-0834). Another option is to contact the **Teatro J.J. Herrera** at Miguel Palacios 12 to see what's on their schedule; ☎ 228-812-0658.

Study Abroad

Xalapa is the home of the **Universidad Veracruzana México**, whose **School for Foreign Students** (*Escuela para Estudiantes Extranjeros*) has an excellent program of graduate, undergraduate, credit, and non-credit courses. Do you have a son or daughter looking for some adventure? Here's a chance to get them out of the house for a bit, and an excuse for a return visit to Xalapa.

The school's offerings include a Cultural Immersion Program that pairs up a student with a "cultural assistant," who works with the student on both Spanish and local culture. An Independent Study Program is meant for students interested in for-credit research, and an opportunity to take undergraduate or graduate-level classes, for credit, at the university. Prices are pretty affordable; individual classes run around US $300 per course, while the home-stay program (where you stay with a host family), runs under US $1,000 for six weeks. Visit the university's website for more information at www.uv.mx/eee.

■ Festivals & Events

There is always an event of some sort – musical, theatrical, novice, expert – in Xalapa on any given day. The established annual events, however, include the entire month of June, which is designated the **month of photography**; look for photographic expositions and conferences. From April to May, the **Expo-Feria** is organized, with a daily schedule of cultural events (dances, plays, music) throughout the city. July 25 is the day of **Santiago Apostle**, marked by fireworks, parades, and music.

■ Shopping

If you want to bring home a gift, stop at **Galleria Artesins**. The blue and white building at 38 Gutiérrez Zamora is filled with beautiful quality, handmade items, including belts, dolls, blankets, hats, baskets, jugs, candleholders, wooden carving, and pictures. The added bonus: most of the stuff is very reasonably priced, and everything is unique. People at home will love you for sure! Open Mon.-Fri., 10 am-2 pm and 4-8 pm; Sat., 10 am-2 pm.

The **Diego Rivera Gallery** sells paintings by local artists, most of which are hung on the walls, gallery-style. One side of the shop is actually a studio, where paintings are in various states of completion. The shop is at 8 Gutiérrez Zamora.

At 44 Ursula Galvan is an **antique shop** with chandeliers, figurines, books, and all sorts of knicknacks – both Mexican and foreign.

One of the main supermarkets here is the **Chedraui**, which has a large branch right in the center at 16 Revolución (a short walk up from Enriquez).

At the corner of Ave. Revolución and Manlio Fabio Altamirano (follow Ave. Revolución uphill two blocks from the main square), **Mercado Jáuregui** is a fun market, selling lots and lots of flowers of all kinds – freshly cut, dried, plastic, individual, bouquets. Religion seems to be a big theme as well, and you can find plenty of crosses for sale.

Besides the gift and souvenir shops, if you're craving a little piece of home, or if you just forgot to pack something specific, you'll see a number of familiar names as you drive into Xalapa on the highway from Veracruz, including a **Costco**, **Officemax**, **Walmart**, and, right in the center near Parque Juárez, a **Sears**. Be prepared to open your wallet a little bit more than you would for the same products at home.

■ Nightlife

With all there is to do in the daytime, I have to wonder how many of you will actually get out at night. Many will probably end up buying balloons, sweet treats (try some *churros rellenos*, fried dough stuffed with caramel), and watching the clowns in **Parque Juárez**. If you see a huge crowd, you'll know that someone is putting on an act.

Others will find a concert or theater show. Most Friday nights you can hear the Orquesta Sinfónica de Xalapa – one of México's very best – playing at the **Teatro del Estado**.

For those interested in a livelier scene, Xalapa has a number of clubs. The disco/bar **Esfinge** near the bus station at 20 de Noviembre (corner of Maestros Veracruzanos) can be easily identified at any hour of the night. Look for the building with the huge sphinx head out front, and listen for the rock music. It's a very trendy spot which, besides serving up drinks and dancing, cures the munchies with pizza, hamburgers, and snacks. It's open 1 pm-2 am. Another hotspot open until the wee hours is **Club Vortex** at 84 Ave. Ávila Camacho.

■ Where to Stay

Hotel Limón, Ave. Revolución 8, ☎ 228 817-2204, is a favorite of budget travelers. Founded in 1894, it sits on a narrow, steep, cobble-stoned street, less than a block away from Parque Juárez. Off-season room rates here are the best in the city; rooms include color TV, and parking is available, There is no a/c. The hotel is charming, with a colorfully tiled indoor courtyard, bright orange and purple coloring, and cozy rooms. The only fault are the thin doors and walls, which tend to echo the snores of guests. But for this price, and this charm, you'll hardly notice. $

Hotel Plaza Xalapa, Enríquez 4, ☎ 228-817-3310. At the corner of Valle and Enriquez, this older hotel overlooks Enriquez, and so some rooms can be a bit noisy. Though the lobby is a little dull, rooms are clean and spacious (if a bit dated), and are very affordable. Credit cards not accepted. $

HOTEL PRICE CHART	
Rates are per room based on double occupancy. Rates lower if single occupancy or sharing a bed. Higher rates on holidays.	
	US $10-$20
$	US $21-$40
$$	US $41-$60
$$$	US $61-$80
$$$$	US $81-$125
$$$$$	Over US $125

Hotel Posada Santiago, Ursula Galván 89, ☎ 228-818-6333, has some small, simple rooms that are clean, with private older bathrooms, and with or without TVs (which will add a few dollars to the price). There is a small, pleasant courtyard that the rooms overlook. $

Casa Inn Xalapa, Ave. 20 de Noviembre Ote. 522, ☎ 228-818-5523 or 0800-715-7788. Right across the street from the bus station, Casa Inn Xalapa has the amenities and services that you would expect in a member of a chain. The lobby has a restaurant and telephones, as well as a credit-card Internet machine. Rooms are very clean, and have modern bathrooms, color TV, room service, and phones, though some of them – especially the inside rooms – can get a bit stuffy since they have no a/c or fan. This explains the higher price for rooms on an upper floor (around 80 pesos more). The hotel seems to cater mainly to business travelers, but is a nice dependable place to stay if you can't make it to the cheaper hotels downtown. There is parking. $

Hotel México, Lucio 4, ☎ 228-818-8000. Looking directly onto La Catedral, the very plain Hotel México is a convenient choice, though the passing traffic can make it pretty noisy at night. Rooms are basic, include a color TV and phone. There is parking in its courtyard. They do not accept credit cards. $

Hotel Posada Casa Regia, 12 Hidalgo, ☎ 228-812-0591. This medium-priced hotel is a quiet, pretty spot to stay, offering simple, clean rooms. $

Hotel María Victoria, Zaragoza 6, ☎ 228-818-6011 or 0800-260-0800. This large handicapped-accessible hotel, a block or so from Parque Juárez, is a modern, fancier option, with single and double rooms, as well as suites (rooms are on the high end of the price range). All rooms have phones, color TV, and a/c. Conveniences include underground parking and a restaurant with a full bar adjacent to the lobby. While you're in the lobby, take a look at the historic pictures of Xalapa on the wall. $$

Villa Las Margaritas, Dr. Lucio 186, at the corner of Julián Carrillo, ☎ 228-815-0611 or 0800-719-4367, www.uv.mx/eee. This pretty hotel has all the amenities (parking, restaurant, laundry service, gym), and clean rooms, at a decent rate. $$

Howard Johnson, Ave. 20 de Noviembre Ote. 455, ☎ 228-812-1925, or 0800-260-5200. This HoJo is really nice, and has a wonderful atmosphere, though it is closer to the bus station (about a 10-minute walk) than to downtown. It has a huge indoor wooden lobby that is open, airy, and filled with plants. Amenities include a gym, spa, restaurant, parking, and laundry. Rates are a bit pricey, but if you're looking for an upgrade, this is a good choice. $$$

Fiesta Inn Xalapa, Km 2.5 on Xalapa-Veracruz Highway, ☎ 228-812-7920 or 0800-504-5000. This hotel is geared mainly to business travelers, and so has all the associated amenities, with little character... and big prices. Some travelers may find its location appealing, especially if you're coming from a long drive and don't want to deal with downtown traffic. Try reserving a room online at www.fiestainn.com.mx for an AARP or AAA discount rate. $$$$

Misión Xalapa, Calle Victoria, at the corner of Bustamante, ☎ 228-818-2222 or 0800-260-2600. One of a number of Misión hotels in México, Xalapa's huge, elegant property, like most of the higher priced stays here, caters mainly to business travelers. The hotel even has two villas and a presidential suite. Rooms are spacious and have a/c, color TV, and a phone. Check the hotel's website, www.hotelsmision.com, for seasonal promotions. Currently, for example, they are offering some package rates. $$$$

■ Where to Eat

The exotic fruits at the market are like nothing you have at home – zapote chico, zapote negro, guanábana, mamey. Try one as a snack and your mouth will be off on an adventure of its own! If your stomach is sensitive, you might want to buy one and try a sliver.

Restaurante Enrico's, 6 Enriquez. A short walk from La Catedral on Enriquez is Enrico's, a popular place for basic, tasty lunches. A *comida corrida*, or pre-set lunch, of soup, chicken, and coffee runs around 50 pesos – and if you're too full when you're done, hop on the trolley tour which leaves right out front. $

La Sopa, 3A Callejón del Diamante, is a popular local favorite almost always bustling with activity. It serves basic Mexican food, and a great lunch *comida corrida* (drink, soup, dessert, and main course). $

DINING PRICE CHART	
Price per person for an entrée, not including beverage or tip.	
$	Under US $5
$$	US $5-$10
$$$	US $10+

Close by, **El Diamente**, 16 Callejón del Diamante, is another local favorite for tasty Mexican dishes. $

Plazo Lefa, 46 Zamora, is across the street from the Foreign Student School, and stays crowded with families, kids, and students, enjoying its pleasant atrium with a covered patio and budget-friendly food – especially the lunch buffet. $-$$

La Churreria del Recuerdo, 158 Victoria, is a little far from downtown, but has lip-smacking *churros*, as well as tasty *antojitos*. $-$$

La Casona del Beaterio, 20 Zaragoza, serves up international fair for lunch, as well as the occasional *enchilada*, at decent prices (almost everything is under 80 pesos). It sometimes has live music. $-$$

Pollos Trico, 20 de Noviembre, across from the Howard Johnson, is a good spot to get food for a picnic. They sell whole roasted chickens for 25 pesos, as well as some basic sides to go with it. $-$$

Another budget option is **Taqueria Tom Mix**, 30 Revolución, Centro. Another location is at 38 Cempoala and Ave. Ávila Camacho, close to Parque Juárez. The small, nondescript restaurant is a place to go if you need something cheap and fast. You can find typical *taqueria* food: *tacos pastor* (small tacos made from thin slices of pork slow-cooked on a rotisserie), *tacos bistec* (beef-steak tacos), *quesadillas*, soups, chickens, *tostadas*, *panuchos* (small fried corn tortillas with a layer of refried beans inside, topped with meat, lettuce and onions), and *tamales*. $

Pelicanos, 108 Allende, has an excellent reputation as a great seafood restaurant – especially for shellfish. The shrimp soup is particularly good. $

For Vegetarians & the Health Conscious

Next door to Enrico's at 6 Enriquez is **Jugos California**, a fresh juice bar almost always loaded with people. They have just about every kind of juice you can imagine; specials are written on a chalk board by the entrance. $

Manantial de las Flores, 102 Galvin. This all-natural food restaurant is a great spot for nature lovers, the health-conscious, vegetarians, and romantics. It's in a neoclassic building that went through the phases of being a Gregorian singing school, a home of spiritual exercises, and a girl's school. Walk through an arched hallway, and around a corner, and you'll find a beautiful quiet outside restaurant in a Franciscan-styled patio, surrounded by plants and nature. Besides the natural/organic meals on the menu, you can buy breads, yogurts, and marmalades. You'll have to make this a lunch spot though. It's open Tues.-Sun., 9 am-6 pm. $$

Restaurante Vegeteriano El Champiñon, 78 Allende, is another vegetarian-friendly spot, serving up quick, no frills, meatless fare. $

Perote

The dusty town of Perote (my hair was one complete shade lighter after my visit), is worth a trip if you're interested in mountain – or should I say, volcano – hiking. The mound in question is the 1,300-foot/4,282-m **Cofre de Perote** (or Nauhcampatépetl in the Aztec Náhuatl language), which rises behind the city, looking deceivingly more like a large hill than the second-highest mountain in the state. From afar, it looks as if it has a square structure at its summit. This is actually the feature that gives it its name – a huge square rock that resembles a treasure chest (or *cofre*).

The area is a natural reserve, known as the **Parque Nacional Cofre de Perote**, and has become an attraction for mountaineers and hikers. It's a somewhat easy challenge, evidenced by the network of well-trodden paths disappearing up the slopes. If you make it to the top (great caution should be taken to not get lost as well as to acclimatize yourself to the elevation first), you can reportedly get a magnificent view of the surrounding mountains and valleys. Perote is not a place you'd like to stay the night and, aside from a few old haciendas outside of town and the volcano, has little else to offer.

■ Orientation & Practicalities

Perote is 53 km (33 miles) west of Xalapa on Highway 140. The unattractive main square is on Francisco I. Madero; to the south is the Cofre de Perote. There are a couple of banks right across the street from the bus station.

■ Getting There & Around

The **drive** to Perote along Highway 140 from Xalapa is very scenic. You'll want to reduce your speed, not just to take in the surroundings – white picket fences marking the borders of cattle ranches, cows and horses grazing on brilliant green fields, huge trees covering the surrounding mountainsides – but also because the road becomes narrow and twisty. With a noticable climb, your ears will be popping the whole way up to Perote, which is at 2,465 meters (8,087 feet) above sea level.

If you go by **bus**, the station is on Francisco I. Madero at the corner of Miguel Hidalgo; to get to the *zócalo* from here, take a left as you exit the bus station and walk two blocks. The bus station has an ATM and a waiting area, but little else.

BUS TRIPS			
Destination	Bus Line	Fare	Time
México City (TAPO)	ADO	137 pesos	4 hours 5 minutes
	AU	122 pesos	
Xalapa	ADO	26 pesos	1 hour 10 minutes
	AU	23 pesos	
Veracruz	AU	71 pesos	2 hours 50 minutes

■ Adventures

Hiking

Basically, you have two choices if you want to get up the mountain.

By Bus or Car: You can drive almost the entire way up the mountain by heading south out of town toward the Cofre and following the bumpy suspension-ruining dirt road up. At its end, you'll have to park and hike the last short bit.

If you don't have a car, you can take a bus up the mountain to the tiny town (800 inhabitants) of El Escobillo. Catching the bus is probably harder than the actual hike itself – sitting on the curb in front of the market as clouds of dust from the nearby dirt road billowed around me, I almost gave up after an hour's wait. In fact, the bus goes up at 8:30 am and 3 pm, returning at 9:30 am and 4 pm. Don't be late on either end. Of course, you can entertain yourself as I did, watching the locals – a few trash collectors wheeling barrels filled with litter or the local dogs who find the loose rubbish and sit in the middle of the street munching for hours, too intent to move for anything. Here, the *cars* drive around the *dogs*.

To pick the bus up, from the *zócalo*, go directly across from the city hall, and head down 16 de Septiembre two blocks, then take a right on the street Barranca de Ocopila (there is no street sign, you'll know you're there when you see a market off to your right). You pick up the bus at the entrance to the market on the next corner, where the road becomes dirt; there are no signs indicating that this is a stop. If you thought that you had been in a second class bus before, well, you haven't been on the Parada Ocopila – an ancient, rickety red school bus with no shock absorbers. The trip takes 45 minutes and costs 9 pesos. Sit on the left side of the bus for your first views of the Cofre. The ride is actually beautiful if you can get your mind off the groans and moans of the bus struggling up the mountain, in second gear the entire way. The drive follows a steep, narrow dirt road that winds past a canyon, through forested hillsides, and alongside hiking trails, before breaking out onto a gorgeous plateau which is a meadow sprinkled with curious looking cacti and grazing sheep. It's as if you've crossed over into another dimension. The bus stops at the church (El Escobillo doesn't have much more than that), before turning around and heading back down.

You'll see some trails behind the church heading out and away from the town, towards the Cofre. The tiny town is also used as a base for some groups that go up the mountain; ask around and you may be able to find yourself a guide.

On Foot: You can hike the whole way up the mountain, though the Veracruz tourist department does not currently have any available trail maps or instructions. There are a number of routes people have beaten up the mountain to its summit, which can make for a confusing journey. You're probably better off with a guide (some Mexican adventure outfitters have offerings). Brave hikers do venture up themselves without a problem, many heading up the mountain to the town of El Conejo, which is about a four-hour hike from the summit.

■ Where to Stay

If you need to stay the night here to get an early start in the morning, the **Hotel Mansión Humboldt**, ☎ 282-825-2937, is a decent, clean choice in a town that does not have much. The hotel is conveniently located on the Xalapa-Veracruz road (Ave. Humboldt Sur 23). Large, clean rooms with phone, cable TV, and bathroom are less than US $20. To get there from the bus station, take a right turn as you exit, then a left onto Humboldt Sur – it's about a five-minute walk.

■ Where to Eat

If you're a cheese-lover, stop at any of the many shops selling *queso fresco* (fresh cheese) along Highway 140 right outside Perote. In town, you can get a cheese-stuffed bread known as *requeson*. As for restaurants, the **Restaurante Molino del Quijote II** (Humboldt Sur 21 – next to the hotel above)

is a popular spot. It serves soups, fish, and a huge selection of filets – peppered steak, lamb, rabbit with mushrooms, as well as a good selection of liquors.

Coatepec

Coffee drinkers may already be familiar with Coatepec; it's known nationwide (and internationally) for its export – superb coffee. The town has the perfect combination of soil, temperature, and altitude to produce some of México's finest. And Coatepec is what you would imagine a coffee town to be like – old colonial buildings with weathered, gray walls, balconies and shady trees; wide streets that see their share of cars, but aren't packed the way a real production center might be; and a couple of large cafés, not boastful or proud, just quietly serving a decent cup. Five miles south of Xalapa, it's a good town to pass through but doesn't warrant much time, unless all you're looking for is a charming hotel. While you're here, be sure to investigate the other local crop, orchids.

■ Orientation & Practicalities

On the western side of the Zona Centro is the Palacio Municipal. From here, if you head west down Aldama, you'll find Parque Miguel Hidalgo and the Parroquia de San Jeronimo. One block to the west of the Palacio Municipal, on Aldama, is the local **bus station**. On a clear day, you might be able to see the Pico de Orizaba in the distance to the south, while to the north is the hill known as the Cerro de las Culebras.

■ Getting There & Around

The local bus from Xalapa will drop you off at the corner of 16 de Septiembre and Jiménez del Campillo; to get to the *zócalo* from here, head west down Campillo. See *Xalapa – Getting Around*, page 196, for directions on how to get to Coatepec.

■ Sightseeing

Mixed in among the everyday houses are some attractive colonial buildings that make Coatepec a good place for low-key sightseeing. After you go in the **Palacio Municipal** to see the mural behind the bust of Benito Juárez, cross the street to check out the **Parroquia de San Jeronimo**

(main church), part of which has been reconstructed after it was partially destroyed in a 1920 earthquake. After that, enjoy the other interesting architecture of the central zone, such as the neat old grey building of the **Papeleria Olimipia** (on Campillo), which doesn't even seem to belong here, or the vivid yellow and red building of the **Benito Juárez Cantonal School** (at the corner of Lerdo and Rebolledo).

■ Adventures

Eco-Travel

You can admire Coatepec's orchids in **Ma. Cristina Arteanias**, a shop at 5 Arteaga (in the *zócalo*) that houses a number of the beautiful plants. Or, a block off the *zócalo*, **El Patio de las Orquidas** at 11 Morelos has more. Look for a red building with a large wooden door. If you're interested in natural plants and medicines, pass by the **Finca La Mision**, at the corner of Aldama and Morelos, which has a number of natural remedies (barks, leaves, seeds) for sale.

Scenes in the movies *Clear and Present Danger* (with Harrison Ford) and *Collateral Damage* (with Arnold Schwarzenegger) were filmed right here in Coatepec, in the **Museo del Café** (63 Zaragoza). At this moment, the old building has a few displays on coffee. If you want to find out more about coffee plantations, with prior reservations you can visit the **Finca Coatepec**, ☎ 228-816-0963, at 32 16 de Septiembre, a private property that can arrange a plantation tour for you.

■ Festivals & Events

Java addicts unite! In honor of Coatapec's coffee fame, on May 15, the town celebrates the Feria del Café (**Coffee Fair**). The caffeinated event brings together artists and businesspeople with expositions, displays, and, of course, plenty of coffee products.

As you may have guessed by the name of the main church, the town's primary festival honors their patron saint San Jerónimo. Similar to nearby Xico festivities, Coatepec's **fiesta de San Jerónimo** (September 30) is celebrated with decorations of flowered arches and regional dances. The flowers (*cucharillas*) are placed on the churches in a colorful, memorable, blanket of beauty.

■ Where to Stay

The beautiful Spanish-styled **Hotel Posada Coatepec**, ☎ 0800-712-6256 or 228-816-0544, is right downtown at 9 Hidalgo (at the corner of Aldama), offering high-quality service, an excellent restaurant, a gorgeous patio, and large themed rooms. They have a villa as well. $$$$

The small but charming **Hotel Posada San Jerónimo**, ☎ 228-816-5486, in the downtown at 26 16 de Septiembre, has spacious, relaxing rooms, and a courtyard lined with *portales* for extra atmosphere. $$$$

■ Where to Eat

Stop by the **Coffino House** at 17 Campillo, a beautiful 140-year-old building with gorgeous wooden doors, and an attractive interior patio detailed with arches underlayed by brick. Get yourself seated on the pretty patio, and enjoy Mexican dishes such as *tostadas de pollo*, *flautas*, and *nachos* with a cup of coffee (of course). A special treat: weekends from 7-9 pm they have Mexican trios and regional dancers. $

Next to the *zócalo*, at 5 Lerdo, is the **Finca Andrade Restaurant**, a great spot that has a fun atmosphere, live music, and a nice range of Mexican dishes, including soups (like *chilpachole de camaron*), salads, pastas, and entrées such as mole, chicken, and trout. Or for an extra flare, try a table-side flaming dish. $

Xico

Xico (pronounced HEE-ko) is, to put it mildly, charming. Long, clean, quiet, cobblestoned roads lined with small, colorful, colonial houses greet the eyes with a warm relaxed welcome. The town, 19 km (12 miles) southeast of Xalapa, is set amid coffee and banana plantations, and near the spectacular Cascada de Texolo (Texolo Waterfall), a short scenic walk from downtown and a place whose beauty has attracted the attention of Hollywood producers.

■ Orientation & Practicalities

Ave. Miguel Hidalgo starts at the main square, and continues down and out of town. On Hidalgo, you'll find the Palacio de Gobierno, and the Plaza de Los Portales, and at the very end, the turnoff for the Texolo Falls.

Orientation & Practicalities ■ 221

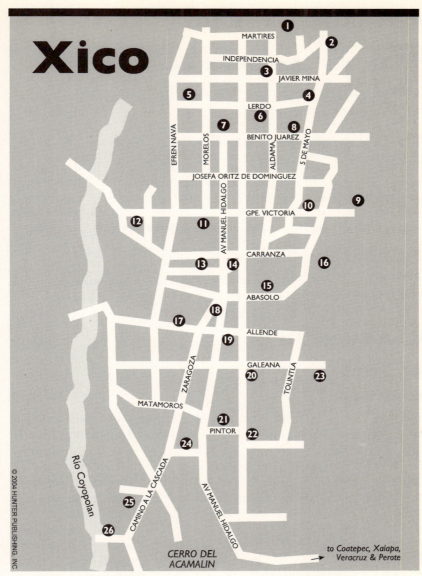

1. Capilla de Cristo Rey
2. Capilla de Carmen
3. Ermita de San Felipe
4. Capilla de San José
5. Plaza de Toro
6. Ermita de Buen Viaje
7. Parroquía
8. Museo Hoja de Maiz
9. Ermita de la Preciosa Sangre
10. Capilla de Guadalupe
11. Ermita de San Isidro
12. Puente Coyopolan
13. Palacio de Gobierno (Government Hall)
14. Plaza del Caracol
15. Ermita del Socorro
16. Ermita de Santa Elena
17. Ermita del Padre de Jesús
18. Los Portales
19. Casa de Cultura
20. Ermita de la Asuncíon
21. Ermita de la Purísima
22. Ermita de San Ignacio
23. Ermita de Santa Teresa
24. Capilla del Llanito
25. Antigua Estación
26. Cascada de Texolo

Getting Around

To get here by **bus**, you'll have to transfer at Coatepec (see *Xalapa – Getting Around*, page 196). The bus will drop you off right in front of the church in the central square. The town itself is very safe to walk around and the lack of traffic makes it a pleasure to explore on foot.

To Cascada de Texolo

The walk to the falls is quite pleasant (a stroll of 30-45 minutes; see below). To get back, you can pick up a local bus marked on its windshield *Cascada Texolo* (5 pesos). It will drop you off at a convenience store near Zaragoza, right before downtown. From the convenience store, go uphill and to the left one block, to get back to Zaragoza.

To Coatepec/Xalapa

Pick up a bus on any corner of Ave. Miguel Hidalgo marked *Xalapa*. Just wave and the bus will stop.

Adventures

On Foot

Town Walk

Start in front of the pretty orange- and yellow-domed main church, **La Parroquia de Santa María Magdalena** (Ave. Miguel Hidalgo and Benito Juárez). There, once you can get your mind off enjoying the astounding number of bird calls and cries, you can appreciate the simple beauty of the Baroque and Neoclassical building, the oldest in Xico. Behind the church is the **Museo Religioso**, a museum dedicated to Santa María Magdalena. Turn down Ave. Miguel Hidalgo (which starts/ends right in front of the church). Take your time strolling along the road made of river rock, admiring the delightful charm of the houses and shops, and enjoying the slow pace and relaxing atmosphere. There are lots of shops on this street selling spices for moles, as well as moles themselves (made from unique blends of different spices creating a milder-than-normal mole sauce), butter honey (a special treat for sweettooths), and wide varieties of coffee (try some to get you in the mood for your later exploration of the Ruta de Café). Some will be handing out samples of delightful selections of locally made *licores* (a low-alcohol liqueur, served warm or cold, made of almost any flavor you can imagine – berry, coffee, fruit). Others sell bottles of the popular drink, *torito* (a mixture of pure sugarcane and fruits and nuts) – varieties are limitless, and include peanut, strawberry, *cajeta* (a caramel-like syrup made from goat's milk), strawberry, or coconut. There are a number of restaurants and cafés as well.

Continue down Ave. Miguel Hidalgo until you reach a split in the road, where you'll want to take the right fork onto Ignacio Zaragoza (to the left Hidalgo continues, and to the right Zaragoza starts). Follow this road walking for about 10 minutes. It's a very pleasant walk, the shops start to die out, replaced by houses and greenery, and you will come to another split in the road.

■ To the left....

The left split takes you on the **Ruta del Café** (the Coffee Route). The area between Xalapa, Xico, and Coatepec is full of coffee plantations. The Coffee Route is part of the tourism department's effort to open this area to visitors. The bumpy, pretty road winds on for about four miles past coffee plantations and wild vegetation.

■ To the right....

The right split will take you to the **Cascada de Texolo** (Texolo Waterfall). The two-km (1.2-mile) scenic nature walk to the falls is on a riverstone road that winds its way slightly downhilll through lush green foliage, and past abundant banana trees. About three-quarters of the way there, you'll reach the final fork in the road. Follow the sign to the right and go down the hill past the parked cars lined up, to the entrance at the very end of the road. On the other side, you'll find a jaw-dropping view. (See *On Water – Waterfalls* below).

WORD TO THE WISE

Author's Tip: If you walk to the falls, don't wear sandals, as the whole route is on lovely (though sandal-unfriendly) riverstone roads. Bring a sturdy pair of shoes. Hiking boots are a great choice, since once you reach the falls, you'll be stumbling over yourself to hike the dirt trails to the bottom. Also, pack a bottle of suntan lotion. The sun can be brutal and there is not a lot of shade either on the walk or at the falls. Bring a bathing suit (there are plenty of spots to take a refreshing dip), and, above all, don't forget the insect repellent. (I did and, after five minutes at the falls, my legs looked as though they had been through a war zone. Thankfully, the tiny flying bugs that found me attractive did not leave itchy bites.)

On Wheels

Nearby villages worth exploring include Teocelo (about 2½ miles/four km south of Xico) and Ixhuacán (about eight miles/13 km farther south from Teocelo). **Teocelo** is a village on the edge of a cliff. There is a wide, hilly main street lined with one-story, multi-colored flat-roofed houses, and the entire village has a rustic charm. To get there, head south leaving Xico.

The much smaller, charming **Ixhuacán** has cobblestone roads lined with houses, and is surrounded by the rich green hills of the Sierra Madre. There's nothing to do here except enjoy the remote feel. To get there from Teocelo, head south until the road ends, and then head west. The road becomes much smaller, and Ixhuacán will be the first village you hit.

Both of these towns, though not far from Xico, will take some time to reach; the roads are small and bumpy, better suited to four-wheel-drive.

HISTORICAL ROUTE

History buffs will be interested to know that in 1519, when Hernan Cortés left the coast to march on Moctezuma at Tenochtitlán, his route took him from Cempoala, up to Xalapa, and on past Ixuahacán, conveniently between the Pico de Orizaba and the Cofre de Perote.

On Water

Waterfalls

The **Cascada de Texolo**, 1.9 miles/three km from Xico, is one of the most spectacular waterfalls in this part of the country, and has reportedly been used as a beautiful lush tropical backdrop for Hollywood movies such as *Romancing the Stone* and *Clear and Present Danger*. You are unlikely to forget a visit here. You can easily spend half the day here, exploring the different trails, taking pictures, and swimming at the bases of different falls.

After passing the parking area (just a section of cars lined up on the sides of the road), you head down the road, and straight ahead you'll see an unremarkable entrance lined by vendors. A little farther in, and you'll come upon an overlook, where your eyes will be assaulted with a wall of rich tropical foliage that covers every inch of a deep ravine. At the bottom, you can see pools of water created by a number of different falls – one under the overlook, and others to its right. To your left if facing the ravine, steps and a steep trail go to the bottom of the main falls, while to your right is a bridge, more lookouts, and trails heading off to La Monja, another smaller falls slightly upriver out of view. If you have time for only one, take the hike down to the left, for gorgeous views from under the lookout. If you have more time, your best option is to start by exploring to the right – less hiking is required, and you'll still have energy when you get back to take the steps down on the left, and to finish that roll of film from down below.

Author's Tip: If you have young children, keep a close eye on them, as the railings on the overlooks are only waist-high and jut out over deep gorges – a bad combination for curious kids. When hiking, be aware of sections that may be roped off for safety reasons, and also for loose gravel on some of the steep dirt trails. It's best to stay on the main trails, even though you'll see a network of shortcut paths heading off into the surrounding greenery. Many of them are very steep, barred by low branches or high grass, and home to biting insects. The main trail may be longer, but you'll be grateful.

The Bridge to the Right....

Head to the right, and you'll see some steps that lead to a rickety wooden bridge (it's safe, I've tried it). From there you can sometimes see people rappelling into the canyon below. To the right is a pool below that you can swim in, while to the left, you'll see lots of people swimming and lounging on rocks dotting the shallow streams, as well as pools caused by the huge nearby cascading waterfall. Cross the bridge and follow a path down into this part of the gorge.

Across the bridge, follow the path to the left, where you should first branch off to another lookout. This is the best one here, offering generous views of the valley floor, and the largest falls. Then continue on the main trail uphill, which heads to the smaller **Cascadas La Monja**. It's about a 10-minute walk to the base of these falls. The trail ends, but you can use the rocks at the falls' base as stepping stones across the shallow crystal-clear stream. Join in the fun – strip to your bathing suit, jump in the refreshing pool, and have someone take a picture of you with the falls crashing down behind. When you're done, the best route back is not wading down the river since you'll have a hard time getting back to the main path. Instead, just go back the way you came.

The Staircase to the Left....

Once you're back at the main lookout by the entrance, you're ready to head down the 365 steps of the steep staircase to your left. There is no elevator at the base (the way down, is the way up), so make sure you're able to go both ways. The hike down is stunning – the vegetation hanging from the surrounding cliffs. Once you reach the bottom of the staircase, you'll be on a short, steep dirt trail (watch your step), which ends at some large rocks on the edge of the fall's base. They are covered with suntanners, swimmers, and amateur photographers. Take a dip. Catch your breath. And don't look up. You'll never want to make the return hike!

■ Festivals & Events

The festival dedicated to the town's patron saint, **Santa Maria Magdalena**, is held from July 18th through the 23rd of each year. It brings parades, fireworks, and activities. Huge arches are erected, made entirely of flowers. As the celebration draws to a close on the 22nd (the patron saint's official day), bulls are set free to run through the streets of the town. That's one wild day to keep marked on your calender.

■ Shopping

Coffee, alcohol, and spices seem to be the addiction here. There are shops all along Ave. Miguel Hidalgo, including 148 Hidalgo, where the **Cafetalera Texolo** has gourmet coffee coming from a coffee roasting machine, as well as many varieties of *licores* stacked on its shelves. A little down the street at 150 Hidalgo, **Derivados Acamalin** is an irresistible shop, its walls stacked with jar upon jar of coffee beans, spices, and all types of moles.

■ Where to Stay

Hotel Real de Xico, ☎ 228-813-0498, at 148 Vicente Guerrero, has 20 rooms, including some spacious junior and master suites. $$

You can also try **Hotel Paraje Coyopolan**, ☎ 228-813-1266, on Venustiano Carranza Sur s/n . The hotel is a couple of blocks from the Parroquia, and sits in front of the Río Coyopolan. Ask them about bicycle and horse rentals. (From the

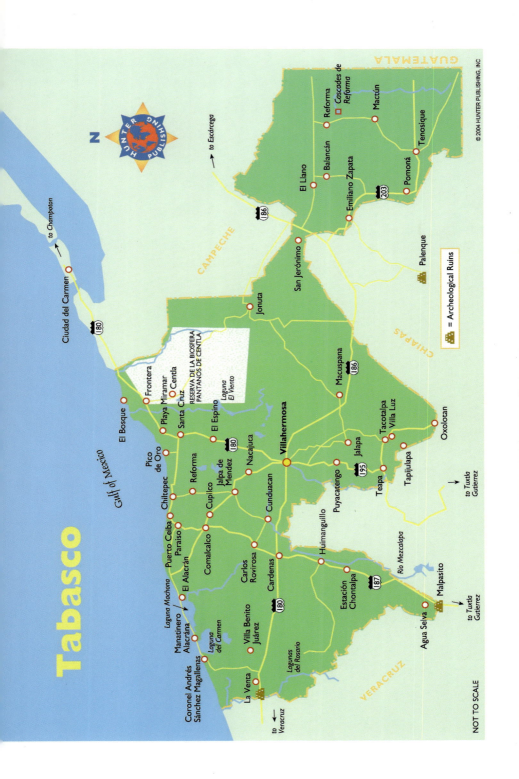

Overfed monkey on the Isla de los Monos, Catemaco (Joanie Sánchez - see page 263)

Above: Puerto Ceiba, Tabasco (Joanie Sánchez - see page 287)

Below: Palapas on Playa Paraiso, Tabasco (Joanie Sánchez - see pages 286-87)

Above: Highlands of Chiapas
Below: El Tajín night-time festival (see pages 144-49)

main Parroquia, go down Juárez and take a left onto Efren Nava, and then the next right). $$

■ Where to Eat

There are lots of great places on Zaragoza to grab a bite. You'll want to try the local specialties – *tamales* (wrapped in *totomoztle* or *xoco* leaves), mole, *xonequi*, and, to drink, a *torito*. The **Restaurante Acamalin** at 162 Hidalgo offers all the regional specialties at great prices (everything under 55 pesos), and a nice relaxing atmosphere – it's hidden away at the end of a plant-lined alley. You're greeted by tile floors, wooden ceilings, and a hot grill. $

Another option, the **Restaurant El Meson Xiqueño**, at 148 Hidalgo, has all the local favorites, and is a bit more formal, with a fantastic indoor patio where you eat alongside beautiful hanging plants, and cages of parrots, including a huge gorgeous guacamaya (a macaw). $

Jalcomulco

Undoubtedly the place to go for adventure (of the Indiana Jones explore-discover-swing-through-the-trees variety) is one hour away from Xalapa, on a scenic curvy road that passes through mango trees, mountains, and canyons, before reaching the tiny town of Jalcomulco. There is not much to the town itself, and, in fact, it is pretty unlikely that you would come to visit unless you had already heard about it through the grapevine. It's not known historically for any particular thing, and it's not on the way to anything else. This has worked out just fine for the adventure outfitters who, after discovering Jalcomulco's superb location, have made it their secret attraction. They pull out pictures of exhausted, smiling rafters, and you're soon booked on the next trip.

Outfitters based in México City, Veracruz, and Xalapa bring vans of would-be adventurers here to take advantage of Jalcomulco's marvelous environs. The nearby mountains make it ideal for hiking and horseback riding, the surrounding jungle makes it heaven for nature enthusiasts (some villas here are in Eden-like settings), and the bordering La Antigua river not only provides food for the town, but has shown whitewater rafters the time of their lives.

■ Orientation & Practicalities

This is a tiny town, so if you're not arriving as part of a tour group, come prepared. There are no banks or ATMs, and no tourist services, other than the adventure outfitters who have offices on the short stretch of the main road as you come into town. Basically, if you don't see it, it ain't there.

■ Getting There & Around

Jalcomulco is 39 km (24 miles) southeast of Xalapa. To get there, take the highway toward Coatepec, where you'll head west, then south past Tuzanapan, following the windy road to Jalcomulco. You can pick up a **bus** at Xalapa (see *Xalapa – Getting Around*, page 196, for directions). Remember for your return trip: buses leave only about every hour. The main street is the one the bus comes in on, while the few streets that make up the rest of the town branch off each side, lined with stores selling ice cold beer (the favorite drink after playing around outdoors all day). If you head a little bit past the end of main street and to the right, you'll see La Antigua river (this section of which is known as *Pescados*) and a few seafood restaurants. On the other side are a number of trails heading into the surrounding hills, and a few nature villas.

Author's Tip: If you just show up here, you probably won't have anything to do. Almost everything worth doing in Jalcomulco, is safer, more fun, and often only available if done with an adventure outfitter – there are many to choose from. Some do have offices on Jalcomulco's main street, and can be approached when you get there (though it's unlikely the activity you want will be available right then). The best thing to do is contact the agencies ahead of time to arrange your adventures. Many will do a day trip – drive you in and then back out from a major city (such as Xalapa or Veracruz), eliminating your need to arrange transportation at all – while others actually have beautiful grounds to accommodate people onsite. The best outfitters do not take walk-ins. For convenience, I've listed adventure outfitters, along with their contact information and offerings, all together below. (This is by no means a list of all the outfitters that go to Jalcomulco.)

■ Adventures

Outfitters

Aventuras Sin Limite, ☎ 279-832-3580 or 279-832-3581. Office in Jalcomulco at 54 Zaragoza. This outfitter is the only one that's locally run in the group, and is very helpful. They have some great offerings, and have a table set up on the main street with pictures and pamphlets. They offer: rafting trips (a three-hour, 18-km/11-mile trip for 400 pesos), rappeling (300 pesos), guided nature walks (100 pesos), tirolesa (see page 231, 350 pesos), Gotcha (see page 231, 350 pesos), horse rides (1½-hour in-town tour for 200 pesos), and a number of packages. My favorite is a three-day camping trip to Coatlemani, a fogotten Totonaca archaeological site near a steep gorge, and accessible only on foot. Here you can still find ancient clay remnants in the dirt. Your own camping equipment is required for that trip.

Río Y Montaña Expediciones, toll free ☎ 866-900-9092 or 55-5292-5032. This is a leading adventure outfitter in México. In Veracruz, it has two lodges in Jalcomulco. One is the "adventure village" known as Picocanoa – a luxurious 24 two- to four-person cabins, set on beautifully manicured (but still tropical and jungle-like) grounds, replete with services such as facials, massages, and a prehispanic steam bath. For the more budget-oriented guests, there's the second lodge, the "tent camp" known as Okavango – a much more rustic, but still appealingly safari-like set-up of tents with private bathrooms. Amenities are shared between the two sites, and include a pool, volleyball court, rope course, bar, and restaurant. From here you take part in guided trips, including rafting, mountain biking, kayaking, tirolesa, and hiking. The camps (particularly Picocanoa) are really nice. You must book ahead of time. The company is based in México City. Check prices and packages at their website: www.rioymontana.com.

Veraventuras (also known as A.C. Aventuras), ☎ 0800-712-6572 or 228-818-9779, www.veraventuras.com.mx, office at 81 Santos Degollado, in Xalapa. This friendly, professional group offers Class III and IV rafting on the Pescados-Antigua River (minimum of two people, 480 pesos), as well as packages including overnight stays (1,600-3,200 pesos for two nights). Some of their offerings include camping, steam baths, rappelling, mountain biking, and tirolesa (see also *Tlapacoyan*, page 159).

Amigos Del Río, ☎ 228-815-8817 or 228-815-2529, office is at 205 Chilpancingo, in Xalapa and 55 Calle Juárez, in Jalcomulco. This outfitter offers rafting (500 pesos for a trip, plus 50 pesos extra for transportation to and from Xalapa), mountain biking (50 pesos per hour), Gotcha (200 pesos per person), bird watching (300 pesos per person), rappelling (300 pesos), and guided walks (50 pesos for two hours).

Amphibian, ☎ 229-931-0997, at 170 Blvd. M. Avila Camacho in the Puerto de Veracruz, is a group that offers trips to Jalcomulco. Give them a call or stop by their office in person for prices and package info.

Selvazul, ☎ 222-237-4887. They have a base camp here with lodges, camping, or hammocks, and offer rafting, Gotcha, horseback riding, and a climbing wall. (See *Tlapacoyan*, page 159, as well.) Offices are in Puebla.

On Foot

Hike

When you go on a hike out here, you *really* get into nature; trails lead in all directions deep into the surrounding hills. I recommend that you take a guided walk or trek, since even if you get verbal directions to the nearby spots of interest (such as the small, picturesque, natural pool known as La Gotera – only a 30-minute walk away), once the trail starts to split a couple of times, you will have no idea which path to take… or, worse, how to get back.

If you do fancy a little walk around by yourself, you can pick up a trail on the other side of the bridge (the hanging one that spans the river is a lot of fun to walk across) from the village. The road to the left takes you past some of the gorgeous reservation-required encampments before continuing its winding way up and away from town. Besides exotic flowers, lush foliage, and coloful butterflies, there are beautiful birds, one of which, the Baltimore oriole, makes a strange-looking nest that you'll see hanging from the treetops (it looks like a sack, dangling from the upper branches). The Baltimore oriole winters in Mexico.

The dirt road to the right winds up and away from town as well, and quickly narrows down to a trail whose popularity quickly becomes evident from the horse greetings on the ground. A 10-minute walk (the trail will still be a wide dirt road) will take you to a high point with a fine view of the surrounding countryside, a good point to turn back. If you continue walking, the trail heads into forests, narrows quite a bit, and starts to branch off in different directions.

Rappeling

This activity is certainly not for everyone, and, after looking at some of the pictures of people dangling from local cliffs, I certainly decided that a 213-foot/65-meter rapel (as one agency offered) was just too much for my poor heart. If you're not afraid of heights, try it out (almost all the agencies offer something) – and don't forget to get a picture of yourself defying death!

Gotcha

This activity is popular especially with the younger visitors. It's paint ball gun wars, played in some sections in the surrounding hills.

On Wheels

Mountain biking is a popular activity here, and with the hilly dirt roads and paths, bikers will have a lot of fun.

On Water

If you get to the river in the afternoon and a wait a few minutes, you are more than likely to see Jalcomulco's most popular activity. Groups come down the river, outfitted with helmets and life-vests, paddling arms slowing down, and looks of exhaustion and exhilaration on their faces – they've gotten their money's worth for sure. They've been **rafting the La Antigua River**. As with most activities in this town, you'll need to sign up with an outfitter, almost all of which promote this as their number-one activity, and most of which have a full range of experience levels, as the river has everything from small rapids to fast-moving expert-level runs. Of course, if you choose one of the latter, this may just turn into a swimming adventure as well!

*Some of the main rivers to raft in Veracruz are the **Pescados River** (Jalcomulco vicinity), **Actopan River** (Actopan vicinity), and the **Filobobos River** (Tlapacoyan vicinity). Most outfitters offer different trips to each.*

In the Air

Do you see wires strung across the river? Or from tree to tree? They're for the much-loved adventure activity known as **Tirolesa** – your chance to fly through the air like Tarzan! Participants attach themselves to the Tirolesa cable, and then slide along the line to the opposite end. Something you've probably never had the chance to do before, and lots of fun.

On Horseback

How about a horseback tour (*cabalgata*). Tours go through the village, and on some of the trails that head into the woods, which in some spots are far more suited to hooves than your poor feet.

■ Festivals & Events

Jalcomulco's celebrations take place May 11 to the 13th, when they put on a fiesta in celebration of the town's patron saint, San Juan Bautista. There are folk dances, music, and parades.

■ Where to Stay

Contact local adventure outfitters listed above for packages that include activities and accommodations. Or try the **Cotlamani**, ☎ 279-832-3582, on the riverbank opposite the town (cross the rope bridge and take the uphill trail to the right). They have a number of air-conditioned rooms and a pool, and they charge 150 pesos per person. $

■ Where to Eat

There are a few restaurants by the river, all of which are a little more expensive than you would expect for this out-of-the-way village, no doubt thanks to the steady trickle of visitors that have made this tiny community a big spot on the map. Almost all restaurants serve *acamaya* (giant river shrimp), which is fished from the local river. If you look out onto the water, you'll see that the rocks are dotted with what look like baskets. You may already have noticed them for sale by the vendors on the main street. They are baskets meant to capture shrimp. The baskets are round, with a hole in the middle that curves around so the shrimp can't escape. Another local dish you may want to try is *crucetas*, a cactus served in broth.

You won't have too many choices of where to eat, so just pick one that looks good, or try the **Restaurante Familiar Beto**, which serves up some good shrimp dishes.

Orizaba

The volcano of Orizaba, known as Citlaltepetl, towers right next to the city of Orizaba. The town sits some 4,000 feet/1,220 m above sea level in the shadow of its namesake, the tallest peak in México at 18,405 feet/5,611 m, and the third-tallest in North America. On a clear day, you can reportedly see it from as far away as the Puerto de Veracruz. But standing in the streets of Orizaba, with an unobstructed view in its direction, you just might not see it if there's a cloud cover.

The town has a cultural mixture that is appealing; you'll find Oaxacan and Pueblan women in the markets, some remnants of its Spanish heritage downtown, and a community proudly respectful of the arts. This is the home of Francisco Gabilondo Soler Cri Cri (a famous Mexican singer of children's songs). As for activities, there are some nearby hills to hike, the volcano for climbers (some use the town as their base), and nearby mountain towns to explore, offering gorgeous (and sometimes harrowing) views of the surrounding valleys and mountains.

Early mornings are the best times for clear views, before the sun and weather decide the day's course. You'll want to keep this in mind for any hikes that you plan, since half the fun is the view from the top.

■ Getting There & Around

By Bus

The bus station is between Sur 11 and Sur 13 at 256 Oriente 6 just to the southeast of the main square. It's about a 10-minute walk. Turn left onto Oriente 6, go down five blocks, then turn right onto Madero Norte and up another five blocks. The station is serviced by UNO, ADO GL, and ADO, and has a spot for hourly storage of luggage. The AU bus station is in the opposite part of the downtown – to the northwest of the center at 425 Poniente 8. The main square is about a 15-minute walk. Head east on Poniente 8, cross a bridge, veer right onto Norte 5, and turn left onto Poniente 4.

BUS TRIPS			
Destination	Bus Line	Fare	Time
Fortín de las Flores	ADO	7 pesos	25 minutes
Huatusco	ADO	32 pesos	1 hour 15 minutes

	AU	30 pesos	
México City (TAPO)	UNO	264 pesos	4 hours 5 minutes
	ADO GL	192 pesos	
	ADO	165 pesos	
	AU	148 pesos	
Xalapa	ADO	101 pesos	3 hours 10 minutes
	AU	86 pesos	
Puebla	ADO	97 pesos	2 hours 10 minutes
	AU	86 pesos	
Tampico	ADO	343 pesos	10 hours 20 minutes
Veracruz	ADO	76 pesos	2 hours
	AU	71 pesos	
Villahermosa	ADO	310 pesos	6 hours 15 minutes
	AU	277 pesos	

You can pick up local buses to Fortín de las Flores and Córdoba in front of the Chedruai supermarket at Oriente 6 and Sur 19, a few blocks to the east of the ADO bus station. Buses take the free (not toll) highway and charge 8 pesos. If you're returning by local bus, bear in mind that their last stop (and main terminal) is, annoyingly, several blocks northeast of the main square. If you dare to take the bus to Maltrata, a mountain village high in the mountains (only available via a local bus), you can pick up a CHYC bus behind the small church of the Virgen de Juquila at the intersection of Poniente 6 and Norte 5.

By Car

From México City, Puebla, or Veracruz, take Tollway 150 the whole way. To get around locally, the Freeway 150 passes through Orizaba, Fortín de las Flores, and Córdoba.

Author's Tip: When you take a local bus, be sure to get a ticket stub and keep it handy while you're on the bus. Many times ticket inspectors hop on board and walk through the aisle double-checking that everyone has paid; if you can't produce a stub – regardless of whether or not you've paid – you'll have to pay again.

1. Cerro del Borrego
2. Alameda Park
3. Mercado (market)
4. Palacio Municipal (City Hall)
5. Palacio de Hierro
6. Mercado (market)
7. Cathedral
8. Parque Castillo
9. Teatro Llave (theater)
10. Iglesia el Calvario (church)
11. Lopez Park
12. Post Office
13. ADO Bus Station
14. Cascada del Elefante (Elephant Waterfalls)
15. Museo de Art del Estado
16. Francisco J Madero Park

■ Orientation & Practicalities

 The main square, known as Parque Castillo, is at the intersection of Madero Norte and Colón Oriente; from here, the streets are labeled *Oriente* (east), *Sur* (south), *Norte* (north) or *Poniente* (west). *Ponientes* head west to east and are located on the west side of Madero. *Orientes* also head west to east, but are on the east side of Madero. *Surs* cross them north to south and are on the south side of Colón. *Nortes* also run north to south, but on the north side of Colón. Street numbers increase as you head away from the center of town, so to get to the city center, just count down.

Emergency Services: Hospital, ☎ 272-724-1480; Red Cross, ☎ 272-722-1480.

Exchanging Money: You'll find a couple of banks near the main square on Oriente 2.

Internet Cafés: Cafés typically charge 10-15 pesos for an hour's worth of computer time. You can find a number of computers near the main square on Oriente 2 (near the corner of Sur 3) at the **Cypercity Café**. The **Rod Pas**, at 74-7 Oriente 2 between Madero and Sur 3, is a huge place with 38 computers, seven flat screen TVs (for video games), and one giant screen TV.

Post Office: The *correo* is at the corner of Ave. Oriente 2 and Norte 6, two blocks east of the main square.

Tourist Information: The tourist information office is on the second floor of the Ex-Palacio Municipal (that big green structure near the central square) on Madero between Ave. Poniente 4 and Ave. Poniente 2. Go up the main staircase and turn left. A helpful staff offers maps and booklets on the city and its environs. Information is in Spanish, but there is a staff person who speaks some English. Open 8 am-3 pm, Mon.-Fri.

UFO SIGHTINGS

I met someone who, in a hike around the mountains with his friend, encountered a split in the trail. One of them took the first path, the other took the second, with the plan to meet up where the trails joined back together. A little into the trail, the first hiker saw a bright light overhead, moving in a strange fashion, then it suddenly disappeared; he couldn't identify it as a plane, a balloon, or a celestial object. When he met up with his friend, he too had seen the same thing moving close by, and he too was just as confused. Before you dismiss this story, know that this is not an uncommon occurrence here. The area around Citlaltepetl (the Pico de Orizaba), has often and long been a place for UFO sightings.

■ Sightseeing

The focal point for the city is the main square, known as **Parque Castillo** (Madero Norte and Colón Poniente). On the north side it has three mismatched domes (one is brightly checked, one is plain, and one is striped) of the **Catedral de San Miguel Arcángel**, built in 1720. Right across the street from the park is the **Teatro Ignacio de la Llave**, built in the late 19th century, a place for operas, ballets, and orchestras. Check the billboards and posters for current events (often there are nightly concerts).

Just to the north of Parque Castillo is the huge green Art-Nouveau iron structure of the **Ex-Palacio Municipal**. Its balconies, adjacent café, and street lanterns might make you think you were in New Orleans. There is a simple reason that this beautiful building sits here, just off the main square, in complete discord with the rest of the city. It was bought in Belgium, completely dismantled, shipped across the ocean, and then put together here in Orizaba in the late 19th century. On its ground-floor terraces is the **Beer Museum**. By the way, you can find the current Palacio Municipal three blocks west of Parque Castillo on Av. Cristóbal Colón Poniente.

On the west side of the center, about four blocks down Ave. Cristóbal Colón Oriente, is the large **Parque Alameda**. As you stroll around the huge square, check out its couple of statues, including the one dedicated to composer Francisco Gabilondo Soler, a Disney-like figure most famous for Cri-Cri the Grilloto Cantor (Singing Cricket), a character as big as Disney's Mickey Mouse. Soler was born in Orizaba on October 6, 1907. As long as you're checking in on the famous, head to the opposite part of the downtown, and hidden away at 180 Ave. Colón Oriente you'll find a narrow old white building with blue trim that proudly states on its entrance that it served as the home of Benito Juárez (though I have yet to confirm this). He was the most celebrated of all México's presidents. Whether or not it's true, you can still check out the pretty yellow balconied courtyard; the building today houses Hector's Gym.

Río Orizaba runs right by the western edge of downtown. Currently, renovations are underway to add a walkway/canal type area. From the bridges (take any road west one to three blocks) you can see what they're up to; unfortunately, though it's shaping up to be pretty nice, it will still be some time before you can really enjoy it.

Do you want to know about God? Across the street from La Catedral, down Oriente, the whole first section of the street is filled with shops dedicated to all things religious. You can find life-size statues, mini-crosses, virgins, saints, images of Jesus, books, candles, cards, charms, oils, incense, tiaras... the list goes on and on.

■ Adventures

On Foot

Hikes

In just about the one place you would least expect to find it – on the other side of the highway behind some gas stations and a hotel – is a hiker's dream: the **Cascada del Elefante**, a waterfall thundering around the bottom of an impressive valley. The lookout is directly behind the Hotel Fiesta Cascada (in fact, you have to walk through the hotel's parking lot). The overlook gives an excellent view of what you came for. Basically, the trail makes a loop. To the left is a staircase labeled *Los Quinientos Escalones* (The 500 Steps). The steps take you all the way down, at which point the trail itself starts. You'll cross a bridge (spanning the creek that flows down the valley center), and follow the trail back up the mountainside, ending up pretty much opposite your original lookout. Continuing, you'll eventually get to the bridge crossing the dam and waterfall, and then onto a trail and stairs, which head back up to the originating side of the trail, a little to the right of where you started.

As an alternative to doing the entire loop, from the lookout, go to your right (opposite The 500 Steps), where a staircase leads down to the dam and falls. This way you can quickly get down to right above the falls, without the big hike. The stairs can be a little steep for children.

The Cascada del Elefante is just outside of town, on the east side of Highway 150D, at the northeast entrance to the city. But you can't easily walk there from downtown, especially since you have to cross the highway.

Though the hill directly west of the city – **Cerro del Borrego** – is only a few blocks from downtown, it is surprisingly hard to find your way there. Pass through and behind the large park dedicated to composer Cri-Cri (Parque Alameda), following Poniente 3 as it turns into Sur 16. About one block down, bear right onto Sur 18, and walk past a couple of houses. If you blink, you'll probably miss the entrance – it's a narrow alley squished beween two buildings, at the very end of which is a tiny sign designating it as the 'entrada' to the hill. A trail goes to the top. Come here in the mornings, when visibility is likely to be good.

Beer Tour

A plaque, next to an easily missed doorway under the outdoor terrace of the Ex-Palacio Municipal, marks the entrance to the **Beer Museum**. The town's link with beer dates back to the 1890s when the Moctezuma Brewery was established in Orizaba; eventually it was joined with the Cuauhtémoc Brewery to create Cervecería Cuauhtémoc Moctezuma, which has seven plants. If the brewery doesn't ring a bell, perhaps one of its brands will – XX, Tecate, Superior, Sol, Noche Buena, Carta Blanca, Chihuahua, Bohemia, and Indio. The three rooms of the museum provide an excellent historical timeline of Orizaba's brews, a few great old factory photos, a display case with old and new bottles, and, in the last room, a selection of old labels and advertisements. If you can read Spanish, you'll be impressed with the informational panels. Admittance is free, and the museum is supposedly open Mon.-Fri., 10 am-6:45 pm, though I've been by in the daytime and sometimes found it closed. Ask for some of the pamphlets on the history of the company (in English), and business cards encouraging you to visit the local production plant for a free tour. To arrange a visit to the plant (Sur 10 and Poniente 9), you'll need to call ahead for reservations, ☎ 272-728-1000, ext. 3241, 3242, or 3243.

Caving

If you're here to climb the volcano, you'll probably have enough fears and worries over crevices, dips, and holes without adding caves to the mix. Otherwise, speleologists gather round. You'll be happy to hear that there are are a couple of different cave systems not too far away, although to really explore them, you'll probably want to get a guide.

The **Grutas de Galicia** and **Grutas las Cruces** are on the free highway between Orizaba and Fortín de las Flores; about halfway to Fortín, you'll see the turnoff marked Grutas de Galicia on your right.

ADVENTURE OUTFITTER

Desafio Turismo de Aventura, ☎ 272-725-0696, a local outfitter at 586 Poniente 3, is a friendly group that organizes caving, rock climbing, rappelling, mountain biking, and hiking. They also offer guided trips up Citlaltepetl (the Pico de Orizaba).

Mountain Climbing

Orizaba owes most of its fame to **Pico de Orizaba**, also known as Citlaltepetl, rising 18,405 feet /5,611 m above the north side of town. It is the third-tallest mountain in North America, and the tallest in all of México. But it is actually considered a fairly easy climb, and those with little high-altitude experience summit it regularly. You'll need little more than crampons and, possibly, an ice axe. This should by no means give you a false sense of security, though. Just as people die on Mount Everest, so they do here. The best season for climbing is from November to March.

There are a couple of different routes to the top, the most difficult and technical are on the eastern glacier, while the most common itinerary is to the northwest. For this easier route, head to Tlachichuca, a town on the northwest side of the peak. From Highway 140 heading north, a few miles after San Salvador El Seco you'll see a turnoff to the east. Tlachichuca has a number of outfitters who can provide acommodations, transportation, and/or a guide. From here, the route normally followed is by four-wheel-drive to Piedra Grande, a camp a little farther up the mountain, where you spend time acclimatizing before leaving for the summit (by way of the Glaciar de Jamapa – Jamapa Glacier) in the wee hours of the morning. It's basically just hiking (though some parts are a bit steep), and ends at the lip of the volcano. Don't forget the suntan lotion!

A guide is inexpensive and well worth it for peace of mind. One local guide service is **Servimont**, ☎ 24545-15009 (Calz. J. Ortega 5, Tlachichulca). They offer packages tailored to your needs. Services include guide, transportation to and accommodation in the Piedra Grande hut (shared rooms), meals and accommodations at Tlachichulca, and, if requested, glacial training. A trip usually lasts two days (to allow for acclimatization). The best way to reach them is by e-mail (refer to www.servimont.com.mx). If you're not renting a car, you can reach the town of Tlachichulca by bus, which many find more economical and relaxing than driving. Because the town is small, there is no direct line from more remote cities such as the Puerto de Veracruz. So most visitors take a bus to Puebla. From there, you can buy a ticket on a local bus (frequent departures) for the two-hour ride to Tlachichulca. There are many stops along the way and the town will be one of the last, so ask the driver to let you know when you get there.

Besides outfitters in Tlachichuca, you can arrange a trip from Orizaba with **Desafio Turismo de Aventura**, ☎ 272-25-0696 (see page 239), or from larger non-local outfitters such as **Río Y Montaña**, ☎ (toll free) 866-900-9092.

Highest Peaks in North America
1. Mount McKinley (United States) . . 20,321 feet/6,350 m
2. Mount Logan (Canada) . . . . 19,524 feet/5,952 m
3. Citlaltepetl (México) . . . . 18,405 feet/5,611 m

On Wheels

Take a pretty drive around the mountains to the town of **Huatusco**, where you will be rewarded with a look at the **Iglesia de Santa Cecilia**. The church is believed to have been built on the ruins of a building honoring the feathered serpent god Quetzalcoátl. When the Spanish tried to build Santa Cecilia on the ruins of the original structure, they were warned against it, and it was foretold that no other temple would stand there. Strangely, after it was built, the church was destroyed by a fire, and, though it continues to be restored, nothing seems to hold.

The town itself is small and unremarkable, with not much of interest, aside from a good view of the Pico de Orizaba on a clear day. To get here, take the highway from Fortín de las Flores north to Cardel; it's about an hour's drive.

As for a visit to really small-time village life, at the end of Highway 123, 23½ miles south of Orizaba, up in the mountains, you can visit the village of **Zongolica**, where you will also find a waterfall.

Historically interesting, the village of **Yanga**, nine miles south of Córdoba on free Highway 150, was a hideaway for runaway slaves in the late 1500s. The area was long an unsettled place, runaways continually raiding nearby roads and villages. The search for stability eventually led to the founding of nearby Córdoba.

On Water

The **Balneario Ojo de Agua** (eye of water) just at the eastern edge of the city near the Río San Juan is a natural spring where you can bathe in its warm waters.

In the Air

The surrounding geography provides the perfect setting for **paragliding** (or, in Spanish, *parapentismo*) over the surrounding mist-covered vegetation. One place for the sport is at the Cerro de las Antenas (Hill of the Antennas)

on Saturdays between 8 and 11 am. To get there, take the free highway going from Orizaba to Córdoba; at Km 76 you'll see a sign with a picture of a paraglider, and a turnoff to the right. From here, it's a short drive to the hill. If you're a real expert, you can investigate the international paragliding competition held each year May 1-4 at the Cerro de las Compañas (check with the tourism office for details).

■ Cultural & Eco-Travel Excursions

When they finally get the **Convento de San Jose** reconstructed, you won't want to miss it. It's a huge old Franciscan convent in the center of the city, in an abandoned and somewhat ruined state. Banamex, the Mexican bank, is funding much of its reconstruction and, though a lot of work has been done, there is much left to do. From the courtyard, it does not look so bad – blackened old walls spotted with windows seem to have survived wonderfully through the years. But when you enter, you can see that time has taken its toll. After being a convent, it was used as a school for priests, and as housing, before being recovered by the city.

The interior has long beautiful hallways with high vaulted ceilings (many standing only thanks to wooden supports), a ruined staircase leading up to second and third floors that are caving in or have already collapsed, and walls covered in graffiti. There is an underground level which you can reach through a courtyard. Over the years it has been ransacked by people coming in search of gold, which Spanish priests were believed to have hidden here. Places such as this were often used to great advantage by Spanish priests, trying to show their god-like powers to the local Indians by mysteriously disappearing and reappearing in different parts of the city. Their secret – hidden tunnels.

The unmarked entrance to the convent is across the street from the Mercado de Flores on Poniente 5, just after you cross the bridge (on your left). You'll see many workers milling around the entrance and working inside. For a number of years the convent has been undergoing reconstruction, and is currently in a dangerous and not visitable state.

Inside the wooden doors of the intricately detailed, beautiful late 18th-century **Museo de Arte del Estado**, you'll find a large collection of paintings by famous Mexican artists (including some contemporary works). The museum is on Oriente 4 at the corner of Sur 23.

Another place to absorb some culture is at the free **Museo Arqueológico de Orizaba**, at 3 Sur 9. It has two rooms with a few glass cases holding fragments of pots, stone figures, jugs, sculptures, and a items related to the ancient indigenous ball game.

■ Nightlife

These are your orders: head to Parque Castillo after 11 pm. Bring your girlfriend. Or your boyfriend. Your husband. Or your wife. Seat them on a bench under the trees. Walk over to the men standing at the corner – you'll see them there, leaning on their guitars, straightening their ties, adjusting their hats. Some will be strumming and humming along, warming up their vocals, getting in tune; others will be quietly watching for a signal from a romantic fool, so in love, only a serenade in the dead of night can express his feelings to his sweetheart. Be that fool. And if you're alone, who said you can't enjoy a serenade too?

At midnight one night I listened to a trio gathered around an SUV. One of the passengers wanted some lively entertainment. After one song he was singing along with the group; two songs and he had gotten out of the car. By the third song, his friends were out of the car singing along as well.

You can find trios of serenaders lined up at the park mainly on weekend nights. And if you want to surprise someone with a traditional serenade, pay their taxi fare and the singers will head to the address you give them.

■ Where to Stay

The **Hotel Trueba**, ☎ 272-724-2930, at 485 Ote. 6 at the corner of Sur 11, is a delightful hotel with an indoor restaurant, modern spacious rooms, color TV, and a/c. It's also conveniently close to the bus station. Credit cards are accepted. $

Also near the bus station, the **Casa Real Hotel & Suites**, ☎ 272-724-0077, is a huge modern hotel with pleasant rooms (a little pricey, though). $$$

HOTEL PRICE CHART	
Rates are per room based on double occupancy. Rates lower if single occupancy or sharing a bed. Higher rates on holidays.	
	US $10-$20
$	US $21-$40
$$	US $41-$60
$$$	US $61-$80
$$$$	US $81-$125
$$$$$	Over US $125

Another option, about four blocks from the bus station, is the **Hotel Aries**, ☎ 272-725-3520, at 263 Oriente 6. It has clean, standard rooms. $

Grand Hotel De France, ☎ 272-725-2311, 186 Ave. Oriente 6, has a really romantic feel to it at night, with a beautiful indoor patio and soft music coming from its restaurant. It has 70 rooms, six suites, parking, and a restaurant; the staff, however, is not the friendliest. $

Hotel Plaza Palacio, ☎ 272-725-9933, 2-Bis Poniente 2, is downtown, and has acceptable older rooms with cable TV. $

Hotel Fiesta Cascada, ☎ 272-724-1596, is a bit inconvenient in its location on the Puebla-Córdoba Highway outside of town (Km 27.5 of Highway 150D, next to a Pemex gas station, behind the Restaurant Orizaba). But it is situated directly in front of the waterfalls and canyon of the Cascada de Elefante. It's a good hotel with a restaurant, waterpark for the kiddies in front, and pool. It has a pleasant, standard rooms or more expensive bungalows and suites. $$

■ Where to Eat

Make a point to stop by the **Mercado Melchor Ocampo** (corner of Madero Norte and Oriente 5) for breakfast. Because Orizaba is so close to Puebla and Oaxaca, you'll find local women with regional recipes making tasty dishes – often everything from scratch.

DINING PRICE CHART	
Price per person for an entrée, not including beverage or tip.	
$	Under US $5
$$	US $5-$10
$$$	US $10+

The **Churros y Purras Chocolateria/Café** at 263 Oriente 6, adjacent to the Hotel Aries, is a delightful spot to satisfy any sweet tooth, serving up *churros* (fried dough rolled in sugar) covered in your choice of either *cajeta* (a caramel-like syrup) or chocolate (try the *cajeta*; you'll love it). *Purros* are the same thing, just in a spiral shape. You can get an order of six for about 9 pesos, and some coffee (15 pesos) or the incredibly rich hot chocolate (18 pesos) to go with it. They have a great selection of breakfasts as well, ranging from *huevos rancheros* to fruit salads. $

The **Dauzon Cafeteria**, 12 Sur 5, is the perfect spot for an inexpensive, tasty lunch. They have a huge display case of cakes and pastries, one of which often accompanies a *comida corrida* for dessert. The best value here by far is the *comida corrida* – for 28 pesos you're given a soup, entrée, and dessert. And the entrées are not the run-of-the-mill fare, but have gourmet pizzazz. Try their health juices as well – carrot, beet, cucumber, orange, melon, apple, tomato – almost any flavor you want. $

The **Gran Café Orizaba** at Madero Norte and Poniente 2, in one side of the building of the Ex-Palacio Municipal, is a popular place to relax with a cup of coffee or a beer during the afternoons. It has a nice ambience during the evenings. $

Romanchu at 208 Poniente 7 is a large, elegant restaurant that serves tasty international cuisine. $$

Fortín de las Flores

Don't let the roadsigns on Highway 150 screaming "Extreme Precaution" deter you from making your way through the misty mountains to the flower-growing town of Fortín, especially if it's during its annual Flower Fair in April. The deep cliff the windy road traces takes only a few minutes to pass.

Though you won't be able to buy any of the local plants, you *will* be able to browse around and admire the unfamiliar tropical species.

The town itself is pretty (everyone seems to have a flowering tree in their yard), but it's not as flower-covered as you would expect. Unfortunately the scent of flowers is not heavy in the air because most of the blooms are grown for commercial use. Most of you will probably be satisfied with half a day here exploring and hiking before moving on to nearby Orizaba (about nine miles/14 km) or Córdoba (14 miles/23 km).

■ Orientation & Practicalities

The main square is the **Parque Principal**, on Ave. 3 between Calle 1 Sur and Calle 3 Sur. The **Palacio Municipal** borders it on the east. The street layout is somewhat similar to Orizaba, forming a gridlike pattern, with streets given a number and a designation of West (*Poniente*), East (*Oriente*), North (*Norte*) or South (*Sur*). *Orientes* and *Ponientes* run north-south, while *Nortes* and *Surs* run west-east. As you get farther from the main square (*Parque Principal*), the street numbers get higher.

Emergency Services: Red Cross, ☎ 271-12-0090.

Exchanging Money: A Banamex is right in the center on Calle 1 and near the Palacio Municipal.

Internet Café: There are a few easy-to-spot choices right around the Parque Principal, including **Compuweb** (daily, 10 am-8 pm, closed for lunch) at the corner of Ave. 3 and Calle 3 Sur.

Tourist Information: The tourist department staff has a desk on the ground floor of the kiosk in the Parque Principal, and actually has a great packet of information compiled on the surrounding activities, including a week-long suggested itinerary. Although everything is in Spanish, they have some maps of the town, as well as photos of surrounding sites posted on the wall, which you may find helpful and inspiring.

■ Getting There & Around

The ADO bus station is on Ave. 2 (almost at the intersection of Calle 6). From the bus station, you can reach the *zócalo* by heading south three blocks and west three blocks until you reach Ave. 1 and Sur 1.

BUS TRIPS			
Destination	Bus Line	Fare	Time
Orizaba	ADO	7 pesos	35 minutes
Veracruz	ADO	69 pesos	1 hour 45 minutes
Xalapa	ADO	75 pesos	2 hours 55 minutes
México	ADO	170 pesos	4 hours 15 minutes
Huatusco	ADO	25 pesos	1 hour 45 minutes
Córdoba	ADO	5 pesos	25 minutes
Coscomatepec	ADO	18 pesos	1 hour

■ Adventures

ADVENTURE OUTFITTERS

Faraventuras/Agencia de Viajes Xochitl, ☎ 271-713-1695, has an office in downtown Fortín (113 Ave. 3 at the corner of Calle 2). They offer trips into the surrounding area to visit caves and waterfalls and observe flora and fauna, as well as more physical activities such as rafting, kayaking, and rappelling.

On Foot

Hikes

As I inched along the shoulder of the tollway, cars whizzing past me, I almost turned back, not believing there could be anything down this road. **El Corazón** (the heart) seemed to be as keen on keeping its secrets as any live heart I had ever encountered. And then, just as I was about to give up, a pulloff appeared. From the safety of the pulloff, I could see that the tollway crossed a long bridge, while on my side a trail headed up and behind a vendor's shack and then cut between tall grass and lots of fluttering butterflies. At its end were the railroad tracks I had been looking for – a sturdy bridge spanning a wide canyon, offering a spectacular view of El Corazón below. From here, you can see the trail of **466 Escalones** (466 Steps), which winds back and forth in a zig-zag design to the floor of El Corazón (the head of the stairs was actually on the other side of the tollway bridge). At the bottom of the steps, appearing as tiny dots from above, you can see a handful of restaurants and a number of swimming pools.

The tourist office has a suggested route that you can follow for a pleasant three-mile hike here. At the valley floor, from the base of the 466 Steps, you head east along the old railroad tracks under and past the tollway, through tunnels, until you reach the *Antiguo Puente del FFCC* (old railroad bridge). Cross over, then loop back down in the direction from which you came (but on the other side of the river). You'll end up passing back under the tollway and be back where you started in around three hours.

To get to El Corazón, a trail heads north and then east from the train station on the east side of town that brings you to the bottom of the valley.

Though it loosely follows the direction of the railroad tracks, you should not follow the tracks themselves. Though they do go through El Corazón, not only do trains use the tracks, but people have been assaulted while walking on them.

Before you head out, stop by the tourist information office and ask for specific directions. The roundabout route that I followed was to walk from the center of Fortín, to the tollway, turning onto it heading back towards Orizaba. After a 10-minute walk down, I found the railroad bridge above El Corazón (a bit more of a dangerous route than necessary).

Author's Tip: Do you have a bathroom emergency? There's a men's and women's bathroom on the ground floor of the Palacio Municipal, right next to a soda machine.

■ Festivals & Events

Fortín's annual **flower fair** can be smelled before it is seen. Held from April 26 to May 10, it's a chance for the town to celebrate the plants it loves, and it's your chance to spend a day wandering around the *zócalo* examining all the stalls that have been set up by local growers, each trying to outdo the next. Vendors are continually arranging leaves and adjusting pots, constantly moving about in their effort to maximize space on their overloaded tables and racks, which will eventually become emptier as the days wear on (the plants are available for purchase). Around the center of town, you'll find performances, parades, musicians playing upbeat melodies on harp and guitar. You'll see an extra number of sweet bread vendors around, carts selling *chicheron* (pork rinds) and *churros*, and stands selling all sorts of goodies for kids – piggy banks, stuffed animals, games, marbles.

■ Where to Stay

The charming **Hotel Posada Loma**, ☎ 271-713-0658, is a small, peaceful place right outside of Fortín at Km 333 on the Córdoba- Fortín Highway. It has eight rooms and 11 bungalows with kitchen and fireplace, and sits surrounded by manicured lawns and gardens, with a clean pool, and a lush tropical setting. $$

In town, the **Hotel Fortín de Las Flores**, ☎ 271-713-1031, at 210 Ave. 2 (between Calle 5 and Calle 7), for all its modern luxuries (pool, restaurant, room service) is still charming. There is a golf club about a 10-minute drive away. $$

■ Where to Eat

For a wholesome, inexpensive breakfast or lunch, try the **Cafeteria las Gardenias** at 216 Calle 3 Sur (right on the main park). Grab a *torta* or some *tamales* for 12 pesos, some *huevos con chuletas* for 30 pesos, or just enjoy a good cup of coffee. $

Or head nearby to the **Cafeteria Y Antojito** at 307 Calle 1, near Ave. 7. It's a good, clean restaurant with similar fare. $

Córdoba

In 1618, 30 families sent by the Spanish arrived and founded Córdoba in an effort to stop assaults and robberies by runaway black slaves who were hiding out in the vicinity. The town is now a city, sometimes referred to as the city of the *Treinta Caballeros* (Thirty Knights), and known nationwide as an industrial producer of sugar and coffee. It's a large town, with over 100,000 inhabitants.

As long as you're in the beautiful *zócalo* itself, you're fine, and even enjoying your visit – weaving in and out of its *portales*, trying to choose the best place café for a stop. Then you're done with the coffee, and spent the 30 minutes or so exploring the *zócalo*. Now what? Well, there's not much else. One block away from the *zócalo*, all madness and hell takes over the streets.

Behind the Catedral (going away from the Palacio), there are just no words to explain the rapidity with which everything deteriorates. You're immediately assaulted with exhaust fumes, horns honking, whistles blowing, people shouting, music blasting from boomboxes, TVs blaring from storefronts... The sidewalks are lined with tall dirty buildings, and crammed with people trying to get out of the way of bold cars driving bumper-to-bumper down too-narrow streets. You would never in a million years guess that that was what lay just feet from the peaceful, relaxing *zócalo*. It's pure madness.

■ Orientation & Practicalities

Avenidas are directed (more or less) east/west, while *Calles* go (more or less) north/south, divided into odds and evens at the *zócalo*. The *zócalo* is at the intersection of Calle 1 and Ave. 1; to the south is Highway 150.

Emergency Services: Hospital, ☎ 271-714-3111; Red Cross, ☎ 271-712-0300.

Exchanging Money: There are a few banks around downtown, including a **Banamex** at Ave. 3 and Calle 3 (Mon.-Fri., 9-4 pm), as well as a **Santander Serfin** (8 am-4 pm, Mon.-Fri., and Sat., 10 am-2 pm). An **American Express** office (Intervia) is at the Hotel Real Villa Florida, 3002 Ave. 1 between Calles 3 and 2; ☎ 271-718-0888; open Mon.-Fri., 9 am-5 pm.

Internet Café: There are a bunch in the wild section behind the Cathedral, as well as one or two on the *zócalo*.

Post Office: The post office is near the *zócalo* on Ave. 3 between Calle 1 and Calle 2.

Tourist Information: The tourist office is on the right side of the first floor of the Palacio Municipal.

Getting There & Around

By Car

From México City, Puebla or Veracruz, you can take Tollway 150 the whole way. To get around locally, use the Freeway 150, which passes through Orizaba, Fortín de las Flores and Córdoba.

By Bus

The main bus station is off Blvd. Córdoba-Peñuela at Avenida 4 between Calles 39 and 41, a couple of miles from the center. There is transportation available at the station to take you there. Luckily, to get out of Córdoba, you don't have to go all the way to the bus station. You can pick up a local bus to Orizaba or Fortín de las Flores, at the intersection of Ave. 11 and Calle 1, about four blocks downhill.

Sightseeing

The very pretty, very typical Veracruz-style *zócalo* on Calle 1 and Ave. 1 is a huge square plaza surrounded on almost all sides by *portales*, under whose arches you'll find shops, cafés, and offices. If this is your first impression of Córdoba, you will be impressed. The long neoclassic building of the **Palacio Municipal** (built in 1905) sits grandly on one side, while next to it (101 Ave. 1) stands another beautiful *portales*-lined building, **El Portal de Zevallos**. It was built in the 17th century, and is the former home of the Hotel Zevallos. More importantly, it's associated with Mexican Independence (significant treaties were signed here). Today, it is a cultural center with exhibits and an artisan shop (Mon.-Fri., 10 am-2 pm, and 4-8 pm) inside its pretty courtyard, as well as cafés where people drink coffee and listen to live music under its arches. Opposite the Palacio Municipal on the *zócalo* is the beautiful baroque-styled **Catedral de la Inmaculada Concepción**, built in 1621. In the understated interior, you'll find a gorgeous main altar constructed of gold. On the last side of the

square, next to the Catedral to the southwest, is the slightly more sedate **Portal de la Gloria**, often referred to as La Favorita as it has hosted a number of illustrious figures, including Benito Juárez; under its *portales* you'll find the **Museo de la Ciudad**.

Where to Stay

The **Hotel Mansur**, ☎ 271-712-6000, right in front of the *zócalo* at 301 Ave. 1, has a fancy gift shop in its dark wooden lobby, and clean standard rooms (as well as some suites) with TV and a/c. $

The simple **Hotel Virreynal**, ☎ 271-712-2377, 309 Ave. 1 at the corner of Calle 5, has spacious, clean rooms at good prices. $

About 15 minutes outside town off the highway, the **Hotel Villas Layfer**, ☎ 271-716-0916, 291 Córdoba-Fortín Highway, next to the Pemex station, is a very good, modern choice with separate villas and a pool. $-$$

Close to the *zócalo*, **Hotel Bello Córdoba**, ☎ 271-712-8122, at Ave. 2 and Calle 5, is a huge monster of a hotel serving the business crowd, with a formal restaurant, a lounge, and ATM inside the air-conditioned lobby. $$

A few blocks outside of downtown, the fancy **Hotel Villa Florida**, ☎ 271-716-3333, 3002 Ave. 1, has a Jacuzzi, pool, restaurant, and tennis court. Rooms are modern, clean, and air-conditioned. $$$

Where to Eat

All along the *portales* in the *zócalo* are cafés with outside tables full of people drinking coffee or relaxing with a beer. The **Café Córdoba** on Ave. 1 (at Calle 3) is a good spot to join in. $

Another is the **Nevelandia** on Ave. 1, right next door, where they have some great espresso and ice cream as well. $

Or you can try the nearby **Café Parroquia** for a light lunch. $

Southern Veracruz

As you head into the southern portion of Veracruz, you enter the area of **Los Tuxtlas** – a tropical landscape of valleys and mountains. The people here work hard in the fields – you'll pass an endless parade of sugarcane, tobacco, and fruit plantations. And because this is your vacation, you won't be forced into the lush fields with a machete, but will instead get to drink in the land's agricultural beauty,

IN THIS CHAPTER	
■ San Andrés Tuxtla	252
■ Catemaco	260
■ Santiago Tuxtla	267
■ San Lorenzo Tenochtitlán	267

and enjoy the region's natural wonders, including waterfalls, *manglares* (mangroves), and a huge lagoon. In the midst of all this you'll find the **San Martín Volcano**, which has a few colorful towns on its side – one known for witches, one known for cigars, and one known for its colossal head. Here, you've reached the edge of the Olmec heartland. If you are up for the adventure, you can continue into the state of Tabasco.

San Andrés Tuxtla

San Andrés Tuxtla is known for its cigars. The town has a couple of factories where they are hand-made. In the middle of the Sierra de Los Tuxtlas, a hilly volcanic region, San Andrés sits between two other cities of interest – the smaller Santiago Tuxtla, and the resorty Catemaco. The drive to town is pretty, passing through cattle ranches and rich green hills, before the windy road curves into San Andrés, a modern busy town on the slopes of the San Martín Volcano. The town is a pleasant place – just small enough not to be overwhelming, with plenty of things to do nearby. But when you return from your daytime explorations, you won't find much to do in town. Hotels here are a little bit cheaper, however, than in the more heavily touristed Catemaco, and the town can serve as an alternative base from which to explore the region, or as a good place to break a long journey.

■ Orientation & Practicalities

Ave. Benito Juárez leads straight into town, passing the *zócalo*, **Plaza Lerdo**. Across the street from the *zócalo* is the cathedral, while another side has the Palacio Municipal. The market is at the intersection of Cinco de Mayo and Bernardo Peña, three blocks west of the *zócalo*. The Casa de la Cultura is two more blocks south on Cinco de Mayo at the intersection with Hernández y Hernández.

Emergency Services: Red Cross, ☎ 294-942-4995; Hospital, ☎ 294-942-0447.

Exchanging Money: There is a **Banamex** in the main square.

Internet Cafés: There are two cafés inside the Plaza Jardin (on Juárez just past the intersection of 16 de Septiembre and Argudin). The first, **Actuals**, has a number of new flat-panel computers running on a fast satellite connection in a pleasantly air-conditioned room. It's open 9 am-11 pm and costs 10 pesos per hour, but it's almost always full. Down the hall, the **Doubleclick Café** has fewer computers (regular monitors, no a/c), but charges a couple of pesos less, and will often have availability if next door is full (9 am-11 pm, 8 pesos).

Orientation & Practicalities ■ 253

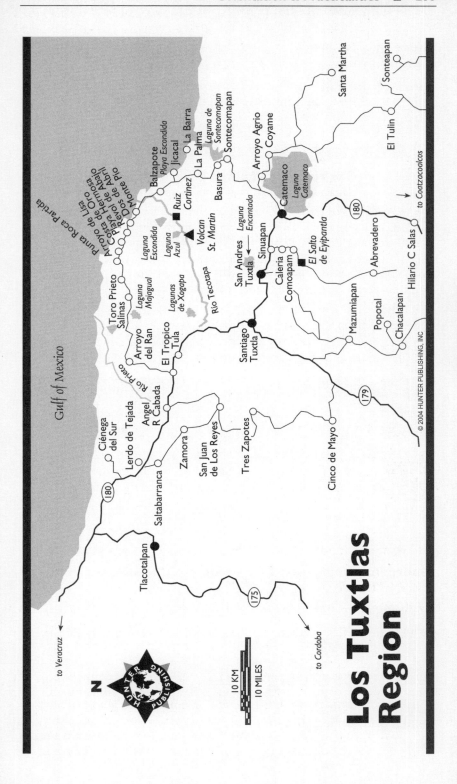

Post Office: You'll find the *correos* two blocks southeast of the Cathedral, at the corner of La Fragua and 20 de Noviembre.

Tourist Information: There is a tourist office on the ground floor of the Palacio Municipal that can give you a couple of general maps, but not much else.

■ Getting There & Around

For the **local bus** to Salto de Eyipantla, Angel R. Cabada, San Andrés Tuxtla, and Catemaco, pick up the appropriately marked bus (TLT-Transportes Los Tuxtlas at the corner of Manuel A. de la Cabada & Cinco de Mayo (by the market).

Probably the fastest and easiest way to get around is by **taxi**. Catemaco and San Andrés are so close that the fare is very affordable. Agree on a price before you get in!

The **ADO bus station** is a good one, with excellent service up and down the coast. The station is northwest of the downtown, about a 10-minute uphill walk from the *zócalo*, off Juárez. The **AU** station is a little closer in, at the corner of Juárez and Romero.

\	BUS TRIPS		
Destination	Bus Line	Fare	Time
Alvarado	ADO	40 pesos	1 hour 20 minutes
	AU	35 pesos	
Catemaco	ADO	5 pesos	25 minutes
	AU	5 pesos	
Xalapa	ADO	127 pesos	3 hours 50 minutes
	AU	112 pesos	
México City	ADO	304 pesos	7 hours 45 minutes
Santiago Tuxtla	ADO	7 pesos	15 minutes
	AU	6 pesos	
Veracruz	ADO	72 pesos	2 hours 20 minutes
Villahermosa	ADO	155 pesos	4 hours 50 minutes

■ Sightseeing

Whether you smoke them or not, you might just have to buy some cigars (*puros*) while you're here. Besides the fact that San Andrés is known nationally and internationally for the quality of its cigars, once you visit a **cigar factory**, you'll be so appreciative of the labor put into each, you'll have no choice but to buy one as a keepsake. One factory to visit is **Puros Santa Clara**, near downtown. It has a display case of their products, and, behind it – much more interesting – a view into a large open room where men and women expertly and efficiently make the cigars.

In the assembly line, each person performs his or her specific task, before passing their part down to the next person.

By some tables, you'll see huge piles and tremendous bags of flattened dried leaves, with people busily deveining them. After the tobacco leaves have been dried and fermented, they're sorted based on size and color, then deveined (as you see here), and placed to age again – the longer the better, but in most cases, for at least another two to three years. At the end of this fermentation period, they're ready to be used. As you'll see, the workers use a *filler*, leaves used to fill the body of the cigar, a *binder*, which is a strong leaf used to hold the filler, and a *wrapper*, which is the tough outer cover leaf that's rolled around the cigar. The cigar rollers are so skilled that the products come out seemingly uniform. But they are pressed into a mold to make them exactly uniform. Finally, the end of the cigar is expertly capped in an unbelievalbly fast and exact process whereby workers fold down the ends of the unfinished cigar, and add a separate leaf to cap it, smoothing it out so it's round, smooth, and uniform – a process that takes about five seconds. Each cigar is bound using a natural bonding glue (a vegetable resin).

In this factory, the next steps are not right within view, but in the next room: since the leaves naturally are the same color, but not the exact same *shade*, another person has the job of sorting the rolled, ready cigars for size and shade, so that when he then puts them into their box, they appear conisistent in color tone. The cigars are put into cedar boxes to retain moisture and prevent them from becoming brittle. A Special Edition box even comes with a humidity gauge.

The different *strengths* of the cigars depend on the leaves, and from what part of the plant they're from. You'll get the strongest "hit" from the bottom part of the plant, and the weakest from the top.

Different types of tobacco (Jamaica, Cuba, Honduras, etc.) are blended together in one cigar, according to a variety of special recipes. A Cuban cigar, for example, is special because it uses high-quality Cuban tobacco, but you can buy a Mexican cigar that uses the same Cuban tobacco.

About 650-700 cigars are produced here each day (the entire process, as you can see, is done by hand). This particular factory opened 40 years ago and is family-owned. They produce cigars of all types and flavors – amaretto, kaluah, chocolate, rum, vanilla, cherry. You can watch the whole cigar-making process unfold for free.

Santa Clara Puros is about one block behind the bus station at 10 Boulevard 5 de Febrero. The Puros y Aromas de San Andrés Tobacco Factory is a couple of houses farther down Boulevard Cinco de Febrero.

Adventures

On Water

Beaches

It's a long bumpy road to the beach from San Andrés Tuxtla. The section of coastline that's accessible from this side of the Volcán de San Martin includes half a dozen adjacent beaches: Punta Roca Partida, Arroyo de Lisa, Costa de Oro, Playa Hermosa, Revol de Abajo, and Dos de Abril. The beaches are wide, with soft brown sand and rough ocean waves, but sometimes littered with trash (especially after holidays).

At the **Costa de Oro**, the last point accessible by bus, you walk a block down a dirt road through a village to get to the ocean. Often, it is deserted, save for a few fishermen. When I was last there, however, the entire village was at the beach, dragging a huge fishing net in to shore. It had been used to trap hundreds of fish at once and the spoils were divided among those who helped haul it in.

The water's a little bit rough for swimming here, but a short walk down toward the **Arroyo de Lisa**, a river that lets into the ocean, provides calm, shallow waters for bathing and, a little upstream, clear green pools flecked with shrimp and tadpoles. As the day wears on, however, this area becomes crowded with people. Unfortunately, with so many people, there is also a lot of trash, making a nice spot unattractive and not worth the effort to get to – and it *is* an effort. If you have the time, patience, and the willingness to really explore, there is a lighthouse at **Punta Roca Partida**.

To get here by public transportation, take a bus to Angel R. Cabada, and pick up a local bus marked *Arroyo de Lisa / Costa de Oro*. Buses come by about once an hour. In Cabada the local bus stop is in front of the Mercado, a block behind where you'll be dropped off. Just turn down 25 de Octobre and you'll see the market on the left. The trip from Cabada will take about an hour – the Costa de Oro is the last stop. Alternatively, take a taxi, or drive. You can take Highway 180 to Cabada, then head north off the highway following the windy road to its end.

1. Casa de la Cultura (Cultural Center)
2. Mercado Municipal (market)
3. Palacio Municipal (Town Hall)
4. Plaza Lerdo (Main Square)
5. Cathedral
6. Cathedral
7. Post Office
8. AU Bus Station

Waterfalls

 The large waterfalls of the **Salto de Eyipantla** are at their best during the rainy season when the water flows down at its max. Wider (60 m/197 feet) than they are tall (45 m/147.6 feet), the falls drain the Laguna Catemaco. Thundering down over a small, rocky cliff, they form a little river whose banks are ideal for picnicking. The *salto* is reached by descending a short (around 200 steps), wide staircase that terminates near the base of the falls. A rocky ledge, perpetually wet with mist and spray, allows you to get a bit closer – right into the arch of an ever-present rainbow. Swimming in the river is not prohibited, but it is a little rough and a bit too deep for bathing.

You'll want to get to the falls early in the day before loads of tourists start arriving, and the place turns from pleasant to madhouse. Unfortunately, the whole area up to the river itself is filled with vendors' shacks and restaurants, spoiling what could be a much more beautiful spot. You can still enjoy a picnic here, however, by heading a little downriver past the vendors to some cleared patches.

To get here, pick up a bus marked *Salto* behind the market (see *Getting Around*). By car, head east on Highway 180 toward Catemaco; a couple of miles out, you'll see a turn-off for Eyipantla. Though the falls are a big tourist attraction for the region, and only 5.6 miles/nine km from San Andrés Tuxtla, the road to access them is surprisingly underdeveloped. You travel down a bumpy road lined with fields of corn and sugarcane, mango plantations, and cow pastures. At the end is a village and a few vendors' shacks. The entrance is a booth, where you pay 5 pesos for access to the area. If you go to the right, there is an alternate entrance (if you've already paid, be sure to have your ticket handy). It takes you to a path leading to a *mirador* (or lookout).

Lagoons

About two miles north of San Andrés Tuxtla, up a dirt road, you'll find the **Laguna Encantada**. The water level in this "Enchanted Lagoon" rises during dry season and drops during the rainy season. To get there, take free Highway 180 east into town. At the fork in town, turn onto Blvd. Cinco de Febrero; about seven blocks before it merges back with Highway 180, you'll see a sign and a road on your left heading toward the lagoon.

Archaeological Discoveries

In 1862, at the ancient Olmec site of **Tres Zapotes**, one of the first of the great colossal heads was recovered. Since then, the site has produced a number of finds, including sculptures, pottery, and stelae – one specifically, Stela C, dating to as early as September 3, 32 BC. Today, the site (believed to have flourished during the Middle Preclassic period – 900 to 300 BC), is nothing but a bunch of overgrown hills and a museum. Here, in addition to a few sculptures, you can see the colossal head that was initially discovered. (Stela C is in México City). The site is about 13 miles/21 km southwest of San Andrés Tuxtla. Head a few miles south on Highway 179; on your right (west) you'll see a road heading towards Tres Zapotes. Alternatively, for a few dollars, you can take a taxi from town. The site is open daily, 9 am-5 pm.

The Olmecs

The Olmecs, or "rubber people," predate any other civilization that has been found in México, probably dating as far back as 2000 BC (to their downfall around 400 BC). Not much is known about them – their language is a mystery (though it is believed that possibly they spoke a Mayan tongue), their origins a puzzle. The colossal heads have distinct features, with prominent thick lips and flat noses. Even their original name is unknown. They were dubbed "Olmecs" in modern times by archaeologist George Vaillant. They are most famous for the huge heads that have been recovered throughout the Gulf Coast at the sites of Tres Zapotes, San Lorenzo, and La Venta (you can find most of them now at the National Museum of Anthropology in México City and in Xalapa's Anthropology Museum). Their sculptures are unique, many depicting a "were-jaguar," a being thought to have been spawned by the meeting of a woman and a jaguar, and characterized in sculptures with a snout, fangs, and human body.

■ Where to Stay

The **Hotel Figueroa**, ☎ 294-942-0257, at 10 Ave. Pino Suárez (two blocks from the main square), was one of the first in town, and is still family-run. The owners are warm and inviting, and have a full case of maps, brochures, and advice that they can provide you (even better than you can find at the tourist office). Rooms are small and basic (fans only), but very clean and inexpensive. This is one of the best values in town. They have indoor parking for a small extra charge. $

HOTEL PRICE CHART	
Rates are per room based on double occupancy. Rates lower if single occupancy or sharing a bed. Higher rates on holidays.	
	US $10-$20
$	US $21-$40
$$	US $41-$60
$$$	US $61-$80
$$$$	US $81-$125
$$$$$	Over US $125

Across from the Figueroa on Pino Suárez near the corner of B. Dominguez is the **Hotel Colónial**, ☎ 294-942-0552, which has inexpensive, basic, older, but clean rooms. $

The **Hotel Posada San Martin**, ☎ 294-942-1036, 304 Ave. Juárez, is a pretty choice, in a quiet, walled-in area just two blocks from the main square; there is a restaurant and bar on-site. Well-maintained, clean rooms come with a/c, cable TV, and phones. $

The **Hotel Del Parque**, ☎ 294-942-3050, at 5 Madero, is conveniently near the *zócalo*. Its rates are on the high end of this range, but it has clean rooms, a/c, a restaurant and café, parking, and accepts credit cards. $

Next door, the **Hotel San Andrés**, ☎ 294-942-0604, 6 Madero, has basic no-frills rooms, which come with TV and fan; if you want a/c, the price of the room goes up about 60 pesos. The hotel has a restaurant and parking, but does not accept credit cards. $

The **Hotel de Los Perez**, ☎ 294-942-0777, at 2 Calle Rascón, has a number of large, comfortable, clean rooms with a/c and TV, as well as parking and a restaurant. $

■ Where to Eat

Most of the restaurants are adjacent to, or part of, hotels, which means they're a little pricey. A good option at the *zócalo* is the **Restaurant y Cafeteria Del Centro**, part of the Hotel de los Perez. It offers both buffet and waitered dining. Breakfast here is especially good; you choose from *juevos rancheros*, bacon, coffee, juice, and more. $

DINING PRICE CHART	
Price per person for an entrée, not including beverage or tip.	
$	Under US $5
$$	US $5-$10
$$$	US $10+

Another choice, the restaurant in the **Hotel Del Parque** (by the *zócalo*) has some *portales* to dine under. $

One of the few alternatives is at the Plaza Jardin (on Juárez just past the intersection of 16 de Septiembre and Argudin). Upstairs is **La Caperucita**, a large restaurant serving tasty Mexican dishes. $

Catemaco

■ Orientation & Practicalities

The town is spread out along the waterfront, with Ave. Playa being the main drag on which you'll find most of the restaurants and hotels. The *zócalo* is two blocks in from the lake on Carranza and Boettinger; the Palacio Municipal is on the *zócalo*.

Exchanging Money: There's a **Bancomer** on the *zócalo*, as well as an ATM on the first floor of the Palacio Municipal.

Post Office: The *correo* is at the corner of Aldama and Corregidora, four blocks east of the *zócalo*.

Tourist Information: The tourist office is on the first floor of the Palacio Municipal (in the *zócalo*).

Getting Around

If you're coming by second-class **TLT bus** (Transportes Los Tuxtlas) from San Andrés Tuxtla, the stop is on a dusty road on the west side of town. To get to the waterfront, hop on the local city bus – one of the newer blue buses you'll see parked nearby. They're called *piratas*, pickup trucks with beds that have been converted to seat how ever many people can pack on. The stop is about six blocks from the waterfront (and ADO bus stop) on Ave. Revolución. From the *zócalo*, head east down Hidalgo and take a left onto Revolución.

The **ADO bus stop** is on the eastern end of the waterfront, about six blocks east of the *zócalo*.

		BUS TRIPS	
Destination	Bus Line	Fare	Time
Catemaco	ADO	6 pesos	25 minutes
	AU	5 pesos	
Coatzacoalcos	ADO	73 pesos	2 hours 30 minutes
	AU	75 pesos	
Santiago Tuxtla	ADO	7 pesos	15 minutes
	AU	6 pesos	
Tampico	ADO	405 pesos	13 hours
Veracruz	ADO	72 pesos	2 hours 20 minutes
	AU	64 pesos	
Villahermosa	ADO	155 pesos	4 hours 50 minutes
Xalapa	ADO	127 pesos	3 hours 50 minutes
	AU	112 pesos	

Adventures

On Wheels

If you don't have a car, and you want to get out of town and explore, you're going to have to try the *piratas*, pickup trucks that have been converted for use as taxis by the placement of wooden planks in the beds for seating. You can take a pirata east of Catemaco around the Lago de Catemaco to Coyame, or you can head north to Sontecomapan on the coast.

Coyame is 12 km (7.4 miles) from Catemaco, about a 20-minute ride down a winding road that traces the edge of the lagoon. The village is best known for its natural mineral water, popularized by the *Coyame* bottling plant. You'll see the plant right at the entrance to the village – a white and blue warehouse with trucks outside. The plant actually sits right on top of the waters themselves. Inside the warehouse, there is a tiled room that has a glass door in the floor; inside the door is a deep well of water. For those unfamiliar with mineral water in its natural form – the water at first appears normal, but if you lower your face to within two feet of its surface, you are overcome with the natural gases. Your eyes water, your nose runs, and breathing becomes impossible. The plant, though a well-known brand in the region, is very small and does not have tours. On a slow day, however, if you ask the manager, you can probably get one without problem. There isn't much else to do here as the village itself is small – a few dirt roads and not much else. There is, however, a little restaurant right by the lagoon (take a right down the dirt road behind the plant). It sits on the edge of a patch of emerald grass and shady trees with a gorgeous view of the expanisve lagoon. Find a spot, have some lunch, and relax.

When it's time to leave, walk up the road a bit, and wave down a pirate heading back to Catemaco. If you continue farther past Coyame, the road becomes a dirt track, passing a couple of villages before eventually ending at Las Margaritas.

Sontecompan is 19 km (11.8 miles) from Catemaco, and sits at the edge of the Laguna de Sontecompan. The ride here is as lovely as you're likely to find, the country road winding its way through hills to the lagoon. The village itself has one main road going through town, and dirt lanes through green hilly fields from house to house. There is a deserted main square, a tiny hotel, and a couple of fruit markets. The real reason to come here, however, besides the pretty the rural setting, is to take a boat launch to the end of the lagoon, which lets out into the ocean. There, you will find a gorgeous stretch of water and beach known as **La Barra** (see *On Water,* below). Farther north from Sontecompan, the road becomes rough, passing a few villages before terminating at Montepio.

As you poke your way through the streets of Catemaco, you will invariably be approached by someone asking if you want to consult a bruja (witch). Are their powers real or not? I have no idea – but many of towspeople seem to think so. Every March, the town hosts an annual witch convention.

On Water
Boat Rides

 Don't miss taking a boat ride on the **Laguna de Catemaco**, the huge lake (it looks more like an ocean) bordering town. The narrated tour initially stays close to shore, making its first stop at a spot where you can buy green clay, whose sulfuric contents are said to cure many ailments. It is meant to be applied to your face. Or you can drink the water (a bottle costs 150 pesos for a six-month supply). The tour then goes out to some islands, the most popular being **Isla de los Monos** (Monkey Island). When I bought my ticket, a little girl trailed me to the boat, insisitent that I have a package of peanuts with me for the monkeys. Her selling point: "You don't even have to open the bag; just give it to them and they'll do it themselves." The monkeys, a colony of Thailandese Macaca Arctoides, were put there by the University of Veracruz who used them for research. Accustomed to boats coming loaded with people, the monkeys are very bold, sitting at the edge of the island, hanging from the ends of branches. And don't be surprised when you see how grossly overweight they are – the university brings them food twice a day, and the boats bring them their snacks hourly. The boat also goes by **Isla de las Garzas** (Heron Island), a bird sanctuary, where you can see hundreds of birds in the branches.

The tour then goes on to visit **Nanciyaga**, where you are offered a tour of the grounds. Nanciyaga bills itself as an ecological reserve, but in fact, it's a well-maintained, thoroughly planned resort – for lack of a better word. The grounds are nice. Wide paths take you past huge trees, a charming rope bridge crosses a dark swampy area, huts are built to prettily complement the surroundings. But the tour focuses more on what services they offer their guests than on information about the natural surroudings (i.e., *here is where our guests can take a steam bath, here is where our guests stay, here is where our guests get massages*). On the plus side, with your admittance fee (30 pesos) you get to taste some mineral water and, if you want, get a facial mud mask. Other attractions: you pass by a hut that usually has a "witch doctor" in residence who, for a fee, can cleanse your aura. You will also see where the annual witch convention is held (in a small outdoor stadium on-site).

Even if you don't take the tour, you still might want to look into renting their kayaks and canoes – ask at the ticket desk for more details. The tour takes about half an hour, and, at its end, the boat brings you back to Catemaco. Pick up the boats near the huge fisherman statue at the waterfront (on Ave. Playa at the end of Boettinger).

From where the piratas drop you off (see *On Wheels*) in **Sontecompan**, turn right down the short road to the edge of the lagoon, where you'll see some restaurants and motorboats lined up at the waters edge. You can rent the entire boat for 350 pesos, or wait until there are enough people for it to go out as a *collectivo*, which shouldn't take too long. Cost is 50 pesos round-trip for the *collectivo*. The boat ride alone is worth the trip. The launch starts by maneuvering through a narrow passageway in the mangroves to get to the lagoon (the dock is actually in a partially enclosed cove surrounded by mangroves – you cannot see the lagoon at all from the launch area). On the lagoon, the boat gears up to high speed for the 20-minute ride to where the lagoon lets out through a channel into the Gulf. The boat will let you out right at the point where lagoon meets sea, on a strip of land with a village, known as **La Barra**.

If what you were hoping for was soft wide beaches, crystal-clear green waters, inviting ocean surf – you've hit the jackpot at **La Barra**. It's a really picturesque spot, one of the best that the Gulf has to offer. On one side of the narrow bar is the lagoon – calm and clear with warm aqua waters – while a minute's walk brings you past a couple of restaurants, and then to the oceanfront on the other side. It's a cleared expanse of spotless sand, marred only by washed up sand dollars and a lonesome palapa. In the early part of the day, you can have the place practically to yourself. After around 2 pm, however, boats of people start to arrive, and the restaurants that had been practically abandoned, fill up completely. Bring suntan lotion, a towel, and something for shade.

Back in Sontecompan, a good spot to rinse off is the **Poza de los Enanos**. To get there from the boat launch area, turn left onto a dirt path and, after a minute or two, you'll reach it. The clear pool of water is surrounded by mangroves; you can often find kids swinging from the trees.

Kayaking

You can explore the lake on your own by kayak. On the *malecón* (at the eastern end), you'll see a vendor with a huge selection of single kayaks (30 pesos for an hour) and double kayaks (35 pesos for an hour), as well as bikes (30 pesos per hour). It may be a bit far for you to head over to the islands on your own (unless you are experienced and know where you're going), but you can certainly have a great time poking up and down the shore. Right around the bend to the east is Playa Expagoya, a good place to pull ashore and join others in swimming and snorkeling.

Waterfalls

Poza Reyna, a private piece of land that calls itself an "ecological park," can be found 27 km (16.7 miles) from Catemaco. It has a pretty waterfall, natural spas, and spots for swimming. They're in a secluded area on the eastern side of the lagoon, up a dirt road past Coyame. Head east (left) up a path after you pass Tebanca.

Spas

There are plenty of places to treat yourself in Catemaco. Most offer the *temazcal* (a prehispanic steambath). In Náhuatl, the language of the Aztecs, *tema* means bathroom, and *calli* means house. They also can give you a mud mask treatment (using local green sulfuric clay) and massages. Two places that specialize as spas include **Nanciyaga** (see below, ☎ 294-943-0199) and **Ecoparque La Punta** (☎ 294-943-0456, at the corner of Ave. Hidalgo and Revolución). The latter offers an eight-treatment session for 400 pesos.

■ Where to Stay

The **Hotel Los Arcos**, ☎ 294-943-0003, at 7 Fco I. Madero, is about two blocks from the waterfront, and has a pool and clean rooms with a/c. $$

A block from Los Arcos, **Hotel Juros**, ☎ 294-943-0084, at the corner of 2 de Abril and Ave. Playa, is a little bit older, but has equally good, clean rooms (your choice of a/c or fan). $

HOTEL PRICE CHART	
Rates are per room based on double occupancy. Rates lower if single occupancy or sharing a bed. Higher rates on holidays.	
$	US $10-$20
$$	US $21-$40
$$$	US $41-$60
$$$$	US $61-$80
$$$$$	US $81-$125
$$$$$	Over US $125

If you get stuck out in Sontecomapan, you have one option, the **Hotel Sontecomapan**, which has old, but acceptable, no-frills rooms with fans only. They have no phone number. You'll find them right after the main plaza on the only main street.

Hotel Berthangel, ☎ 294-943-0089, at 1 Madero, is right across from the *zócalo* and has acceptable older rooms. $

Also in front of the *zócalo*, **Hotel Las Brisas**, ☎ 294-943-0057, at 3 Carranza, has large decent rooms with fans only, though they say they will be getting a/c soon. $

A better choice on the *zócalo* is the **Hotel Catemaco**, ☎ 294-943-0203, which has a pool and a/c. $$

Nanciyaga, ☎ 294-943-0199, www.nanciyaga.com, calls itself an "ecological reserve." There are 10 basic wooden cabins set in an attractive jungly area on the lagoon. A stay includes use of the kayaks and mineral spas. You can also pay individually for use of the property's other facilities, which include a *temazcal* (steam bath), massage parlor, and a witch doctor. Though it is somewhat commercialized, celebrities often visit Nanciyaga for its "natural" appeal; a couple of Hollywood movies were filmed here. To get here, head east from Catemaco following the road to Coyame. After four miles/seven km you'll see the sign for Nanciyaga on your right. $$

The **Hotel Finca Real**, ☎ 294-943-0222, off the *malecón*, is one of the more expensive choices here. It's a pleasant hotel with a pool and a view of the lagoon. $$$

Camping

The **Trailer Park La Ceiba** (no phone number) is on the western end of Ave. Playa, and is marked by a pink restaurant with a palapa roof. $

The **Hotel Playa Azul**, ☎ 294-943-0001, at Km 2 on the road to Sontecompan, is a modern hotel that's "ecologically run." It's a step up from tent living – services include cable TV, a/c, pool, and restaurant. Rooms are are fine, but basic. They also offer camping spots with hookups. $-$$

■ Where to Eat

Most of the restaurants are on the *malecón*, serving up the town's specialties: *mojarra* (a type of perch caught in the lake), *anguila* (eel), *tegogolos* (snails), and *langostinos*.

DINING PRICE CHART	
Price per person for an entrée, not including beverage or tip.	
$	Under US $5
$$	US $5-$10
$$$	US $10+

The **Restaurant-Bar La Isla**, a block from the lagoon at the corner of Ave. Hidalgo and Revolución (near the ADO stop), has a good selection of *mojarra* prepared in different ways, including *mojarra en tachogovi* (with hot sauce), *chilpachole* (spicy crab soup, typical of Veracruz), or *chile y limon*. They also have some good shrimp dishes and soups. $$

The **Restaurant-Bar Cabana Aloha**, on the western end of the *malecón*, has tables looking onto the lagoon, live music, and offers a selection of fish, *langostino*, and shrimp. $$

The **Restaurant-Bar La Ola**, next to the dock, is a popular seafood place right on the lagoon. Live music keeps it packed during high season. $$

Next door, the **Restaurant-Bar Jorge's** sells the local fish plates, along with a good ceviche. $$

Santiago Tuxtla

Santiago Tuxtla, a sleepy town 13 miles/21 km west of San Andrés Tuxtla, has a few cars, a few people, and one huge head. A remnant of the Olmec civilization (not a by-product of the town's ego), the colossal sculpture is known as the **Cobata head**, and it sits proudly at the town's center in the Parque Olmeca. You can find other archaeological artifacts from the area (as well as a few more colossal heads) across the street in the arcaded building that once held the Palacio Municipal, but it is now the **Museo Regional Tuxteca** (open daily, 9 am-5 pm).

This is a quieter place to spend the night Catemaco or San Andrés Tuxtla (the sidewalks roll up pretty early), but there aren't a lot of hotel options. Try the **Hotel Castellanos**, ☎ 272-727-0300, in front of the park at 5 de Mayo and Comonfort. It's a large hotel with garage, restaurant, and rooms with TV and a/c. $

Grab a bite nearby at **La Joya**, corner of Comonfort and Juárez; they have an excellent, inexpensive *comida corrida* for lunch. $

East of Los Tuxtlas, heading towards Tabasco, you go straight through what was once the heartland of the Olmec civilization. In this swampy area of rivers and lowlands and mosquitoes, the Olmecs thrived. Bizarre, but true. Today there's not a lot left to see. The major cities you'll encounter are nothing but industrial centers. Acayucan, Coatzacoalcos, and Minatitlan are not worth visiting. Investigate San Lorenzo Tenochititlán, then continue to Villahermosa.

San Lorenzo Tenochtitlán

It's a small archaeological site, down a long bumpy road, but San Lorenzo was a great center for the Olmecs – one of the oldest of the Olmec sites, dating from 1150 BC to 900 BC. Findings at the site include hundreds of overgrown mounds (probably houses supporting a population of around 1,000), a buried drainage pipe, eight colossal heads (which probably represented rulers), and a crude ball court. Evidence also suggests that the Olmecs traded widely, ate dog as part of their diet, and were cannibalistic.

Broken and destroyed artifacts indicate San Lorenzo's destruction in 900 BC was a violent one – probably a revolt or invasion. Most of the recovered pieces have been moved to museums elsewhere, though the site has a museum (open daily, 9 am-5 pm). The site's location is often referred to simply as Tenochtitlán. To get there from Acayucan, head southeast on the road toward Oluta/Tenochtitlán. Tenochtitlán will be the last stop on the small winding road, about 20 miles.

Tabasco

Tabasco is hot and wet. Its sweltering summer heat is sticky and ever-present. Plants drink it up – everywhere you look it's green and thickly vegetated. Animals thrive on it – parrots and toucans and crocodiles and manatees all call this home. Humans, well, who

IN THIS CHAPTER	
■ Villahermosa	269
■ The Coast	286
■ Western Tabasco	288
■ The Sierras	289
■ Eastern Tabasco	291

could and did survive in such a place has a lot to do with what you see today. The Olmec civilization appears to be at its beginnings. In western Tabasco (and southern Veracruz), a thousand years before the birth of Christ, in the land of swamps, heat, and disease-carrying mosquitoes, against all that would drive you or me away, the Olmecs put together their civilization. Then they disappeared. And the Maya came. Using the swamps to their advantage, they traded. And then the Spanish came, and they too struggled with and grew a few settlements in the inhospitable swamps. The state is infused with history and indigenous cultures. But it's also a vibrant economy and a modern state – tosome degree at the expense of the environment. Oh, it's still jungle and swamp and insect land, but deforestation has taken a dramatic toll. And oil development has brought money, growth and modernization (look at Villahermosa). Plant disease, such as lethal yellowing of the palms, has started to kill off the thick groves of coconut palms. And the more exotic animals too have started to disappear – hiding in the far, remote reaches of the state. To explore Tabasco properly, you'll have to venture into the hinterlands. Just don't forget the mosquito repellent.

Villahermosa

In complete defiance of the swamps, rivers and wetlands that would seem to keep civilization and modernity at bay, Villlahermosa has struggled, survived, and flourished. But it was not always so promising. The city was originally founded in 1519 by Hernán Cortés, under the name of Santa María de la Victoria and in a location on the Río Grijalva. It turned out to be a bad spot – the settlement was continually plagued by pirate attacks.

In 1596, the Spanish picked up the town and moved to a new spot. The subsequent years, however, proved no better, and though the settlement was finally declared a city in 1621 (and renamed **Villa Hermosa de San Juan Bautista**), the pirate attacks continued, and the town's search for a better location continued. In 1666 it moved to Tacotalpa, and in 1795 it moved again – this time to its present location.

Villahermosa is the state's capital, as well as a huge petroleum and agricultural center. It's a sprawling, modern city – a place more urban than cultural. You'll find McDonald's and Burger King, large supermarkets and huge office supply stores, a downtown with offices, shops, and hotels crowded together, and streets full of people with an agenda. It's not so bad though – some of its natural surroundings have been incorporated into its design. The Río Grijalva flows through the center of town, and the lagoons that permeate the city are manicured and landscaped. All in all, if you expect a city, you'll enjoy yourself. Just don't forget to specify a/c in your hotel – this is Tabasco, and it gets *hot*.

■ Orientation & Practicalities

Emergency Services: Cruz Roja/Red Cross, ☎ 993-315-5555; Hospital, ☎ 993-315-2015.

Exchanging Money: There are a number of banks around the downtown, many on Juárez, including a **Banca Confia** at 518 Juárez, a **Bital** at 601 Juárez, a **Banco Mexicano** at 1401 Ave. Méndez, and a **Banpais** at 1010 Madero. You'll find banks at the Tabasco 2000 complex as well, including a **Banamex** at the corner of Vía 2, and a **Bancomer** at 103 Ave. Los Ríos.

Internet Cafés: You can find places to check your e-mail in the downtown center (*Zona Luz*).

Post Office: The *correos* is right off the pedestrian walkway (Lerdo de Tejada) at 131 Sáenz.

Tourist Information: There are a few tourist information booths throughout the city, including one at the airport and one next to the entrance of the La Venta Park Museum (Ave. Adolfo Ruiz). The main state tourism office is across the street from Tabasco 2000 (1504 Paseo Tabasco); it's a pain to get to, and there's no need to bother – the smaller booths can provide you with an excellent map and booklet on the state in English or Spanish.

Villahermosa

1. Tabasco Park
2. Tabasco 2000
3. Convention Center
4. Planetarium
5. Palacio Municipal (Town Hall)
6. State Government Buildings
7. Tomás Garrido Canabal Park
8. La Venta Museum Park
9. Museum of Natural History
10. La Polvora Park
11. Esperanza Iris Theater
12. Museum of History & Archeology
13. ADO Bus Station
14. 2nd Class Bus Station

Getting There

By Air

Villahermosa's airport is serviced by **Aerocaribe**, **Aerolitoral**, **Aeroméxico**, **Aviasca**, and **Mexicana**. See page 20 for contact information. Domestic flights depart regularly for destinations throughout México (including México City, Poza Rica, Tampico, and Veracruz). Internationally, AeroMéxico offers direct service to Houston in the United States, and (if you're feeling a little bit adventurous) Aerocaribe has flights to Havana, Cuba.

The airport is 13 km (eight miles) east of town. To get to downtown, you'll have to take a taxi.

By Car

Villahermosa sits at the crossroads of several highways. Coming from points to the west, follow Highway 180 east; from points east, follow Highway 186 west; from the north, follow Highway 180 south; and from the south, follow Highway 195 north.

If you're driving the tollway route from México City, the amount you'll pay in tolls adds up. Be sure you have enough cash on hand. A regular car on the autopista for the entire route will pay around US $50 one-way).

By Bus

The large, busy, hot, crowded **ADO** bus station (also serviced by UNO and AU) is at the corner of Mina and Merino, many blocks north of the downtown. To get to the center, walk south down Mina, and at the second large intersection, take a left onto Col Méndez Magaña. The station has luggage storage, and a taxi rank. If you have luggage, you'll want to take a taxi for sure. The ADO station has good coverage throughout the coast.

BUS TRIPS OUTSIDE TABASCO			
Destination	Bus Line	Fare	Time
Merida	UNO	486 pesos	8 hours
	ADO GL	344 pesos	8 hours

	ADO	293 pesos	7 hours 45 minutes
México (TAPO)	UNO	748 pesos	10 hours
	ADO GL	541 pesos	10 hours 20 minutes
	ADO	467 pesos	
	AU	417 pesos	
Oaxaca	ADO	342 pesos	11 hours 40 minutes
Orizaba	ADO	310 pesos	6 hours 15 minutes
	AU	277 pesos	
Palenque	ADO	68 pesos	2 hours 5 minutes
	Altos	57 pesos	2 hours 10 minutes
Poza Rica	ADO GL	496 pesos	10 hours 30 minutes
	ADO	419 pesos	9 hours 45 minutes
Reynosa	ADO	835 pesos	24 hours 15 minutes
San Andres Tuxtla	ADO	155 pesos	4 hours 50 minutes
	AU	138 pesos	
Tampico	ADO GL	676 pesos	14 hours
	ADO	562 pesos	14 hours 15 minutes
Tuxtepec	ADO	176 pesos	5 hours 50 minutes
Veracruz	UNO	387 pesos	7 hours
	ADO GL	279 pesos	7 hours
	ADO	244 pesos	6 hours 10 minutes
Xalapa	UNO	456 pesos	
	ADO GL	323 pesos	7 hours
	ADO	298 pesos	7 hours 40 minutes

BUS TRIPS WITHIN TABASCO

Destination	Bus Line	Fare	Time
Balancán	ADO	96 pesos	2 hours 40 minutes
	TRT	80 pesos	3 hours
Cardenas	UNO	39 pesos	45 minutes
	ADO GL	28 pesos	
	ADO	22 pesos	
	AU	20 pesos	
	Sur	16 pesos	
Comalcalco*	ADO	39 pesos	1 hour 25 minutes

	TRT	34 pesos	1 hour 45 minutes
Emiliano Zapata	ADO	68 pesos	2 hours
	TRT	60 pesos	
Frontera	ADO	34 pesos	1 hour 5 minutes
Paraiso	ADO	48 pesos	1 hour 40 minutes
Puerto Ceiba	ADO	51 pesos	1 hour 50 minutes
Teapa	OCC	32 pesos	30 minutes
	Altos	29 pesos	1 hour 5 minutes
Tenosique	ADO	95 pesos	2 hours 50 minutes

*The first ADO bus does not leave until around noon, while the TRT does not leave until later in the evening. For more frequent service, you'll need to head across the street to the second-class bus station and take one of the much more frequent (though slower) second class buses.

■ Getting Around

The city is big, and the main spots of interest are somewhat far from each other. To get around, you can certainly walk (bring a map), or you can pick up any of the **combis** (VW vans) you'll see zooming through the streets. Many pack in so many people that their rear end practically scrapes the ground. That's OK, wave it down, and you can pack in too. For the more conventional, there are plenty of **taxis** that can take you places pretty cheaply.

You can get to many points in Tabasco through AU or ADO, though on a limited schedule. For more frequent, and slower, service, there is a **second-class bus station** three blocks north of the ADO station on Blvd Ruiz Cortines. Head north on Mina and then turn right (east) onto Blvd Ruiz Cortines.

Another option is to **rent a car** and not worry about public transportation at all. There are a number of car rental agencies in the city, including the following.

- **Hertz**, ☎ 993-316-4400, 1407 Paseo Tabasco, near Tabasco 2000
- **Avis**, ☎ 993-312-9214, 602 Juan Álvarez
- **Dollar**, ☎ 993-315-4830, 600 Paseo Tabasco
- **Budget**, ☎ 993-314-3790
- **Advantage Rent A Car**, ☎ 993-351-3218, 911 Ave. Velódromo de la Cd. Deportiva)
- **Ardavi National**, ☎ 993-312-5419, 309-3 Melchor Ocampo

Templo de la Virgen de la Asunción in Cupilco, Tabasco (see page 280)

Prehispanic statuary, Tabasco

Cascadas de Agua Azul, Chiapas (see page 307)

Woman in typical clothing of Chiapas

■ Sightseeing

Plaza de Armas is the main square, just south up a hill off the Zona Luz. Interestingly, unlike many towns and cities along the coast, you will not find the Palacio Municipal here. Instead, it's out on Paseo Tabasco in the Tabasco 2000 area (see below, page 277). The main square is a quiet, pleasant park, on the north side of which you'll find the **Palacio de Gobierno**, and on the south side the **Iglesia de la Concepción La Conchita**. The cute little church was built in the early 19th century to house a statue of the Virgin of the Conception. It's been rebuilt a couple of times, most recently in 1945.

The city's cathedral – **La Catedral de Nuestro Señor de Tabasco** – is up Paseo Tabasco at the corner of 27 de Febrero. It's a tall, beautfiul neoclassical cathedral with two towers, an interesting sculpture in its courtyard, and a plain interior. The cathdral is actually still under construction and has been since the '60s; the 18th-century cathedral that originally stood here was destroyed in the '30s.

To the east of the plaza is Río Grijalva and the **Puente de Solidaridad**, a fairly new pedestrian bridge. The bridge is used mainly by locals to cross to the other side of the river, but is also a good spot to get a nice view of the surroundings. Don't be surprised if, right next to the bridge, you see long lines of people queuing up to take a boat across the river. Why they simply don't walk across, instead preferring to wait up to 20 minutes for the boat to return, is beyond me. Boat rides can be picked up right next to the bridge, for a few pesos over and back; on the other side of the river is a residential area.

South of the Zona Luz, on the banks of the Río Grijalva, is the Centro de Investigación de las Culturas Olmeca y Maya (**CICOM**). The zone includes the Biblioteca J. Ma. Pino Suárez (library), the Casa de Artes José Gorostiza (art center), the Teatro Esperanza Iris (theater), La Ceiba (art school), and the **Museo Regional de Antropología Carlos Pellicer Cámara** (Anthropology Museum). The anthropology museum, dedicated to the indigenous cultures of Tabasco, is the main attraction. Most visitors, after staring in awe for a few minutes at the huge Olmec head at the entrance, take the elevator up to the top (third) floor to begin the tour. At the top, you'll find artifacts from many of México's indigenous cultures, including the Totonacs, Zapotecs, Mixtecs, Mexicas, and Remojadas. The mezzanine has Olmec and Mayan pieces, as well as the museum's most important artifacts, including the gorgeous Pellicer Vase. Finally, the first floor has some larger Olmec and Maya pieces. Open daily, 9 am-8 pm; there's a fee. The museum is at 511 Periférico Carlos Pellicer Cámara (near the intersection of Ave. Esperanza Iris).

The best-known attraction in Villahermosa is the **Parque-Mueo La Venta**, an open air museum/zoo with a number of ancient pieces from the nearby Olmec site of La Venta, which was being threatened by oil exploration and recovery. With little option but to move the pieces from the site to ensure their saftey, Tabascan scholar/poet Carlos Pellicer went to work. His brainchild was the park – where he could put the archaeological artifacts back in the jungles where they were discovered, instead of a more traditional museum setting. After much lobbying, Pellicer finally received approval for his idea, and an allottment of land for his project; he quickly went abiout creating his vision and, on March 4, 1958, his work paid off, and the museum opened its doors for the first time.

It's far better to see the items in their original environment, but if that's not possible, the La Venta Park is a good alternative. When you enter, the first thing you will see is a pit that serves as the home to a group of howler monkeys; this is the first of a few animal displays around the park. Though you will find more animals here, including macaws, toucans, parrots, crocodiles, snakes, pumas, and jaguars, the animal exhibits should be considered a bonus to your visit, not the main attraction. There are few of them in relation to the size of the place, and often the animals stay hidden. On my visit the jaguars remained in their dark den, the birds totaled two quiet macaws, and the crocodiles never emerged from their abandoned-looking swampy cage. But the monkeys were numerous, chatty and fun.

Past the monkeys, you'll enter a room that has some artifacts on display in traditional museum style, providing a history lesson on the Olmec culture, and, specifically, the La Venta site (look carefully, some of the items in this part of the exhibit are reproductions, not originals).

Once you've covered the basics, it's out of the room and into the "jungle," where paths lead you through large wild-looking plants into clearings where you find each piece on display, set up as it was originally found. The trees and plants are huge and varied; they include ceiba and mahogony trees and medicinal plants; in the brush and running across the path you'll see some of the smaller non-ferocious animals. As you walk along the path, you'll see a number of monuments, stelae, and sculptures, including some colossal Olmec heads. Thought to represent rulers, the heads are made of basalt. Two gorgeously detailed altars (or thrones) are also worthy of mention. Altar 4 shows a seated man exiting a niche or cave, and Altar 5 shows the same, but in his arms he holds a were-jaguar baby. Other figures on the altar hold struggling babies as well.

The were-jaguar is a common feature of Olmec sculpture, originating from the union of a human and a jaguar. A shaman's transformation into a jaguar through his wearing of the skin of the beast is represented on this Olmec ceramic vessel from Veracruz. His mask, with lolling tongue and pointed fang, only covers half his face, showing that he is in the process of change.

Another interesting monument is Stela 3, a relief of two men in ceremonial headdress, one of whom has a goatee.

A leisurely stroll through the park will take about an hour or two. When you purchase your ticket, maps will cost you an extra dollar or two, but it's not really necessary to get one — paths clearly lead you through the whole park. Guides, some bilingual, are at the entrance offering their services. They might help explain some of the pieces, but if you want to take your time poking around the animal exhibits you may not need one.

Parque Museo La Venta is on the Laguna de Las Illusiones on Blvd. Adolfo Ruiz Cortines, northwest of the city center. It's about a 25-minute walk from downtown. Starting at the *malecón*, head straight up Paseo Tabasco, then take a right onto Blvd. Adolfo Ruiz Cortines. Unless you have your walking shoes on, you might want to take a *combi*, bus (marked *Tabasco 2000*), or a cab. The park is open Mon.-Sun., 8 am-5 pm; zoo is closed on Mondays. Admission 50 pesos.

When you leave, take a walk around the **Laguna de Las Illusiones**, a beautiful spot with a pretty walkway, and lots of colorful birds. There are even boats to take you out on the water. If you need more to do, next to the park's entrance you'll find the Museo de Historia Natural, or walk another two short blocks up Paseo Tabasco to the Tabasco 2000 complex.

The huge rhinocerous sculpture across from the Museo La Venta marks the entrance to the **Museo de Historia Natural** (Museum of Natural History) on Blvd. Adolfo Ruiz Cortines). The museum is not focussed specifically on Tabasco, but mainly dedicated to the planet's history, containing exhibits on the evolution of the universe, life, mankind, and natural resources. It does, howoever, have a section deciated to Tabasco's geography. Open Mon.-Sat., 10 am-7 pm, Sun., 10 am-5 pm. There is a admission fee.

The **Casa Museo de Cultura Popular Angel E. Gil Hermida**, right outside the center at 810 Ignacio Zaragoza, is a good place to see the crafts and artistry of the local indigenous cultures. Open Mon.-Sat., 10 am-5 pm, free.

Villahermosa

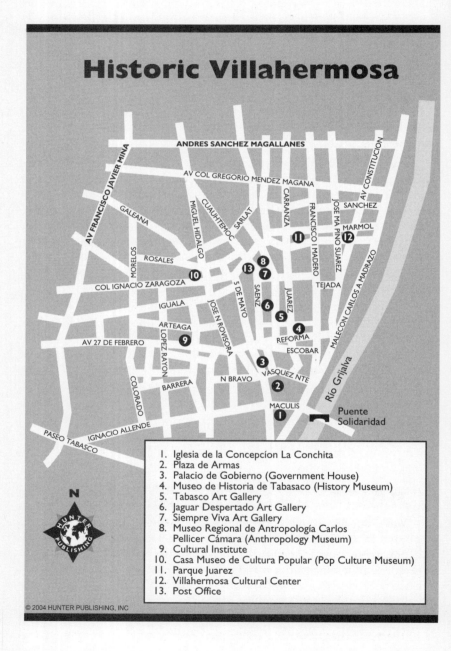

The **Tabasco 2000** complex is a collection of modern commercial and government buildings from the '70s and '80s. Here you'll find the Palacio Municipal, the city's convention center, banks, hotels, restaurants, a modern planetarium, a huge shopping center (modern and upper crust, with boutiques, department stores, and movie theaters), and a big plaza with walkways and pretty fountains.

■ Adventures

On Foot

The heart of the city for the pedestrian is the **Zona Luz**, downtown's city center, parts of which have been converted into a pedestrian zone. Restaurants and cafés line the way, many with outdoor tables and musicians putting out upbeat melodies. Shops of all sorts sell clothing, knick-knacks, and accessories. These are great spots to duck into when the heat of the day becomes unbearable – they're almost always air-conditioned! There are stands selling souvenirs, snacks, and juices. Street entertainers (mainly clowns) follow kids around, twist balloons into shapes, and try their best to make you smile. During the daytime, the Zona Luz is always bustling with action; at night, however, shortly after dark, businesses start to close, and the area empties out. The Zona Luz runs parallel to the river along Calle Juárez.

Be sure to visit the art galleries in the zone. The **Casa Museo Carlos Pellicer Cámara**, at 203 Calle Sáenz, was the house where Tabasco's famous poet Carlos Pellicer was born. Inside the museum, four rooms house a collection of his personal effects, including photographs, books, documents, furniture, clothing, and a mock set-up of the tiny quarters he lived in (a narrow corner space under a staircase). It's an intersting museum, even if you're not quite sure who he was. (Open Mon.-Sat., 10 am-8 pm, and Sun., 10 am-4 pm; free.)

CARLOS PELLICER CÁMARA

You'll see his name everywhere you go here. Pellicer was born in 1897 in Tabasco. He was an acclaimed poet and a devout scholar with a love for nature (often reflected in his works). He also had a passion for archaeology. Eventually, he became director and curator of the National Institue of Bellas Artes, going on to set up museums throughout México, including Villahermosa's Parque Museo La Venta.

A few houses down on Sáenz is **El Jaguar Despertado Art Gallery**. You won't see any art on the first floor, but if you head up the staircase, bypassing the café and offices, the gallery on the third floor has work by various local artists. (Open Mon.-Sat., 9 am-10 pm, Sun., 10 am-3 pm; free.)

The Casa de los Azulejos (House of Tiles) at the corner of Juárez and 27 de Febrero houses the **Museo de Historia de Tabasco**. The exterior decorated with tiles from Barcelona, and the interior is an elegant combination of columns and arches. The museum itself has a collection of pieces representing the history of Tabasco. (Open Tues.-Sat., 10 am-8 pm, Sun., 10 am-5 pm; 25 pesos.)

From the Zona Luz, it's a short hop over to the *malecón* for a walk along the river. Head east down Ave. 27 de Febrero. It's pleasant, but the sidewalk is narrow, and it runs alongside a busy thoroughfare. If you keep walking down the *malecón*, you'll pass a huge overpass and statue, eventually reaching CICOM (see *Sightseeing* above).

On Wheels

In order to see more than cosmopolitan Tabasco (where a quarter of the state's population lives), you'll have to visit some of the smaller towns. The state is small, but the roads, though not always the fastest, connect the main regions pretty well. In the smaller towns, you'll have a chance to see real Tabascan life.

One of the towns closest to Villahermosa, **Nacajuca**, is where most of the state's largest indigenous population – the Chontal Maya – lives. The town is particularly known for the handicrafts that the locals produce.

Just north of Nacajuca is **Jalpa de Mendez**, which is also known for its craftsmen – and specifically, for its intricately decorated *jícaras* (dried, hollowed gourds used as dishes or cups). You can also find a museum, the **Casa Museo Coronel Gregorio Méndez Magaña**, where the Colonel (a Tabascan hero) was born. The museum has some war paraphernalia, and some of Méndez' personal effects (9 am-8 pm daily; free). While you're in town, swing by **Cupilco** (a few miles north) and see its pretty – and crazily colored – church.

To get to Nacajuca, head north out of Villahermosa, following the road and signs to the town 28 km (17.3 miles) away. Continue northwest less than a mile to Jalpa de Mendez, and just nine miles beyond that, Cupilco. There's a gas station here.

On Water

A fun twist on the traditional boat tour, Villahermosa has a dinner boat ride. The ***Capitán Beuló*** takes you out on the Grijalva River for a two-hour dinner cruise that serves typical Tabascan cuisine (including *pejelagarto* and fresh seafood). The boat leaves from the *malecón* Madrazo; Tues.-Sat. at 3:30 and 7:30 pm, Sundays at 1:30 and 3:30 pm; ☎ 993-312-9217. $$$

Archaeological Discoveries

The road to **Comalcalco** may not be paved with brick, but the site itself sure is. The ancient city, 35 miles/58 km northwest of Villahermosa heading toward the coast, represents what was probably the westernmost fringe of the Maya civilization. Here, amidst the heat, the mosquitos, and the coastal flatlands, the Maya built Comalcalco, a city of a few hundred buildings that flourished around 800 AD. The interesting thing about Comalcalco is that, unlike the other cities the Maya built, which were stone, this one was made out of brick. In fact, the ealiest Maya buildings were made simply of compacted earth. Researchers think that this innovation came about because there was no stone in the area; so they sought out, and found, an alternative.

When you enter the site, down the path and to your left (north), you'll see **Plaza Norte** (North Plaza), made up of Templo 1 (the first and tallest building), and Templo II and Templo III (directly in front). A little farther down the path and to the left is the **Gran Acrópolis**. On the acropolis are Templo VII and Templo VI (with a mask of the sun god). Climbing higher, you'll find the rooms of the **Palacio**, as well as the **Patio Hundido** (sunken patio). To the right of the Palacio are two more small temples (Templos IV and V), and a last one (the farthest north), known as the **Tomb of the Nine Lords of the Heavens**, with a beautiful relief inside.

As you walk around the buildings, you may be interested to know what you can't see. Curiously, most of the bricks that the buildings are made of are carved on the interior face – that is, on the side that usually faces the adjacent bricks. The carvings are thought to be representations of animals, humans, and plants. It's believed that some of the symbols represent the mason's signature. In one of the most mind-boggling (if true) articles that I've read, archaeologist Neil Steede observes that the symbols closely match symbols found on Roman bricks.

As one researcher puts it:

"The illustrated bricks of Comalcalco are pieces to a grand puzzle, whose completed, final image may reveal a Roman Christian presence in the Americas a thousand years before the arrival of Columbus."[1]

Shown above are some typical mason's signs found on Roman bricks (left) and Comalcalco bricks (right). Many additional similarities are found between mason's signs from Comalcalco and those from Roman, Minoan, and ancient Greek sites.[2]

At the site's entrance, a museum displays some artifacts recovered from the site. It has a café. The site is open 10 am-5 pm; admittance fee. To get here by car, head west on Highway 180 towards Cardenas; at Cardenas, turn north (right) onto Highway 187 heading for Comalcalco. It's slow driving, and will take you about an hour to get there. Alternatively, you can get here by *combi*, or by first- or second-class bus (see *Getting Around* above). If you decide to take the bus, be aware that you won't be dropped off right at the ruins, but at the town of Comalcalco. From there, you can take a taxi to the ruins (a couple of miles outside of town).

■ Cultural & Eco-Travel

Nature Park

Okay, it's a little commercialized, but it does give you a look at Tabasco's main ecosystems. **Yumká** is a nature park that has been spruced up with animals and guides to give people a safari-like experience. The park is about 15 minutes by highway outside of the city, and encompasses savannah, jungle, and wetlands. You pay for a tour through walking trails in the jungle, on a trolley ride through the savannah, and on a boat tour of the lagoon. Unfortunately, it's more like a fun twist on a zoo than a true experience in the Tabascan wilderness – many of the animals roaming around are not native to México, imported instead from Africa and Asia. So, in addition to the crocodiles, jaguars, deer, mon-

---

1. Steede. Neil. "The Bricks of Comalcalco," *Ancient American*, 1:8, September/October 1994.

2. Fell, Barry. "The Comalcalco Bricks: Part 1, the Roman Phase," Occasional Papers, Epigraphic Society, 19:299, 1990.

keys, macaws, iguanas, and birds, you'll see giraffes, rhinoceroses, antelopes, zebras, ostriches, elephants, and hippos. There's a shop and restaurant at the site. Hours are 9 am-4 pm, daily. You'll have to pay for a guided tour. The park is 16 km (10 miles) from downtown, near the airport; to get there you'll have to take a taxi.

Chocolate Plantation Tour

Near the town (and ruins) of Comalcalco, there are a couple of factories that grow and process the locally grown cacao beans – chocolate factories! **Hacienda La Luz** will give you a look at their operation (other nearby plantations include Hacienda Brondo and Finca Cholula). Talk to a tourist representative in Villahermosa, ☎ 993-316-3633, for more information.

■ Festival

During the time of the **Feria de Tabasco** (State Fair) special open-air buses dedicated to taking people to the fair show up everywhere. At night, they have flashing neon lights and loud blaring music. The driver's assistant hangs by a foot and an arm out the doorway, calling at people who pass by, joking with them, doing his best to get people onboard; and the buses fill up quickly – kids with ice cream dripping over their hands climb on, families of five and six squeeze onto a bench, and women dressed to the nines carefully find themselves a seat (sometimes next to men dressed to the nines... as women!). Miss one, and the next bus comes along in a few minutes, the show repeating itself over and over – and you arent even at the fair yet! The fair itself is lots of fun. There are carnival rides, theater performances, folk dances, cockfights, and musical entertainment. There's a rodeo and a stockyard with livestock showing and selling. There are games and foods and souvenirs. *Try* not to overindulge. It all takes place for a few weeks at the end of April and beginning of May.

■ Where to Stay

The **Hotel Cencali**, ☎ 993-315-1999, near the Laguna de Las Illusiones (at the corner of Juárez and Paseo Tabasco), is a pretty hotel in a colonial building. It has a pool, and a lobby with a beautiful painting by local artist Montuy, representing the Mayan-Quiche legend on the creation of the universe. The hotel has air-conditioned rooms, and everything from standard accommodations to presidential suites. $$$$

Centrally located near the Zona Luz, the **Hotel Madán Villahermosa**, ☎ 993-312-1650, at 408 Francisco Madero, has a good restaurant and comfortable air-conditioned rooms. $$

The **Hotel Miraflores**, ☎ 993-312-0054, at 304 Reforma, is two blocks from the river, and has a lively restaurant and bar, parking, room service, cable TV, and comfortable clean rooms; the hotel also has two large suites. $$

The **Hotel Tabasco**, ☎ 993-314-9156, at 31 Lerdo (at the corner of Juárez), is centrally located, has a friendly staff, and basic rooms with fan or a/c (add 60 pesos). This is on the lower end of the price scale. $

HOTEL PRICE CHART	
Rates are per room based on double occupancy. Rates lower if single occupancy or sharing a bed. Higher rates on holidays.	
	US $10-$20
$	US $21-$40
$$	US $41-$60
$$$	US $61-$80
$$$$	US $81-$125
$$$$$	Over US $125

The **Hotel Hyatt Regency**, ☎ 993-315-1234, is the luxury accommodation in town, towards Tabasco 2000, near the intersection of Blvd. Adolfo Ruiz Cortines and Paseo Tabasco (106 Ave. Juárez). The 206-room building has a couple of restaurants, pools, tennis courts, a fitness center, parking, and room service. Rooms are what you would expect at this price level. $$$$$

The **Hotel Camino Real**, ☎ 993-316-4400, is next to the Tabasco 2000 complex at 1407 Paseo Tabasco. It caters to a lot of business travelers, and so has the associated amenities, including a convention room, restaurant, bar, laundry service, pool, and parking. $$$$$

The **Hotel Oriente**, ☎ 993-312-0121, at 425 Madero, is downtown, and has good basic rooms with fan or air-conditioning (for 80 pesos extra). $

The **Hotel Plaza Independencia**, ☎ 993-312-1299, is in a good spot a block south of the Plaza de Armas (123 Independencia) within view of the river. It has a pool, restaurant, parking, and good, straightforward, clean rooms at good prices. $$

The **Hotel Maya Tabasco**, ☎ 993-312-1111, is a little to the north of the center at 907 Blvd. Adolfo Ruiz Cortines. It's a good quality hotel with clean, large, air-conditioned rooms, as well as a pool, restaurant, parking, and shuttle to the airport. $$$$

If you want to try a reliable name, the **Hotel Howard Johnson**, ☎ 993-315-4912, at 404 Ignacio Aldama, has comfortable air-conditioned rooms, and is nicely adjacent to the pedestrian walkway. $

A good budget choice, near the Zona Luz, is the **Hotel San Francisco**, ☎ 993-312-3198 at 604 Madero. It has decent air-conditioned rooms. $

In Paraiso

The **Hotel Sabina**, ☎ 993-333-0016, at 115 Ocampo, is right in front of the main square. Rooms are clean and air-coniditioned. They do not accept credit cards. $$

■ Where to Eat

Tabasco is such an urban center, there's something to suit just about any taste – you'll find Italian, Japanese, Chinese, Spanish, and international restaurants mixed in among the Mexican restaurants.

DINING PRICE CHART	
Price per person for an entrée, not including beverage or tip.	
$	Under US $5
$$	US $5-$10
$$$	US $10+

With so much water around, you won't be surprsied to discover that typical Tabascan cuisine has something to do with fish. River fish such as the *robalo* (snook) is typical, as is the bizarre-looking *pejalagarto*, an ugly fish with crocodile-like jaws and teeth. Other Tabascan dishes include *carne salada con chaya* and *pochitoque en verde*; in smaller local restaurants you can sometimes find rabbit or armadillo on a menu. Desserts include *tortas de plátano* or *empanadas de queso*, and to drink, *chorote* or *pozol* – drinks made from ground corn and cacao, thick and yummy, once you acquire the taste for them.

You can find **Los Tulipanes** (511 Carlos Pellicer Cámara) near CICOM and the river. It offers Tabascan specialties (including the *carne salada con chaya*) and sometimes live music. It's closed Mondays, and only open 1-9 pm during the rest of the week). $$$

Another good spot with Tabascan as well as Mexican dishes is the restaurant **Madán** (the same one referred to under Hotel Madán above, at 408 Ave. Madero). It's often busy at lunch time. $$

If you're out for a morning walk, and would like a Tabascan breakfast, about seven blocks north of the Zona Luz you can find **Las Jícaras** at the corner of Merino and Constitución, open 7 am-11 pm. $

El Mirador at 105 Madero is open lunch to dinner, and has mostly Mexican dishes, but also some seafood, including a couple of variations of the river fish *robalo*. $$

El Torito Valenzuela is another spot for typical Mexican food, and has a good lunch; it's conveniently a block from the pedestrian walkway (towards the river) at the corner of Ave. 27 de Febrero and Madero. $$

Restaurants that go easy on the stomach include a **VIP's** at 403 Madero (at the corner of Reforma and open until midnight), which serves grilled chicken, burgers, steaks (basic international fare). Along the same lines, there's a **Sanborn's** around Tabasco 2000, at 1310 Ave. Ruiz Cortines, open until 1 am. $$

There are also a number of pizza joints (you'll find that Mexicans have taken a great liking to the tomato pie). Try **Di Bari** at 712 Méndez or **Douglas Pizzas** at 105 Lerdo. $$

Or, if you're *really* missing home, you can find a number of fast food chains in the Zona Luz on the pedestrian walkway, including a McDonalds, Burger King, and Kentucky Fried Chicken. You'll also find a number of burger and fast food joints all around Tabasco 2000. Don't expect prices here to be like what you find at home, however. You'll pay about twice as much as normal for the luxury of having that grease and fat in the wonderful land of Tabasco. $-$$

Vegeterians tired of eating fish (or those that can't eat fish) can try **Aquarius**, a vegetarian restaurant with two locations – one at 309 Mina (near the bus station) and one at 513 Zaragoza (near Parque Juárez). $$

The Coast

Tabasco's coast is a network of lagoons, rivers, and wetlands where vegetation grows abundantly. Most of the land is made up of tiny strips, bordered on one side by lagoon, on the other by ocean, and every now and then welcoming a river into its folds. The lagoons are wide and quiet; pretty spots to explore if you can find a boat. And the coast is wild and remote. There is the hot, busy coastal town of Paraiso, with beaches easily accessible, but most of the coast still has a raw, untouched beauty to it. Even the beaches that could accommodate hundreds of people are in many cases utterly deserted off-season or mid-week. The beaches have row upon row of coconut palms growing in thick groves beside the wide brown sand. Waves crash on the shore – a bit rough in spots, but the water is always warm and often shallow.

The busy town of **Paraiso** is the main town on the coast (though it is actually around six miles inland). Highway 187, after passing through miles of green, flat countryside makes this its second-to-last stop. There's not much of interest to visitors in the town – aside from its main square, a modern plaza with a simple white and grey church. This is the San Marcos Church, built during the '70s – two towers, three naves, and an interior with lots of arches. There's also a restaurant where you can grab a snack.

From here, you have your pick of beaches. The main one, developed specifically for tourists, is the **Centro Touristico El Paraiso**. It's a

15-minute drive (or second-class bus ride) from Paraiso, and is the first beach you'll hit on the coast if you head northwest. A rocky turn-off in the middle of groves of trees marks the entrance (you'll see a sign). Down the road is a guard's hut (empty when we visited) and a parking lot meant to accommodate hundreds of cars. At the edge of the parking lot, up towards the beach, you'll see the center itself, a huge modern cement complex with restaurant, restrooms, and lots of unused space. Beyond this eyesore, however, is the beach – a wide expanse of fine soft sand (typical Gulf brown) that continues down the coast as far as you can see. Hundreds of coconut palms tower and sway in the wind, making the beach feel remote and tropical. Directly in front of the center are rows of picture-perfect palapas lined up back-to-back, put there for public use. It is everything you might imagine a Tabascan beach to be – a little wild, somewhat remote, and very tropical. Much of the year when it's not a holiday or weekend, the center is completely deserted – restaurant closed, parking lot empty, palapas abandoned. You can have the whole beach pretty much to yourself. At peak times hwoever, those facilities do fill up – children playing, families arriving with tables, chairs, and food, teenagers bathing – and public transportation won't be a worry.

If you leave the Centro Turistico El Paraiso, you'll have to go back through Paraiso to reach the other popular beach on its eastern side. If you continue west, however, you'll follow a road that winds its way along the coast and a series of huge lagoons. The closest beach, 12 miles west, is **Nuevo Paraiso** (where you can find swimming and recreational boats), followed another 13 miles down by **El Alacrán** (a village that sits on the edge of the Laguna Machona, where you can find boats to take you fishing). A few miles beyond that is **Manatinero Alacrán**. It sits on a strip of land with the ocean on one side, and two lagoons on the other . The Laguna Machona is on the west and the Laguna del Carmén on the east. On Laguna del Carmén is a section known as **El Pajaral**, where you can find huge colonies of birds. Fishermen from town can take you on a boat tour to view them., Another 14 miles down is **Coronel Andrés Sánchez Magallanes** at the edge of the Laguna del Carmén; you'll find a beach here as well. Beyond this, 25 more miles, and you'll hit the border of Veracruz. The road west past of Paraiso is deteriorating badly from the severe storms that sometimes hit the coast; driving can be difficult and roads impassable in some spots.

On the eastern side of Paraiso, nine miles away, is **Puerto Ceiba**, on the edge of the Laguna Mecoacán. From Paraiso, you can pick up a local bus near the main square, at the corner of M. Ocampo and Galeana, for the 20-minute ride to the village. It's a quiet town, made up mainly of fishermen. From the docks, you can find fishermen to take you into the clear lagoon for a tour or for fishing (a boat rental will cost around 150 pesos). Since the village is somewhat sheltered from the ocean in an inlet, you won't find any easily accessible beaches. You will, however, find excellent seafood – this whole area specializes in oysters (farmed locally), clams, *pigua* (crayfish), sea bass, *mojarra* (a type of fish) and *pejelagarto* (a delectable – if nnpleasant-looking – fish popular for its delicate white flesh).

Another good place for a delicious seafood lunch is five miles farther west at the village of **Chiltepec**. Five miles beyond that, and you'll find the Playa Azul, a fine spot for fishermen, but without much for anyone else.

You'll need to follow Highway 180 north to get to the *far* eastern side of the Tabascan coastline. Just as you turn to follow the coast, a road leads to the ocean, where you find the Playa Miramar, a popular local attraction.

The next place you hit is the major town along the coast – **Frontera**, a busy port on the banks of the Río Grijalva. It was in this area (known as the Centla region) that Hernan Cortés was given the enslaved princess La Malinche (aka Doña Marina) – one of the people that would give him a voice in the New World. She spoke Maya and Náhuatl (the language of the Aztecs). Another companion of Cortés was a Spanish castaway who had learned to speak Maya as well. This enabled him to communicate with Moctezuma.

From Frontera, to the north, you can take a road to the coastal point of **El Bosque**, where there is a lighthouse, a pleasant beach, and boat rides onto the river. To the south of Frontera is the Reserva de la Biosfera Pantanos de Centla, which is basically a huge marshland area devoid of towns, but filled with birds. From Frontera, Highway 180 continues along the coast for 23 km (14 miles) more before crossing over into the state of Campeche.

Western Tabasco

■ Adventures

Archaeological Discoveries

In the swampy region of western Tabasco, almost at the border of Veracruz, lies an ancient center inhabited thousands of years ago. The site of **La Venta** (dating to 1000 BC), is believed to have been the greatest of the Olmec citiesm. Many of its monuments were moved to Villahermosa when oil expansions and development threatened to destroy what nature – for millenia – had not. The site, therefore, is largely stripped. Most of the monuments, stelae, sculptures, figurines, altars, and four colossal heads were shipped to

the Parque Museo La Venta in Villahermosa. There are however a few things that remain, specifically the buildings themselves, and a few artifacts, including one colossal head. The site's main structure is the Great Pyramid – a huge 34-m (111.5-foot) volcano-shaped clay mound; it is surrounded by a number of smaller mounds. The buildings would at one time have been colorfully painted. During the excavations, distinctive mosaic masks formed by blocks placed on the ground were found buried; the mosaics are thought to represent jaguar masks, and are probably offerings (today housed at the museum in Villahermosa). The site was destroyed and abandoned sometime around 400-300 BC. There is a museum at the site. Open daily, 10 am-5 pm; admission fee.

To get to La Venta, follow Highway 180 west from Villahermosa about 130 km (80.6 miles), at which point you will see a turnoff to the north (right) for La Venta (near the border with Veracruz).

A very small Zoque Indian archaeological site is near Tabasco's border with Chiapas. This is **Malpasito** (250-400 AD). The site has

some excavated platforms, but more important are its carvings of geometric designs and animals. The site is a little remote for the everyday tourist, and will probably be of most interest to those coming here to camp at Agua Selva nearby. Open 10 am-5 pm; free.

■ Cultural & Eco-Travel

The eco-tourism center **Agua Selva** is at the very southwest corner of Tabasco, bordering the states of Chiapas and Veracruz. It's a remote reserve doing its best to provide ecological activities, but is so far out of the way for most visitors, that not many venture there. Its surroundings include mountains, over 100 waterfalls, caves, and forests, and you can take guided hiking tours (lasting several hours to several days). Among its attractions are the Malpasito ruins (see *Archaeological Discoveries* above). There are some cabins and campgrounds here as well. From Highway 180, head south on Highway 187 about 150 km (93 miles). Agua Selva is in the mountains to the west. If you're interested in visiting, the best thing to do is contact a tour agent in Villahermosa to set you up with the accommodations and transportation from the larger town of Huimanguillo (the tourism office can put you in touch with a good agent).

The Sierras

Leaving Villahermosa, heading south towards Chiapas on Highway 195, the land becomes increasingly rugged as you enter Tabasco's Sierra region. Here, after winding through some lush green hills and pretty rural countryside, you get within a few miles of the Chiapan border, and find the town of **Teapa**. From here you can find the **Grutas de Coconá** (Coconá Caves) a mile or so away to the north. The huge network of caves (eight galleries can be explored) were discovered in 1876, and opened to the public in 1967. A marked road heads north from Teapa toward the caves (open daily, 9 am-5 pm; fee). A little to the south of Teapa you'll find the sulfur hot springs of **El Azufre** (from Highway 195, right after you cross the border into Chiapas, you'll see the turnoff). There are restaurants, cabins, and facilities for bathing here.

If you're feeling adventurous, you can leave the area of Teapa, and head east on the local road that winds past sugar cane plantations to the town of **Tacotalpa**. Curiously, this town, though seemingly in the middle of nowhere, was the capital of the state of Tabasco up until 1795, at which point it was moved. There isn't much to see in the town, but if you're coming by bus, and want to continue on, you should head to the plain, unattractive, main plaza, where you'll find the unremarkable 18th-century church, and the bus ticket counter to continue south to Tapijulapa and Oxolotan.

If you're driving, you'll see a fork at Tacotalpa – north goes to Xalapa and south to Oxolotan. As you leave town, you'll once again start a winding trip through the hills. Often shrouded in haze, they seem to get greener and greener the farther you go. You'll also hear the famous Tabascan bugs getting louder and louder.

Soon you reach **Tapijulapa** (22 km/13.6 miles from Tacotalpa), a picturesque village with narrow streets and houses. Here you'll find a couple of nature attractions, including the sulphur springs and waterfalls of **Villa Luz**. To get to them from the town (which sits on the Oxolotán River, you'll find boats to take you onto the river and over to the waterfall's dock (which has facilities). A short distance from the dock, you'll find the former house of former governor Tomas Garrido Canabal. From here, follow the trail to the right to reach a cave where there are sightless fish. This is the **Cueva de la Sardina Ciega** (Cave of the Blind Sardine). On the Sunday before Easter of each year, the town has a Sardine Fishing Festival here, where, after a ritual is performed, *barbasco* is thrown into the water to knock the fish out, making it easy for the townspeople to catch them.

Continuing along past Tapijulapa, the scenery becomes even more wild, gorgeous and remote, winding among mountains and hills, and climbing steadily. If you come by bus, be prepared for a wild ride. Every local who needs a lift is picked up, the bus sometimes getting so full it can do nothing but chug slowly along the ever-tightening curves. Even then, going slow as molasses, you'll feel as if a strong wind could topple you over the unguarded road's steep edge into the deep valleys below. But you're lucky in one sense. The bus can get so full you won't be able to see out the windows! I counted 25 schoolchildren getting off my bus, yet the aisles were still packed solid with men and women, crammed in shoulder-to-shoulder. But eventually you'll see the tiny village of **Oxolotán** around a bend in the road.

Next to the main square, the village has a convent built in the 1550s, used by Dominican friars in 1633, and shortly thereafter abandoned. This is the **Templo y Convento de Santo Domingo de Guzmán Oxolotán**. It's so out of place in this tiny Zoque Indian village that you'll have to blink twice. It towers over the main square, a huge deep red building with bright yellow trim. Inside, there's a cavernous hall with a wooden roof and stone walls; an interior door leads to a museum with beautiful original paintings from the 17th and 18th centuries, an 18th-century wooden altarpiece, 17th-century sculptures of saints, and photographs of its initial remodeling. There are also explanatory panels on the site in both Spanish and English, describing the convent's construction and restoration. Open daily, 10 am-5 pm; free.

To get to Tacotalpa by bus, pick up a local second-class bus at the Teapa bus station; buses go out *packed*, so buy your ticket as soon as you get there. There is no limit on the bus – once all seats are sold, standing aisle spots start to go. Once you get to Tacotalpa, to continue south, you'll have to once again go by second-class bus. You'll find the ticket booth in the main square; to get there from where you get dropped off (bus station), turn right as you exit the station, take a left, then the first right, then a left at the park. Ask if you're unsure; the locals are friendly and eager to help. The bus heading south will say *Oxolotan* on its window, takes about 1½ hours to make the 17-km/11-mile trip, and costs around 13 pesos each.

Eastern Tabasco

Heading east from Villahermosa, Highway 186 takes you across the state, dipping a little into Chiapas before taking you up and out to the westernmost portion of the state (bordering Guatemala). It then continues up into Campeche, Tabasco's region of rivers and marshes. The most important river through this area is the Usumacinta, which starts in Guatemala, continues through Chiapas, cuts across Tabasco and eventually joins the Grijalva River. There are few towns of interest along the eastern portion of the state; most of the area is just farm and cattle land.

Adventures
On Water

Off Highway 186, shortly after the turnoff for Estacion Macuspana, are the remote jungle-shrouded waterfalls known as the **Cascadas de Agua Blanca**. You'll have to hike a little from Las Palomas to get to them.

Continuing on Highway 186 heading west, you cross into the state of Chiapas, and are presented with the choice of continuing north on Highway 186, or south onto Highway 203. If you head south, you cross back into Tabasco and hit the town of **Emilano Zapata**, which has a pretty waterfront where you can take boats onto the water for sightseeing or fishing; also, during March, the water recedes, forming sandbars.

About 66 km/40 miles farther along the highway, you'll get to **Tenosique** on the banks of the Usumacinta River. Boats here take you out onto the river and past the Boca del Cerro – a deep jungle-filled gorge.

Archaeological Discoveries

There are vestiges of Tabasco's ancient past out in the western Tabascan plains. The village of **Balancán** is the place to start. It has a museum, the **Museo Arqueológico Doctor José Gómez Panaco**, where you can find Mayan artifacts as well as pieces recovered from the nearby ruins of **Reforma**, including a disk representing the Mayan calendar. The ruins, believed to have flourished around 600 AD, lie on a flat, green plain, and are still somewhat wild and unexcavated. But you can see a few stelae, as well as waterfalls, also created by the Maya, nearby. A contemporary of Reforma lies to its south – the largely unexcavated Maya site of **Pomoná** (600-900 AD). Beautiful reliefs have been found on some of its buildings.

To get to Balancán, at the point where Highway 186 splits north and south, follow it north, and just before you cross into Campeche, take the road turning off the Highway heading east. The road quickly becomes completely straight; follow it for about 24 km (15 miles) until you reach Cuatro Caminos, where you'll head south (right) another five miles to Balancán. The museum is at the corner of José N.

Rovirosa and Calle Zaragoza, and is open daily, 9 am-8 pm; admittance is free.

To get to Reforma, from Cuatro Caminos continue east (instead of turning), until you reach Adolfo López Mateos (28 km/17 miles), where you'll turn south (right); nine miles down you'll find the site. Reforma has a museum and restrooms. Open 10 am-5 pm, daily; there's an admittance fee.

To get to Pomoná, from Emiliano Zapata, just continue south on Highway 203. Just before you reach the village of Gregorio Mendez Magaña (about 14 miles before Tenosique), take the turnoff on your left. There's a museum at the site. Open 10 am-5 pm, daily.

Oaxaca

South of Veracruz looms the state of Oaxaca. Highway 175 from Veracruz pushes right into its northern half, unmindful of the mountains that rise up, the vegetation that looms closer and greener, or the wildlife that diversifies and multiplies, as the population thins out. Oaxaca's northern half is wild and remote – mountains and cloud forests, inhabited by only a few communities that dot the highways. As you head south, the land slowly becomes more populous approaching the Valles Centrales (Central Valley) and the beautiful city of Oaxaca itself; beyond that, you hit the Sierra Madre del Sur, and then the Pacific Ocean. Of its population, 30% (16 separate groups) are indigenous. The Mixtecs and Zapotecs make up the largest groups.

IN THIS CHAPTER	
■ Tuxtepec	295
■ Ixtlán de Juárez	301
■ Guelateo	302

Local handicrafts and festivals have made it a favorite of visitors seeking a unique cultural experience. Its cultural diversity is only outdone by its biodiversity – 50% of México's plant species, and 40% of its mammals call Oaxaca home. And then there is the beautiful colonial architecture of Oaxaca (the city) and the miles of coastline, including the lovely bays of Huatulco and Puerto Escondido.

Tuxtepec

Tuxtepec sits in Northern Oaxaca almost at the border of Veracruz, on the banks of the Santo Domingo River (which eventually, farther north, becomes the Papaloapan River). It is busy, smelly, and crowded, and if you've never been to Oaxaca, you're going to wonder what all the fuss is about. A short drive away, there are a couple of villages that must be left over from the Garden of Eden.

Take a look anddecide for yourself.

■ Orientation & Practicalities

The river is on the south side of town; the main square is on the eastern side of town, three blocks from the river, at the corner of Ave. 5 de Mayo and Allende. It is bordered by the Palacio Municipal, on whose second floor you can find a tourism office. The Correos is two blocks to its south west, at the corner of Ave. Independencia and Hidalgo.

■ Getting There & Around

Pick up a local **bus** to get to the Valle Nacional/Monte Flor/Jacatapec region. The terminal for the *Lineas Unidas Tuxtepec/Valle National* bus line is on Ave. Libertad (near M. Ocampo).

To get to the area by **car**, simply head south on Highway 175. You'll hit (sequentially) Jacatapec, Monte Flor, then, farthest out (35 miles from Tuxtepec), Vallve Nacional.

For other bus travel, the ADO station is at the corner of 1 de Mayo and Calle Sebastian Ortiz.

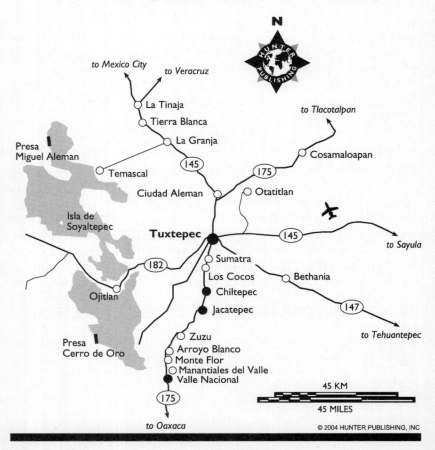

BUS TRIPS			
Destination	Bus Line	Fare	Time
Coatzacoalcos	ADO	112 pesos	3 hours 10 minutes
Cordoba	ADO	74 pesos	2 hours 20 minutes
	AU	76 pesos	
Xalapa	ADO	134 pesos	3 hours 40 minutes
	AU	119 pesos	
México (TAPO)	ADO	250 pesos	6 hours 25 minutes
	AU	224 pesos	
Oaxaca	ADO	186 pesos	7 hours
Veracruz	ADO	78 pesos	2 hours 20 minutes
	AU	71 pesos	
Villahermosa	ADO	16 pesos	5 hours 50 minutes

Adventures

Drives

Valle Nacional

You'll probably get a couple of strange looks as you walk through the village of Valle Nacional. With little by way of a *zócalo*, little by way of a main street, and little by way of a population, there's almost no reason to go. But come prepared for a visit, and you'll have some fun.

If you follow the road that heads behind the church, you'll pass the Palacio Municipal, and, shortly thereafter, come to the end of the road. There you'll see a path start, heading up a hill, behind some tied-up horses, and into a fenced pasture of cows. A minute's walk past lazy cattle and huge cow-patties, and you'll come upon your destination – a picturesque, untouched river. There's a large bank on one side, with smooth riverstones and rocks scattered about, leading up to the green pasture you came through. The river itself is clear, wide, and warm. It's a perfect spot to come with a picnic, take a dip in the shallow waters, then set up a fishing pole. You can literally see the fish in the water. You'll want to ask in the village first, however, to be sure it's not a restricted time of year. If you have a kayak, even better – there are a few rapids to keep you entertained.

"LA DORMIDERA"

A bizarre plant, nicknamed *La Dormidera*, moves when you touch it. The plant, which grows as a ground cover in short clusters (similar to clovers) resembles the clover somewhat, except that it has a number of short fan-like leaves coming from its stem. Try brushing your finger across its leaves; the plant responds by bunching its leaves together, in a reaction that is disturbingly sentient. You can see and play with the plant a little before the beginning of the trail that heads toward the river.

Monte Flor

About 10 minutes north of Valle Nacional is the village of Monte Flor, a place that's something like unwrapping a birthday present – you'll be surprised and delighted by what you find. Have the bus drop you off, or pull your car over, at the museum. Museum? Yes, museum. The tiny village, barely a blip on the map, has a **Museo Comunitario Monte Flor**. The museum is in a small, two-room, baby-blue building that looks something like a house, set right next to the road. You'll usually find the museum keepers sitting on the porch out front doing their best to get in a good siesta. As for what's inside – some years ago, during construction work around the nearby school, an old Indian tomb was discovered buried in the ground. Estimated at 1400-1521 AD, it had a skeleton inside, along with a few pieces of pottery, vases, and bowls. The main room of the museum has the skeleton on display, which they believe to be a person around 33-35 years old, and of high status; the social level has been guessed at based on the fact that the skull was squeezed into an oblong shape (in prehispanic times, when the skull of a baby girl was still soft, it was clamped so that it grew in an elongated shape). Other than the skeleton, you'll find a few display cases, a couple of vases of exceptional quality, some stamps, and a few jewelry pieces. It's a tiny museum, and there aren't many displays, but where else are you going to see a skeleton laid out in Northern Oaxaca? Open daily, 7 am-7 pm; 10 pesos for adults, 5 pesos for children.

Though it may seem they're pulling a joke on you, the museum caretakers are being truthful in their directions; if you follow the short path down the hill behind the museum, you'll come upon an indescribably gorgeous oasis. At the bottom of the hill, there is a natural spring that bubbles out of the ground from behind some rocks, forming a crystal-clear, aqua-hued pool and river. Stocky, gnarled, vibrantly healthy trees surround the pool, while, sprouting out of its center, is a gigantic tree. Its roots are half above the water; from its highest branches vines drop down. Lush green grass surrounds both side of the spring. The setting is where you would imagine elves and fairies live – it's as if the spring water embued the surroundings with a magical dust that brought out life and beauty. You'll find a few villagers where the spring seeps through the rocks, collecting water for their homes; farther down the river, local women do their laundry, and kids cool themselves from the heat of the day. You don't have to visit the museum to come here, just head through the field next to it, and follow the path down.

Jacatapec

About a 10-minute drive north of Monte Flor, you'll find the village of Jacatapec. From the road, it doesn't look like much – a few houses lined up along the street, trees surrounding everything else from view. There are two entrances to the river, which is a few feet away – the *viejo* (old) bridge and the *nuevo* (new) bridge. Take the old one. The old bridge is a long, rope-strung, wooden-planked, hanging bridge suspended over a gorgeous, wide, slow-moving river. If you were to close your eyes, and imagine the perfect spot for relaxation, it would be on the river in Jacatapec. The river is a deep emerald green that moves slowly by. At times it doubles the beauty of a nice day, reflecting the sky like a mirror. At other times, it offers glimpses into its transparent depths. If you stand on the bridge, you can even watch the fish swim by – as huge shadows slowly gliding past, or as silver flashes coming from within the water as the sun glints off their sides. The banks are quiet, surrounded by hanging trees, coves, and the shadows of nearby mountains. You'll even see a few swans swim by. If you're interested in fishing, you should ask around first – at certain times of the year, fishing is prohibited so the fish to multiply.

On Water

In the nearby town of Temascal, you'll find the huge lake around the **Presa Miguel Alemán**, a dam created for hydroelectric purposes in the 1950s. Here you can rent a boat to take you around islands in the middle of the lake for about 150 pesos. Be sure you bring your camera and binoculars along, because this is no ordinary lake. Once you're able to get past the shock of how impressive it is, in both size and beauty, you're going to want to explore as much of it as possible. It resembles something you might have drawn as a child to depict paradise: an enormous lake, more like a sea than an enclosed body of water. There are tropical islands shaped like hills, dotted with palm trees, and inhabited by ocelots and wild boars; hundreds of birds in the distance fly low over the waters; a wide, sandy shoreline has an occasional pig or duck resting in the grass; a couple of fishing boats are pulled up on shore. It's enchanting.

To get here by bus, you can pick up an AU or other second-class bus from Tuxtepec. It's about a two-hour ride (25 pesos) passed sugarcane fields and rolling hills, until you reach Temascal, where the bus drops you off at the end of a long road; you'll see the dam straight ahead. Head toward the dam. When you reach the guards, turn right and continue walking uphill for about 15 minutes until you come to the end of the road. You'll see a sign saying *Dique* and pointing left. Follow it a short distance down, until you see a gravel entrance past some seafood restaurants, and continue down to the *presa*.

To get here driving, follow Highway 145 north back into Veracruz; after Tres Valles, at the town of La Granja, turn left (west) onto a road that terminates at Temascal.

On the opposite end (southern side) of the Presa Miguel Alemán, at **San Pedro Ixcatlán**, you'll find you'll find more boats to take you onto the *presa*. Take a trip to the very pretty island, **Isla de Soyaltepec**. To get here by car, head west on Highway 182; at the town of La Sorpresa, you'll see a road going north toward San Pedro Ixcatlán and the *presa*.

■ Where to Stay

The **Hotel Mesón**, ☎ 287-875-1200, 1684 Blvd. Benito Juárez, is conveniently near the ADO bus station (by the Chedraui supermarket). It has 65 rooms, a restaurant, parking, and suites. Rooms are clean and come with air-conditioning. Credit cards are accepted. $

HOTEL PRICE CHART	
Rates are per room based on double occupancy. Rates lower if single occupancy or sharing a bed. Higher rates on holidays.	
	US $10-$20
$	US $21-$40
$$	US $41-$60
$$$	US $61-$80
$$$$	US $81-$125
$$$$$	Over US $125

The **Hotel El Rancho**, ☎ 287-875-0722, at 435 Blvd. Manuel Ávila Camacho, has pleasant, clean rooms (suites available) with a/c, cable TV, and parking. There's a restaurant on-site. $

The **Hotel Posada Guadalupana**, ☎ 287-875-1195, at 584 Independencia, has a friendly staff, and clean, spacious rooms; it's currently being expanded and remodeled. Even with a/c costing about 50 pesos extra, it's still at the lower end of the price scale. A great bargain. $

The **San Juan Hotel**, ☎ 287-875-1939, at 108 Ave. 1 de Mayo, is a cute simple hotel with restaurant, and clean rooms. $

The **Hotel Tuxtepec**, ☎ 287-875-0944, at 2 Matamoros (at the corner of Independencia), has basic rooms with fan or a/c at good prices. $

The **Hotel Central**, ☎ 287-875-0966, at 565 Independencia, is centrally located and has good, basic, air-conditioned rooms. $

■ Where to Eat

If you get out and explore the city, I doubt that you'll have any interest in eating here. Let me explain. Around the bus station, you'll find plenty of vendors at their markets, stalls, and shops. It seems, however, that the most popular

DINING PRICE CHART	
Price per person for an entrée, not including beverage or tip.	
$	Under US $5
$$	US $5-$10
$$$	US $10+

thing to sell – for everyone – regardless of where the vendor is set up (street corner, storefront, sidewalk...) is chicken: chicken hanging from hooks, chicken laying on tables, chicken in plastic bags, chicken with head and feet, chicken without head and feet, chicken with head (no feet), chicken with feet (no head), chickens turning yellow, chickens turning orange, chickens turning brown.... And all the chickens – every single chicken that you see – is sitting out in the heat and sun (which in the summer can be extreme in the city), aging and yellowing and creating a putrid odor that's hard to escape. I've never seen anything like it. The dilemma then, is where you can eat that doesn't use those chickens? Well, that's a tough one.

Your best bet is either to stick with canned food (there is a Chedraui supermarket one block away from the ADO bus station on Blvd. Ávila Camacho). Or try the vegetarian restaurant at 1115 Ave. Libertad between Matamoros and M. Ocampo, where you'll find the Restaurante Vegetariano Sal Y Pimienta. Or else find the cleanest looking place that you can. The best-looking restaurants I passed were in hotels. The San Juan Hotel (see above) has a good, clean restaurant that may be worth trying, as does the Hotel El Rancho (see above).

Ixtlán de Juárez

Driving south from Tuxtepec along Highway 175, the scenery becomes increasingly beautiful as the road curves and winds its way between mountains; this is the one of the more remote and less inhabited sections of Oaxaca. A few hours south of Tampico, (about 40 miles north of Oaxaca), you'll arrive at the village of Ixtlán de

Juárez. The Zapotec community of Ixtlán has taken advantage of its location in the Sierra Juárez Mountains and the biodiversity of its surroundings (eagles, ocelots, jaguars, tapirs, and toucans are among the few species that are said to live in the region), and developed locally initiated ecotourism projects. Local guides here can bring you to good places for hiking, mountain-biking, and birdwatching. Most of the trips are within a few hours of town. You can visit caves (El Arco), explore a hill known for supernatural phenomena (Piedra del Sol), hike into a cloud forest (Los Pozuelos Hill), hike to a waterfall, or go fishing for rainbow trout. To find out more about the trips, lodging, and bike rentals, contact the local ecotourism agency, **Shiaa-Rua-Via**, ☎ 951-553-6075. Their office is in front of the main square in town.

Guelatao

A couple of miles south of Ixtlán, you'll find Guelatao – the first home of former president Benito Juárez, who was born here in 1806. There are a couple of statues dedicated to the former president in the downtown.

THE ZAPOTECS

The Zapotecs ("people of the zapote tree" from the Náhuatl name *Tzapotecatl*) are an indigenous people of the Oaxaca Valley; today's descendants come from a civilization that developed and flourished from 300 BC to 950 AD. One of the culture's most famous achievements was Monte Albán – a hilltop capital and religious center built around the year 500 BC in the Oaxaca Valley. Former (four-term) president Benito Juárez was a Zapotec Indian.

■ And Beyond...

Oaxaca is a beautiful state, and a place you could easily spend a lot of time exploring. If you decide to drive, you'll want to take particular care along its highways, as the winding mountain roads are narrow and prone to mudslides during the rainy season. Be sure to consult the State Department's travel advisory and road condition reports, and, above all, plan on having a great time!

Chiapas

If you're in Tabasco, it's an easy and mandatory side-trip south across the Tabascan state border to visit one of Chiapas' most spectacular attractions – the ruins of Palenque.

IN THIS CHAPTER	
■ Palenque	304
■ Farther Into Chiapas	311

If the name doesn't already bring some kind of image to mind, let me set you up: mist-enshrouded mornings, lush-green Chiapan rain forest covering nearby hills, massive, magnificent, detailed, ancient ruins… it's beautiful, impressive, inspiring and unforgettable.

Much of Chiapas is still rough, rugged, and wild. The Lancandón jungle covers large parts of the east, giving an aura of mystery and romance. Indigenous Maya, somewhat isolated from the rest of the country by rough mountains, retain their language and their culture; exotic wildlife and tropical jungle, also sheltered by the state's geography have found some of their last refuges here; deep canyons, majestic waterfalls, and steamy rainforests pop up at every bend.

But there's also another side of Chiapas. The indigenous natives are impoverished, the government corrupt, and the quality of life poor. And the jungles harbor guerrillas intent on a revolution against all this – the Zapatistas. Since 1994, rebels have been at work in Chiapas, led by the infamous Subcomandante Marcos. The effects of the movement in many cases don't bother the tourist who sticks to main routes and well-visited areas. It is, however, something you should keep on the radar if you're considering a visit. Consult travel advisories and warnings, and pay attention to what locals are saying; don't travel around at night, and stay out of the remote countryside.

SUBCOMANDANTE MARCOS

The rebel Zapatista army is led by a masked man referred to as Subcomandante Marcos. If you see a picture of him, he's usually shown smoking a pipe. The man is believed to be, though it's never been confirmed, Raphael Sebastián Guillén Vincente, student of philosophy, ex-lecturer, and leftist.

Palenque

■ Orientation & Practicalities

Emergency Services: Hospital, ☎ 916-345-0733.

Exchanging Money: There are two banks with ATMs, a Bancomer almost two blocks west of the main park on Juárez, and a Banamex one more block over.

Post Office: The Correos is just north of the main park at Calle Indpendencia and Ave. Bravo.

Tourist Information: The tourist information office is one block from the main park at the intersection of Juárez and Abasolo.

■ Getting There & Around

By Air

There is an airport three km (1.9 miles) north of Palenque (town); it's serviced by Aerocaribe, ☎ 800-531-7921, and has flights to Cancún, Merida, Guatemala, Ciudad Flores, Villahermosa, and Tuxtla Gutiérrez.

By Bus

There are a few different bus stations near each other at the end of Juárez near the *Monumento Cabeza Maya*, providing first- and second-class service. They are serviced by ADO, Cristóbal Colón, and Autotransportes Tuxtla. There is particularly frequent service to and from Villahermosa. To get to the ruins, take one of the many *combis* that you'll see driving around; it's about eight km (five miles) to the site.

By Car

So you're not here yet? What are you waiting for!? From Villahermosa, it's a *quick* drive. You'll want to head west on Highway 186 until you reach Catazajá (149 km/92.3 miles), where you'll turn south onto Highway 199 (another 25 km/15.5 miles). The whole drive takes about two hours. If you plan on driving farther south down the gorgeous winding mountain Highway 199 toward San Cristóbal de las Casas, go during the daytime, lower your speed, and read on below. The trip is only 191 km/118 miles, but expect it to take five to six hours because of the steep mountain roads.

Getting There & Around ■ 305

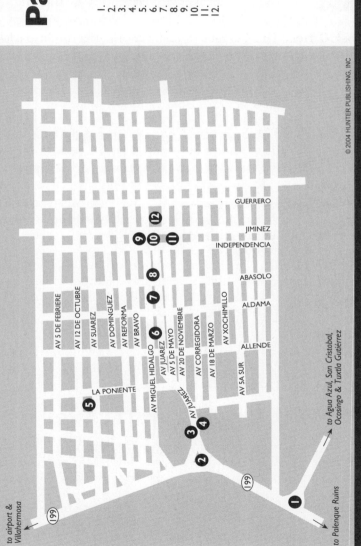

Palenque

1. Monumento Madre Chol
2. Monumento Cabeza Maya
3. Gas Station
4. ADO Bus Station
5. Market
6. Banamex
7. Bancomer
8. Casa de las Artesanías
9. Palacio Municipal, Post Office
10. Main Square
11. Casa de la Cultura
12. Santo Domingo Church

NOT TO SCALE

■ Cautions

As this book was being rresearched, the US State department issued an announcement about violence against foreigners in the remote southeast regions of Chiapas (east of Ocosingo, which is on Highway 199). While this announcement has since expired, and no new specific warnings have been noted, before driving or taking the bus deeper into Chiapas, doublecheck State's travel warnings and advisories. Recently, some Zapatista activity has been noted around Agua Azul. In addition, for years, the situation has been a cause for concern, especially along Highway 199 south of Palenque to San Cristóbal de las Casas. Be cautious.

During my recent travels, I was told by Mexican tourism representatives that there was not a safety concern along the Chiapan Highways. A week later I met a couple of foreign tourists who had a friend that had been pulled over and robbed at gunpoint on a bus in Chiapas. Typically, the highly touristed areas pose few problems. Stay on the main highways, and travel only during daytime. If you're taking the bus, make it a first-class or deluxe.

Another concern, that you'll want to be particularly aware of in this area are the road conditions. During rainy season (June to around September), the areas between San Cristóbal de las Casas and Palenque, as well as the areas between Tuxtla Gutierrez and San Cristóbal de las Casas, often have problems with sections of the roadside giving way and sliding down the mountain sides. Even in the southern portion of Tabasco, on my way to Oxolotan, a portion of the roadway had fallen off before I arrived; the local bus just continued along without a care in the world, driving around the gaping hole that had removed half of one lane in the road. Again, keep your ear to the ground and ask around – usually your hotel, tourist representatives, and locals you meet along the way will know how things look.

■ Tour Operators/Travel Agents

If you want to see some of the gorgeous surrounding sites such as the ruins of Yaxchilán and Bonampak, Misol-Há, or the Cascadas de Agua Azul and you aren't up for driving, consider one of the tour operators that specialize in the area; they're knowledgeable, have transportation, and can get you to amazing places you might not want to hunt down on your own. **Viajes Shivalva**, ☎ 916-345-0411, at Plaza Artesenía, **Viajes Yax-Ha**, ☎ 916-345-0767, at 123 Calle Juárez, and **Viajes Toniná**, ☎ 916-345-0384, at 105 Calle Juárez, are all reputable and competitive.

Taaaaaaaaxxxxxi!!!

Maya Pakal . . . . ☎ 916-345-0112

Hidalgo . . . . ☎ 916-345-0288

■ Adventures

On Water

Driving south of Palenque along Highway 199, about 18 km (11 miles) out, you'll see a sign indicating the turnoff for another gorgeous nearby attraction, the **Cascada Misol-Há**. The waterfalls take their name from the Río Misol-Há which creates the cascade as well as a pretty pool of water at its base. Whether or not you want to go for a swim in the cool waters (and after a day in the Chiapan humidity you'll probably be dying for it), you can balance your way across some rocks to explore a small cave behind the falls themselves.

Not to be outdone, the nearby **Cascadas de Agua Azul** will quickly banish the Misol-Há falls into the nether regions of your mind. From Misol-Há, continue on Highway 199 south towards Ocosingo for another 46 km (28.5 miles), and you'll see a turnoff for the falls, which leads another few kilometers to a parking area. The waterfalls thunder down in an absolutely breathtaking display; the colors of the pools that are formed explain their name (Blue Waters). Swimming here is allowed, but the rocks, rapids, and current make it more suitable for admiring longingly from the banks. On weekends and holidays the place gets pretty crowded with families. If you come during this time, get here early in the day; Mexican families don't arrive in full force until a little after lunchtime. There are some restaurants here if you need to grab a bite, and there are places for camping (which is popular), but you'll want to check things out first to see how acceptable it will be. Trails lead farther down the river as well. If you opt for hiking, stick to the paths, try to stay off deserted stretches, and take a partner. As in Palenque, once you get away from the crowds, your chances of being harassed increase.

To get here or to Misol-Há, you can take a *combi* from downtown Palenque. Be aware though that *combis* don't actually go up the path to the site; they drop you off at the highway entrance, and you'll need to walk the rest of the way yourself. Don't forget the (DEET) mosquito repellent – there are biting bugs of all kinds in that beautiful green vegetation, though you'll hardly notice if you're protected.

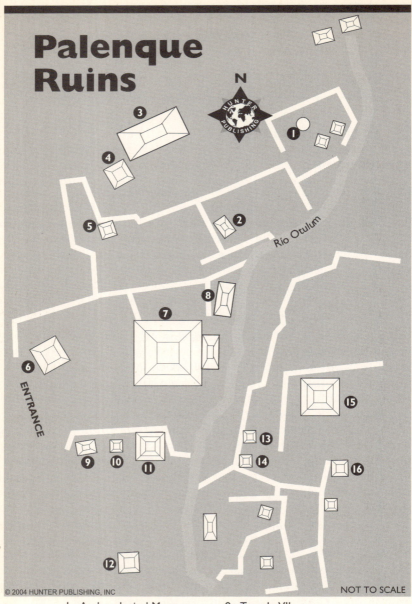

Palenque Ruins

1. Archaeological Museum
2. Ball Court
3. North Group
4. Temple of the Count
5. Temple X
6. Temple XI
7. El Palacio
8. Otulum Aqueduct
9. Temple VII
10. Temple XIII
11. Temple of the Inscriptions
12. Temple of the Jaguar
13. Temple XIV
14. Temple of the Sun
15. Temple of the Cross
16. Temple of the Foliated Cross

■ Archaeological Discoveries

The Ruins of Palenque

Palenque was a huge site in its time (during the Classic Period, 300-900 AD), and served as a primary center for the Maya. Today, though much has been recovered from the jungle and restored to some of its glory, there is still a huge portion of the city hidden away in the surrounding vegetation. Which means that, though you'll spend hours just wandering from site to visible site, there are trails heading off into the surrounding greenery where ruins still lie buried and waiting for archeologists to start their work. If you do venture down one of these paths, you'll want to be particularly careful not to get too far out, since in any remote areas away from the well-touristed portion (and particularly here in Chiapas) there is always a slight danger of harassment.

As you enter, you'll be heading toward some of the most restored buildings in the site. One of the first buildings you'll see when you enter is on your right – Temple XII, also referred to as the **Temple of the Skulls**. Next to that, you'll find the pyramid that yielded its hidden treasures to archeologist Alberto Ruz Lhuillier – the

Temple of the Inscriptions

Templo de las Inscripciones (Temple of the Inscriptions). The pyramid is fascinating. Inside, down an interior stairway, Lhuillier discovered the tomb of Pacal – a Maya ruler of Palenque (615-683 AD). In a vaulted chamber at the bottom of the stairway, was Pacal's sarcophagus, decorated with outstanding bas-reliefs. You'll also notice the walls decorated with the stucco reliefs of the Nueve Señores de la Noche (Nine Lords of the Night). The sarcophagus lid, a five-ton slab, portrays the image of a man in a semi-reclined position, with head upturned. One of the most interesting of its interpretations is probably due in part to the great mysteriousness surrounding Maya civilization. Some people believe that the image on the lid depicts an ancient astronaut shooting up to the stars (they claim that the body positioning seems to be very similar to that of present-day astronauts). The interior stairwell is a favorite of most visitors, though it is currently closed.

As you explore, you'll be impressed with the number of bas-reliefs and inscriptions, which are helping archaeologists understand the city. You'll want to investigate the other main structures at the site,

The Palace

including directly in front of the Templo de las Inscripciones, **El Palacio** (the Palace), which is a complex of rooms and buildings. To your left is the **Templo del Conde** (Templo of the Count, named after Count Waldeck who spent time here studying the site), the **Grupo Norte** (the North Group), and the **Juego de Pelota** (ball court). Behind the Palacio and to the right are the **Templo XIV**, **Templo del Sol** (Temple of the Sun), **Templo de la Cruz** (Temple of the Cross – which has the oldest known depiction of someone smoking, as well as – very curiously – an image of a cross), and **Templo de la Cruz Foliada** (Temple of the Foliated Cross).

Temple of the Count

Are you wondering why you continue to see representations of the cross on the buildings here? When the Spaniards first landed in the New World, they were confounded by reports of explorers seeing the cross on many buildings and temples. In fact, before Christianity was ever introduced to the New World, the Maya were using the cross as a religious symbol. The roots go back to the Maya belief in the creation of the world. They believed that the fundamental axis of the world was the First Tree of the World – a huge ceiba tree with roots in the earth, and branches in the heavens. The symbol that was used to represent the tree was a cross – every Maya village had a ceiba tree at its center, and those that didn't placed a cross there instead.

For your day of adventuring and creeping around the ruins, be sure you go prepared. Bring insect repellent. Also be sure to wear a hat, apply sunscreen, and bring a bottle of water. Forgetting water is one of the most common mistakes that tourists make. After a few hours hiking around the ruins (and to thoroughly enjoy them, you'll more likely end up spending

Temple of the Foliated Cross

most of the day there) you'll be parched; shops on-site are not known for their reasonable prices.

At the entrance, you'll find guides willing to take you around and tell you the history. These can be good, especially if you're on a tight schedule, as they know where they're going and what to show you. Sometimes however, there's something to be said for "discovering" the ruins on your own – climbing the temple, picking the path that seems most interesting, or just sitting under a tree and taking it all in. And don't forget to visit the museum as you leave (you've paid for it with your ticket). Admission costs about 50 pesos, free on Sundays. Open daily, 8 am-5 pm.

■ Where to Stay

Because it attracts so many tourists, you'll have a nice range of hotels to choose from. During holidays, prices jump. In the lower price category, there is the **Hotel Kashlan**, ☎ 916-345-0297, at 105 5 de Mayo. It has clean, decently priced rooms. $$

HOTEL PRICE CHART	
Rates are per room based on double occupancy. Rates lower if single occupancy or sharing a bed. Higher rates on holidays.	
	US $10-$20
$	US $21-$40
$$	US $41-$60
$$$	US $61-$80
$$$$	US $81-$125
$$$$$	Over US $125

The **Casa Inn**, ☎ 916-345-0104, at Km 27.5 on the highway to Palenque, has a gym, tennis courts, and a restaurant. This is a member of the Casa Inns chain. They have good clean rooms. $$

The **Chan Kah Resort**, ☎ 916-345-1100, at Km 30 oo the road to Palenque, is a beautiful spot to spend your visit. Its a marvelous natural setting of bungalows, with a pool and restaurant. Credit cards accepted. $$$$

The **Hotel Maya Tulipanes**, ☎ 916-345-0201, at 6 Cañada, has 72 tidy rooms with a/c and cable TV, as well as a restaurant, pool and parking. $$$$

The **Hotel Ciudad Real**, ☎ 916-345-1315, is at Km 1.5 of Highway Pakal-Na (toward the airport). This is a good hotel that offers a restaurant, bar with live music, and pool. Rooms are pleasant, with air-conditioning, cable TV, and room service. Credit cards are accepted. $$$$

The **Villas Kin-Ha**, ☎ 916-345-0533, at Km 2.7 on the highway toward Palenque, is another on the cabana theme; accommodations are air-conditioned (at the lower end of this price scale). $$$

Another spot to try is the **Hotel Misión Palenque**, ☎ 916-345-0241, at the Rancho San Martin; it has air-conditioned rooms as well as suites, a pool, a bar, and a restaurant. It's at the bottom end of this price scale. $$$$$

■ Where to Eat

La Selva is a popular spot serving traditional food, and has a number of seafood dishes; it's on the road to Palenque. $$-$$$

DINING PRICE CHART	
Price per person for an entrée, not including beverage or tip.	
$	Under US $5
$$	US $5-$10
$$$	US $10+

The **Restaurant Maya** at the corner of Hidalgo and Independencia has some well-priced regional foods. $$

Restaurant Virgo is at 5 Hidalgo and has an open-air restaurant. $$

Farther into Chiapas

If you've come into Chiapas from any other state, the first thing you'll have noticed is how wild, rugged, and green your surroundings became. The farther into Chiapas you go, the more gorgeous it becomes. Highway 199 toward San Cristóbal de las Casas has spectacular scenery as you wind your way through the mountains (although your stomach might do a few lurches as you look out the window – especially if you're not driving). And Chiapas has many more beautiful attractions tucked away – among them, San Cristóbal de las Casas (a lovely and unforgettable colonial city), the spectacular Cañon del Sumidero (a deep, deep canyon), and the beautiful Laguna Miramar.

But that's another book altogether.

Appendix

Useful Words & Phrases

Hello	Hola
Goodbye	Adios
Good Morning	Buenos Días
Good Evening	Buenas Tardes
Good Night	Buenas Noches
yes	sí
no	no
good	bueno/buena
bad	malo/mala
please	por favor
thank you	gracias
thank you very much	muchas gracias
you're welcome	de nada
excuse me (physically)	perdóneme
excuse me (sorry)	discúlpeme
How are you?	¿Cómo está?
Good, and you?	¿Bien, y usted?
Do you speak English?	¿Habla usted inglés?
I don't understand.	No entiendo
I don't speak Spanish.	No hablo español
I don't know.	No sé
What's your name?	Cómo se llama?
My name is	Mi nombre es....
Where....?	¿Dónde...?
When...?	¿Cuándo...?
men	hombres/señores
women	damas/señoras

Time

What time is it?	¿Qué hora es?
One o'clock	la una
Two o'clock	las dos
It is two oclock	Son las dos
...quarter past two	...dos y cuarto
...half past two	...dos y media
noon	mediodía
midnight	medianoche
afternoon	tarde
morning	mañana
evening	noche
today	hoy
tomorrow	mañana
yesterday	ayer
day	día
week	semana
year	año

Weekdays

Monday	lunes
Tuesday	martes
Wednesday	miércoles
Thursday	jueves
Friday	viernes
Saturday	sábado
Sunday	domingo

Months

January	enero
February	febrero
March	marzo
April	abril
May	mayo
June	junio
July	julio

August	agosto
September	septiembre
October	octubre
November	noviembre
December	diciembre

Around Town

store	tienda
I need...	Necesito...
Where is/are ?	Dónde está/están?
How much is it?	¿Cuánto cuesta?
Do you accept credit cards?	¿Aceptan tarjeta de crédito?
Do you have....?	¿Tiene...?
Do you have change?	¿Tiene cambio?
money	dinero
bank	banco
credit card	tarjeta de crédito
telephone	teléfono
pharmacy	farmacia
post office	correos
stamp	estampilla

In the Hotel

Do you have a room?	¿Tiene usted una habitación?
Can I see the room?	¿Puedo ver la habitación?
for one person/for two people	para una persona/para dos personas
a single room/a double room	cuarto sencillo/cuarto doble
with one bed/with two beds	con una cama /con dos camas
air-conditioning/fan	aire acondicionado/ventilador
hot water/cold water	agua caliente/agua fria
bathroom	baño

Planes, Trains, & Automobiles

car	carro
gasoline	gasolina

gas station . . . . gasolinera
full . . . . lleno
oil . . . . aceite
tire . . . . llanta
road . . . . carretera
airport . . . . aeropuerto
airplane . . . . avión
bus . . . . autobús
ticket . . . . boleto
bicycle . . . . bicicleta
stop . . . . alto

Numbers

one . . . . uno/una
two . . . . dos
three . . . . tres
four . . . . cuatro
five . . . . cinco
six . . . . seis
seven . . . . siete
eight . . . . ocho
nine . . . . nueve
ten . . . . diez
eleven . . . . once
twelve . . . . doce
thirteen . . . . trece
fourteen . . . . catorce
fifteen . . . . quince
sixteen . . . . dieciséis
seventeen . . . . diecisiete
eighteen . . . . dieciocho
nineteen . . . . diecinueve
twenty . . . . veinte
twenty-one . . . . veintiuno
twenty-two . . . . veintidós

thirty	treinte
thirty-one	treinte y uno
forty	cuarenta
fifty	cincuenta
sixty	sesenta
seventy	setenta
eighty	ochenta
ninety	noventa
one hundred	cien
one hundred and one	ciento uno
two hundred	doscientos
one thousand	mil
two thousand	dos mil

Bibliography

Busenberg, Bonnie. *Vanilla, Chocolate, & Strawberry, The Story of Your Favorite Flavors*. Minneapolis: Lerner Publishing Company, 1994.

Carroll, Patrick J. Blacks in Colonial Veracruz. Austin: University of Texas Press, 2001.

Coe, Michael D. & Koontz, Rex. *Mexico, From the Olmecs to the Aztecs*. London: Thames & Hudson 2002.

Coe, Michael D. *Mexico*. New York: Thames & Hudson, 1988.

Goodwin, William. *Mexico*. San Diego, CA: Lucent Books, Inc., 1999.

Cortés, Martín Cerón. *Huellas de Xalapa*. Xalapa: La Rueca Ediciones, 1998.

Hamnett, Brian. *A Concise History of Mexico*. Cambridge, UK: Cambridge University Press, 1999.

Hunter, C. Bruce. *A Guide to Ancient Mexican Ruins*. Norman: University of Oklahoma Press, 1977.

Joseph, Gilbert M. & Henderson, Timothy J. *The Mexico Reader, History, Culture, Politics*. Durham and London: Duke University Press, 2002.

Nolen, Barabara. *Mexico is People*. New York: Charles Scribner's Sons, 1973.

Pearce, Kenneth. *A Traveller's History of Mexico.* New York, Northampton: Interlink Publishing Group, 2002.

Sabloff, Jeremy A. *The Cities of Ancient Mexico.* New York: Thames & Hudson, 1997.

Vigil, Angel. *The Eagle on the Cactus, Traditional Stories from Mexico.* Englewood, CO: Libraries Unlimited, 2000.

Index

Accommodations. See also Camping: credit cards, 45, 64; hotel expectations, 64–66; price scale, 63–64; tipping, 51
Air travel, 20–23
Aldama, 101–103
Ameripass, 24
Aquariums, 173
Archaeological discoveries: Costa Esmeralda, 155–156; El Tajín, 139, 142–149; Gulf Coast, 68–69; Palenque, 309–310; ruins of Zempoala, 163–164; San Andrés Tuxtla, 258–259; San Lorenzo Tenochtitlán, 267; Tabasco, 288–289, 292–293; Tampico, 120; Tlapacoyan, 160–161; Tuxpan, 134–135; Veracruz, 180; Villahermosa, 281–282; Xalapa, 206–207
Art galleries, 207–208, 279

Bathrooms: accommodations, 65–66; archaeological sites, 69; availability of, 43; Fortín de las Flores, 248
Beaches: Chachalacas, 164; Ciudad Madero, 115; Costa Esmeralda, 155; Gulf Coast, 71; Matamoros, 97; San Andrés Tuxtla, 256–257; Tabasco, 286–288; Tampico, 122–123; Tuxpan, 134; Veracruz, 177
Beer tours, 239
Biking: Jalcomulco, 231; overview, 71–72; Tampico, 121; Veracruz, 176
Bird watching: Cardel, 164; coastline, 100; Costa Esmeralda, 154; La Mancha, 162; Matamoros, 95–96; Veracruz, 177
Bullfights, 73, 83
Buses, 24–28

Camping, 66, 157–158, 266
Cardel, 164
Catemaco, 260–266
Caving, 67–68, 239
Cenotes, 102
Chachalacas, 164
Chiapas: overview, 303, 311–312; Palenque, 304–311; safety and crime, 16, 48–49, 306; tourism information, 75

Chocolate plantation tour, 282–283
Cigar factories, 254–256
Ciudad Mante, 109
Ciudad Victoria, 103–107
Climate, 3–4
Coatepec, 218–220
Combis, 274, 282, 304, 307
Córdoba, 249–251
Costa Esmeralda, 153–158
Crime. See Safety and crime
Cultural & eco-travel excursions: Coatepec, 219; Costa Esmeralda, 156; Ixtlán de Juárez, 302; Orizaba, 242–243; Papantla, 143–144; Villahermosa, 282–283; western Tabasco, 289; Xalapa, 207–210
Culture & customs, 18–20
Customs regulations, 23, 32–37
Cuyuxquihui, 142

Dances, 143–144, 149–150
Danza del Volador, 143–144, 149
Dining: archaeological sites, 69; credit cards, 45; drinks, 62–63; health matters, 57; local fruits, 61–62, 213; markets, 58, 152; price scale, 57; regional specialties, 60–61; spices, 62; tipping, 51; vegetarian, 214–215; where to eat, 57–61
Disabled travelers, 41
Diving, 102, 179
Driving, 23–24, 28–31

E-mail, 41, 73
Eco-travel. See Cultural & eco-travel excursions
Ecology, 4–7
Economy, 17
El Tajín archaeological site, 139, 142–149
Embassies/consulates: Gulf Coast, 75–76; Matamoros, 95; Nuevo Laredo, 81; Reynosa, 88
Entertainment, 72–73

Fauna, 5–6. *See also Bird watching*
Ferries, hand-drawn, 87
Festivals: beaches, 71; Coatepec, 219; Costa Esmeralda, 156; Fortín de las

Flores, 248; Jalcomulco, 232; Matamoros, 97–98; Nuevo Laredo, 82–84; overview, 53–57; Papantla, 149–150; Reynosa, 90; Tampico, 123; Tlacotalpan, 190–191; Tuxpan, 135; Veracruz, 180–181; Villahermosa, 283; Xalapa, 210; Xico, 226
Firearms, 50, 68
Fishing: Aldama, 103; Ciudad Victoria, 105; coastline, 100; Costa Esmeralda, 154; Matamoros, 97; Nuevo Laredo, 82; overview, 69–70; Tamaulipas, 69; Tampico, 123; Tlacotalpan, 190; Veracruz, 179
Flora, 6–7
Food. See Dining
Fortín de las Flores, 245–248
Fruits, local, 61–62, 213

Geography, 3
Goldsmithing, 208–209
Golf, 120–121, 176
Government, 16
Guelatao, 302

Haciendas, 208
Handicrafts: Tabasco, 51; Tlacotalpan, 189; Veracruz, 51; Villahermosa, 277; Xalapa, 210
Health matters, 45–48, 57
Hiking: Fortín de las Flores, 247–248; Jalcomulco, 230; Orizaba, 238; overview, 66–67; Perote, 216–217; Reserva de la Biosfera de El Cielo, 107; Xalapa, 200; Xico, 223
History, 7–16
Horseback riding, 232
Hotels. See Accommodations
Hunting, 68, 81, 97
Hurricane ratings, 4

Insurance: car, 24, 30, 50; medical, 47–48
Internet cafés: availability, 41, 73; Ciudad Victoria, 104; Córdoba, 249; Fortín de las Flores, 246; Orizaba, 236; Papantla, 139; San Andrés Tuxtla, 252; Tampico, 110; Veracruz, 166; Villahermosa, 270; Xalapa, 192–194
IVA (Impuesto de Valor Agregado), 45
Ixtlán de Juárez, 301–302

Jalcomulco, 228–232

Kayaking. See Rafting / kayaking

La cucaracha, 91
La Mancha, 162
Laundry, 44
Lodgings. See Accommodations

Markets (mercado): bathrooms in, 43; dining, 58, 152; health matters, 46; shopping, 50–51; Tampico, 124
Matamoros, 92–99
Measurements, 38–39
Mexipass, 20–21
Military checkpoints, 31, 49
Money matters: credit cards, 30, 45, 64; overview, 44–45; safety and crime, 48
Mountain climbing, 240–241
Museums: archaeological sites, 69; Ciudad Victoria, 105; Córdoba, 250; Matamoros, 96; Ocampo, 108; Santiago Tuxtla, 267; Tampico, 115–117; Tuxpan, 133; Tuxtepec, 298; Veracruz, 175–176; Villahermosa, 275–276, 280; Xalapa, 198, 204, 206–206, 208; Xico, 222
Music. See Nightlife

Nature parks, 282
Nightlife: Gulf Coast, 72; Orizaba, 243; Papantla, 151; Tampico, 124–125; Veracruz, 182–183; Xalapa, 211
Nuevo Laredo, 78–85
Nuevo Progresso, 92

Oaxaca: Guelatao, 302; Ixtlán de Juárez, 301–302; tourism information, 75; Tuxtepec, 295–301
Ocampo, 108
Orizaba: accommodations, 243–244; car tours, 241; caving, 239; dining, 244–245; mountain climbing, 240–241; nightlife, 243; orientation, 235–236; paragliding, 241–242; sightseeing, 237–238; travel, 233–235; UFO sightings, 237

Packing, 39–41
Palenque, 304–311
Papantla: accommodations, 151–152; Danza del Volador, 143–144; dining, 152; El Tajín site, 144–149; festivals, 149–150; nightlife, 151; orientation, 139–140; shopping, 150–151; travel, 140–142

Paragliding, 241–242
Passports, 34–37
People, 17–18
Perote, 215–218
Pickup trucks (piratas), 261
Post offices, 43
Poza Rica, 136–137
Price scales: accommodations, 63–64; dining, 57

Quiahuiztlan, 161

Rafting/kayaking: Catemaco, 264; Jalcomulco, 231; overview, 70–71; popular rivers, 158, 161, 231; Tamaulipas, 71; Tlapacoyan, 159–160; Tuxtepec, 297; Veracruz, 179–180
Rappeling, 230–231
Reserva de la Biosfera de El Cielo, 107–109
Reynosa, 88–92
RV sites. See Camping

Safety and crime: biking, 71; Chiapas, 303, 306; hiking, 67; overview, 48–50; State Department warnings, 74, 306
Sailing, 134, 179
San Andrés Tuxtla, 252–260
San Lorenzo Tenochtitlán, 267
Sand dunes, 164
Santiago Tuxtla, 267
Shopping: markets, 50–51; Nuevo Laredo, 84; Papantla, 150–151; Tampico, 124; Tlacotalpan, 189; Veracruz, 181–182; Xalapa, 210–211; Xico, 226
Spas, 265
Spices, 62, 222
Study abroad, 209–210
Sulphur (sulfur) springs: Tapijulapa, 290; Tinajitas, 162; Xalapa, 205–206

Tabasco: caving, 67; coast overview, 286–288; eastern overview, 291–292; local fruits, 61; mosquitos, 3; shopping, 51; the Sierras, 289–291; tourism information, 75; Villahermosa, 269–286; western overview, 288–289
Tamaulipas: Aldama, 101–103; border, 77–78; Ciudad Victoria, 103–107; fishing, 69; hunting, 68, 81, 97; kayaking, 71; Matamoros, 92–99; Matamoros to Aldama, 99–101; Nuevo Laredo, 78–85; Nuevo Laredo to Reynosa, 85–87; Reserva de la Biosfera de El Cielo, 107–109; Reynosa, 87–92; shopping, 51; Tampico, 109–127; tourism information, 74
Tampico: accommodations, 125–127; adventures, 117–123; dining, 127; festivals, 123; markets, 124; nightlife, 124–125; orientation, 108–112; shopping, 124; sightseeing, 114–117; taxis, 117; travel, 112–114
Taxes, 44–45
Taxis, 31–32, 51
Telephones, 41–42
Time zone, 37
Tinajitas, 162
Tipping, 51–52
Tirolesa, 231
Tisniche, 190
Tlacotalpan, 188–191
Tlapacoyan, 158–161
Tourist information, 73–76
Tourist season, 51–57
Travel: getting here, 20–24; safety and crime, 30, 48–49
Traveler's checks, 45
Turtles, 100, 156
Tuxpan, 131–136
Tuxtepec, 295–301

UFO sightings, 236

Vaccinations, 48
Vanilla, 150–151
Veracruz (state): along the coast, 161–164; Catemaco, 260–266; central overview, 138–139; Coatepec, 218–220; Córdoba, 249–251; Costa Esmeralda, 153–158; Fortín de las Flores, 245–248; Jalcomulco, 227–233; local fruits, 61; northern overview, 129–131; Orizaba, 233–245; Papantla, 139–152; Perote, 215–218; Poza Rica, 136–137; rafting/kayaking, 70; San Andrés Tuxtla, 252–260; San Lorenzo Tenochtitlán, 267; Santiago Tuxtla, 267; shopping, 51; southern overview, 251–252; Tlacotalpan, 187–191; Tlapacoyan, 158–161; tourism information, 74; Tuxpan, 131–136; Veracruz, 165–187; Xalapa, 191–215; Xico, 220–227

Veracruz (town): accommodations, 181, 183–185; adventures, 174–180; archaeological discoveries, 180; dining, 185–187; festivals, 180–181; nightlife, 182–183; orientation, 165–166; sightseeing, 171–174; travel, 166–171
Villahermosa: accommodations, 283–284; adventures, 279–282; archaeological discoveries, 281–282; art galleries, 279; combis, 274, 282; dining, 280, 285–286; festivals, 283; orientation, 270–271; sightseeing, 275–278; taxis, 274, 282; travel, 272–274

Waterfalls: Catemaco, 264; eastern Tabasco, 292; Orizaba, 238; Palenque, 307; San Andrés Tuxtla, 257–258; Xico, 224–226

Witches, 262

Xalapa: accommodations, 211–213; adventures, 198–206; archaeological discoveries, 206–207; art galleries, 207–208; dining, 213–215; festivals, 210; goldsmithing, 208–209; haciendas, 208; nightlife, 211; orientation, 191–194; shopping, 210–211; study abroad, 209–210; sulfur springs, 205–206; theaters, 209; travel, 194–196
Xico, 220–227
Xicoténcatl, 108

Zapista movement, 15–16, 303, 306
Zempoala (Cempoala), 163–164
Zoos, 117, 276